I Talked
with a Zombie

Other Interview Books by Tom Weaver and from McFarland

Attack of the Monster Movie Makers: Interviews with 20 Genre Giants (2014)

Earth vs. the Sci-Fi Filmmakers: 20 Interviews (2014)

They Fought in the Creature Features: Interviews with 23 Classic Horror, Science Fiction and Serial Stars (2014)

I Was a Monster Movie Maker: Conversations with 22 SF and Horror Filmmakers (2011)

Science Fiction Confidential: Interviews with 23 Monster Stars and Filmmakers (2010)

Eye on Science Fiction: 20 Interviews with Classic SF and Horror Filmmakers (2007)

Science Fiction Stars and Fantasy Film Flashbacks: Conversations with 24 Actors, Writers, Producers and Directors from the Golden Age (2004)

Return of the B Science Fiction and Horror Heroes: The Mutant Melding of Two Volumes of Classic Interviews (2000)
(A combined edition of the two earlier Weaver titles *Interviews with B Science Fiction and Horror Movie Makers* and *Science Fiction Stars and Horror Heroes*)

Other McFarland Books by Tom Weaver

Poverty Row HORRORS! Monogram, PRC and Republic Horror Films of the Forties (1993)

John Carradine: The Films (1999)

By Tom Weaver with Michael Brunas and John Brunas

Universal Horrors: The Studio's Classic Films, 1931–1946 (McFarland, 1990)

By Tom Weaver, David Schecter and Steve Kronenberg

The Creature Chronicles: Exploring the Black Lagoon Trilogy (McFarland, 2014)

I Talked with a Zombie

*Interviews with 23 Veterans
of Horror and Sci-Fi Films
and Television*

Tom Weaver

McFarland & Company, Inc., Publishers
Jefferson, North Carolina

The present work is a reprint of the illustrated case bound edition of I Talked with a Zombie: Interviews with 23 Veterans of Horror and Sci-Fi Films and Television, *first published in 2009 by McFarland.*

LIBRARY OF CONGRESS CATALOGUING-IN-PUBLICATION DATA

Weaver, Tom, 1958–
I talked with a zombie : interviews with 23 veterans of horror and sci-fi films and television / Tom Weaver.
    p.   cm.
Includes index.

ISBN 978-0-7864-9571-9 (softcover : acid free paper) ∞
ISBN 978-0-7864-5268-2 (ebook)

1. Horror films—History and criticism.   2. Horror television programs—History and criticism.   3. Science fiction films—History and criticism.   4. Science fiction television programs—History and criticism.   5. Motion picture producers and directors—Interviews.   6. Motion picture actors and actresses—Interviews.   7. Television picture producers and directors—Interviews.   8. Television actors and actresses—Interviews.   I. Title.
PN1995.9.H6W35   2014   791.43'6164—dc22   2008035960

BRITISH LIBRARY CATALOGUING DATA ARE AVAILABLE

© 2009 Tom Weaver. All rights reserved

No part of this book may be reproduced or transmitted in any form or by any means, electronic or mechanical, including photocopying or recording, or by any information storage and retrieval system, without permission in writing from the publisher.

On the cover: Leggy Tarantella (Tandra Quinn)—and her leggier friend—await visitors to the *Mesa of Lost Women*, 1953.

Design by Marty Baumann (www.martybaumann.com)

Manufactured in the United States of America

McFarland & Company, Inc., Publishers
Box 611, Jefferson, North Carolina 28640
www.mcfarlandpub.com

To
Jeanne Bates
Phil Brown
Alan Caillou
Ben Chapman
Robert Clarke
Robert Cornthwaite
Hazel Court
Richard E. Cunha
Arnold Drake
John Fiedler
Gary Gray
Tod Griffin
Val Guest
Betsy Jones-Moreland
Carolyn Kearney
Phyllis Kirk
Bernard L. Kowalski
Kay Linaker
Teala Loring
Paul Marco
Michael Pate
Mala Powers
Kasey Rogers
Herbert Rudley
Hans J. Salter
Herbert L. Strock
Frankie Thomas
Burt Topper
George Wallace
Mel Welles
Robert Wise
Jane Wyatt

ACKNOWLEDGMENTS

As always, a huge "Thank you!" shout-out to the incomparable Marty Baumann, the Astounding B Monster himself, designer of this book's cover. Check out his website www.bmonster.com to see more of his amazing artistry.

Thanks, too, to the many other colleagues who make these interview books of mine possible: Ron Adams, John Antosiewicz, Mike Barnum, Ted Bohus (*Chiller Theatre* magazine), John and Michael Brunas, Bob Burns, Jim Clatterbaugh (*Monsters from the Vault* magazine), Kevin Clement (*Chiller Theatre* magazine), David Colton, Glenn Damato, Joe Dante, Richard Devon, Yolande Donlan, Mike Elmo, Kerry Gammill, Arthur Gardner, Jimmy George, Mike Gingold (*Fangoria* magazine), Bruce Goldstein, the late Alex Gordon, the late Val Guest, Arch Hall, Jr., Richard Heft, Jan Henderson, Sandy and Georgia Horvath, Whitey Hughes, Joe Indusi, Kent Jones, Joe Kane (*VideoScope* magazine), Richard Kiel, Bob King (*Classic Images* and *Films of the Golden Age* magazines), Ruta Lee, the Lincoln Center Performing Arts Library's Dynamic Duo of Christine Karatnytsky and Christopher Frith, Tim and Donna Lucas (*Video Watchdog* magazine), Dave McDonnell (*Starlog* magazine), Scott MacQueen, Boyd Magers (*Western Clippings* magazine), Leonard Maltin, Greg Mank, Mark Martucci, Burr Middleton, Kenny Miller, John Morgan, Barry Murphy (proofreader extraordinaire), Ray Nielsen, Robert Nott, Mark Phillips, the Photofest gang, Paul Picerni, Oconee and Jeannie Provost, Fred Rappaport, Fred Olen Ray, Alan Rode, Robert Rotter ("Glamour Girls of the Silver Screen" website), Mary Ray Runser, Dan Scapperotti, Rich Scrivani, Tigger, Tony Timpone (*Fangoria* magazine), Terry Tousey, the late Jon Weaver, Stephen B. Whatley, the whole gang at the Classic Horror Film Board (http://monsterkid classichorrorforum.yuku.com) and Lucy Chase Williams.

And an extra-special "Thanks!" to Preston Neal Jones, who provided the interview with Hans J. Salter, Universal's resident musical genius during the studio's monster movie heyday.

Abridged versions of the interviews featured in this book originally appeared in the following 'zines:

Richard Alden: "Richard Alden: Inside *The Sadist!*," *The Phantom of the Movies' VideoScope* #54, 2005
Eric Braeden: "The Amazing Dr. Forbin," *Starlog* #344, April 2006
Ann Carter: "Amy and Her Friends: The Ann Carter Interview," *Video Watchdog* #137, March 2008
Robert Colbert: "Rendezvous with Yesterday," *Starlog* #352, January 2007, and "Timely Destinations," *Starlog* #359, October 2007

Acknowledgments

Robert Conrad: "The Night of the Wild Stuntmen," *Starlog* #349, October 2006
James Darren: "Tunnel Vision," *Starlog* #359, October 2007
Maury Dexter: "The Little Studio of Horrors," *Chiller Theatre* #22, 2005
Pat Fielder: "Married to the Macabre," *Starlog* #355, May 2007, and "Pat Fielder," *Western Clippings* #81, January-February 2008
Richard Gordon: "Sven-Garlic!," *Monsters from the Vault* #19, 2004
Ron Harper: "Under Ape Rule," *Starlog* #345, May 2006
Charles Herbert: "So You Wanna Be a Kid Actor...?," *Classic Images* #371, May 2006
Jimmy Lydon: "*Rocky Jones ... Space Ranger*," *Films of the Golden Age* #50, Fall 2007
Lee Meriwether: "4D First Time," *Chiller Theatre* #22, 2005, "Catwoman in Conversation," *Starlog* #343, March 2006, and "Timely Destinations," *Starlog* #359, October 2007
Laurie Mitchell: "Queen of Outer Space," *Starlog* #346, June 2006
Tandra Quinn: "Dance of the Spider Woman," *Starlog* #365, May 2008
William Reynolds: "Reynolds Rap," *Starlog* #359, October 2007
Betta St. John: "Dancing with Lions," *Starlog* #347, July 2006
Hans J. Salter: "The Ghost of Hans J. Salter" by Preston Neal Jones, *Cinefantastique* Volume 7, Number 2, 1978
Jay Sayer: "The Saga of a Corman Stock Player," *Cult Movies* #41, 2005
Olive Sturgess: "Working with the Bad Boys," *Films of the Golden Age* #47, Winter 2006-07
Frankie Thomas-Al Markim-Jan Merlin: "Spacemen's Luck," *Starlog* #331, February 2005, and "Spacemen's Pluck," *Starlog* #332, March 2005

TABLE OF CONTENTS

Acknowledgments vii

Richard Alden 1

Eric Braeden 10

Ann Carter 26

Robert Colbert 49

Robert Conrad on *The Wild Wild West* 69

James Darren on *The Time Tunnel* 78

Maury Dexter 90

Pat Fielder 121

Richard Gordon on *Svengali* (1954) 139

Ron Harper on *Planet of the Apes* 146

Charles Herbert 159

Jimmy Lydon on *Rocky Jones, Space Ranger* 171

Lee Meriwether on *4D Man* and *Batman* 181

Laurie Mitchell 198

Tandra Quinn 212

William Reynolds 232

Betta St. John 250

Hans J. Salter (Interview by Preston Neal Jones) 269

Jay Sayer 285

Olive Sturgess 304

Frankie Thomas, Al Markim and Jan Merlin on *Tom Corbett, Space Cadet* 317

Index 343

Richard Alden

I didn't want to come off as a coward in The Sadist
*but I also didn't want to come off as some Hollywood hero,
like Batman or something.*

In 1958, America reacted with horror as Nebraska teenager Charles Starkweather and his 14-year-old girlfriend Caril Fugate embarked on a bloody Great Plains rampage. The first crime scene was Caril's home in the seedy Belmont section of Lincoln, where one of the three victims was her own mother. Hunted by police and National Guardsmen, the teens claimed seven more victims in Nebraska and Wyoming before their murder spree reached its finish line at the end of a roadblock-crashing 110 M.P.H. police pursuit. At the trial, Charley blocked every effort by his lawyers to have him declared insane and on June 25, 1959, the mad dog killer, now 20, went to the electric chair, where it took him four minutes to die.

In 1963, Charley and Caril's serial-killing career became the inspiration for a low-budget indie called *The Sadist* from Arch Hall, Sr.'s, Fairway-International. Arch Hall, Jr., and Marilyn Manning, stars of Fairway's *Eegah* (1962), were top-cast as the young thrill killers, holed up at an out-of-the-way auto salvage yard and terrorizing three schoolteachers (Richard Alden, Helen Hovey, Don Russell) whose car has broken down en route to a Sunday afternoon Dodger Stadium baseball game.

Written and directed by TV veteran James Landis, *The Sadist* emerged as a harrowing motion picture and a highlight in the early acting career of Richard Alden, playing the phys ed teacher menaced by the goonish psycho Charlie Tibbs (Hall) and his mute moll Judy (Manning). Born in Toronto, Alden started out in TV production before turning to acting in the early 1960s, when he film-debuted in the Mounties-and-Indians adventure *The Canadians*. Now, four decades later, he is a veteran of scores of U.S. and Canadian films and TV episodes, and has recently authored a novel and two screenplays.

I got into show business by starting as a stagehand with the Canadian Broadcasting Corporation in Toronto. I worked my way up from there and became a "script assistant" [production assistant] and then a floor director and so on. Then I left, like a damn fool, and went to Hawaii, KHVH-TV, and worked there as a director—I did news, I did sports, I did their children's show called *Captain Honolulu* and I did a lot of commercials. Things didn't work out in Hawaii too well, I didn't get along with the station manager, so I left and came to California and tried to get into television production. Unfortunately, I didn't know a damn soul. Even with all my experience, I couldn't get any work, I couldn't get a job as a *page boy*, even, at NBC or CBS or anything. But I'd always had a feeling that acting might be something I could do, and I drifted into the acting through living in theatrical boardinghouses in Hollywood, where a lot of actors lived. I started going to workshops with them, and I thought, "Well, I'll give it a shot, and if it doesn't work out, I'll go back to the CBC and try to resume my career up there."

In these acting workshops, were there any actors I might have heard of?
Bobby Pickett was in there, the guy who did "Monster Mash." Then there was Donna Douglas, who did *The Beverly Hillbillies*, and also Elaine Joyce, who did [the 1976 TV series] *City of Angels*. Now she's married to Neil Simon—she really moved up in the world [*laughs*]! I started going to these workshops and within two months I got my first film, a 20th Century–Fox picture called *The Canadians* [1961] with Robert Ryan. It was a good, strong supporting part, I played a gunfighter in the thing. That sort of started it out. Then I did another one for Fox, *The Two Little Bears* [1961] with Eddie Albert and Jane Wyatt, and that was a pretty decent part. Robert L. Lippert was the executive producer on those films, he did a ton of pictures for 20th, and I got to know his daughter Judy, who took a liking to me. There was no chance for it to *go* anywhere, though, she was like a beach ball, fatter than hell [*laughs*]. But *nice*. Also, I was still in a semi-married state, you might say, with a girl back home. I didn't want to have any affairs anyway, because I'm very loyal—never cheated in my life. So Judy and I were just friends. Then Judy introduced me to Jim Landis and he and I hit it off pretty well and became good friends. I liked him very much, he was a great guy. I had a lot of respect for him, 'cause I have a tremendous reverence for writers. So we became friends, and then he told me about this film *The Sadist* and I was with him during the writing of it, and a couple of my ideas went *into* it. Landis had to push like hell to get me on the film. Almost everybody else in *The Sadist* were relatives or friends of Arch Hall, Sr., and I was the only one who really had to read to get in the damn film. Is Jim Landis still with us?

The Writers Guild tells me he died in 1991.
I wouldn't be surprised—he smoked like a chimney, all the time. Jim really knew his stuff, I'll tell you; man, what he could do with no money...! That picture *The Sadist* was done for peanuts, I don't know if Arch, Jr., told you that or not.

He wasn't quite sure what the budget was. Vilmos Zsigmond the cinematographer once said it was $33,000.
I thought it was $25,000. I can tell you what *I* did it for: I got zilch. I did it for a showcase—I thought it might help my career. By the way, my hair was blonde, the same color as Arch, Jr., so for *The Sadist* it was dyed black to contrast with Arch, Jr.

You mentioned helping Landis a bit with the writing of The Sadist...?
I didn't help him with the writing, I just gave him the idea for something going wrong with the car—I suggested the fuel pump, and he liked that idea. I was over to his home all the time. He lived on the fringe of Burbank, right around the [Los Angeles] river bottom, which is a place where everybody used to ride horses. As a matter of fact, I used to have a horse over there, a quarter horse, and one day I rode my horse over to his house. I knew where he worked, his desk was at this particular window, and so I rode the horse right up and put the horse's head right in the window over Jim's desk [*laughs*]! He was writing something *else* at that time, *The Sadist* came later. He was always writing *some*thing. He was a talented guy.

You mentioned having to audition.

At Fairway, I had to read for the role of Ed Stiles, the leading man. I read for Arch Hall, Sr., and Jim. As far as Jim was concerned, I had the part, but he had to convince Arch, Sr., that I'd be right for it. I liked Arch, Sr., I thought he was a great guy. Did you ever see the movie *The Last Time I Saw Archie* [1961]? It's a World War II service comedy based on Arch Hall, Sr., and Bob Mitchum played him.

Written by Arch, Sr.'s, friend William Bowers, who's also a character in the movie.

Right, and Bill Bowers was played by Jack Webb. Bill wrote *The Gunfighter* [1950] and *Support Your Local Sheriff!* [1969] and we were very close friends, Bill and I, up until he died. He was an incredible character, a marvelous, talented writer.

Did you ever get an inkling what Arch, Sr., thought of having his life made into a movie—and being depicted as a goldbrick and a conniver?

I had a feeling that Arch wasn't so pleased about *The Last Time I Saw Archie*—I heard something from Bill on that! Arch, incidentally, had a wonderful voice. He does the narration at the beginning of *The Sadist* and he's also the voice you hear on the car radio, announcing the ballgame and so on. I liked the man very much and often wondered why he did not make it big as an actor. He had a noble head, a handsome man with a great voice.

And Arch Hall, Jr.?

I liked Arch Hall, Jr., too, *very* much. I liked *every*body. Marilyn Manning, I don't know what *she's* doing these days. Helen Hovey I never got to know her very well, but she was a very nice lady. She was Arch Hall, Sr.'s, niece. We shot the movie up in Saugus, so it was a bit of a drive every morning.

How much of a crew?

A little tiny crew. Seemed like maybe eight or nine people at the most. I don't think some of 'em were professionals. The man who worked sound told me he played with [musician] Johnny Rivers' group.

Was The Sadist *non-union?*

Oh yes it was, and I took a big risk with that. SAG *did* visit the set one time when I wasn't around. As I told you, I didn't take anything [any money for acting in it]. They gave me some expense money, I think $200 in expense money to eat with and things like that, and that was all. I was flat broke, of course. Actors are doing it now, they're doing non-union things to survive. Even some *names* [well-known actors] are doing them. Actors get tired of not working. SAG now seems to be in such disarray, with all sorts of internal problems. It seems to be the union's just for the big guys, the big money-earners...

Prior to The Sadist, *Arch, Jr., had only done two or three movies, Helen Hovey none—and Don Russell wasn't even an actor! What were these people like to work with?*

This was the wonderful thing about Landis: He actually gave Arch, Jr., an awful lot of line readings, and Arch just sort of aped what Landis did.

Landis wouldn't have had to do that with Marilyn Manning—she didn't have any lines!

No, and he didn't do it with me, he left me alone. But he really worked with Arch, Jr. Landis read the lines and then Arch would copy him. Landis really worked hard with Arch, Jr., and he made Arch do a good job, he really did—I think he gave a helluva performance in that thing. I don't know what background Helen Hovey had, but I thought she did a very good job, she played it very honestly. Marilyn Manning managed to stay in character, and

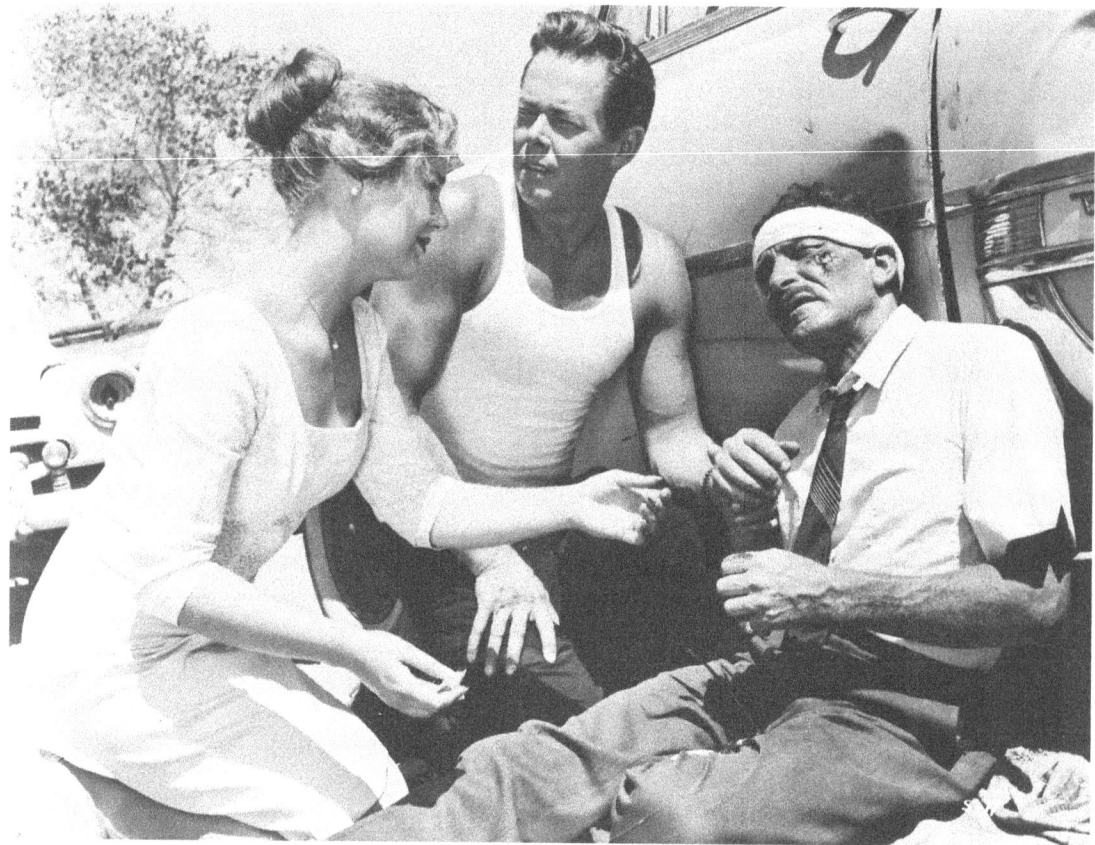

A professional actor, Richard Alden (center) was joined in the cast of *The Sadist* by one-shot actress Helen Hovey, a member of Arch Hall's family, and the movie's production manager Don Russell.

that's not always that easy when you don't have lines. He may not have *been* an actor but Don Russell *seemed* like a very well-trained actor. (And a very nice guy.) Even the two cops who ride up on motorcycles, who were real cops—even *they* did a pretty good job.

And as for working with them, they were all great and I got along great with everybody. We *all* got along good and we were all pitching in. If I could do anything to help on the side, I was happy to do it. Helping maybe to dress a set a little bit, or if they needed a hand here or there. I didn't do *much* of it, but anything I could do, if Jim asked me, I'd do it. I think *The Sadist* took about six weeks, and I was there every day for six weeks.

What challenges were there to playing your character?

Well, it's hard to play a part like that and not look like a coward. But if you're sitting looking at a .45 automatic that can blow your head off, I think the phony Hollywood heroics are [inappropriate]. I tried to do it like I would in *real life*. One reviewer wrote something along the lines of "Stiles was a coward." Well, there was a shot in *The Sadist* that that reviewer must have missed, a moment when Stiles coulda got away. After Stiles shoots the gasoline into Charlie Tibbs' face and blinds him, Stiles looks off and he sees that he can run away and never be caught. But he doesn't, he stays to protect the leading lady [Helen Hovey], because he sees that Tibbs is heading towards her. But there's a shot that Jim Landis, included, purposely, where Stiles looks around and there's *nothing* [to prevent his escape] and he can just take off and save himself, and leave the girl to face her own death. But Stiles didn't do it. So he really *wasn't* a coward at all.

What time of year were you shooting?

It was shot in the summertime, so it was like 120 degrees up there. In the scene where I got shoved into the trunk of that car, it was hotter than Hell in there [*laughs*]! Also—another one of my ideas—it was my idea to *scream* at Arch Hall, Jr., in the scene at the end where I'm charging at him as he's reloading his gun. The first time I did it, in rehearsal, it *worked*—it scared the hell out of him, and he didn't get to fire the shot. I got the idea from reading *Tarzan* books when I was a kid. The books said that the lion would roar as it leapt at its prey, sort of to freeze 'em on the spot, and the lion would get to 'em before they could move. Actually, lions don't do that at all, except in Edgar Rice Burroughs [*laughs*]. But I thought I'd use that [in *The Sadist*], and when I ran at Arch, to give myself a couple of extra seconds to get to him, I let out that scream and Arch just froze—he didn't expect that at all. And I *did* get to him. So in *life* it would have worked. But the *next* time, Arch was ready for me [*laughs*]!

I love the cloud of dust you kick up as you're charging at him. Like the Road Runner!

In school I used to be a very fast sprinter. But here's what you're actually seeing there: As I took off towards Arch, I had scooped-up handfuls of dirt in my hands and I threw them behind me, so it looked like an explosion, so that I'd have a cloud of dust behind me as I screamed and shot out at him like a bullet. That was *my* idea, to do it that way.

When you first found out that your character would be killed at the end of The Sadist, *what was your reaction?*

Didn't bother me at all. I was killed in *The Canadians* too—I was a gunfighter in that, and I was stampeded over a cliff! I've been killed several times, on [TV's] *The Virginian* and everything else.

What's your best scene in the movie? Or just a favorite scene?

I like the death scene. I kinda had the chance to *do* something, rather than just stand there and pontificate [*laughs*]. I didn't want to come off as a coward in *The Sadist* but I also didn't want to come off as some Hollywood hero, like Batman or something. I tried to just play it as honestly as I possibly could, the way a guy *would* in that situation, because, man, when you're faced with a weapon like that, you can't make many mistakes.

Arch, Jr., told me that a lot of the gunshots in The Sadist *are real.*

Yeah, we had live ammunition on that set. Like when Arch was shooting at me, through the boards as I was running away, that was live ammo. We didn't have the budget to do it with special effects, so that was real live ammo we used. It was such a low-budget film, we couldn't do anything *else*!

And your attitude about being in scenes where live ammo was being used?

Oh, nobody cared [*laughs*]—nobody cared at all. I had confidence that Arch wasn't gonna kill me, and that Jim wouldn't let it get *too* out-of-hand. We all knew that it was such a low-budget film, we couldn't [have stunt doubles]. We had to do everything ourselves.

Where did you see The Sadist *for the first time?*

We went to a screening in Los Angeles, at a theater down on LaBrea and Olympic or somewhere around there. It was just for the cast and crew and friends. Incidentally, I have

Alden took chances reel and real in *The Sadist*: Having live ammo fired in his direction by star Arch Hall, Jr. (left), and working for no salary in the non-union production (both Screen Actors Guild no-nos).

difficulty looking at myself on the screen, I don't like it at all. I had a funny experience: I went to a screening of it once, later on, where I wasn't in the audience, I was in the projection room. For some reason, looking at it from the projection room, I wasn't self-conscious and I was more objective about it. But when I'm sitting in the audience, I don't like it at all! Just "once removed" and it was all right to look at. Bob Ryan [star of *The Canadians*] told me he never saw *any* of his pictures, he couldn't stand to see himself—a *lot* of actors don't like to see themselves. Incidentally, it's funny to me to see *The Sadist* now: I see myself with a 30-inch waistline, and now it's 36! But I still work out and all that stuff.

Arch, Jr., told me you worked out with weights before going into each scene.

    I do things like that to relieve tension. It just helps me. I did it on *The Canadians*, too,

I did a whole bunch of push-ups before I did my very first scene ever, to loosen myself up and so on. I was a little tense—I was just starting out as an actor. I'm a far better actor now than I was then. I *hope* so, after all these years [*laughs*]!

Would you have worked for the Halls again?

Oh, yes! They did another one with a friend of mine that I got into it, a guy named Carmen Bonacci, about a brassiere salesman [*What's Up Front!*, 1964]. I've gotten a lot of other actors work, I can tell ya. But it doesn't seem to work the other way around for *me*! Oh, and Landis wanted me to do another one and I didn't want to do it, I didn't think I was right for it. It was a thing called *Tender Grass* [a.k.a. *Jennie: Wife/Child*, 1968] and I recommended Jim Reader, a friend of mine out of Pasadena Playhouse. His first movie, and he got a starring role in the movie [*laughs*]! And he did a good job with it.

The Sadist—*was that your biggest part in a movie?*

I guess it was the biggest. I've had other leads—I did a thing called *The Pit* [1981] that we shot in Canada. I played the father of the young boy [Sammy Snyders] who was the central character. It was about little monsters living in a pit in the woods and the kid can see them but nobody else believes that they exist. Lew Lehman directed it. He told me that I was the only one in the film that "matched" from shot to shot—you have to do the same thing [make the same movements] in every shot. He said I was the only one he didn't have to worry about when he was cutting from one angle to another, with me he had no trouble with the continuity at all. But a lot of the others in the cast were theater actors and they weren't used to doing that technique. Lew had worked with John Huston [on *Phobia*, 1980], and Huston cut his films in his head. Lew tried to do that and it didn't work quite so well, I don't think, because he had trouble putting it together [*laughs*]!

When you first saw The Sadist, *what did you think of it?*

I liked it pretty much. I'd love to be able to do it again, of course—I'm a much more experienced actor now than I was then. I thought it would do all right [box office-wise], but then Arch, Sr., went and apparently, according to Jim Landis, roadshowed it in various cities all around the country. Like one theater in New York and one theater in Chicago and one theater somewhere else, and it never got the exposure. Then I understood from Landis that Hugh Hefner was interested in blanket-releasing it in drive-ins, but that Hefner couldn't take it because it wasn't first-run any more. That killed it for me. If it had played in drive-ins, I'd have been pretty well-known, as well as Arch Hall and everybody else. I did the movie for that reason. But it all fell apart when it came to the distribution, so it didn't do me any good. My big gamble, to try to have it do me some good, didn't pay off at *all*.

But I'm glad I did it, because I'd never done a lead in a film before. It was fun, it was an education. Working with Jim was great, and Vilmos Zsigmond was a fabulous cameraman so it was great to work with him too. It was a great experience, I loved doing it. I never went into acting for money anyway—it was for the love of doing it. Money was never important to me. I couldn't believe they even paid me.

When they did *pay you!*

[*Laughs*] Well, after *The Sadist* I got paid for various things, naturally. I did a lot of work in Canada too. My parents were up there and I kept going back and forth to Canada all the time, and that really hurt my career here. Because if you leave town for ten minutes, your agent forgets you. You gotta stay here all the time. That was a big mistake I made.

You must have had other jobs throughout your acting days.

Oh, yes, I've had to do all kinds of other things to survive. I was never able to work just as an actor. I thought [the TV series] *Hogan's Heroes* was going to materialize into something. I started out doing German soldiers on it and they liked me because I could do a German accent and they made me the bartender [a recurring character]. It was only a few lines in each show, nothing much, but it was a lot of fun to be a part of it. I got to know a lot of the guys—Dick Dawson and I became friends. Then Bing Crosby Productions, which produced *Hogan's Heroes*, was going to do a show called *The Queen and I*, and they did the pilot, and I was going to be the bartender on the ship. But the show never went. So I've had a lot of close calls but never got the steady gig which everybody needs.

I came within a hair of a series up in Toronto called *The Starlost* with Keir Dullea, which was [an outer space show] like the Bill Shatner thing *Star Trek*. It came down to me and one other guy [Robin Ward], a guy a lot cuter than me and about ten years younger, and he got it over me. I thought I had *that* series pretty much locked-up but I didn't, I missed out on that. Then he beat me out of another part, too, later on [*laughs*]. They were doing the [1980s] *Alfred Hitchcock Presents* thing in Toronto and Eli Wallach was coming in to do the guest star, and I was auditioning for the second guest star. Eli Wallach, I wanted to work with him so bad, my teeth ached. I gave the reading of my life, Rene Bonniere the director told me that I gave a terrific reading, and I walked out of there feeling ten feet tall. Well, I didn't *get* it, they sent it down to Universal and *again* they went for the other guy, a very handsome guy. He couldn't act worth a damn, he just was wooden as hell, but he *looked* good. He was a nice guy and all that, *and* he just had that good look, which means a lot. I was really disappointed. While they were shooting it, I ran into Eli Wallach in a Toronto restaurant called Jingles where all the show people hang out, and I told him how badly I'd wanted to work with him. It's like playing tennis with Jimmy Connors or Bjorn Borg or somebody, it really validates you when you work with fine actors. Only actors understand this but it gives you even greater legitimacy when you work with really good people. I would have loved to have worked with Eli Wallach.

What are you doing these days?

They're interested in me for the lead in a [writer-producer] Stephen J. Cannell film up in Vancouver called *It Waits*, a horror film—there's a creature that lives in the wilderness and it's terrorizing the area. If I do it, and it looks pretty good, I'll play a senior forest ranger getting near retirement. In case it does happen, I'm growing a beard for it now. [Alden does not appear in this 2005 movie.] I also wrote a couple of screenplays, one of which, *Heart of Malice*, I sold to an independent film company called 50 Curb Productions. Another one I've written, called *Easy Street*, is I think a pretty good script but I haven't been able to sell it yet.

For Alden, seen here in a recent shot, the hunt for acting jobs goes on. He's also written a couple screenplays on spec.

Have any of your screenplays been produced yet?

No, not yet. Then I wrote a book about coming out [to Hollywood] to be an actor—it's all the things I would tell (say) a nephew back in Chicago or some place. I wrote it but I've never done anything with it! Some people have read it and liked it. It's real honest, it's the way it really *is* when you're trying to be an actor in this town, and the horrible disappointments and the mistakes that actors make. And that *I* made. Like leaving town and going up to Canada for two weeks, and staying for a *year*. Of course I *did* work up there, but it doesn't matter what you do up *there*, down *here* is all they care about. All of the mistakes I made, I tell people what they were and to try to avoid them. Of course, they'll all do the same things anyway, probably [*laughs*]. You can't put an old head on young shoulders.

And what final words on The Sadist?

It's fun to look back on—I have it on disc, and sometimes I look at it. All I can see is that small waistline of mine, that I wish I still had [*laughs*]! I did other things that I like better, but I'm glad I had that experience. Now that you tell me Jim Landis is gone, I feel badly that I was not around him near the end of his life. *The Sadist* was his shining moment. He was not good at kissing ass and this probably prevented him from going further. I thought the budget was $25,000 but even at $33,000 Jim worked miracles. What might he have done with a million…? Jim Landis was a vivid personality and I will miss him.

ERIC BRAEDEN

> *I have only now become fully aware of how good a picture [*Colossus: The Forbin Project*] really is. I realize now why Steven Spielberg was on the set almost every day when we shot it.... A lot of today's top directors were very influenced by* **Colossus**, *apparently....*

In the 1970 science fiction thriller *Colossus: The Forbin Project*, Eric Braeden starred as Dr. Charles Forbin, inventor of a super-computer designed to ensure a safe future for mankind; disaster ensued. The following year, playing the U.S. president's senior science adviser in *Escape from the Planet of the Apes*, he set out to save mankind from domination by apes; again, disaster followed. Then in 1997, playing multi-millionaire magnate John Jacob Astor in a certain James Cameron–directed mega-hit, Braeden boarded the *Titanic*!

Off-screen, fortunately for Braeden, things have gone a great deal better. The actor (real name: Hans Gudegast) has progressed from a struggling German-American supporting actor, resisting Hollywood typecasting (villainous and Nazi roles), to the co-star of TV's popular World War II series *The Rat Patrol* (1966–68), to one of the deans of daytime drama: For over a quarter-century, he has starred on TV's top-rated soap *The Young and the Restless* and has received multiple Emmy nominations (Outstanding Lead Actor in a Daytime Drama Series) for his performance as Victor Newman. (He won in 1998.)

Braeden, now marking his forty-fourth anniversary as an actor, was recently (August 2005) saluted by the American Cinematheque with a *Forbin Project* retrospective screening at which he made a personal appearance.

The Colossus *screening at the Egyptian Theater the other night—how did that go?*

I was more than pleasantly surprised. I have only now become fully aware of how good a picture it really is. *Now* I fully appreciate it. I realize now why Steven Spielberg was on the set almost every day when we shot it. Oliver Stone is also impressed with the film, I've heard. And when I did *Titanic*, after I did the scene where I came down the stairs in the first-class dining room, James Cameron turned to me and he said, "Never." I thought he was saying something about [the way I had done] the scene, so I was about to become slightly belligerent [*laughs*]—I said, "What do you mean, 'Never'?" And Cameron said, "You don't remember the last line in *Colossus*?" Turns out that he, too, is a big fan of the film! So a *lot* of today's top directors were very influenced by *Colossus*, apparently—they loved that film. I never fully appreciated it until Saturday night.

How did you find out that Spielberg was on the set every day? Did he make an impression on you in 1968, even though he hadn't really done *anything yet?*

He was sort of known as the little *enfant terrible* at Universal Studios. I was not aware of him, except I heard that this young director was very good. Stanley Chase, the producer, knew him—Stanley Chase, being a producer, was aware of the young, budding directors. Spielberg asked for permission to come to the set, so ... there you are.

When you were offered the lead in Colossus, *I know that you initially had reservations—and with very good reason!*

When I was offered *Colossus*, I was doing *100 Rifles* [1969] with Burt Reynolds, Raquel Welch, Jim Brown and Fernando Lamas in Spain. Tom Gries directed that, Tommy Gries who was also the originator of *The Rat Patrol* that I'd done before. I got a call, an agent saying that [Universal] would love to do a screen test with me for a starring role in a picture called *Colossus*. I had a week off, so I flew back from Madrid to L.A. and did the screen test and then flew back to Spain, where my wife and I shared a huge flat with Fernando Lamas and [his wife] Esther Williams. When the next call came in from my agent, he said, "Guess what? They loved your screen test, and Lew Wasserman wants you to star in the picture." Lew Wasserman, the president at Universal Studios and the most powerful man in Hollywood. I cannot begin to describe to you the feeling of elation, the unparalleled euphoria I felt. There was a pause, and then he added, "*However...*" I said, "What?" He said, "He wants to change your name [from Hans Gudegast]." I said, "You must be kidding." He was not kidding. I said, "*Never*. I simply won't do it," and I hung up. Within seconds, I went from euphoria to almost utter depression and dejection.

And the reason why *Universal was insistent on a name change?*

Lew Wasserman very specifically said no one with a German name would star in an American picture. But then I had time to think about it ... four weeks to think about it. I talked to my wife about it for a long time, we took long walks in Madrid, and as she and I talked, slowly one softened one's attitude when one began to bandy about the idea of doing it. And my wife reminded me of having played the son of Curt Jurgens on Broadway in a play [*The Great Indoors*] with Geraldine Page and Clarence Williams III, done in 1966, the Eugene O'Neill Theatre, and Jurgens then told me, "Listen, go back to Germany. You'll play nothing but Nazis in Hollywood. That's our fate." I said, "*I* will make a difference. I will be the one that gets out of that trap somehow." And *Colossus* was that escape. And up to that point, I never *was* burdened with the typical German accent, so I thought I had a chance to get out of it. I finally then thought of the careers of [Maximilian] Schell and Hardy Kruger and various others and thought, "Well ... I guess I have to bite into the sour apple." To change from Hans Gudegast was a *very*, very difficult thing to do. Long story short, we came up with a

Eric Braeden first came to the attention of television audiences as Capt. Dietrich, German commanding officer of a World War II armored unit, and nemesis of the Allied commandos who comprise *The Rat Patrol*.

name that was somewhat close to my emotional life. From the village I came from in Germany, called Bredenbek, I took the first part, Breden. In order for it *not* to be pronounced *breedin'*, I spelled it B-r-*a*-e-d-e-n. And Eric's a Nordic name—it could be British, could be Swedish, could be German, could be Norwegian, could be *any*thing. Hence, Eric Braeden. It took me a while to get used to it, but ... in retrospect, I'm glad I did it.

At the time when you did Colossus, *were you at all "into" science fiction?*

[*Flatly*] Not at all. Still couldn't care less. And knew nothing about computers. Am *still* a technophobe of sorts. I have enormous admiration for people in science, but that was not one of my stronger points in school, because we had people who taught physics and math who I did not *like* particularly, to be honest with you. It's amazing how important teachers are. However, after having done *Colossus*, I was often approached by computer science students [who recognized Braeden as its star] who said, "Oh, my God," and dah-dah-dah, and, "Can you tell us how...." I mean, they'd ask about things like "the heuristic programming section," and I had no idea what the fuck they were *talking* about! I would say, "No, no, no—

In *Colossus: The Forbin Project*, Braeden played "the father of Colossus," a computer programmed for peace—he *thinks*.

I'm so far advanced in this stuff that I really cannot burden you with it. Also, it's a secret, so I can't talk about it...." [*Laughs*] And I knew *nothing*!

But, no, I was never really "into" science fiction. *Reality* is so fascinating to me, history is so fascinating to me, that I cannot divorce myself enough to deal with science fiction. I hate to say that in your magazine [this interview originally appeared in the sci-fi-oriented magazine *Starlog*], but that's the truth. I'm so *fascinated* by reality that I am not fascinated even by *fiction*—not at all.

Do you happen to know if you were the first choice for the starring role?

Early on, they had either Charlton Heston or Gregory Peck in mind, but then they changed their mind about that. Stanley Chase insisted on a relative unknown. That's when I came into the picture.

Colossus *seems to have been Universal's answer to MGM's* 2001: A Space Odyssey *[1968], a big hit. Did you get the feeling that Universal was trying to emulate the success of* 2001*?*

That I don't know. They probably were; if *2001* was a big hit, then I'm certain that is what they wanted to do. I mean, studios all want to do that, I guess. As an actor, when you go into [a new project], you don't have these "overviews," you are obviously more concerned with interpreting the role and you're concerned with issues that pertain to us actors, and that means relationships with directors and fellow actors. I was just very, very impressed with [*Colossus* director] Joe Sargent. I can't say anything but the nicest things *imaginable* about him: He was the warmest, nicest director I've ever worked with. Hands down. No question about it. He's an actor's director. He had been an actor himself, he understood actors, and you never had that feeling of there being a gulf between the two. He's a wonderful man and a great director, and when I now see the film, I realize just how good he *was*. He was *damn* good. For example, when you watch the crowd scenes in the computer room, he did a wonderful job with an essentially static set. Not too much action, as it were. As I sat in the balcony of the Egyptian and saw it on that huge screen, I said to myself, "You know, I never really paid him enough homage." I just am *so* impressed with what he did.

You mentioning the "static" set reminds me to tell you: Last night as I re-watched the movie, it occurred to me that Colossus *might be the most exciting movie—that has no action—that I've ever seen.*

That's very interesting that you say that, that's *nice* that you corroborate my feeling about that.

To me, Colossus *isn't just a good science fiction movie, it's a darn good movie, period.*

I don't see too many movies. The reason I don't is because I can't sleep after them most of the time. I stay up 'til four, five in the morning [thinking about the fact that] I want very badly to *write* [movies], I want to *direct*, I want to do all that, and I know damn well I won't. So I often don't see them. I used to see Woody Allen films, or Ingmar Bergman films, and ... I can't sleep afterwards, because I so *badly* want to do it then, and know full well what my limitations are. So now I won't frustrate myself with this stuff.

A massive amount of actual computer stuff was brought into Universal to dress the lab set.

It was overwhelming, and very impressive to a novice.

I've read that parts of Colossus *were shot at U.C. Berkeley.*

Yes, at the [Lawrence] Livermore National Laboratory. Then we went to Rome, which was an interesting experience. The scene we did there was shot on the Tiber, near one of

Forbin's (Braeden) dream of seeing the countries of the world join hands and hearts becomes a nightmare when his all-powerful Defense Department supercomputer Colossus, impregnably installed inside a mountain, sets itself up as supreme dictator.

Rome's oldest synagogues. I was in Rome filming scenes of *Colossus*, and I could have been almost concurrently doing *another* film that a producer at Universal offered to me—he offered me the chance to play one of the male leads, and I couldn't do it. The producer was Leonardo Bercovici, and the movie was *Story of a Woman* [1970] with Bibi Andersson. I wanted to do that film simply because of Bibi Andersson, not because of the others in it but Bibi Andersson, because I've been a big fan of Ingmar Bergman's films. However, James Farentino ended up doing it. I would have *much* preferred to have done that [over *Colossus*], although as I now see *Colossus* in retrospect, I must say it was of fundamentally greater importance than *Story of a Woman* [laughs]!

What can you say about your co-stars, Gordon Pinsent [a JFK lookalike playing the U.S. president] and Susan Clark [Forbin's colleague and, later, lover]?

Gordon Pinsent was wonderful to work with. A gentleman, and a damn good actor. When I saw *Colossus* again on Saturday night, I thought, "*Damn*, he was good." Working with Susan was a pleasant experience.

You and Susan Clark had a nude scene of sorts in the movie.

Susan had some difficulty, contractually with Universal, over that issue, I think, they fought a little over that. That's all I remember, vaguely, sort of in the back of my mind. I know that there was some controversy in regard to that, *some* issue involving whether she wanted to be seen in the nude or not.

And your feeling about being asked to do it...?

Look, I'm basically European—you think I give a shit whether someone is nude or not [*laughs*]? I think it's great. To have any reservations about it, to me, is sick. To me, that is *sick*. In other words, the notion that people have strange feelings about seeing a nude body, to me, is the height of sickness. *That*, to me, is perverse. *Totally* perverse. *That* is how we were born! You think God was ashamed when He created us? I mean, this is utterly ludicrous! To impose these kinds of restrictions, and shameful feelings, upon the nude body is *sick* and *perverse*, and whoever's responsible has, as far as I'm concerned, done mankind an *enormous* disservice. That's as simple as it is. There's *nothing* wrong with a nude body. *Nothing* at all. It ought to be celebrated—the Greeks did it, and as far as I'm concerned they were far more civilized, when it comes to that, than the barbaric monotheists who decry the human body in its nakedness—I resent the hell out of that. The nude body ought to be *cherished* and it should be *deified*, as it used to be in the old times. What's happening now, about that, is *sick*.

According to the books, you and she both wore body stockings in that scene.

I certainly did not. Of *course* not. What the fuck would I wear a body ... [*trails off*]. Let's put it *this* way: Under the *sheets*, one wasn't completely naked, no, of course not. But

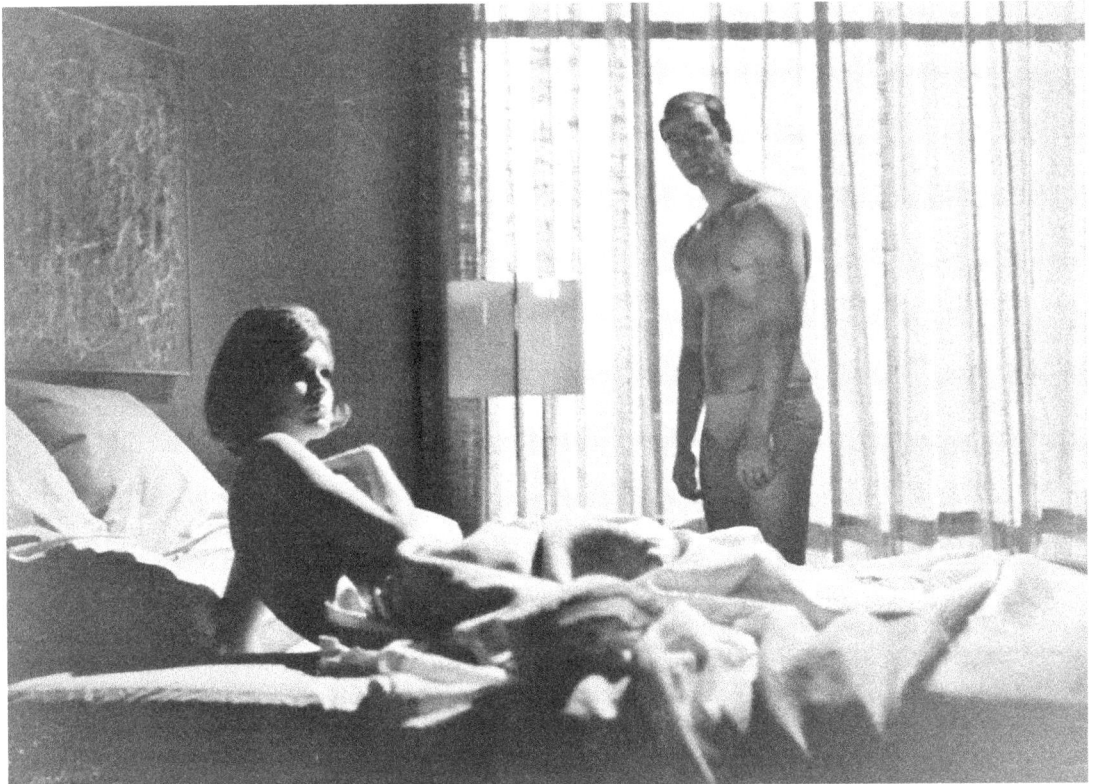

Susan Clark may have hesitated to do a nearly nude scene in Colossus, **but European-born Braeden "[didn't] give a shit."**

then you almost never are, unless it's specifically called for. You don't want to embarrass the actress, unless she is open to that, or whatever. No, you don't want to do that. Besides that, to be frank with you ... unless you're an exhibitionist, it's not the most sexual surrounding [a movie set], when you have nothing but crews around. That is not very conducive to sexual scenes ... it is *not*.

James Bridges, who wrote Colossus, *had mixed feelings about the way it came out. He thought that Joseph Sargent humanized the people too much. He felt the movie should have been "colder."*

I disagree with Bridges, even though I can see, intellectually, where he's coming from. It's an interesting point. There *is* a tendency in Hollywood to sort of sentimentalize things a little bit, but in *Colossus* I don't think it was overdone, not really.

I'm afraid I don't enjoy movies where you can't identify with the characters.

I guess he was thinking of *2001*, wasn't he? But those characters in *2001* were fuckin' boring [*laughs*]. Utterly boring! The story was fantastic, but *they* were boring. And *that*, in turn, has partly to do, I think, with the director. In other words, directors who have *enormous* egos very often will.... [*Pause*] I don't want to get into Stanley Kubrick. But some directors, they see it as an auteur, they see it as a novelist—in other words, the story [becomes] bigger than the individuals involved. But if it's devoid of humanity, if it's devoid of recognizable human traits, then ... what do *I* care? I don't give a damn. It just doesn't interest me. I think it's more reflective of the inner life of a director than almost anything else, don't you? And Joe Sargent could not have done that if you *paid* him. He's just a warm human being, he's a *mensch*.

I can't think of too many science fiction movies in which the star has more screen time than you do in Colossus. *Except for a few minutes, you're in it from start to finish.*

At the Egyptian, with my son who came along, my wife who came along, we watched it and ... I did a pretty good job, yeah [*laughs*]! Again, I have to say, I sat back and I thought, "I'll be damned. This was a pretty damn good movie!" I was sitting up in the balcony, not expecting anything, and I was so pleasantly surprised, and suddenly realized this was really a damn good film. I sort of had tears in my eyes at the end, and I thought, my God, I never really thanked Joe Sargent enough for the wonderful job he did as a director. Nor did I thank the production designers enough. Or the producer, Stanley Chase, who put the whole thing together. The technical aspects of it, and the directorial accomplishment, was just tremendous, and I never really gave the film enough credit and enough respect. Now I have enormous respect for it. It became visceral when I saw it again.

In Colossus, *the computer's cameras are everywhere, and Forbin talks about the loss of privacy being intolerable. I couldn't help but think of our twenty-first century world and all its surveillance cameras, and some people starting to get their backs up about it. Could you talk about* Colossus *as it relates to privacy concerns today?*

Look, all new things are born of necessity, and terrorism is here to stay for a while, I'm absolutely convinced of it. Because a large part of the world is pissed off at the Western world. That obviously necessitates a kind of surveillance that will require installation of cameras and all kinds of biometric things and identity things. Living in this day and age, you sort of say, "Yeah, I understand the need for it." I *am*, to be quite frank with you, amused by the *paucity* of it, at airports. I mean, it's a joke as far as I'm concerned. And this business of arbitrarily selecting every fifth person or tenth person on line at the airport [for a more thorough search] is ridiculous. How 'bout *looking* at the person? I mean, *please*! I know it ain't politically correct, but you cannot be politically correct and let some obvious candidates, people who look suspicious, go through. They single out some gray-haired old lady in a fuckin' wheelchair—I mean, give me a *break*. This is *outrageous*. It's *stupid* and outrageous. So you know *part* of that is just a p.r. job. I don't want to get into the details of it, but I remember being on an Air Canada flight not too long ago, and I had warned them, prior to getting onto the plane, about three characters I had observed. Lo and behold, one of 'em started shit on the plane: He went to the toilet, started smoking, started all kinds of ruckus, and said "I hate America!" and "Down with America!" I was sitting up in first class and became aware of the commotion and, long story short, two F-16s escorted us back to LAX.

If you *really* want to do security, you take certain people aside and ask them some questions. To me, that's very obvious. *However*, in our democratic society, you may get sued for coming to the wrong person. It's a difficult problem, an enormously difficult problem. But look at the surveillance cameras in London, how they helped identify [the July 7, 2005, subway bombers]—so it *can* work, it *does* work. And it's something we have to live with.

Knowing all those cameras are around makes me *feel safer, and makes other people feel very threatened.*

With a "European tinge to his quality," Braeden gave his *Colossus* role "stature as well as attractiveness," according to one reviewer. It was his first starring movie, Stanley Chase's first film as producer and Joseph Sargent's first as director.

It's a tough question to answer. I have no succinct answer. I'd rather err on the side of security. Wouldn't *you*?

Pffft! Oh, absolutely!

And, as far as I'm concerned, the wrong people are doing the screening. Give me a break. It's a fucking joke, it's pathetic. They should be trained, they should be government people. Stop this *nonsense* of privatizing everything—what's *that* bullshit all about? The lowest bidder gets the job, gets the contract. What does that *mean*?

And with lives at stake!

Barely educated people are now doing the screening. It's *outrageous*. What is this mantra about privatizing everything? It's ridiculous. There are certain functions that government-supervised and government-educated people should *do*, period. With certain requirements. One of which is that you can *read*!

I've read that Universal bollixed up the release of Colossus—*they did a real half-assed job of it, perhaps partly because they were more interested in promoting* Airport *[1970].*

They didn't do a damn thing with it. But I think that also had to do with the fact that this was a very bad time for movies. Remember, there was then the beginning of a recession in the country. Let me tell you *that* story: For a period of about three years, between '70 and '73, [Hollywood] made almost no films. Around that time, I was approached by a wonderful agency called Chase-Park-Citron, the Rolls-Royce of the agency business then, and Herman Citron took me to Hillcrest Country Club here in Beverly Hills and had lunch with me, and said, "You'll be a big star one day ... but, do me a favor, don't do any television right now. But you gotta be patient now, because they'll make no films for a while." What nobody knew was how long the recession would last. But I had a child by that time, a family to feed, hence, after a while, I said, "Wait a minute. I can't wait *this* long." Hardly any films were being financed. That is the time period during which you had Tony Curtis, Anthony Quinn, Jimmy Stewart, Rock Hudson, all kinds of people, suddenly starting to do television, because no films were being made. So I started doing television. And that was, in a sense, the end of the film career. That is the brutal reality of Hollywood. I guest-starred on all kinds of shows ... and became so utterly bored with it that I said, "I want *out* of this business." Then I was offered the thing I've been doing now for 25 years....

The Young and the Restless.

Correct. I looked at it with great trepidation. I signed a deal for, I think, three months—and wanted *out* after three months. Then of course they dangled the inevitable financial carrot, and I succumbed ... and the rest is history, 25 years later.

Incidentally, after *Colossus* I was approached to do James Bond. I was at lunch with "Cubby" Broccoli at his house, very pleasant, very nice, and he said, "Do you still have a British passport?" A lot of people thought I was a Brit. I told him I did *not* have a British passport, and that was the end of that. He said that no one who was not a subject of the British Commonwealth, either British or Irish, or Australian or I think even Canadian, would have worked in the part, could play the part of James Bond.

That would have been a heck of an opportunity.

No question about it. But to be honest with you, at that time I wasn't even that interested. No, because it was sort of derivative. I mean, how can you replace Sean Connery? You can say what you want, but he's the only James Bond that I would ever take a look at.

You and me both.

So it didn't interest me in the least.

Escape from the Planet of the Apes—*do you recall the details of getting that part?*

Nope. They were just interested. Don Taylor directed, another nice man—he's passed away now. A nice man and an actor's director. The whole group was just a very pleasant group of people. [Stars] Roddy McDowall and Bradford Dillman and Kim Hunter ... it was a pleasant experience. I'm just glad I didn't have to play one of the apes! I felt sorry for those actors. They came there at three or four in the morning. Imagine that, every morning, and a four-hour makeup job. That is just absolutely horrendous. I have nothing but respect for that. Then at night they had to take the damn makeup off.

I'm going to guess that you had not seen the previous Apes *movies.*

No.

The Apes *pictures ... you'd think they'd be silly movies,* kid's *movies, with talking apes running around. But there are some intelligent ideas in a few of 'em, especially yours.*

To be honest with you, I think the character I played, Dr. Hasslein, had rather a reasonable position. [Hasslein wanted to sterilize apes Cornelius and Zira so that world-dominating apes would not descend from them.] Don't you think? I remember standing at a party afterwards, with Steve Allen and his wife [Jayne Meadows], and telling them that I thought Hasslein's position was reasonable, and they were just aghast! I never forgot that reaction. I said, "No, just *think* about it...." It made a great deal of sense, what Hasslein said.

Think of, now, the debate raging in *all* societies as to the causes of xenophobia. Xenophobic outbreaks usually are a result of unwanted immigration. The question now, here in America, is a very legitimate question. Most Americans came as legitimate immigrants to this country, and went through hell and high water to get here. Illegal immigration is truly a reason for outrage, as far as I'm concerned. It has *nothing* to do with being xenophobic, it simply has to do with the fact of saying, "*Wait* a minute. *Every*one else who came here, including myself, applied in regular ways to become an immigrant." You fulfill certain quotas and what have you, you wait for your time, you get a green card, and that's how you go about it. *Why* now, all of a sudden, should millions come in here without having to go through that process? Well, the hypocrisy, of course, lies with Big Business. They usually say, "We don't want these non-registered immigrant aliens in our country," but on the other hand, they profit from it enormously, and *that* is why it goes on. You know that and I know that. Agriculture in California would suffer immeasurably if it weren't for that cheap labor that comes across the border; the entire clothing industry would suffer; a myriad of restaurants all over California would suffer—it goes on and on. It's a vexing problem, isn't it? It's an enormous problem. Or *is* it a problem? Maybe it isn't!

That was the interesting thing about Hasslein: He goes off the deep end in Escape, *he becomes "the villain of the piece" ... but, dagnabbit, he's convinced that he's doing the right thing, and I in the audience am not sure that he* isn't *right.*

Exactly. That made it an interesting part. Look: America's a country of immigrants, and I would say that over 90 percent—*vastly* over 90 percent of the people who have come here, who are now Americans, their forefathers came through the regular channels of immigration. It ain't easy to get into this country. It is damn tough. Well, why all of a sudden should it now be made so easy for millions of others to come across the border? Not to speak of enormous danger as far as terrorists are concerned. Terrorists *are* a reality. It's not a figment of someone's imagination, it is reality. Those porous borders south of here ... it's horrendous. And don't tell me that the United States government, with all of its extraordinary technological know-how, wouldn't know how to close those damn borders. It's *bullshit*. Of *course* they can. It's one of the great hypocrisies.

In an old interview, you talked about the reaction you got from kids after playing that part in Escape from the Planet of the Apes.

[*Laughs*] I would walk through Westwood, where my family and I lived at the time, and parents would be walking with their kids, and they would say, "Oh my God, that's the terrible man who shot the baby chimp." Of course, you live with that, as an actor. When you play the bad guy, there's always the mixture of ... there's a smile on people's faces, yet, if they're young enough, they're shocked. But I was used to that, I played so many bad guys.

Did you watch your own movies when they came out?

I've seen *Colossus* altogether three times—the other night was the third time. *Escape from the Planet of the Apes* once. The part in *Escape*, obviously, was an example of all the *bad* characters, the bad guy types I played. And I had developed such distaste for that, that I could have screamed. That goes along with something that has been a motivating force in

Audiences perceived Braeden's *Escape from the Planet of the Apes* character to be villainous for wanting to sterilize Cornelius (Roddy McDowall) and Zira (Kim Hunter)—but the actor thought, and still thinks, that that course of action had its merits.

my private life, and hence I created what is called the German-American Cultural Society, because I was sick and tired of the dehumanization of German characters. The fate of most German actors, as we discussed before, was to play these terrible characters. In those days, I played all *kinds* of heavies—American heavies, Russian heavies, Italian heavies, any heavy you can imagine, I've run the gamut. But I was *tired* of that, and that's why I love doing what I'm doing now [*The Young and the Restless*], and I've loved it for the last 25 years. Or at least 24 of the 25, because the first year I hated it. But after about a year I began to realize that I'd been given a chance to play aspects of a human being that I was never given before. *Never, ever* given before. In *all* of his shadings. That's why daytime, I think, has an enormous advantage over nighttime and over most films: You touch upon aspects of a man's character that you normally don't get to play. In films, you have a good guy and a bad guy; in nighttime TV, it's also clearly divided between good and bad. But in daytime TV, the character I play is very complex, capable of coldness and brutality and capable of enormous affection and tenderness and vulnerability. *That* you don't get to do very often in the other media, you really don't. I think perhaps I've contributed a little bit to our medium in that I insisted on playing all kinds of aspects of the character. I've enjoyed that part of it *enormously*, and I'm extremely loyal to this medium for that reason. I regret dreadfully not to have painted a large canvas, as it were, namely film and nighttime, because obviously by virtue of the fact that [*The Young and the Restless*] plays during the day, a lot of people *don't* get to see it, although over 120 million people a day *do* watch this stuff all over the world. But yet ... if one were to do a successful nighttime series, or if one were to have this kind of longevity in films, then a larger group of people would see it. *That* I regret, but otherwise, as an actor, I've been allowed to do things in daytime that I was never allowed to *do* before, and I'm eternally grateful.

And you work under tighter conditions than the actors in nighttime shows and in movies.
   There are some performances that we do in one or two takes, and I'll be damned if they don't compare very favorably with what you see at night and in film, where they have 10 or 20 or 30 takes. And we out-act most of those guys against the *wall*. I want to see most nighttime actors, or film actors, or stage actors, come on our set and do between 10 and 40 pages of dialogue a day, in one or two takes. I'm known as someone who works very fast, and considering that, sometimes you look at it and say, "I'll be damned. That's really not bad." Having *said* that, I would obviously rather star in films—who wouldn't? But very few people are given that chance.

Even before The Young and the Restless, *in the 1970s, you'd already pretty much disappeared from feature films.*
   After *Escape*, its producer Arthur Jacobs wanted me to star in a film called *The Aquanauts*. It was going to be some huge, underwater, bottom-of-the-sea adventure—I have no memory now exactly what it was about, but it sounded very exciting and he wanted me to star in it. But then Jacobs passed away. We had already done some testing on sound stages at 20th Century–Fox when he passed away, but *The Aquanauts* never came to fruition.

How did you like working with Jacobs on Escape *and, briefly,* The Aquanauts?
   Oh, he couldn't have been nicer. Jacobs used to have parties at his house in Beverly Hills, and I never go to Hollywood parties—that's been a rule of mine as an actor. Unless [the hosts] know you don't want *anything* from them. I'd just rather remain arrogant and distant. If they want something from me, fine, otherwise, I couldn't care less. I've always

told that to my son [screenwriter Christian Gudegast] as well: "Remember one thing: In this town, familiarity breeds contempt. Be aware of that. Stay distant, stay mysterious, stay *away*." I remember other actors coming up to me, asking, "How come you weren't at *this* party or *that* party?" I would say, "What? To blow smoke up someone's orifice? I couldn't care less." That's what most people don't realize: Schmoozing and socializing in this business, as an actor, is, I think, absolutely counterproductive. It means *nothing*. It means *absolutely nothing*. However, I succumbed to the invitations to Arthur Jacobs' because he promised to have ping pong tournaments [*laughs*], and anything with sports, I immediately go to, if it's a competition. So we'd have ping pong competitions with Walter Matthau and Dick Zanuck and all kinds of people. *That* was the only way he got me there. Those were pleasant Sunday afternoons, and a lot of people came by, and ... so that was different.

It was sports that brought you to America, and sports again bringing you to Hollywood.

I had won the German Youth Championship, with a team that I was on—we were the smallest team ever to win the German Youth Championship in track and field. My disciplines were discus, javelin and shot-put.

According to your publicity, you received a track scholarship to Montana State University.

First I was in Texas for about four weeks, then I went to Montana and worked as a cowboy on a ranch of a German rancher who had come [to America] at the turn of the last century. He was already rather old then, obviously, and had a ranch near Missoula, Montana. I worked as a cowboy for a while, and then applied to University of Montana, Missoula, on the track scholarship. They accepted it, and I was there for a year. But the scholarship only covered tuition, not my living expenses. So I worked in a lumber mill from six to two in the morning, outside of Missoula, in a place called Bonner. I worked on the "green chain"—that means, in the winter, from six to two in the morning, you work [out of doors], just a roof over your head, the rest is open. You imagine how cold *that* was.

I can't imagine.

Ten guys on one side of the green chain, ten on the other side, and freshly cut boards come out of the sawmill, and you're responsible for certain-sized boards, and you stack them all night for eight hours. That was my job from six to two in the morning. I was home by three o'clock, got up at seven, went to my first class at eight and listened to lectures on philosophy or humanities or political science or whatever it was. I'd be dead tired. I went to track and field practice at two in the afternoon ... then I slept for an hour ... and then I went back to work. That was my first year in Montana. And then I said, "This shit has gotta *stop!*"

[Laughs] *I feel exhausted just hearing about it!*

Through my girlfriend and *her* friends, I met a guy called Bob McKinnon, who was on a swim team, and he was looking for a partner to go with him up and down the Salmon River in Idaho, the River of No Return. It's called that because no one had ever *returned* from an attempt to go *up* against the rapids and down again. You have to differentiate between *that* and going down the rapids in a rubber raft—that's relatively easy. Try, in a 14-foot-long Crestliner aluminum boat, with a 40-horsepower Johnson motor in the back, going *up* the river, and then down again. No one had ever done that. I asked him, "What's the upshot?," and he said, "We'll make a documentary film. Then we go to California." I said, "I'm *in*." Anything to get away from that hellhole that I was in at the time—although Montana is beautiful.

We made the river trip, sponsored by Johnson Motors and Alcoa Aluminum. I almost died on that trip three times. The part of it that was filmed, was filmed on only two miles near an accessible road on the Salmon River. The most dangerous parts were *not* filmed. The part that was filmed was on the tamest part of the river. It was done by an inadequate photographer, a guy from Missoula who didn't know his ass from a hole in the ground. But we made our documentary, which was called *The Riverbusters*. It almost cost me my life, but it brought me eventually to California. We were actually sponsored to take a bigger boat and go up the Amazon and down again—and thank God *that* didn't work out!

And then you began acting.

Well, at first, of course, I didn't know a soul in Los Angeles. So I started parking cars. And I worked for a furniture moving company, moving furniture. And learned how to curse in English [*laughs*], whilst carrying a refrigerator up some stairs. There was an old American guy on top carrying the top part, I was at the bottom, and an old lady was saying, "Now, don't touch *this*" and "Don't touch *that*." We were barely holding on to this enormous weight, and—I'll never forget it—the old guy said, "Lady, will you shut the fuck *up*??" I was trying to translate from German into English—"'Shut the fuck up'? Wait a minute—he's turning a verb into a noun!" I'll never forget the moment: I remember the time of day, I remember where on the steps it was, and I *loved* it—"Shut the fuck *up*," it sounded wonderful! That's how I learned how to curse.

So, yes, sports have always been an enormously important part of ... not only my physical wellbeing, but my psychological wellbeing. My father died early on, I grew up in the postwar years in Germany and it was an enormously tough time. I don't want to get into that.... I'll write a book about that shit one day. He died when I was 12, and that makes you a very angry young man. The thing that saved me was sports of one sort or another, mostly track and field, and from ice hockey to boxing to soccer to ... I did *every*thing. It got my mind off things.

Things such as...?

The first four years of my life were spent under bombs. Every night, every single night, they bombed the shit out of the town I was born in. I viscerally remember the nightly bombings, and then *daily* and nightly bombings. It leaves enormous ... scars. It leaves you with an enormous amount of impotent anger. Your father dies, you grow up with three brothers, and you have fights all the time ... if not with the brothers, then with whoever looks at you cross-eyed.... [*Pause*] So sports was an avenue *out* of that complexity of emotions, those conflicts, that anger. Coming to America, obviously, I continued with track and field, and later on with soccer—in L.A., I began to play for a Jewish soccer team called the Maccabees. By then I had become politically aware, because I had seen for the first time, in a theater on Beverly Drive and Wilshire Boulevard in Beverly Hills, a film about concentration camps. It was *Mein Kampf* [1961]. I was then 19 or 20, and it was the first time that I saw what actually happened in concentration camps. In German high school, we had not discussed it; we discussed everything *up until* the Second World War, and then Hitler was dealt with sort of ... derisively, but not really seriously. So my first introduction to this horror was in 1961. I'll never forget it ... it was, obviously, one of the [eye-opening] moments of my life. I wrote letters full of vitriol and anger back to my mother and asked, "That is what my father's generation was part of?" (He was dead, I couldn't ask *him* questions.) You go through that whole *enormous* upheaval of anger and shame and guilt and fury. Very little has been done about *my* generation's reaction to all that ... it's one of the most difficult things to deal with, because there's nothing you can do to undo it. I began to play soccer for the Maccabees:

Whilst playing the Nazi characters on *The Rat Patrol* and all that, I played soccer with a Star of David on my chest every Sunday. We had seven Israeli players (tough players, very good players), two Brazilians, a Mexican and two Germans, and we won the U.S. Championship, 1972–73. One of the proudest moments in my life.

And, as you mentioned earlier, you co-founded the German-American Cultural Society.

Our main aim is German-Jewish dialogue. We have Jewish members and non–Jewish members, it's consciously and intentionally a mixed group, and we discuss issues that pertain to this subject matter. I also have very close relations to Israel; I go there, often as a guest of the Israeli Ministry of Tourism. I have a deep sense of solidarity with that country. Obviously, if you think for five minutes, you realize that Israel is also largely a product of the Holocaust and that, as Germans, we have a responsibility—*my* generation has a responsibility, first of all, to make sure that none of this horror ever occurs again. That you do by insuring that democracy remains intact, that no one is allowed to invoke the so-called "emergency laws," Article 48 of the Weimar Constitution that allowed Hitler to create an emergency, meaning that he shut down all opposing press and incarcerated anyone who opposed him. It allowed that bastard to take over completely and suspend all democratic rights. *That* we must never allow again. There is danger in this country right now, because there are fewer and fewer people taking over more and more media. That is an enormous danger, and it leads to oversimplification. We *need* a diversification of news, a diversification of opinions, in order to insure that a democracy survives. That is the true lesson to be learned and extrapolated from the Nazi experience.

Getting back to your TV career, I want to bounce a few titles off of you. Kolchak: The Night Stalker?

[*Laughs*] We did that one [*continues to laugh*], I think on the *Queen Mary*. [*More laughs*]

And you were the werewolf.

[*Laughs*] Allen Baron was the director, who was an old friend, and we had a lot of fun doing that. It was funny ... it was funny....

Wonder Woman?

[Lynda Carter] was extraordinarily beautiful. Just extraordinarily beautiful. And that wonderful actor, Ken Mars, was in it too. Beyond that, I don't remember a damn thing. What I remember of *Wonder Woman* is nothing except the fact that she was just

As the star of the daytime drama *The Young and the Restless*, he has been a television fixture for nearly three decades. In July 2007 Braeden (www.ericbraeden.com) received a star on the Hollywood Walk of Fame.

an extraordinarily beautiful and gracious woman. One of *the* most beautiful women I've ever worked with, and I've worked with a few.

And the movie Piranha *[1978]?*

[*Pause*] I didn't *do* that.

I know you didn't, I was wondering why.

Well, let me *tell* you why, because it's interesting. I was offered that part, and I went down to the location, and it was so haphazard that I turned around and said, "No, thank you." It just was so shoddy, the whole thing, that I said, "Not interested," and turned around before I started.*

A little while ago you mentioned your son. What's he doing now career-wise?

I'm proudest of his accomplishments, because he does what I have always wanted to: He *writes*. And he's a damn good writer. He goes under the old name of Gudegast, Christian Gudegast, and he wrote *A Man Apart* [2003], and he's writing all kinds of other things right now, very successfully. And he will direct soon. You will hear from him. No question.

I read a bunch of old interviews with you, and almost invariably the interviewers mention in their intros that you don't suffer fools gladly, that you're very intense, that you're arrogant. How come I find myself talking to a pussycat? What have you done with the real *Eric Braeden?*

"Arrogant" isn't really the right word, it is a sense of integrity, it is a sense of knowing who I am, and I will not kiss someone's ass in order to get somewhere. Either buy what I have to offer, or don't—and I don't give a *damn*. I am really *most* cooperative when I work with people if they approach me on an equal footing. But when I detect *any* kind of condescension, I'll come *after* you. I'll come after you so fast, you have no idea. And I don't give a shit who you are. I don't give a damn whether you're a cop, I don't give a damn what director it is—and directors often have the tendency to megalomania. As soon as I notice any of that shit, I come after you. You *will* know that I am around.

If you approach me in a decent manner, if you treat me as a human being, *with* respect, I will treat *you* with respect. Immediately. No questions asked. Let me give you an example: I cannot *stand* it when I'm with some friends of mine, American friends, who will deal very arrogantly with busboys or with waiters. *I cannot stand that.* I've been one myself. It's important to deal with another human being with respect, *regardless* of what they do, I don't give a *damn* what they do, whether they are janitors, whether they are busboys, whether they are doctors, what*ever* it is. If I see a human being in you, and we relate as human beings, that's fine. If you try to be condescending with me in *any* way, I'll come after you. That's as simple as it is. I do not suffer people who use authority arbitrarily. I'll fuckin' come *after* you. But if you treat me as a human being, with respect and with decency, you can have *any*thing.

According to Joe Dante, director of Piranha, *Braeden did* start, *and does* very briefly appear (two underwater shots) in the finished film. *"Eric dutifully showed up at the USC Olympic swimming pool to shoot some underwater shots in pre-production. One look at the kiddie crew, the rubber fish and general all-around air of 'Let's put on a show in the barn' was enough for him. He did what was asked, then that night or the next day I got a phone call from him, very apologetic, saying, 'I can't do it, I just can't!' And, believe me, I understood! We must have looked like the most rag-tag bunch of bumpkins. I couldn't blame him, I told him there were no hard feelings—and there* weren't. *His departure led to my hiring Kevin McCarthy to play Dr. Hoak, and Kevin and I have been friends ever since. I always looked for something for Eric in subsequent pictures, but the only part I ever came up with was Victor Scrimshaw in* Innerspace *[1987]—and we know who got that one [McCarthy again]!"*

ANN CARTER

*As a child I had an imaginary playmate,
who had to have a place at the table.
I think a lot of kids do.... You might have had one too!*

The following introduction was adapted from one written by *Video Watchdog* editor Tim Lucas for *VW* #137 (March 2008), where this interview originally ran:

If this magazine has any guiding aesthetic, it is our appreciation for the dark beauty and the wisdom that can be found in the fantastic cinema. There is no greater, more seminal embodiment of these aesthetics than the chillers produced at RKO in the 1940s by Val Lewton. Likewise, few characters in the fantastic cinema are more personally meaningful to us, and our readers, than little Amy Reed, the troubled protagonist of Lewton's *The Curse of the Cat People* (1944).

It's doubtful that anyone reading this could fail to recognize an aspect of themselves, or the child we once were, in Ann's most famous performance. Despite its exploitative title and status as a sequel to 1942's *Cat People*, *Curse* was not a horror film, but rather an intimate psychological study of the troubles that can arise from adults' common inability to address children as equals, and their condescending invention of fancies to amuse them. Playing a Sleepy Hollow youngster with a vivid fantasy life, complete with ghostly companion (Simone Simon), Carter's performance has been highly praised by some movie historians, and even by the movie's co-director Robert Wise in the book *Fearing the Dark: The Val Lewton Career* (McFarland & Co., 1994): "One big asset [to *Curse*] was the little girl, Ann Carter.... I'm always struck by how good she is and how consistent her performance is through the whole film. Ann Carter just had one of those marvelous bits of chemistry for the screen that some actors have. She just clicked on the screen and that was it."

I was born in Syracuse, New York, on June 16, 1936. My dad was with the Dodge division of Chrysler Corporation—he worked there for 38 years—and my mom was a stay-at-home mom. When I was born, my mother, who was 40, became quite ill. I was an RH baby; that's an immune problem where the mother's body rejects the baby because they have different blood factors. She was in good health *until* I was born, but then she had arthritis and some kidney problems and other complications. *And*, she just could not deal with the cold weather any more. Moving to California helped: When I was three, Mom and I moved out to Palm Springs, and my dad was sorta back and forth because California and Detroit, where he was working for Chrysler on defense-related projects. Then after Palm Springs, Mom and I moved in with Mom's sister, my Aunt Stell (short for Estelle), and *her* husband, my Uncle Jack. First we lived with them in Glendale, on Idlewood, for a very short time, and then [we moved] to a place near Olympic and Robertson in West Los Angeles, with Dad there again part-time.

So who got interested in you becoming an actress, you or your mother?

Mom had always been very interested in the theater, and wanted to be involved in that herself, but her father would not allow it. Now, I was only four years old when this all began and so I only know what Mom has told me, but when we lived in West Los Angeles, one day she and I were on a bus and someone from 20th Century–Fox saw me and told my mom that I should be introduced to a producer-director named Herbert Brenon. I *was*, and through Mr. Brenon I got to try out for a one-line part in Fox's *Last of the Duanes* [shot in April–May 1941]—and I got the part! I was just too little, I do not know anything about *Last of the Duanes* except for what my mom said, but she was vvvvery focused and I'm sure she told me exactly what happened. It was a Western and I was held by some actor [J. Anthony Hughes] and all I had to say was one line, "That's not the man, Daddy." When it was time for me to say it, the actor gave me a little pinch [as a cue] and I said it. And that was that [*laughs*]! So Herbert Brenon was responsible for getting me started, but all I remember is that he was an older gentleman *then* and he wore a hat all the time, and that's *all*!

Your first fantasy film was I Married a Witch *[1942] with Fredric March and Veronica Lake.*

I remember *I Married a Witch*, that one I do have in my head, because it made such an impression. I played Veronica Lake's little daughter and in the last scene, I was supposed to come flying down a staircase on a broomstick. The broom was suspended by a wire from a boom, and it was quite a big deal for them to make a little seat on it for me. Doing it was *so* exciting that that has stayed in my mind. I got on the broom and I don't recall being afraid, it was just ... exciting! I was five then.

So the broom swung down over the staircase, with you sitting on it, as though it was flying.

Yes, on a wire attached to the boom. I remember being fitted for this thing, and the guys making sure the kid wasn't gonna *really* fly [*laughs*]! But I've never seen the footage, Mom said it ended up on the cutting room floor.

In the movie as it exists, you simply run into the room "riding" a broomstick.

Something like that, yes. And I remember them doing my hair over one eye to make me look like Veronica Lake [known for her "Peek-A-Boo Bang"].

The first movie in which you had a decent-sized part was Commandos Strike at Dawn *[1942], where you were the daughter of Paul Muni.*

Oh, I was six when we did that one, and I have so many memories of it! Part of it was shot at Columbia, but a good part of it was shot in Canada because, up at Mill Bay, which is north of Victoria on Vancouver Island, the area looks almost the same as the Norwegian fjords, and

Ann Carter reads a textbook between takes on the set of *I Married a Witch*.

Her hair styled to recreate Veronica Lake's trademark "Peek-A-Boo Bang," Carter very much looked the part of Lake's young daughter in *I Married a Witch*'s comic climax.

Commandos was set in Norway. They built the schoolhouse and the little village and all of that, right there at Mill Bay. We spent a very long time that summer [1942] in Canada, at the Empress Hotel, where I remember how high the beds were; kids had to have steps to get up on them! That was during the war, and because of fear of a Japanese attack, there were little boats in the harbor, right in front of the Empress, in case we had to evacuate. Now *that* was very exciting! In the movie there was a wedding scene with dancing, and we [the Carter family] were friends for, gosh, almost 40 years after that with the lady who did the choreography, Wynn Shaw, a dance teacher in Victoria. Wynn was a very close family friend until she passed away in the early '80s. Of course, knowing Wynn kept a lot of memories of *Commandos Strike at Dawn* "alive" for me.

We were on a ship, the *Prince David*, for some scenes. The [real-life] commandos on that ship also were in the movie—as Germans [*laughs*]. They got dressed up as Germans and they marched down a road into the village that had been constructed for the movie, which was pretty exciting. I was told by my mother that after that whole marching scene was shot and the rushes sent back to Columbia, the technical advisers at the studio noticed that all the German helmets were on backwards [*laughs*], so they had to redo *all* of it!

I remember Paul Muni becoming very, very angry with me. He was ill then, and in this one scene I was sitting on his lap, and he forgot his line. And I prompted him. And that was not good. *Not* good! He said [*ominously*], "Where is this child's *mother*?" He was pretty upset!

If there was fear of a Japanese attack and boats for evacuation in front of the hotel ... was that any place to bring a child?

[*Pause*] Gosh, I never thought of *that* [*laughs*]! I don't know! Part of the movie was set at the school, and there were a *lot* of us children in that scene, it was supposed to be a whole school. So actually there were quite a few children there. Was that any place to bring a child?, I don't know.... I didn't ever *think* about that before! But, luckily, there *was* no Japanese attack on us [*laughs*] and we had such a pleasant time up there, really, really wonderful.

But you did get killed in your other war movie, The North Star *[1943].*

A Russian village was constructed on the Goldwyn lot for *The North Star* and, yes, I *was* killed in that. I was strafed from a plane, supposedly! I had to run down an alleyway, and all of the little explosives were under the ground, going off to make it look like the plane was strafing. I had to fall down, and there was a mattress kind of thing buried under a little bit of dirt at the place where I had to fall. I had to do that a *few* times. According to Mom, the "blood" that was on me was glycerin and red dye, and Ann Harding held me as I was supposed to be dead. In that movie were Ann Harding, Anne Baxter and Ann Carter

Carter gave one of moviedom's great child performances as Amy Reed, caught between her dreamworld and reality in *The Curse of the Cat People*. The haunting fantasy was in some ways autobiographical for producer Val Lewton, embodying some of the stranger aspects of his childhood.

[*laughs*] — Ann Harding was the mom, Anne Baxter was the older sister and I was the younger sister. I have good memories of that one ... except fallin' down and gettin' killed [*laughs*]. I was offered a contract with Goldwyn after that movie, but Goldwyn never picked up the option.

In Val Lewton: The Man in the Shadows *[2008], the documentary produced by Martin Scorsese, you talk on-camera about being able to identify with Amy, your character in* Curse of the Cat People, *because you were an only child, and surrounded by adults all the time.*

That's right, I really *was* somewhat like her: a little bit of a dreamer; I enjoyed fantasy; my mother read to me so much. She and I had a routine whenever I was working: After [a day's work], we would have dinner, either at home or somewhere, and I would have a bath, and then she would help me learn the script and the lines and so forth for the next day. And for every movie, she would first talk about the whooole picture, the whole idea, the whole plot, so that I *understood*, so that I was *not* just some little parrot reciting lines. And I *was* "alone" like Amy, an only child, so we were similar. My father was around a lot when he wasn't back east, but he wasn't as directly involved with the movie thing as Mom, Mom just really concentrated on that.

How did you get your parts? Did you have an agent?

I did, and it was Earl Kramer, Stanley Kramer's uncle. I saw in the Val Lewton documentary that Mr. Lewton knew Stanley Kramer quite well and I thought that was interesting, I never knew that.

And Lewton was briefly connected with the Kramer movie The Member of the Wedding *[1952], which you were in, which makes me wonder if he was the one who suggested casting you.*

How interesting. I don't know!

After playing a few small, sometimes uncredited parts, you were practically the star of Curse of the Cat People.

That was probably the most enjoyable experience of all, followed closely by *The Two Mrs. Carrolls* [1947] and *Commandos Strike at Dawn*. I have nnnno bad memories at all on *The Curse of the Cat People*. Nothing. It was pleasurable because I thought it was a great story; it was fun; and it was also fascinating to me because of the set. It was all shot on a set at RKO except, of course, the exterior of Mrs. Farren's [Julia Dean] mansion and a few other exteriors. They took this set [the backyard of the Reed house] and made it "summer"; then it was "fall" with the guys up on the catwalks throwing leaves which drifted down; and then it was "winter" with the guys throwing gypsum and un-toasted corn flakes out of boxes — that was the snow. It was absolutely beautiful.

Your co-stars?

Kent Smith and Jane Randolph were just fine, and Julia Dean, who played Mrs. Farren, was very interesting to me. When she told the Headless Horseman story, she really got into that. I was pretty awed by her: She was very good and very involved in her part. Elizabeth Russell played Mrs. Farren's daughter Barbara, who resented Amy. Our relationship was good, but she was ... scary-looking! She *was*, she was cruel-looking: very, very thin, and with those very high cheekbones. The way [Nicholas] Musuraca, the cameraman, lighted her, he made her look really forbidding. I wasn't *scared* of her, but ... she was a little intimidating! Oh, and I remember how they decorated that old mansion, with all of those bizarre

Among Amy's (Carter) "imaginary friends" in *Curse* are a butterfly, a ghost, and, in this publicity shot, a statue in front of the spooky Farren house.

stuffed birds and other creepy things, and the way they made the place look eerie and dark. It was very impressive to me. Incidentally, I've been asked if I was ever afraid during [the making of] *The Curse of the Cat People*. No! Never! Not even in the scene on the bridge, when the Headless Horseman was supposed to be riding by. Because I knew the whole story, plus the fact, I was on a set with a *lot* of other people. So, no, I was not afraid.

What do you remember about Simone Simon?

She was very kind to me. I remember particularly her dress, her gray chiffon dress with the stars all over it. (She always had that same dress except for the wintertime scenes when she wore the white fuzzy cloak thing with the hood.) The stars would fall off and I would go around picking them up. This seemed to me to be my purpose or something [*laughs*], part of my *job*, I was supposed to pick up all the stars and give them back to her! Looking back, that was funny. The same sort of thing happened on *Commandos Strike at Dawn*: When we weren't working, my stand-in and I spent our time on the set picking up nails to give back to the carpenters, who had been complaining they couldn't get any more nails because of the [wartime] scarcity of metal. Apparently I was always going around collecting things to give to people!

Simon once told an interviewer that you were "amazing." According to her, one day on the set when people were talking about the fact that Italy had just surrendered, you asked, "Unconditionally?"

I *did*? [*Laughs*] Oh, my goodness, I don't remember that at all. But, see, that's what happens when you're always surrounded by adults and you hear all these big words!

Do you remember Sir Lancelot, who played the family retainer Edward?

Because I didn't know any better, I always called him "Mr. Sir Lancelot" [*laughs*]. And he *let* me! He was great. He had a very musical speaking voice, he sings in the movie, of course [Edward sings "Ruben Ranzo" as he vacuums], and he also sang a bit on the set, between takes. I liked him very much. He was a warm, friendly guy to me. I was really impressed with him!

How funny, you've had more and nicer things to say about him than anybody else!

[*Laughs*] Well, he was very warm and interesting to a seven-year-old, he was fun. The other people were very nice and all that, but they didn't go around singing and laughing like Mr. Sir Lancelot!

The movie started production with Gunther von Fritsch directing, and then when he fell way behind schedule, Robert Wise made his directing debut by taking over.

Watching the movie the other night, I noticed that in the opening credits he goes by Gunther *V.* Fritsch, probably because it was during the war. I referred to him as Gunther Fritsch; the "von" wasn't part of his name, as far as I remember. On the *Curse of the Cat People* DVD, the audio commentator [Greg Mank] talked about how exacting Mr. Fritsch was, a perfectionist and so forth, and that's probably what put him behind. He was quite a soft-spoken man, quiet and gentle. I don't remember anything bad, no pressure or anything. He explained things, and you could figure out what he wanted. Of course, I feel the same way about Robert Wise. I can't think of any ways in which they were different, I remember Robert Wise as a nice guy too. So it was just really enjoyable. Gunther Fritsch, Robert Wise, *every*one was just pleasurable.

I recently heard that there was a rumor that I was told not to smile in that movie because I was missing a front tooth. Well, I have no memory of missing a tooth at that time. My husband Crosby and I got out the album of *Curse of the Cat People* stills that we have, and we started going through and looking at all of them and, gosh, there was *not* a lot of smiling going on, because it really wasn't that kind of movie. *However*, there was one still of the scene at the end, when Kent Smith and I are at the Dutch door to the house, and I was smiling this big smile, and Crosby and I were *scrutinizing* it to see if there were any gaps [*laughs*]! Then we got out the DVD and looked at that scene in the movie and we could see that there *was* a tooth missing. Not a middle tooth but the one "next door" [the right lateral incisor]. So that "rumor" *was* true!

Val Lewton—any recollections of him?

I remember seeing him on the set, always a very nicely dressed in a suit and tie and so forth. But I don't remember any conversations.

For him, Curse *was very autobiographical; he was a lonely only child, tried to escape from reality, etc. He even had a "Magic Mailbox Tree" that got him in hot water.*

So *that's* where that came from. I learned a lot about his life from the [*Man in the Shadows*] documentary. It was so sad!

On the set of *Curse* with starry-gowned Simone Simon and director Gunther von Fritsch.

If a person did have a Amy-like childhood, doesn't he have to get over it at some point? Should he start makin' movies about it?

He definitely did hang onto all those sad memories. I wonder if some of the stress and anxiety contributed to his heart problems that caused him to pass away so young. He had his first heart attack at around 40, and died at 46. Oh, that's terrible.

What happens to the Amys of the world who never get their acts together? Do they all become Val Lewtons?

They may feel similarly but just think of the amazing work Val Lewton gave us. They won't all become Val Lewtons, because who has the talent that Mr. Lewton did? Now, as a child I had an imaginary playmate, who had to have a place at the table. I think a lot of kids do. Mine was a girl; I don't remember her name, and I have no one to ask.

Who made room at the table? Who did you tell about your imaginary friend?

I remember just my parents. My parents were very accommodating about it; I think most parents are. *You* might have had one too! But I don't remember my children having imaginary playmates at all.

What do you think of the parenting that goes on in Curse? *I see a terrible father giving this poor suffering child so many mixed messages, I want to smash him like a bug!*

[*Laughs*] The father teaches Amy that a tree is a mailbox, and then he gets angry with her when she uses it as a mailbox—that *was* a mixed message, wasn't it? And Amy's parents

In 1943, Julia Dean (left) was an eminent Broadway actress of yesteryear who had lived in retirement for 13 years prior to accepting the role of the reclusive Mrs. Farren in *Curse*; "I was pretty awed by her," says Carter.

are a little distant, I think. Kinda cold. Not as warm and approachable as they probably should be or could be. But then, if they'd been warm and approachable, there probably wouldn't be that *story*, because Amy wouldn't have had the need for the friend.

The movie took 33 days to shoot and you worked 32 of 'em. Did you feel any pressure at all, working just about every day and being pretty much the star?

No, there was *no* pressure. And, incidentally, I never ever expected or aspired to be a star; I just didn't think of that. No, I was just *in the movie*. My parents would always say to me, after a movie came out, "Well, you coulda done *this* better," "You coulda done *that* better," etc. I think [that that was good], and I always felt that way too. I feel that way while seeing 'em *now*, a lot of times! "Oh, why did I do such-and-such?," "I wish I'd done such-and-such." My mom and dad kept me normal, I think. They didn't ever buy into using a word like "star" or anything like that.

Were you ever tired or upset on a movie set when you were young, or were you always a pro?

I don't remember being tired or upset, even though there were a few [trying moments]. I recall going down into a well in *Commandos Strike at Dawn* with Paul Muni, and the rope got going swinging, and I banged my head on the side. Of course I went "Ouch!" and I remember, when I saw the movie, listening really carefully and being able to hear that "Ouch!" [*laughs*]. And in *Ruthless* [1948] where I was playing Diana Lynn as a child, we were up at a little lake near Los Angeles. This lake was supposed to be a river so they had fire hoses going under the water to make it look like a river, and I was with two boys in a canoe. There were weights on the side of the canoe, making it tip over, and it just did not go well for take after take after take, the canoe didn't turn over properly. I didn't mind being dumped in the water, but if there was anything that was a little difficult, I guess it was doing those retakes, because you were soakin' wet, you'd been in the water, you had to get out, you had to start from Square One with the wardrobe, the hair, the makeup, the whole business, over and over. That was a little tough, but it was okay.

Was your mom on the sets of all your movies?
Oh, absolutely, every second.

A lot of former kid actors, high-profile ones, are always beating the drum about how horrible it was. But from most of my interviewees who acted as kids, I hear nothing but positive things.
It wasn't horrible at all. At least, it wasn't for me. For me, it was just the opposite. I would say that the only negative thing was having to go to all these lessons my mother made me go to, which were dancing lessons, singing lessons, diction lessons, drama lessons and so on. A kid would want to be off doing some other things. For instance, I don't know how to ride a bicycle. I never was allowed to ride a bicycle, 'cause you might fall down, hurt yourself, do something that "shows." That doesn't particularly bother me any more, I don't care about riding bicycles today [*laughs*]. But I sure remember thinking, "Oh, gosh, I don't *want* to go to another lesson!"

And the higgledy-piggledy way a kid actor "goes to school," now and then on a set — is that any way to get an education?
Oh, it was great, it really was, because most times it was one on one. Even when it was not one on one, it was one teacher and just a few kids, it wasn't like a regular class. And it was fun. I remember some great teachers — they called 'em welfare workers then. There were several that we remained friends with, they became family friends until they were gone. One was Amelia deFerris from *The Two Mrs. Carrolls*, a really wonderful woman — but demanding. My handwriting, up until *Two Mrs. Carrolls*, was less than okay, it was sort-of scribble, and Mrs. deFerris taught me to write much better. Another, Birdina Anderson, went to Canada with us for *Commandos Strike at Dawn*. She was wonderful, and we were really good friends until she passed away in the '60s. I think you learn more one on one, whether it's just 15 minutes at a time or what*ever* it is. It wasn't always just a few minutes, but even if it *was*, the teacher and I were so close to each other and we had a one-on-one, and you can't beat that.

What kid actors were your friends?
I especially remember Gigi Perreau, and also Claude Jarman, who was in *The Yearling* [1946].

You talked a minute ago about watching your own movies and thinking you should have done this or that better. Are there any of those moments in Curse of the Cat People*?*
Oh, yes! As I watch myself walking down the street to the Farren house, I think, "Oh, you look so stilted walking like that! Why didn't you relax?" And there are times when I think

In her second performance as Irena (after 1942's *Cat People*), Simone Simon projects no sense of malice; indeed, a now ethereal and gentle Irena fits in well with the other trappings of *Curse*'s Christmas ending (Carter at right).

I could have maybe read a line a little better. There are, in every *one* of my movies. I can't change it now, but I can't help thinking it! "You could have made it a little more believable."

In all of your movies, what was your worst "Damn, why did I do it that way?" moment?

 The worst? In *Blondie Hits the Jackpot* [1949], I was supposed to be sort of a stuck-up, rich, snob brat kid, and I think I read some lines very, very badly. I cringe when I look at that! And I cringe when I see myself in *The North Star*, because I just sound like a little parrot in some of the lines. Why did they let me get by with that? Why didn't they make me do it again?

Now the opposite: Name a scene in Curse of the Cat People *where you nailed it.*

 That's hard! That'd be very much like bragging, and that is ... hard [*laughs*]! Something I did well? Well, I think that I did a good job in the close scenes with Simone Simon. And at the mansion with the old lady, Julia Dean as Mrs. Farren; I think I also did a good job interacting with her, with her telling the story and so forth. *She* was so believable, and so forceful and so "into" what she did, that it really affected me, and I think that was good.

And, acting-wise, name a few high spots from other movies.

I think in *The Two Mrs. Carrolls* with Humphrey Bogart, the scenes that I had, particularly with him. With Barbara Stanwyck too, but mainly with Humphrey Bogart, in the beginning, the talking that we did together. I thought that went well. *He* was so good, and that helped me a lot, what the person that I was with was like. And he and I got along *so* well—he was great, he really was. I think he "pulled me along," he affected me so much that it made it easier. His nickname for me was Tonsils, and that was because, [for a scene] at the beginning of the movie, I was sitting on the arm of a couch or something, talking to him, and between takes, I yawned. And he peeeered into my mouth, down my throat, and said, "Oh, *Tonsils*," and that was *it* [*laughs*], it was "Tonsils" after that. He was a *really* nice man, a very warm, nice man.

Were you enough of a movie buff that you knew in advance who some of these stars were?

Yes. I really always loved to go to the movies with my mom and Aunt Stell. Oh, remember the flowered nightgown I wore in the [*Curse*] scene where I was supposed to be having

In *Curse*'s conclusion, the bloodhounds tracking Amy through a wintry Sleepy Hollow midnight were played by Rosie and Annie; "I *loved* them!" Carter still recalls.

the nightmare? Aunt Stell made that nightgown—it had little purple flowers. I remember it so well 'cause I had it for a while after that. She made it for me to wear in the movie, and then I kept it. Years later, when I saw the colorized version of *Curse of the Cat People*, they made so many mistakes with the colors of the things we had on. I remember being so annoyed: In the colorized version, the long party dress I wore [in the backyard scene with the Magic Mailbox Tree] was yellow, but it was really *blue*. I loved that dress so much because it was so pretty. And I remember quite a few other things that the colorizers got wrong. Boy, they were wrong a lot! I have a copy of that color version and I don't like it. I like the black-and-white because color takes away from the eerie feeling.

Audiences who went to the movies in 1944 to see a movie called Curse of the Cat People *and saw what they saw—do you think they were disappointed?*
I have pictures of advertising for the movie, and the marquees, and, my goodness, they've got monsters on there and everything. Boy, if people went to the movie looking for that, they certainly had to be ... [*laughs*] ... at least disconcerted by it! I hope they liked what they saw, but they didn't *go* there for that, they went to see something more ... zombie-like! I couldn't understand why they called it *Curse of the Cat People*. Well, yes, I guess I do understand why, but the movie wasn't like that. That title got people *into* the theaters, but I'm sure they were expecting something waaay different.

Lewton wanted to call the movie Amy and Her Friend.
I remember hearing that.

Where did you see the movie for the first time?
In Syracuse [her home town]. I remember being interviewed at the WSYR radio station by a man named Vadeboncoeur, and *Curse* was going to be shown at Loew's. You know how Loew's is spelled; well, I could not figure out how you pronounced it, and I kept calling it Leo's. And I couldn't get *his* name right either, Vadeboncoeur; I kept calling him Vandabunker! At the end, I said, "Thank you, Mr. Vandabunker. I'll see you tonight at Leo's!" [*laughs*]—my mom later got after me about that! But that was a long French name, Vadeboncoeur, for a seven-year-old to figure out!
Mr. Vadeboncoeur had a daughter, Joan, who was just a little older than I, and she and I became good friends. I remember Joan coming to California and visiting, but mostly it was [the Carters] visiting back there. Well, Joan and I sort of drifted apart, it has been more than 50 years since I've seen her. Anyway, the other day I got a call from Brandee

Only-child Ann with her mom in the 1940s.

Brooks at Turner, the publicist on *Val Lewton: The Man in the Shadows* which is going to be playing on Turner Classic Movies, and she said, "I'd like to know if you could do a phone interview on the third of January with a person who is with the *Post-Standard*." The *Post-Standard* is the newspaper in Syracuse. Brandee said, "I can tell you her name, it's here in my notes somewhere. It's Joan, and the last name is Va ... Vade ... Vadeb...." She got partway through the name, and I got butterflies in my stomach, and I said, "Vadeboncoeur...?" And she said yes! I had *goose pimples* all over! When we hung up, I thought, "Oh! I want to tell my mom!" [*pause*]—and it was the worst feeling: I have no one, who was there back then, to tell. And that's not good! But I can't wait to talk to Joan. I hope she remembers me, 'cause I sure remember her.

How did you feel after seeing Curse of the Cat People *at that Loew's in Syracuse?*
  I felt pretty good. But it's *always*, to me, difficult to see myself, it makes me cringe just a little bit. "What's everybody else thinking?," "Is it okay?," thoughts like that.

*Did you go up on the Loew's stage or do any*thing*, or were you just in the audience?*
  No, I was just there. The time when I talked [about the movie] was when Vadeboncoeur interviewed me on WSYR Radio.

Have you ever seen the original 1942 Cat People—*the story of your "parents," so to speak?*
  It's important to me now, when I see the two movies, that in the first one, my future parents are good friends and nothing more. I also find that "Dad" [Kent Smith] is pretty clueless about how his relationship with Alice [Jane Randolph] is affecting Irena [Simone Simon]. Of course, the mood of the two stories is the same, with the ancient curse affecting us all.

Did you know that Curse of the Cat People *was used, back in the day, as a training film by child psychologists?*
  My mother told me that it used to be shown at UCLA, in the psych department. And I can see why. I think it realistically and gently presents the imaginary friend aspect of a child's life in a way that shows what's going on in the child's mind. *Not* belittling or denying that, but showing *why* she needed this friend. The return of the father's deceased first wife was just kind of "the scary part."

Have you ever been to Sleepy Hollow?
  No! Thirty years ago or so, my husband and my son David and I took a trip east, and from New York City we went up the Hudson to Saugerties, because I wanted to see the farm where my mom's family lived when she was little. We also stopped to see friends in Syracuse and Camden Village and so forth, up there in upstate New York. Oh, I *should* have gone to Sleepy Hollow, I really should have, and I didn't. I will go back and see it someday, if I can.

Did you ever see Sleepy Hollow *[1999] with Johnny Depp?*
  No.

Prior to being approached about appearing in the Lewton documentary, were you aware of how many fans Curse of the Cat People *had? And how many you have?*
  No, not at all! I figured that [my acting days] were a long time ago, and that I could enjoy the fact that I was able to do what I did, and that was kind of *it*. Having had to give *Curse of the Cat People* so much attention over the past year, I keep thinking how wonderful it would have been to get together again with some of the other people who were in it, but

most of them died years ago, and now Simone Simon has passed away [in 2005]. They're all gone now except for Jane Randolph and me.

You were so good in Curse, *and the movie got some good reviews. Were you surprised that you went back to small and uncredited parts after that?*

I didn't think about it then at all. You did what you did. *Now,* looking back ... I dunno. Maybe the parts just didn't come up.

Unbilled both times, you were in two more fantasy films, The Boy with Green Hair *[1948] and* A Connecticut Yankee in King Arthur's Court *[1949].*

Even though I was older when I did *The Boy with Green Hair,* I remember it only vaguely because I wasn't that involved. Mostly I just remember Dean Stockwell and his green hair, and the scene where I was standing there with a group of kids. I was holding a little Asian baby—that *wet* all over me. They evidently didn't have any plastic pants on it or anything, and my dress was soaking wet and I was ... pretty uncomfortable [*laughs*]! That's my big, wonderful memory of that! But, oh, now, *Connecticut Yankee* was a lot of fun because it was Bing Crosby and William Bendix, and they were un-be-liev-a-ble together. We ruined—no, *they* ruined so much film, because we'd start filming and they would start clowning around, and they were hysterical. Of course the footage was not usable, but it was fun!

Eleven-year-old Ann tries to keep a straight face while acting opposite funnymen William Bendix (left) and Bing Crosby in the fantasy-comedy *A Connecticut Yankee in King Authur's Court.*

I was playing a peasant girl and I had to be very sad and cry, my father was dead [in the movie], and that was hard with them around because of all their horseplay. Gosh, they did the funniest stuff...!

Your acting career sort of petered out around the time you were battling polio.

We're quite sure that I got polio over the Fourth of July [1948] vacation when my parents and I went with some friends on their boat over to Catalina Island, 26 miles off Los Angeles. I was 12, we were at the isthmus, and my mother told me that people were dumping all this awful stuff in the water from their boats near us, sewage and so on, and she didn't want me to go in there. But my dad said, "Oh, let the kid go," and so I did go swimming off the boat. And I got sick on the 13th of July, and that's just about the right amount of time for incubating the polio virus. I *could* have gotten it somewhere else, but we always thought it was from that Catalina trip. I started being sick with symptoms like summer flu. The doctor came to the house (which doctors did then) and he said, "Oh, it's summer flu," but it lasted for a *long* time. But then it was over ... or so we thought. But then a few years later, when I was in *The Member of the Wedding* with Julie Harris, I was standing with some other kids on a soundstage [representing the exterior of Harris' house], and the director Fred Zinnemann looked at me and said, not to anyone specific, but sorta to *every*one, "What is wrong with that child? She's leaning to port!" And I *was*, I'd started going all crooked. That was kind of the beginning of figuring out that something was wrong. Turned out the muscles were all gone on one side of my back. I started going to doctors and then, at White Memorial Hospital in Los Angeles, I had an electromyogram, a very unpleasant test where they stick needles in the muscles, and while those needles are in there, you flex the muscles!

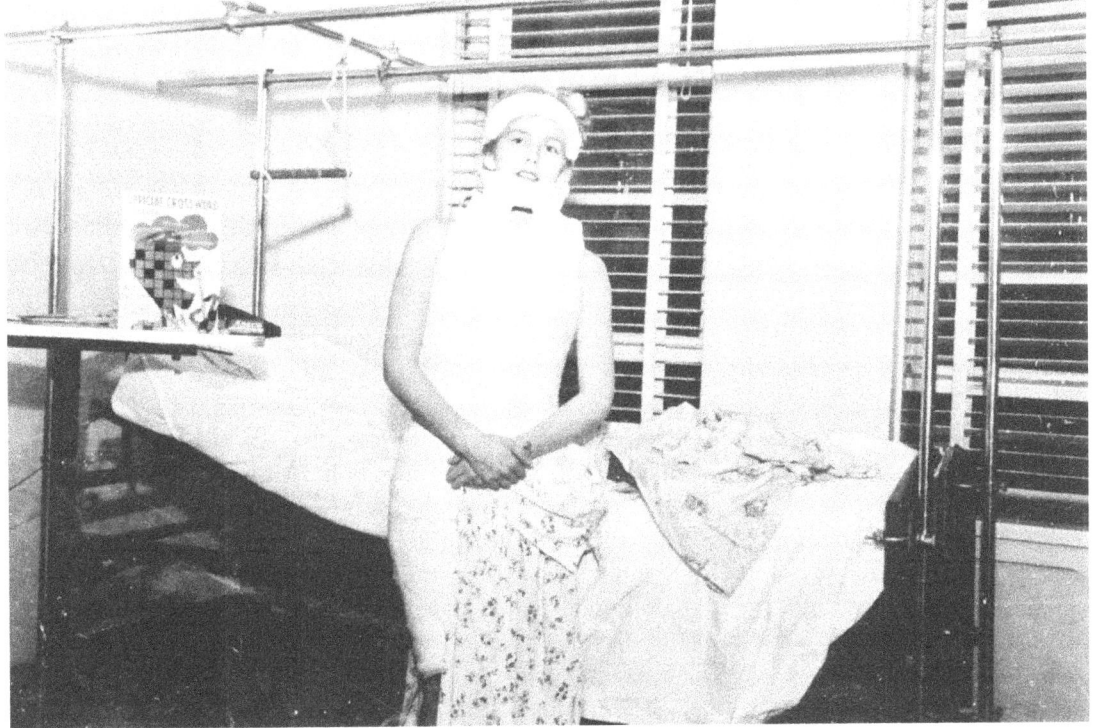

Ann in the early 1950s, confined by polio to a body cast.

That test tells them which muscles have had polio. Then I had to swim every day at the Hollywood Athletic Club and go to physical therapy three times a week to get me strong enough to carry around a cast, because the casts were huge and weighed 55 pounds each. I had one cast for a while, and then they took that cast off and put *another* cast on. During the time when I was wearing a cast, I had to have home school; in that cast, I could only kneel down or lie down, I couldn't go to school and so forth. At home I had a hospital bed and a trapeze thing to pull myself up, and teachers came to the house. Then after the casts, I had a brace which I could wear and go to regular high school. Now that I look back on it, it was a torturous thing, that brace! It was like a boned corset with a metal framework in the back and leather straps under my arms, and then I could put clothes on over it. However, I had to make sure not to lean back against anything, because the metal parts would make holes in my clothes. And as I moved around the house, I had to try not to let that metal ding the walls and furniture.

*I call the Internet "The Worthless Researcher's Best Friend" and I take every*thing *with two grains of salt. Did you know that, according to several sites, you were killed in a 1978 car accident?*

I have been told about that, and that's kinda creepy ... that gave me a few little goose pimples. But as Mark Twain said, "The reports of my death are greatly exaggerated!" [*Laughs*]

Around the time you were coping with the polio, your dad and mom were making another contribution to show business: They helped bring Lawrence Welk to prominence!

That's right! At some point about 1950, '51, Dodge was looking for someone to sponsor on television, and my mother was all excited about [the TV series] *The Lawrence Welk Show*, she thought it was wonderful. She urged Dad to pay attention to the Welk show and urged him to present that as a good idea for Dodge to sponsor. My dad really was not a "music person," he really didn't care about the music that much, but at my mother's constant nagging about it, really [*laughs*], he recommended *The Lawrence Welk Show* to Detroit, and Dodge wound up sponsoring Lawrence Welk. *Then*, years later, when my dad retired from Dodge, Lawrence Welk said to him, "Okay, Bert, I worked for you all these years, now you can work for *me*." And my mom and dad retired out to Lawrence Welk's Country Club Village in Escondido, California, a mobile home park, and they managed it for years. So they and Lawrence Welk always were very, very close.

Once you conquered polio, you never did act again, did you?

After that, I wanted to go to college, and I did, Occidental College in Los Angeles. My agent Earl Kramer called while I was in college and wanted me to go on an interview for the movie *Not as a Stranger* [1955] and I said I couldn't because I had a final that day. And *oh my gosh*, that was not taken well by him nor by my mother. But it was a choice I made, and I made it, and that was it, and I was sorry that they were unhappy, but ... it's what I did! I wanted to finish college, I wanted to teach, I wanted to get married and have a family and so forth. I really didn't realize it at the time, but it just broke my mother's heart. She used to bring it up once in a while in a very wistful way. I didn't realize it then but, being a mom now, I do: It was so important to her that I continue in movies and in radio — I did *Lux Radio Theatre* a lot, and [starting at age 11] I had a disc jockey show on KFWB for a while. *Mom* enjoyed all of this, and she knew I enjoyed it, which I did, very, very much. And, again, I was the only one [an only child]. As Jane Randolph says to Eve March in *Curse of the Cat People*, "You know these fond fathers with their only chicks," and that's how *both* my parents were. I was the focus, and it was tough on them when I didn't go on with what they thought I should, Mom especially because she was so involved. But I became a wife, a teacher and a mom. Crosby and I have been married 50 years and it was what I needed and what I *wanted* to do.

Did you get married first or become a teacher first?

I got married in my graduate year at college [1957], and the next year I started teaching. I taught high school and junior high, and a little time as a substitute. But the teaching that I liked the best was teaching continuation high school, and of course my ninth grade drama class, where we put on various productions.

Did your kids watch your movies on TV?

When my children were young, yes, every once in a while there would be a movie of mine on TV, and my name a few times was in *TV Guide*. I remember getting after my children from time to time about something or other, and their saying to me things like, "Oh, *you* just think you're so smart 'cause your name's in the *TV Guide*!" [*Laughs*] They'd put me in my place! Oh, and I re-

Carter in college in the 1950s; "it just broke [my] mother's heart" that she chose college and a teaching career over a continuing career in the movies.

member what happened one time when I got after my daughter Carol about something. I've always had very good hearing, and when my kids would mutter behind my back (as kids do—I certainly did), I would hear 'em. Well, this one time I got after my daughter Carol, and then stomped away; I'd "said my piece" and walked away down the hall very dramatically, to underscore how angry I was. And I could hear her say to her sister Gail, "What does she want, an Academy Award?" [*Laughs*] That's what you get for hearing too well!

Why did you move to Washington state?

I always loved it up in this part of the world, I've thought it was beautiful since we did *Commandos Strike at Dawn*. I used to come up and visit [choreographer] Wynn Shaw from time to time, sometimes with my family and sometimes alone, and I continued to think, "That is *so* beautiful." Well, once we didn't have any more ties with California (my mom died in '77 and my dad in '79), I said to my husband, "Let's at least go up there and look around" [as a possible new place to live]. Well, he got a job up here and we relocated.

You make where you live sound pretty middle-of-nowhere—but nice!

It's east of Seattle, about 40, 45 minutes (depending on traffic) from downtown Seattle. You have to go through Bellevue and Issaquah, and then up into the mountains, heading up towards Snoqualmie Pass. It's beautiful, it's like going to the Alps [*laughs*]. But our whole area is growing, which is good and it's bad. A lot of the older residents here are very unhappy about it. But we've been here so long, 25 years, that we don't feel that we're "invading." Located where we are, in the valley going down from the pass, we get more weather.

Ann and Crosby Newton on their spring 1957 wedding day.

This place is known for pretty bad winds, and it's a little bit interesting because we have sky-high Douglas firs, and when the winds kick up, you worry about them. But it's very pretty here; I'm looking at squirrels right now out in my backyard, where I have a feeder. We see a lot of animals right by our house, we have elk and a lot of raccoons and deer and so forth.

Did you continue teaching in Washington?

When we moved to Washington, I went to travel school and became a cruise-only travel agent, and did that for four years, and really loved it, because I think cruises are amazing. I also *went* on a lot of cruises; you have to be able to tell people about various ships and lines. Then when my son David's son Ryan was born, because his parents went to work, I took care of Ryan during the week until he started going part-time to day care. He was about four when he started going to day care, to socialize with other kids—which is a good thing! If a child doesn't socialize ... well ... they become Amy. Or they become *me*. I got in a lot of trouble when I first went to school. My mother did not let me go to school until the legal limit, which [in California] was seven. I didn't start school 'til I was seven because she didn't want to send me one day sooner than she *had* to. I started out in second grade—I never went to kindergarten or first grade—and I got in *so* much trouble initially because of not being socialized. I mean [*laughs*], I wasn't some kind of wild *thing*, I was socialized [with grown-ups] but not with other kids my age. I would *kick*; I got in a lot of trouble for kicking; and for just not "getting it" about how to get along with other kids.

So when you did Curse of the Cat People, *you were seven but had not been to school one day of your life.*

That's correct.

Teacher Carter (indicated by arrow) with her ninth-grade drama class (Roosevelt Junior High School, Glendale, California, 1964).

Ann in 1984.

Why didn't your mom want you to go to school until you were seven? So that you'd always be available if movie work came up?

I don't know that it was *only* for work; it was probably partly for work. But it was partly because ... I was "it." My dad was in Detroit a lot, and Mom wanted me home. Ryan, incidentally, reminds me so much of the way Amy was in the movie. He's *so* very creative, fantasy-wise. He's now 11, and for years I've been able to say to him, "Ryan, tell me a story," and he makes one up on the spot, full of all this fantastic stuff *that makes sense*. I don't know how he does it but his creativity and sensitivity make me think of Amy. And *he's* an only child. It's amazing to me how imaginative he is. What he wants to do when he grows up is to design games for Xbox or PSP, and I think that would be great!

You recently had yet another health scare.

Yes, I had stage 3 ovarian cancer, which is ... pretty bad. It will be three years the 20th of this month [January 2008] that it was diagnosed. I went to different cancer treatment

Undergoing chemotherapy (March–August 2005), Ann poses with nurse Shirley; "I really don't feel bad about going around bald—but it's *cold*!").

Cancer conquered! Ann crosses the finish line in the Cancer Institute's July 2006 5K SummeRun fundraiser in downtown Seattle.

places and didn't feel right about any of them, and I was really confused and scared. 'Cause ovarian is ... awful. Well, *all* cancers are awful, but ovarian is so sneaky, and you usually don't find it 'til it's too late. But I had a wonderful OB/GYN, and one day I asked his partner-associate what *he* would do, and he said, "I would be sure to see Dr. Saul Rivkin at Swedish Cancer Institute in Seattle." I went down there with my husband, and as soon as we went in there, it just felt right. I am so thankful that it happened that way, because Dr. Rivkin gave me hope and a very, very aggressive chemo treatment. At one point I overheard him say to my husband, "She's *tough*," and I thought to myself, "Good. I *want* to be tough." Well, I got through it, with help from my family and friends who did the right kinds of things that loving family and real friends do.

*I guess if you can bounce back from polio, and from your death in that car accident, you can do any*thing*!*

Oh, yes, am I not amazing [*laughs*]? I consider myself so fortunate to have the opportunity to have all the fun of this happening to me right now!

You're starting to strike me as almost Amy-like, where this second lease on life has made life more magical to you.

It really has. You have a whooole different outlook once you've gone through those things.

By "the fun of what's happening to me now," you mean all the attention because of your appearance in Scorsese's Val Lewton: The Man in the Shadows.

I remember the day Mikaela Beardsley [the documentary's line producer] first called me. I'm a pretty wary person, actually, and because my son's in law enforcement, and an ex-Marine, he has said to us, "Be careful." I got this phone call out of the blue from Mikaela, who said, "Is this Ann Carter?," and I thought, "Oh-oh." I said, "Well ... ummm ... yes...," but there were red flags all over the place because I was being careful. But as I talked to her, I realized she was just asking if I'd be willing to come to New York and be interviewed for this documentary, and she was offering me a great opportunity. After that first conversation with Mikaela, I called my husband and children, I told my friends ... it was great. Oh, I was *so* excited! My husband and I went to New York at the end of January 2007, and it was so much fun! I did not meet Martin Scorsese, and *that* I regret. The hotel where we stayed, the Buckingham on 57th Street near Seventh Avenue, was right across the street from his office. There was a "debate" about where they were going to shoot my interview—I didn't care!—and they decided that it would be easy to do it in my hotel room, so we did. I talked on-camera for about an hour. It was exciting in New York, and we had a great time.

You look smashing in the documentary. Just terrific!

Thank you! I'm just so happy to *be* here, 'cause I had such a scary time with the cancer.

You have three kids, and how many grandkids?

Ann Carter Newton today.

I have one wonderful grandson, Ryan, and two great granddaughters. [*Pause*] I mean, I have two *beautiful* granddaughters—I have no *great*-granddaughters [*laughs*]. Not *yet*!

So you will *be a great-grandmother one of these days.*

I hope so. And I'll *love* it.

ROBERT COLBERT

I wasn't ever badly injured on Time Tunnel *in spite of all of the rolling and tumbling and swordfights and fistfights and rifle fire. God Almighty, I fought everything but a camel on that show!*

For Baby Boomer SF fans, one of the big events of the fall 1966 TV season was the premiere of producer Irwin Allen's latest adventure series *The Time Tunnel*. Different from Allen's other shows in its semi-anthology setup, it starred Robert Colbert as Doug Phillips, head of the government's Project Tic Toc—a scientific complex beneath the floor of the Arizona Desert, and incorporating a tunnel whose occupants can be sent into the past or future. Or *both*, as Doug and his associate Tony Newman (James Darren) learn when they find themselves haplessly hurtling back and forth through the ages, often from one historical hotspot to another, despite the ongoing efforts of their project co-workers (Lee Meriwether, Whit Bissell, John Zaremba) to return the reluctant time travelers to the here and now.

The one-season series is now new on home video from Fox Home Entertainment and, to commemorate its debut, Colbert sends his mind back in time (cue the kaleidoscope effects and the trippy music) to the beginning days of his acting career. Our first stop along the infinite corridors of time: Okinawa, Japan, where Army M.P. Colbert has just made his stage bow in a touring production of *The Caine Mutiny Court-Martial*...

I got drafted by the Army in '54 and sent to Fort Ord, and from there, after basic training, I was sent to Okinawa. They put me in the M.P. division, and I was a clerk-typist makin' a fast 33 bucks a month. I had an opportunity to get a job at Radio Free Asia KSBK; I would go up there for four hours a night and get two dollars an hour, so that was an extra eight dollars a day, an *enormous* amount of money for me. I was doing the disc jockey job, spinnin' records and talkin', and then while a record was playing I'd run down the hall and grab a sheet off of the ticker tape and run back and do the news. I ran the whole station by myself for four hours every night.

A woman named Joretta Hayes, originally from Aberdeen, South Dakota, was in charge of Air Force Special Services in a town called Naha, Okinawa, and she heard me night after night on the radio and she became intrigued with my voice, and so she would call the station asking me to come down to Naha to try out for a play she was producing, *The Caine Mutiny Court-Martial*. I told her I had no interest in doing that, because the eight dollars a night was very important to me. I did not have time to perform my duties as a clerk-typist *and* run the radio station at night, *and* do anything else. To do her play would mean I'd have to give up my radio job, and, boy, that job was awfully important to somebody makin' 33 bucks a month.

She said, "Oh, come down and just try out for it. Read the part, see what you think. You might be interested and have some fun." So I did, I went and I read for the part of Greenwald, the Jewish attorney. Those were, to this day, the greatest lyrics [lines of dialogue] I ever had—his soliloquy about how his grandmother was melted down into a bar of soap in Germany, and everything else. It was just an amazing experience. So I opted to give up my job at the station and go down and do this play, and we performed it in various places, including the Ryukyuan Islands. One little adventure took us to an island where we performed *The Caine Mutiny* in front of a small—*small!*—American contingent, and a *huge* Ryukyuan contingent. Well, except for about four [Ryukyuan] corporals and a pfc, they couldn't understand a damn word we were sayin'! And then I fell through the stage at one point, it was so rickety! It was the funniest experience in my life, it was a hoot and a holler, and I'll never forget it as long as I live.

And that's when you got hooked on the acting?

Yes. When my service time was pretty much over on Okinawa and I was heading home, I thought, "I might give this [acting] a little try when I get back." After I was discharged, and I was living in Portland, Oregon, I started doing a little theater with the Oumansky theater group. We did theater in the round, a lot of little plays here and there, and I did some Shakespeare at the Portland Civic Theater. While I was doing *The Little Hut* in a theater in the round at a place called Amatos Supper Club in Portland, Mickey Shaughnessy saw the performance. He was a nightclub performer, and he also was in movies like *Don't Go Near the Water* [1957] with Glenn Ford and *Designing Woman* [1957] with Gregory Peck—he was pretty hot at the time. He saw *The Little Hut* and he came up to me afterwards and introduced himself and he said, "Listen, if you ever wanna come down to L.A., I have an agent in Beverly Hills. I'd like him to meet you and see if they'd be interested in handling you. I think you got a career in films and various stages of the theater." I said, "Well ... when's the next plane?" [*Laughs*]

Despite so-so ratings and a season's-end cancellation, *The Time Tunnel* with Robert Colbert (pictured) has stood the test of time, popular in reruns and now out on DVD.

Oh, I need to tell you that, prior to meeting Mickey, I had been hired to do a couple of TV commercials in Portland. One of them was for Arthur Murray's Dance Studio and the other was Tonkin Mercury Ford, up in Portland. I was scheduled to do these two, live one-minute commercials and I went over to NBC and I was standing around there, waiting to do the Tonkin Mercury commercial and watching, on a monitor, the TV show that was airing at the moment, which was called *State*

Trooper with Rod Cameron. Rod Cameron was in this horrific fight scene, and I knew that when the fight was over, then it'd be time for me to do the commercial. Well, the stage manager threw me a loop: Suddenly he went, "Seven, eight, nine, ten," and pointed his finger at me! Shocked and ill-prepared, I turned to the camera and I said, "Tonkin Mercury! Bigger on the inside! Bigger on the outside! Wider safety vision! Larger trunk space!" ... and I just went blank, with about two-thirds of the commercial left to go. The stage manager said, "Don't worry, don't worry. I was just giving you a little test there, a chance to practice." But I was shook. I pulled the copy out of my pocket and I started re-reading it, all shook up, and finally I got to where I was thinking, "I'm okay again."

The stage manager said, "Okay, seven, eight, nine, ten and ... *boom*," and he pointed at me. I went, "Tonkin Mercury! Bigger on the inside! Bigger on the outside! Wider safety vision! Larger trunk space!..."—and then I went blank again. I was standin' there, just lookin' at the camera, not havin' a clue how to get myself out of this thing. Finally, after about 40 seconds of dead air time, I was [off the air again]. *And* I was informed that it was no longer necessary for me to do the Arthur Murray spot ... I could go home.

In other words...

In other words, I was fired. I went home and I was *so* depressed. I had let myself down, I thought I'd just ended my career. Well, I sat down that evening and I wrote a poem called "Endeavor." It was the first time I had ever written anything. It was a pretty long poem and I wrote it in this space in my life when I was so depressed and thinking that I had failed.

Now, flash-forward. At Mickey Shaughnessy's suggestion, I flew down to Beverly Hills to meet with the Lillian Small Agency. It was a good, solid, small agency—it wasn't William Morris but it was the next best thing. A class act. Green as can be, I was there and they brought me into this room where there was a big conference table with 10, 12 people sitting around it. I was standing in this room with all these people looking at me and one of 'em said, "Do you have any film on ya?" I said, "Oh, no, I don't. I've done some stage work and that's about it." They said, "Can you *do* anything?" I said, "Well," I said, "I just wrote a poem and I could recite that for you." [*Sarcastically*:] Well, *that* lit up the room, they just couldn't *wait* for *that*! But anyway, they said, "Sure, recite the poem." So I went ahead and I recited "Endeavor" for them. It went on for a bit, it was a lengthy poem, and after I got to the end of it there was a little silence as they were looking at me. Then they said, "Listen, would you mind stepping out into the outer office for a few minutes? We'd like to meet a bit here...." I did, I sat out there for probably 20 minutes, it seemed like about ten hours, and then they came out and they said, "We've decided to take you on." And, by God, the next day they sent me out on an interview for a movie called *Under Fire* [1957]. That was my first movie.

Incidentally, *Under Fire* also featured an actor named Gregory LaFayette, and around that time Gregory married [actress] Judy Tyler, who had just finished the Elvis movie....

Jailhouse Rock [1957]. The big one.

They got married, and they drove off on the honeymoon ... and up around Wyoming, they collided head-on with another car. It killed Judy immediately, and Gregory was knocked unconscious. When he revived and they told him that she had passed, why, even though he wasn't physically hurt all *that* bad, he died instantly. From the shock of finding out Judy was gone, Gregory LaFayette died. Gregory was a sweet guy, we had gotten to be buds and everything, and I was waiting for him to come back from the honeymoon and we were gonna hang together and do some things.

I remember meeting Lance Reventlow [playboy son of jillionaire heiress Barbara Hutton] and thinking, "Jesus, here's a kid who's set for life." When you meet some boy whose mother is the richest woman in the world and he's got everything while *you're* out there trying to pay the rent, you just go, "Wow. What a lucky guy." A few years later, he's dead [in a plane crash], and you're still cookin' along, makin' babies and havin' a life long after [the deaths of] people you might have been a bit envious of, or had a desire to have a little taste of their kind of life. That's happened to me so many times: I looked up at so many people who then just *went*. So long, long ago, Bobby quit wishin' that he had some of the stuff *they* had!

So one day after this agency said they'd take you on, you got an acting job.
    That's right, a small part in *Under Fire* as an Army guy. I got the first job I went on, and pretty much never stopped working. I did a couple things over at Allied Artists, *Joy Ride* and *Macabre* [both 1958], little B movies over there, one thing leading to another.

Macabre *was William Castle's first horror movie.*
    We used Lance Reventlow's home. He had this home where half of the swimming pool was inside the house: You could dive in it in the living room and swim around, or go outside by swimming down under the bottom of this huge pane of plate glass that went down into the pool [a living room window], and come up in the outdoor part of the pool, which overlooked the city. It was quite a deal, I've always loved that idea, and would like to incorporate it into my home after I get rich from the sale of these *Time Tunnel* DVDs [*laughs*]!

Was that where you met Lance Reventlow?
    Yeah, Lance was there with his girlfriend. We were there for a few days, and I don't remember any time he *wasn't* there. He was home watchin' us shoot the movie and havin' as much fun as *any* of us.

Why does a guy with all the money in the world want to rent out his house to movie people?
    Isn't that something?, that never even entered my mind.

No offense, but I don't want any of you guys shootin' in my *house!*
    It certainly wouldn't have been for the money. He might have had some tie-in with Bill Castle or his partner Robb White or one of those guys. Yeah, why *would* he do that? *I* certainly wouldn't [*laughs*]!

You had a much bigger part in Have Rocket—Will Travel *[1959] with the Three Stooges. What can you say about that?*
    I could tell you that at the time I was no Three Stooges fan. All I remember about that is [leading lady] Anna Lisa, who might have been a little taller than me [*laughs*]! I'm 6'2", so she was a big woman. I sure did like that Anna Lisa—I remember *that* part! But as far as any particular memories, like with the Three Stooges, I don't have *anything* to report except that, years later, I was a golfer and I played in the Hollywood Hackers, and Moe and Larry Fine were Hollywood Hackers and I got to know 'em. So, many years after we did *Have Rocket—Will Travel*, Larry Fine and I had many a laugh together. I don't think I ever even told him I was in the movie. He may or may not have known it himself, I dunno, I don't think we ever brought that up. But I always loved Larry because we had a lot of fun on the golf course. Anyway, movies like *Have Rocket—Will Travel* and *Joy Ride* and *Macabre* were all part of my "dance" on the way to signing with Warner Brothers and kinda settling down to where I didn't have to go around on interviews all the time.

Did you enjoy hobnobbing with the stars at Warners?

I was still a relatively new kid in town, and I was just as much a fan as *any*body. I spent a lot in the green room at Warner Brothers watching people who were stars to me walk in. I was just sittin' there goin', "Wwwow, look at *that*...!" Oh, I remember one time sitting at Paramount, in the commissary, when Cary Grant and Sophia Loren were doing *Houseboat* [1958]. In that commissary, you couldn't hardly hear the person you were having lunch with, from all the silverware clanging and the plates and the people talking—it was just a cacophony of mixed noises. All of a sudden, in walked Cary Grant and Sophia Loren ... and the minute they hit that room, it was like a *wave* going across the room as it became silent. You couldn't hear a glass tinkling, you couldn't hear a bit of silverware, not any voice, not a *sound*. It was the most incredible moment I ever witnessed as a spectator to stardom, it was something I'll never forget.

Six-foot-two Colbert had a leading lady (Anna Lisa) who nearly rose to his altitude in the Three Stooges comedy, *Have Rocket—Will Travel*.

Mostly you were in TV stuff at Warners.

They signed me to a contract and I did just a *ton* of shows. Warner Brothers had a "marriage" with ABC where any TV series Warners made, ABC would put on the air. We used to laugh, we called any new series "The Wind-Up Warner Brothers Series Doll": They'd wind it up and if it was any kind of a hit, they'd make four more just like it. That's when they had *Hawaiian Eye, Bourbon Street Beat, The Roaring Twenties, Surfside 6, Cheyenne, Maverick, The Alaskans*, you name it, on and on and *on*. Most of my stuff was TV, of course, but I also did a [Warners] movie where I played a killer, a thing called *A Fever in the Blood* [1961] which I loved because the cast was just awesome. Hell, you look at who was in that thing, we had Herbert Marshall, and Efrem Zimbalist, and Jack Kelly, and Don Ameche, and Carroll O'Connor—it just was more damn fun!

Warners was getting ready to do a movie called *Black Gold* [1963], a story about guys drilling for oil, on the order of that old Clark Gable-Spencer Tracy film *Boom Town* [1940], and I was really looking forward to having a shot at the lead. I was sent down to wardrobe, where I thought they were going to put me in the wardrobe for *Black Gold*. But I didn't come out lookin' like Clark Gable, I came out lookin' like Jim Garner. This was at the time when Jim Garner [star of the hit Warners series *Maverick*] was fighting with Jack Warner because Garner wanted more money and they wouldn't give it to him, so he walked. That pissed Jack off, he and Garner ended up in a blood feud, and Garner was blackballed in this town for about two years, they wouldn't let him work. So now, as I was walking down the main street of Warner Brothers on my way to a screen test or something, *every*body was hangin' out of the windows and lookin', they thought Garner was back on the lot [*laughs*]!

Turns out they wanted to put me on *Maverick* as a new Maverick brother named Brent, a younger brother. When I found that out, I said, "Jesus, don't do that! Give me a break, Garner's the hottest thing in the damn TV world, I don't wanna be associated with trying to replace him. You can put me in his boots but I can't fill his shoes!" But anyway, they did it, and it was okay, I didn't get damaged *too* much out of it, and I had some fun working on *Maverick* with Jack Kelly and Roger Moore.

Between guesting on so many Warners shows, and being a regular on Maverick, *they musta had you hoppin'.*

Just about every *week* I was in a different show, workin' constantly, working amongst all these stars and just havin' the time of my life over there. Even when there was a strike by the writers, why, Warners gave birth to a guy named "W. Hermanos," which was Warner Brothers in Spanish, and "he" wrote a lot of scripts. What Warners would do is, they would take the script for an episode of, say, *Bronco*, something that had already been shot and shown, and they'd eradicate *Bronco* on the title page and type over it *Cheyenne*. And then they'd replace, throughout the script, the names of the *Bronco* characters with the names of the *Cheyenne* characters. They would even take a Western script, again say *Bronco*, and make it a *Bourbon Street Beat*, a modern-day deal. And now, instead of jumpin' on a horse, you'd be climbin' into a taxi [*laughs*]! All of a sudden we were redoing old scripts that were all written long before the writers' strike, and we just kept workin' as if there was no strike at *all*. I always wanted to change my name to W. Hermanos and go down to the Guild and collect all those residuals that that puppy must have made [*laughs*]. There must have been millions waitin' for this dude down there, that nobody ever got!

Why did you leave Warners?

I was the only one at Warner Brothers who ever got out prior to the end of his contract—and not by any grand design! A friend of my wife, a restaurant man back in Philadelphia, came out and wanted to open a restaurant in L.A. and he wanted me to be his partner. I thought, "Well, that sounds like a good idea. Everybody wants a restaurant." So I put up the money and we opened this restaurant in Beverly Hills called The Corner and it was a huge success. *But*, people started stealing food and booze and everything out of there. You don't realize what it can do to your bottom line when turkeys and hams and cases of champagne suddenly start disappearing. My father died and I went off to Oregon, to the funeral. When I came back, I pulled up to the restaurant and all across the eaves of the building was written COCKTAILS—HAPPY HOUR 5–7—TWO COCKTAILS FOR 75 CENTS and so on. I'm goin', "What the hell is this?" I go in the bar, and there's a marshal standing there with a chain on his wrist, he was chained to the drawer of my cash register, and every dime that went in the cash register, *he'd* put in a bag. We were in the throes of some kind of a bankruptcy.

Finally we had to close the restaurant. My partner took bankruptcy and he went broke, and I owed $80,000, which in 1961 was more money than I'd ever seen in my life. I didn't take bankruptcy, but we owed all these people—banks, the purveyors, the meat people, the liquor people, the produce people, you name it, we owed 'em. No, *I* owed 'em, 'cause my partner took the bankruptcy. Here I was, just deep in debt and didn't know what the hell to do, and they were startin' to say they were going to garnishee my wages and so forth at Warner Brothers. I went to [head of Warners TV production] Bill Orr and his assistant, [writer]

Hugh Benson, and I told 'em my circumstances. I said, "Listen, if you guys would let me out of my contract, if I'm able to say that I'm unemployed, I can negotiate with these people at so-much on the dollar and see if I can pay my way out of this thing before I go broke and lose my credit and everything." Well, by God, they took it up to Jack Warner and they decided, "Okay, this is a rare thing but we're gonna do it. And maybe, Bob, you'll come back and be with us after you get this all squared away...."

Released from my contract, now unemployed, I went around to all the creditors. I had $3700 in the bank. I went to the bank that I owed about $18,000 to, and I got them down to where they'd take 1500. And then I went to the meat people and the liquor people and the produce people and *all* these people, I paid 'em all off at 10, 20 cents on the dollar. Squaring things with all these people cost me $3500, so I still had 200 bucks in the bank. Then, the next day, I signed with Universal for 2100 bucks a week!

How much had you been making at Warners?

Maybe $700 a week! So within about ten days, I'd paid off the $80,000, and I was making three times more money a week than before. Pretty soon I had a lot more than 200 bucks in the bank and I was out of my contract at Warner Brothers—I was the only one that got out.

Speaking of Bill Orr, the guy who helped me get out of my Warner Brothers contract: He was in charge of Warner Brothers Television, he was *God* there, and I always loved him because he was fair with me, and so was Hugh Benson—they liked me. When I got the Golden Boot Award a couple of years ago [on August 10, 2002], I saw this man, almost a ghost-like figure, sitting in a wheelchair, unrecognizable. But it was Bill Orr, and he was also being honored with a Golden Boot Award that night. He couldn't talk, he must have had a stroke or something, but he could listen. I went over to him with a lot of love, and I leaned down and I said, "Bill, I've always thought the world of you. You were very instrumental in helping me. Not only putting me under contract to Warner Brothers but, when I was having problems with that restaurant and you weren't letting *any*body out of their contract at the studio, you let *me* go, and that saved my *life* at the time. You made it a happy ending at a very sad point in my career. I loved ya then and I love ya now." He just looked up at me with eyes that were totally alive—they were just dancin' around in his head with a feeling of joy, like he almost wanted to reach out and kiss me. He couldn't hardly move and he couldn't talk, but his eyes said everything. And I'm delighted to have had that moment, because a few months later he died. But I'd had that little opportunity to share my feelings with him. Bill Orr was a tough cookie, but I liked him a lot, I just thought the world of him.

At Universal, on the Boris Karloff TV series Thriller, *you were in an episode called "The Bride Who Died Twice."*

The bride was Mala Powers from *Cyrano de Bergerac* [1950], which was, and still is, one of my favorite movies—I just love [playwright Edmond] Rostand's lyrics. "Bride Who Died Twice" was directed by Ida Lupino, and she was a mean, mean lady. There was an old man with long gray hair in the show, playing a prisoner I believe; he must have been in his eighties or nineties, *very* old, *very* feeble, but a sweeter man you never saw in your life. Well, he was having trouble with his dialogue, and Ida was *unmerciful* with this fellow, she rode him and rode him. He was just in tears. I'd been really looking forward to meeting Ida Lupino but, boy, after I saw the way she treated this old man, I couldn't wait to be done with that show so that I could just forget about her because I was so disappointed with what she did.

She was very good to me, very nice, but the way she treated that man, I couldn't wait to get off the show.

What are your memories of landing the leading part on The Time Tunnel?

My agent sent me out to 20th, to meet Irwin Allen. I went in, I met him and I sat there with him, and he was interviewing me. There was no mention about any screen test or anything, we were just talking and so forth. Then he took me into a room where he had his storyboards—black-and-white drawings, 11×14s, maybe a little bigger, allll around the walls of this room, depicting practically every scene in this upcoming *Time Tunnel* pilot ["Rendezvous with Yesterday"], which was set on the *Titanic*. There were renderings of costumes, *all* kinds of stuff. I thought, "This is really incredible. Such great detail...."

Had you ever met Allen before? Were you even aware of the kind of movies and TV series he'd done?

I didn't know Irwin from a *rock*. I didn't know what his past was, I didn't know at the time how many other shows he had going. But he was telling me about how this pilot was going to be *the* most expensive pilot ever filmed—it was like a half a million bucks, and that was a *lot* of money in '66. When I saw the storyboards and all this other stuff, and he was tellin' me how much money they were gonna spend on it, and that Michael Rennie would be in it ... it was quite impressive. And it was like *he* was tryin' to sell *me* on the idea of goin' to work for him.

Free of his Warners contract, Colbert made a lucrative move to Universal and guest shots on series like Boris Karloff's *Thriller*.

Rather than trying to figure out if he wanted *you* working for *him.*

I don't know where he knew me from, but apparently when I came in, I was the one he wanted, 'cause that was that, I had the job. And I *wanted* that job, once I saw Irwin's dog and pony show there. I saw the storyboards, and found out that it was gonna be *the* most expensive pilot ever filmed, and that Michael Rennie was going to be in it—I loved Michael from *The Day the Earth Stood Still* [1951]. There was nothin' about it that made you *not* want to *do* it! I didn't know Jimmy Darren or Lee Meriwether or anybody from Adam's off ox, but I wanted the part and he said, "Well, you *got* it." Then he took me over to meet Paul Zastupnevich to get some wardrobe.

One suit of clothes for practically the whole run of the series!

[*Laughs*] That's right, I didn't know I was only gonna get one shot at wardrobe! As you remember the pilot, Jimmy's character went off in the middle of the night and jumped into the Tunnel and went back in time to the *Titanic*, and I had to rescue him before it went down. So I had to dress in the costume of the time, 1912 or whenever it was. The Norfolk suit was very appropriate, so that when I got on board the ship I wouldn't look conspicuous, I would just look like one of the passengers. That's how the Norfolk suit came about.

And then you had to wear it in ev-er-y other episode, too.

Yeah, and I tell you what, I soon got real sick of that puppy! About ten years ago, Jimmy was offered $6000 for one of the green sweaters he wore in the show. I can't imagine what ten Norfolk suits would have been worth to the fans!

The Titanic *episode was the first you shot, and* directed *by Irwin Allen.*

As a director, he was very low-key. Competent. Great authority. There was a lotta respect for him among the crew and the cast. When he was around, we all deferred to Mr. Allen as the leader of the pack, and everybody was very pleasant to him, and vice versa, he was always nice to us. But, as I say, he was a very low-key director, he would go about his business, he didn't raise his voice. He'd get a little frantic *once* in a while, if he got in a bind, and it just became kinda comical. Incidentally, he had a comb-over that was one of the best I've ever seen. But one time he walked in front of a Ritter, which is like a big fan—it's a

Dressing in an old-fashioned coat for *Time Travel*'s first episode somehow led to his having to wear it in *every* episode, Colbert reports (pictured: Colbert, left, with James Darren).

huge, three-, four-blade airplane propeller inside a cage, and when they fire that thing up, it would be a huge wind machine. Well, when Irwin walked in front of it, you couldn't see the Ritter for the hair that flew up off the back of his head, straight up in the air! So he had to be very cautious about his hair [*laughs*]. He only directed the one *Time Tunnel* episode, although I did a movie-of-the-week thing he directed, *City Beneath the Sea* [1971], that had a pretty good cast in it.

During the shooting of the other Time Tunnel *episodes, was he on the set much?*

He didn't come down much when he didn't have reason to; he monitored it from afar. It was a rare visit by him, and when he did come, he usually brought somebody [a set visitor]. If he was showin' someone around the lot, why, he'd bring 'em to *Time Tunnel*. Irwin was as big a fan as any of us, and, hell, he'd bring people like Joseph Cotten ... Edward G. Robinson ... Victor Mature ... one time I met Bill Lear, of the Lear Jet, and *his* family. We used a Lear jet in the pilot, and Irwin and Bill knew each other, and I got to meet Bill Lear, which I thought was really cool. Bill brought four of his daughters along, and one of 'em was named Shanda. Shanda Lear [*laughs*]. I thought *that* was cool, too. The four daughters were cute as hell, but I was a happily married man, so all I could do was look. So you never knew who was gonna come wander around the set with Irwin, and it was always fun to have all these people that you were just a *fan* of, coming around to visit with you and wanting to meet you and sit and talk to you and take you to lunch. I was havin' a lot of fun.

Once things got rolling along, talk about a typical week as the star of The Time Tunnel.

Jimmy and I would work usually in the field. Most of it was shot on the back lot at 20th or, if we had to go to location, out at the 20th Ranch, Malibu Canyon and various places. So we would do five days in the field, Jimmy and myself having whatever adventure the episode was about. Then after we'd done our five-day shoot, the "Tunnel people" [actors Lee Meriwether, Whit Bissell, John Zaremba, etc.] would come in on the sixth day and they would work on the Tunnel set, doing various scenes that were interspersed throughout the script. Outside of the pilot, Jimmy and I never, except on *rare* occasions, worked with them. We hardly ever crossed paths or even *saw* each other.

The Tunnel itself was one of the attractions of the show—very elaborate.

For the pilot, they had two back-to-back stages and we used *both* of them for the Tunnel. The Tunnel went from one stage right on through to the other, another 40, 50 feet. After that, they just used the half of it [used one stage]. At the back of the Tunnel they put a scrim that showed sort of an infinity type of twirl, and away they went on one stage.

Your approach to the role?

Hit my marks and payday was Friday night!

Can I ask what payday was?

I think I got about 3500 an episode, somewhere in that area. I don't remember exactly but it wasn't much more than that.

What would you like to say about working with James Darren?

I always thought the world of Jimmy—he's a talented guy. And he looks today pretty much like he did when we did the show, he looks like it's still '66 and he just stepped off the set. The portrait in the attic must be ripped and rancid and smelly by now [*laughs*], because he looks *great*. Back when we did the show, I think Jimmy was prematurely gray, and he dyed his hair. *Now* he has a little bit of gray that he lets come through. But it's just

James Darren and Colbert could land in any century, past or future, in creator-producer Irwin Allen's series *The Time Tunnel*.

so funny, he's one of those guys that never ages, he's just the same size, the same look exactly as he did 40 years ago. Jimmy's a terrific guy, everybody likes him, he's got a lot of buds, and they all usually are from the crowd in Philly [South Philadelphia]—he's a real home boy. We didn't hang together, but—friends? I think he hung the moon, I just love the guy, he's a wonderful dude to me. He came over the house a few months ago and we had a great time.

And Lee Meriwether?

Aaah. She's a princess. She's more beautiful now than she was *then*—she's a stunning-looking woman today. You talk about a high-class, top-flight human being, why, she's *it*. She gets an 11 in every aspect of her life. She *loves* the theater, she works all the time, she's married to a wonderful guy, Marshall Borden, and she's got Kyle and Lesley, her kids, and her little granddaughter Ryan. Lee Meriwether is one of the most beautiful, one of the finest, classiest women I've ever met in my life.

What were the side benefits to being at Fox at that time? What other things were going on that you were glad to be able to see?

Well, we had [the TV series] *Peyton Place* and *Batman* and *The Green Hornet*, and huge sets for the motion pictures that were being filmed. And the commissary was jammed with anybody and everybody you'd ever want to know. It was an exciting time. Even in the old days at, say, MGM, back in the '30s, '40s, '50s, I don't think *they* could have had any more fun than we did.

When television came in, it was the illegitimate kid, and nobody associated with movies wanted anything to do with it. It was the little bastard child that wasn't ever going to amount to anything and was never gonna live past puberty. Well, TV just kept getting better and better and better. And, wow, I was there through that transition period and saw [TV] grow—and then of course we still had motion pictures on the side. I don't think there *ever* was a more exciting time in the film industry, to have been on the planet and working there, than my years. If, early on in my life, someone had predicted how wonderful it was gonna be, I would have been a doubting Thomas. I went out there trying to get a little piece of it, and I got *buckets* full of absolute Heaven.

Are you interested in science fiction at all?

I am a huge fan, as I think back on H.G. Wells and his works and other great sci-fi treasures of the past. I've enjoyed Rod Taylor's *The Time Machine* [the 1960 movie] and a myriad of other wonderful things. *However*, when it comes to NASA and so on, if you were to ask me if I was interested in *that*, my answer would be … not much. Not much. As far as wanting to spend eight minutes on Mars or the Moon or any other goddamned rock out there in the galaxy, I have no interest in it. To spend 15 minutes on a spaceship, wondering if you're ever gonna come back—it would be of *no* interest to me. If they offered me a free ride on the next space shuttle, I'd have to check my calendar. I just have *zero* interest in what the hell's goin' on out there in space. I want to see what we can do to take care of what

Time out: Colbert strums to the delight of co-star Lee Meriwether.

we got *here*. To me, NASA and all of that is just a bunch of people playin' with science and having a wonderful time at the taxpayers' expense, when I think what we should be doing is spending those billions and billions of dollars *not* putting space stations in the sky, but on doing something to get hospitalization for people who can't afford to get out of pain.

I look at [NASA's exploits] like, "Okay. I'm glad to have seen some of this stuff" ... but it's just people up there, strokin' themselves about ... I dunno ... puttin' a Rover on Mars, let's say. Okay ... well, if you must, you go ahead. But how 'bout doin' something for mankind and humanity *here*? This planet amazes me—what it *is*, what it puts *out* and what it *does*, from a flower and an insect on up. I just look at it and go, "Wow. This *is* the magic show. This is un-be-*liev*-a-ble." And yet, what is more abused than this planet and what is taken for granted more than this planet? My interests are in the present and how we can improve something [our world] that turns more into a bucket of worms every day.

On a lighter note, can ya talk about some of the Time Tunnel *guest stars you particularly enjoyed?*

Well, right off the bat, Michael Rennie [the *Titanic* captain in "Rendezvous with Yesterday"] was just the best, and we ended up spending a lot of time together. We were just buddies, chasin' chicks and drinkin' Margaritas and havin' a good time. I had a good relationship with Michael, we had fun. We didn't play golf or anything, we just were drinkin' buddies at a club that's no longer there, it's now the Maharishi Mahesh ... uh ... Yogi Center for ... uhh ... Spiritual Wellbeing ... or ... [*Pause*] Well, whatever *that's* all about [*laughs*]!

What club was that?

There was a little restaurant up Sunset where we used to hang out, and that's where Michael Rennie used to drink, along with Ted Knight. Ted and Michael Rennie and I, we used to hold court in this bar, and we had some wonderful times. God, when I think back on the people that I met on *Time Tunnel*. Carroll O'Connor was on the show ["The Last Patrol"], playing a modern-day general and also one of his own ancestors back in the War of 1812.

And, in the 1812 part, doing kind of a Charles Laughton imitation.

Yes, very Charles Laughton-ish! Eduardo Ciannelli ["The Ghost of Nero"], now *there* was a class act. A total gentleman. He treated me like a prince. Somehow or other, he almost kinda *adopted* me. He couldn't have been kinder. And I was like a fan of *his*. Boy, he just stood out to me. I wish I could have spent a lot more time with that man. He was quite a bit older than I was and all, but my experience with him, working with him, was one of the best I ever had. And Victor Jory ["Pirates of Deadman's Island"] was another one of my favorites. He was a man who ran with John Wayne and Ward Bond and all those guys back in the hard-hittin' Western days—hard-drinkin' guys. Victor was a wiry, thin guy, but he was the toughest of *all* of 'em. When Victor got a little bit in his cups, nobody wanted to mess with him, and if they did, they ended up goin' through a *wall* some place, 'cause Victor was the toughest, meanest son of a gun that ever walked the planet. When he hit you, you stayed *hit*. So Victor and I became good friends.

Speaking of getting hit, who was your stuntman?

My stuntman was my brother. Glen was the same height, nine years younger than I am, and just one of the greatest physical specimens you ever saw.

He was your stuntman right from the get-go?

No. Paul Stader was the stunt coordinator on the show, and he assigned himself as my stuntman. But at some point in the early stages of the show, I expressed a desire to have my brother be my stuntman. Well, Paul wanted the job of being my stuntman so bad he could taste it—it meant a whole lot of extra money to him, because that was totally separate [from his stunt coordinator paychecks]. So when I said I wanted Glen, well, it wasn't the most popular thing I ever said in my life. I had to go through quite a bit in order to be able to get Glen the job, because doubling me meant a couple of hundred grand a year to Paul and it was nothing he wanted to lose. Paul was my same height and coloring and everything, he was a fine double for me, but not anywhere near as good as my brother; with my brother, you could hardly ever tell when he was working and when *I* was working. So I fought like hell and got Glen the job.

And Stader's attitude about this?

Well, it was like somebody coming in and taking that money right out of his pocket. I hadn't realized the significance of it. These [stuntmen] didn't want my brother there at all, because they were all close to Paul who had hired them in the first place. Anything Paul felt toward my brother had to trickle down from him to them in a heartbeat. Denver Mattson [another stuntman], *alllll* these top dudes didn't want anything to do with my brother. Well, they all ended up just respecting Glen completely, man. Before we finished the series, Glen was the most popular guy on the show in the stunt department. They thought he hung the moon, that he was the handiest, that he could kick anybody's ass. Glen was awesome: He could do everything *they* could, and better, faster, more convincingly. My brother ran the gauntlet of everything they had to do and nobody could touch any of the stuff that he could handle, he was just terrific.

After that first season ended, we thought we were gonna be coming back the next year, and during this hiatus Glen raced Triumphs. He got badly injured in a Triumph accident up in Idaho somewhere and he ended up in the hospital. One of his ribs had punctured his heart or lung, and he had broken an arm and stuff, but he was anxious to get back to L.A. So he got out of the hospital too soon, he jumped on a plane, and the pressurization wasn't just right and he formed blood clots. He then had to have a very serious operation where they had to tie off the veins to his legs, and he never recovered from that. He's still alive, but he's never had the use of his legs again ... he's never been anything like he was. He was the most incredible physical specimen and stuntman and motorcycle rider and fighter—he could hit you, and before you landed on the ground he'd hit you eight more times [*laughs*]. I never saw reflexes like this. He's up in Oregon, and ... that was my stuntman....

You got your brother work on the show—how about your actor friends? Were you able to get them into guest spots?

I always was good about that. A lot of actors wouldn't help their *mother* get a job. We had a saying when I started out in this business: "It's not enough that you succeed, but your *best friend* must fail." [*Laughs*] I wasn't that kind of guy. If I was going on an interview, I'd tell my buddies, I'd say, "Come on along, what the hell," and we'd go out and *fight* for it. And sometimes they'd get the job and I wouldn't! But as far as getting people work on *Time Tunnel*, outside of my brother, I can't remember if I did or not. I woulda got 'em on *Time Tunnel* if I'd have had a Chinaman's chance, but we never knew what was coming up, we'd never know what the next show was going to be about. It wasn't a thing where I could say, "Hey, we got a great part comin' up in the next episode" because they'd give us our script on Friday night for the next show we'd start shooting on Monday. So it was never a thing where I had an opportunity to say, "Well, here's a good part for you here...." I never really had that shot on *Time Tunnel*.

When we see Doug and Tony passing through time—floating through that weird kaleidoscope—is that really you and James Darren?

That was Jimmy and me. We were each rigged up with a harness, and we were hangin' in front of a huge blue scrim. They had big Ritters [wind machines] on us as we hung suspended against this blue backdrop. And later, of course, they superimposed those kaleidoscopic images [over the blue]. So, yeah, that was *us* up there, twisting and turning! [Darren remembers things differently on page 80.]

The show had a lot of action. Did you ever get hurt in any way?

In one fight scene, don't ask me which episode it was, there was a bench, probably about four feet long, and it got involved in the fight somehow. I either hit it or it hit me, I don't exactly remember how it went down, but I *do* remember I ended up with a gash in my forehead that required me to leave the set immediately and go have about 20-some stitches. Of course they were very small stitches, because nobody wanted to damage my beautiful face [*laughs*]. I was gone a very short time, maybe a couple of hours, and then I was back on the set working. I'm sure they didn't even *miss* me!

Did they cover it up with makeup?

That's right. But I wasn't ever badly injured on *Time Tunnel* in spite of all of the rolling and tumbling and swordfights and fistfights and rifle fire. God Almighty, I fought everything but a camel on that show! For the role of that scientist, they shoulda got Ali instead of Bobby [*laughs*]!

Could they even make *a show like this today? In 2006, is any kid going to sit down and watch stories about the War of 1812 or Dreyfus or any of that?*

Oh, I think so. It was a fun thing to do, every week you had something interesting—history is *always* interesting. When you have a show where you can go backwards or forwards in time, it strips away allllll the barriers of boredom! You don't know what's coming up next.

I've gotten the impression that you liked Irwin Allen a bit better than some of the other stars of his series that I've talked to. What was good and what was bad about working for him?

Well, I liked him, I had no reason not to. And I respected the fact that he had 250-something people working [on his series], and that's a lot of families, a lot of food, a lot of bread. I've always respected the guy who put the knife and the fork on the table. He wasn't anybody that I would wanna *hang* with, because he came from a whole different mindset than I did. But to dislike Irwin Allen would be pretty picky, because he didn't really interfere much in what you did. He didn't have the most gregarious personality in the world, he wasn't a "hail fellow well met" kind of guy, but, Jesus, he was busier than a cranberry merchant. Poor Paul Zastupnevich—if anybody disliked Irwin, I would think [it would be him]. And I think I heard later in life that he *wasn't* the biggest fan of Irwin. Paul worked night and day putting all of those costumes out on all of those shows. Especially *Time Tunnel*, because every time we went to do the next episode, he had a whole new cast of people he had to outfit.

Because it was almost like working on an anthology series—different demands every week.

Right, the other [Allen series] were a little more laid-back once he got 'em set up. But if *anybody* got abused by Irwin Allen, it was Paul Zastupnevich. You didn't hear it from him, but you could see the exhaustion in the guy and you always kinda felt sorry for him.

But I have nothing bad to say about Irwin; in fact, when he passed away, I was a pallbearer. His wife Sheila [actress Sheila Mathews] lives up the street from me here in Malibu; she and I were always friendly.

[Fox TV executive] William Self told me that one of the problems with Time Tunnel *was the expense of the sets. Unlike all the other Irwin Allen series, all of which had one basic set,* Time Tunnel *needed lots of new sets every week.*

I never heard that, but it was sure the truth. Incidentally, part of the reason it was sometimes interesting working on *Time Tunnel* was because it *was* like an anthology, really. Every week we had a whole new cast and a whole new setting, new wardrobe, whatever. As an actor, it was a hoot, because you never got bored, you never knew who you were going to be working with the next week or where you were going, because you didn't have time to analyze future episodes, you just showed up, worked hard (about 14 hours a day), went home and waited for your next script, which usually came out about the night that you finished.

So why wasn't The Time Tunnel *more of a success ratings-wise?*

You have to look at the shows that we were up against us on Friday night. There was *Man from U.N.C.L.E.*, there was *Wild Wild West*—

After reaching the end of the *Tunnel***, Colbert returned to television guest spots, including a** *That Girl* **episode with Marlo Thomas.**

There was Tarzan *too. Oh, as a kid I just couldn't stand the fact that half the shows I liked* were all on at the same time*!*

In that time slot, there were lots of shows that were of interest to the public, we were just *one* of them, and you couldn't watch *every*thing—we didn't have the ability in those days to do anything but watch one channel at a time. No VCRs, nothing. So we lost a lot of audience. But the people who did watch it, they were an amazing group of people. Teachers throughout the country would build classroom assignments around the episodes because—even though we weren't historically accurate—we provoked enough interest that the kids would do reports on Robin Hood, or Krakatoa, or whatever. And it was real easy for the teachers to assign stuff, so the teachers just loved us! We had a real solid core of followers. I think if *Time Tunnel* had gone another year, we would have gone *seven* years. It had the appeal. Certain people just thought of it as a nighttime marvel. I went to Roadtown, in Tortola, down in the British Virgins. I was at the Moorings, sailing one of those big 60-foot Morgans [a yacht], and one day I happened to walk from the Moorings into Roadtown. I started at one end of town and by the time I got to the other end of this small town, there were alllll these people following me—I looked like the Pied Piper of the Saloon Set! *The Time Tunnel* was the biggest hit on the island. I found out later that, throughout the British Virgins and so forth, that little puppy was big-time television. In England they *still* show it, apparently, because I get fan mail and different things from England, from people who are just nuts about it. You'd think it was in prime time and just released. Out here [in California], on my lineup of TV stations, it's shown six days a week, every morning except Sunday. So it's had a "shelf life" bar none—I don't know of any other show with such a limited original viewing audience that still runs with the frequency of *Time Tunnel*.

Recently, on Conan O'Brien's TV show, Tom Hanks said The Time Tunnel *was his favorite TV show as a kid, and that he would do slow-motion tumbling on his sofa, imitating you and James Darren.*

I had no idea! But, y'know, in addition to the "regular" fan letters, I've had 100 fan letters from people saying that their careers were dictated by and based on their interest in *Time Tunnel* when they were kids. This one gal is a scientist, she designs aircraft over in London, and she said that she got interested in becoming a scientist because of *The Time Tunnel*. There've been lots of people like that. So it was an interesting show, it had a lot of merit. Sure, it was crude in some ways but, God, it's still something that stands up today in many ways, which is hard to believe.

When The Time Tunnel *was cancelled, what was your reaction?*

We'd already been picked up [for a second season], and we were home on hiatus, when we found out it was being cancelled. So we were in shock, because we all expected to come back. At the end of the first season, we'd had a huge party for 256 people and their families, that worked on the show. We had 256 actual people getting a salary off of the thing, and we had the biggest blast you ever saw on one of the big sound stages—I *think* it was the stage where we had the Tunnel set. We had a huge party there after we were picked up, Irwin was happier than hell, and everybody else was too; we were all happier than clams. We went home and about three months later we were told that ABC had changed their mind and cancelled it, and that was the end of that. It was a *big* letdown. As I mentioned, I thought that if it went another year, it would have really been a hit. Our ratings weren't very high; our share, whatever the hell that was, was mediocre, but, Jesus, we were up against everything in the world. There wasn't enough share to go *around* for that hour that we were on.

A few years after Time Tunnel *shut down, you were in that Irwin Allen movie you mentioned earlier,* City Beneath the Sea.

Yeah, a movie-of-the-week type of thing. I was one of the leads, and Jimmy did a little cameo in it. It had a pretty good cast of "outsiders" [actors not associated with Irwin Allen] who came in and worked with us, like Stuart Whitman and Robert Wagner. Stu Whitman didn't want to do it, I think he'd heard some horror stories about Irwin. He called me and asked me what I thought, and I said, "Come on, suit up and get in here, you'll have fun." Somehow or other, between when I talked to him and when he showed up on the set, he injured his shoulder badly—really tore it up doing something, I forget what. He could hardly move that arm, so we shot the whole show with him with one side of his body immobilized. Robert Wagner, to me, was always very aloof. He came from a very wealthy family, and he had a high opinion of himself as I recall—there was just something arrogant and different about Bob. I'd meet him some place and say hi, and he wouldn't know me from Adam's off ox no matter *how* many times he met me. He was that kind of a fellow, just from a different breed than I was. Then Bob's daughter Natasha, his youngest daughter, had a horrible crush on my boy Clayton. Oh, she wouldn't let him out of her sight, and he finally had to set things straight, because he didn't feel the same way she did. But, boy, she had her sights set on my son, I remember that. I thought, "Gee, it'd be funny if I end up being related to Robert Wagner!" [*Laughs*]

Wrapping up, give me a few "quick takes" on some other sci-fi credits of yours. First, "Sabotage," an episode of Irwin Allen's Land of the Giants *in which you appeared.*

I don't remember much. I haven't seen it since I did it, if I saw it *then*.

You were in Amazon Women on the Moon *[1987], in a spoof of 1950s sci-fi movies like* Cat-Women of the Moon.

I was an astronaut along with Steve Forrest and John Travolta's brother Joey, and a *monkey*. On the Moon, the Amazon gals ended up feeding my character to the giant spiders* and the *other* two guys get laid. I think even the *monkey* got laid, I don't know, but *I* didn't! *Amazon Women* was a funny piece, almost like a *Hellzapoppin* kind of show, we laughed a lot and I had fun making the damn thing. I liked Joey Travolta; I haven't seen him since, but we've talked. He's out in the Valley now, running some kind of an acting studio. And Phil Spector's victim Lana Clarkson was one of the Moon girls. The scenes where we were walking around on the Moon surface were shot at Vasquez Rocks.

Wearing a spacesuit out at a place like Vasquez Rocks—does that get hot and sweaty?

Not like I was when I was at Warner Brothers doing [the TV series] *The Alaskans* with Roger Moore, in real sealskin coats and pants and fur-lined stuff—in July! To get back to your question, yes, it was hot in those spacesuits on *Amazon Women* but, Jesus Christ, I boiled on hot sets 100 times, so that was nothing new.

Is it possible that the people who made Grand Tour: Disaster in Time *[1992] thought to put you in that movie because of your* Time Tunnel *connection?*

It could have been, the film certainly had some of those [sci-fi time travel] aspects. In it, I wore this white, godlike outfit, and I *was* a godlike kind of character, with superpowers. That was filmed in Eugene, Oregon, and I loved the location because we were right on the river and nice accommodations, and I'd be riding my bicycle and visiting with people in

---

*Viewers learn of Colbert's character's grisly death-by-giant-spiders via a dialogue exchange; no such scene was shot.

Still pals today, Colbert (right) and Darren, here seen with actress Phyllis Davis, attend the occasional sci-fi con and autograph show.

this quaint little college town. I remember having a very, very nice time on location with some great people, and it was an interesting little movie.

You said before that you do think that a new version of Time Tunnel *would "work" today.*
　I just think there's a *tremendous* market for it. If I knew somebody who wanted to invest in something in that area, I would say, "Go ahead, put it into *this* type of thing" [a *Time*

Tunnel type of show], because it just opens up the world of imagination, it runs the gamut from reality to fiction to surrealism to anything you *want*.

You're now retired from the acting, correct?

I retired about 12 years ago, but I'm thinkin' about suitin' up again. I still look good. And, you know, the money has just gone crazy. I have enough to last me the rest of my life I'm sure, I own a very expensive piece of property out here in Malibu, but I wouldn't mind suitin' up and goin' back in and doing a little more work on this high dollar that they're puttin' out today. So if you run across any producers who think I'm dead, let 'em know I'm still here!

If you could go into the Time Tunnel and go to any period, past or future, and spend a little time, where's the first place you'd go?*

I'd probably go to the Roaring Twenties. That was a very exciting, wide-open time where government was making all the rules and everybody was breakin' 'em. I *like* that! They were dancin' and laughin' and drinkin' their bathtub gin and havin' more fun than is allowed. So that would be one of the time periods that I would go to, along with many other times that I would be interested in glimpsing and being a part of.

---

*The same question is asked of James Darren (page 89) and Lee Meriwether (pages 188–189).

ROBERT CONRAD ON
THE WILD WILD WEST

> *There were too many injuries [sustained by* **Wild Wild West** *stuntmen], too many people getting hurt.... I knew that there was going to be a death comin'. I just felt it in my body, that someone was going to die.*

For fans of movie and TV action, it can take years of study and research to tell when a star is being stunt-doubled, and by whom. But even a kid can tell when a star is doing his *own* stunts—and, on a personal note, that's one of the reasons this writer became *the* #1 Knee-High Fan of the TV series *The Wild Wild West* (1965–69). It was a Western series, a spy series and often a sci-fi series, which made it a "triple"—but for this member of the kindergarten crowd, it became a towering home run because Robert Conrad, playing James T. West of the United States' post–Civil War Secret Service, was not only in the thick of every fistfight, but was also doing his own riding, leaps and death-defying falls.

Conrad, however, was not the only player with the heart of a lion: During the four years that the CBS series ruled the ratings roost, he assembled one of the best stunt teams in TV history, a cadre of rough'n'tumble pros also more than happy to put their bodies on the line to deliver the ultimate in TV action. To commemorate Paramount Home Entertainment's Spring 2006 release of *The Wild Wild West: The Complete First Season*, Robert Conrad reminisces about the stuntwork that helped make the series a TV classic.

Let me tell you where I'm comin' from before we even start: When I was eight or nine years old, Wild Wild West *was my favorite show, and that hasn't changed very much in the years since.*

Thank you. You'll enjoy it more now. I got a copy of the Season One DVD sent to me, so my grandson and I sat down and I put it on and the two of us watched some of it. We enjoyed 'em.

Being "physical" as an actor—I assume that's something that's always been important to you.

Welllll, not really. *Wild Wild West* was written for stunts, it was written for action, and consequently [action] was there every day, every scene. Our show couldn't really take the time to coordinate a sequence so the viewers didn't know that it was a stuntman. *Wild Wild West* just didn't lend itself towards *having* a stunt person doubling me all the time. So that's why I did all my own stuff. I was a stuntman when I started in the business, so it was something that I could do.

What were a couple of the early TV shows and movies you did stunts in?

God, there were so many. This was long before *anyone* was born [*laughs*]. Do you remember [the 1950s TV series] *Highway Patrol*? I did my own stunts on *Highway Patrol* and on *Lock Up*, and from there I went on and on. It all began when I belonged to the Beverly Hills Health Club and there was a man there named Henry Rackin, who was the casting director at Ziv [the prolific TV production company]. He asked me if I could ride a horse, and I told him, "I can ride like the *wind*." Subsequently he hired me to play a non-speaking part as an Indian. That gave me an introduction to that wonderful company Ziv that had these shows like *Lock Up* and *Highway Patrol* and so on. Anyway, in that show where I played the Indian, I did my own stunt and I did it well, and that started me [acting *and* doing stunts] over at that company. Then I went to Warner Brothers and did *Hawaiian Eye* [1959–63], and on that show I did probably 50 percent of my own stunts. (But *Hawaiian Eye* was not the kind of show where there were a lot of stunts I had to do.) Then from *Hawaiian Eye* I went into the *Wild West* series, and it was just natural for me to do my own stunts once again.

Try *this* on for spies: In the 1965-69 series *The Wild Wild West*, Robert Conrad and Ross Martin were James West and Artemus Gordon, Secret Service agents in the Old West contending with conventional security threats—and also *un*conventional ones, from ghosts and an opera phantom to sea monsters and a flying saucer.

Whitey Hughes, the Wild West *stunt coordinator, says that CBS told him early on that they didn't want Robert Conrad two feet off the floor. How were you able to get your way and do most of your own stunts, with CBS having that attitude?*

I did *all* my own stunts, not "most" of 'em.* I even did the acrobatic stuff—I'd done [acrobatics] as a kid in grammar school. Whitey Hughes I hired to be a stunt coordinator, and *as* the stunt coordinator he was told [by CBS] that they didn't want me to get injured. But CBS didn't know that I *hired* Whitey Hughes [*laughs*]! I said, "Whitey, who hired you?"—and then would do my own stunts. As stunt choreographer, I think he did a wonderful job.

Who put together the stunt team that became so "famous"? Was it you or you and *Whitey?*

I put the stunt team together. Whitey didn't know some of the people, like for instance Dick Cangey [Conrad's real-life Man Friday and a stuntman on *Wild Wild West*]. The stuntmen were Whitey Hughes, myself, Red West, Cangey and Tommy Huff, who went on to be one of the top stuntmen in the industry—he passed away just a few months ago [in 2006].

---

*According to Whitey Hughes, stuntmen Louie Elias and Chuck O'Brien were two of Conrad's stunt doubles on the show. Later in this very interview, Conrad talks about his last-season stunt double Jimmy George.

He became one of the best. And Dick Cangey has passed away [in 2003]. Oh, and another member of the stunt team was Bobby Herron, who doubled Ross Martin. That was our group.

In Season One fight scenes, Jim West strikes a lot of martial arts–type poses, but in later seasons he's doing more boxing-type stuff.

The reason for that is, I had been studying karate with one of the top instructors in that art form, and I thought I'd introduce it [to TV] in *The Wild Wild West*. You'll notice that I'm pronouncing the word karate the way people do here [kah-*rah*-te], but when you *do* karate you pronounce it karate [kah-rah-*tay*]. It means "empty hand"—kara is empty and te is hand. Anyway, I did it in *Wild Wild West*, and then everyone started picking up on it. In fact, [karate] awards started being given to people who couldn't *spell* it! So I said, "Awww, nuts. I'll go back to boxing," and I did.

Dick Cangey used to tell me that you were really into boxers and that there was a boxing ring on the Wild West *stage, and that was the reason people like Floyd Patterson appeared on the show.*

That's true, I liked boxing and boxers. Floyd Patterson ["The Night of the Juggernaut"]—what a nice, nice man Floyd was. I certainly liked Wilhelm von Homburg [who played various *Wild Wild West* villains]—he was a great fighter who wasn't given the credit he was entitled to. Von Homburg was *crazy*—nuttier than a fruitcake. He just was full of life, he just loved wine, he loved women and he loved song. But I loved working with him and I loved boxin' with him. Roland LaStarza [also seen on *Wild Wild West*] gave Rocky Marciano one of his best fights. We had Roland do our show because he was an outstanding fighter.

When I interviewed Wild West *writer Ken Kolb, he said that at one point during the run of the show, you wanted to actually box some well-known prizefighter, and CBS put the kibosh on that.*

I was going to fight in Japan. But what happened was, we did an episode ["The Night of the Fugitives"] with a saloon scene where I jumped from the top of a staircase and grabbed a chandelier and swung, but I fell and broke my skull. It wasn't that CBS said no, because CBS said no lotsa times and I just ignored what CBS said [*laughs*].

The stuntman you were supposed to kick as you swung on that chandelier, Jerry Laveroni—he wasn't there to *kick, which is why you fell.*

There's always been the question of, did Jerry Laveroni back away from the kick [chicken out], or was Laveroni late in timing? I like to think he was late. Laveroni's still around, and I'll tell you where he works: He does security for the New York Yankees. Thanks for bringing his name up, because he was another one of the regulars.

The fall from that chandelier had to be your worst mishap on the show, and you've talked about it several times. What was the second *worst?*

There were a lot of times when I was injured or where my body was shaken up. There were just so many, I can't individually recount 'em. But there weren't any that put me in the hospital except the chandelier. I jumped through a "blind wall" once. In an episode set in a prison ["The Night of the Bars of Hell"], I smashed through the wall and fell a ways, and two guys [stuntmen Bill Catching and "Red" Morgan] were supposed to catch me. They missed me, so I only caught part of the table I was supposed to land on, instead of the center of it. That shook me up pretty good.

Conrad's passion for boxing meant that star, stuntmen et al. often donned gloves between takes on the set of the spy-fi series. Right to left, boxing great Roland LaStarza, trainer Ralph Gambina, Conrad, stuntman Whitey Hughes and Conrad's sparring partner Rocky.

Even great stunt teams have their "off" days: In "The Night of the Bars of Hell," Conrad burst through a wall intending to land on a padded, breakaway card table—and missed it by *that* much.

You name for me, now, 'cause you're so knowledgeable about actors and stunts: Who were the three actors who've done their own stunts?

Well, you ... Bruce Lee?

No, he didn't do his own stunts. Bruce Lee did his own martial arts but when it was time for him to fly out the window, he had a stuntman. The three actors who did their own stunts were Robert Conrad, Douglas Fairbanks [Sr.] and Jackie Chan. I once went up to Jackie Chan at a charity and I said, "I really like your work" and "Take care of yourself." And he said, "Well, I model my work after *you*." I was very flattered.

Did anybody ever "worry" about the fact that every Wild West *super-villain had the same henchmen—the same stunt guys—every week?*

No, because I think the way they were dressed and made-up, unless the viewers were really paying attention, they wouldn't notice. The stunts went by so quick.

William Witney was one of your directors—

He, for some reason, didn't like me, and I don't know why. What was his problem with me? You can tell me, I don't care. I'm 71 years old now.

Off the top of my head I don't remember exactly what he said to me. I could Xerox that part of my interview with him and send it to you.

Nahhhhh, it's okay, he's dead and it's history. If you coulda remembered, I would have loved hearing it. But I don't care to read it.

Witney told me you had to jump over something that was going to explode once you cleared it— and that you told the guy with the detonator to blow it up when you were right over *it. You and the stuntmen, putting your bodies on the line every time—weren't there moments of suspense?*

Yeah, just about every time we did a stunt! But we'd high-five and say, "Let's get it on."

I'm reaching for the book with my William Witney interview—you promise not to get mad at me, right?

Oh, hell, I won't get mad. I didn't get mad at *him* when he was still alive! No, I'd appreciate it.

Okay, I'm reading from my book now. He told me he couldn't stand you and Ross Martin ... "they were a couple of prima donnas" ... "they would be late, they'd hold things up" ... "Bob would go back to his dressing room in between scenes"...

That was *it?* Unfortunately, all that stuff isn't true. I never went back to my dressing room. I sat on my chair [on the set], because it was more fun bein' with the guys than it was sittin' in my dressing room alone. Why would I go to my dressing room?

In one of your voiceover episode intros on the new DVD, you talk about Michael Dunn, "Dr. Loveless," trying to do a stunt—with disastrous results!

In that episode ["The Night of the Murderous Spring"] we made a rail for him, like for a train, from a second story level down to [the soundstage floor], and he was supposed to escape coming down that rail in a railcar. And he fell when he was on the second story. But he'd insisted on doing his own stunt. We could have got a midget [stuntman] but Michael wasn't gonna have it. So he got hurt, and that's the reason Dr. Loveless is in a wheelchair in that episode.

The Wild West *wardrobe man Jimmy George, who looked a lot like you, did some stunts for you in the last season, after that chandelier debacle.*

Yes, Jimmy did do some of the stunts. To Jimmy's credit, he had a lot of courage, but I dismissed him after a couple of stunts. He didn't have the moves. He had the courage but he didn't have the moves.

You did him a favor. I think he got hurt on half the stunts he did!

Yeah, so I cut him loose. I still talk to Jimmy, and I spoke to Red West just last week— Red's in Tennessee. And when Whitey Hughes got the Golden Boot [a prestigious award for Hollywood Western veterans] in 2002, I was the one who presented him with it.

At a certain point, did you have any say in the scripting of Wild Wild West? *"I want x-number of fights per episode," etc.?*

I never cared about the scripting. I was happy with the way they were writing it. I remember at one point they were analyzing the show's success, sitting in their rooms wondering why it was so popular. And someone said, "Well, it's Ross Martin and his disguises

Conrad (right) and his fourth-season *Wild Wild West* stunt double Jimmy George at a 1986 reunion of *WWW* stuntment arranged by this writer's brother Jon Weaver.

and costumes, and it's Robert Conrad and his action sequences. So we'll write action for Conrad and we'll write disguises-and-costumes for Ross, and we'll stay on the air as long as we want."

At ten years old, I coulda told 'em that.
    That's what the show was all about.

How often did somebody get whacked in the fight scene?
    Accidentally punched? Not too often. Cangey caught one once [sustaining a broken nose in "The Night of the Avaricious Actuary"], and Tommy Huff once [split open near his eye in "The Night of the Fugitives"]. But not too many times. We were pros. There were a lot of times when the stunt guys got *hurt*, like Red West took out a piano one day—he hit his head on a piano keyboard ["The Night of the Running Death"]. And in another one, Cangey took out a *wall* [*laughs*]. On and on and on. But that's what they got paid for. That's why they were called *stuntmen*.

Outside of the show, you also socialized with some of the stuntmen.
    Yes, we even had a football team, and we won 44 games in a row. They couldn't find anyone to beat us. Jimmy George was a better football player than he was a stuntman—he was an outstanding football player.

Then you and Cangey would go to the rodeos.
    We *worked* the rodeos [made personal appearances, Conrad and Cangey doing fight scenes, and Conrad singing]. And I got hurt—I dislocated my shoulder doing one of the

rodeos. We were working on cement, but to make it look like it was an authentic rodeo they covered the cement with dirt. Cangey had to knock me off my horse and drive me into the ground. But the dirt had been removed by the animals walkin' back and forth, so when Cangey hit me, he drove me into the cement. Me with my dislocated shoulder, for the rest of that rodeo I sang!

Was it disheartening when CBS ordered that the fights be less violent in the last season?
No, 'cause we kept up the pace, ignored CBS again. But it was time for the show to go. There were too many injuries, too many people getting hurt. Whitey Hughes went in an ambulance [clipped in the head by a horse's hoof after a saddle fall in "The Night of the Golden Cobra"]...Red West went in an ambulance...Jerry Laveroni and Jimmy George got hurt...

You went in an ambulance, after the chandelier stunt. But Dick Cangey told me you were uncooperative, that you wouldn't lie down on the stretcher. Believe me, I know that feeling of, "Hey, if I just stay on my feet, I'll be okay."
Exactly. I thought I'd get better if I could ride in [the passenger seat of] the ambulance and not be strapped down in the back. I was in and out of consciousness, though, so I think they should have strapped me in anyway [*laughs*]! I realized, at some point when I was in the hospital, that I couldn't remember arriving there, and I didn't know where I was. So, yeah, it was time, I felt, for the show to go.

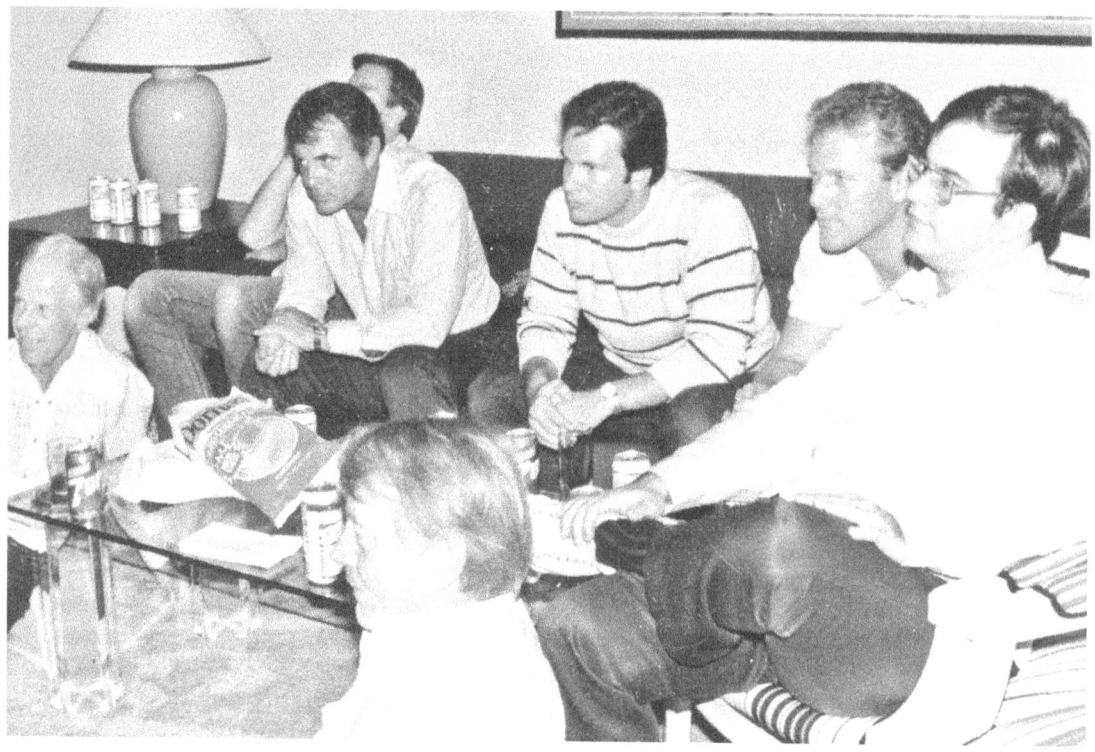

Watching a montage of *Wild West* **stunts and fight scenes at the 1986 reunion are, left to right: Whitey Hughes, Conrad, person obscured, Red West (on floor in foreground), Jon Weaver, unidentified and Tom Weaver.**

Jim West and his wild wild stunt team, almost two decades later. Left to right, Tommy Huff, Red West, Conrad, Dick Cagney and Jimmy George.

How often do you watch a Wild Wild West?

I had not seen a *Wild West* in *20 years*. But I'm gonna continue to sit down with my grandson and watch the shows. It'll be a treat for him.

If you could only show one Wild Wild West *fight or stunt to your grandson—"Look at the crazy stuff Grandpa used to do"—which one would it be?*

The *two* stunts that I would show him would be the one in the prison, through the wall, and the other one would be the chandelier one where I got injured. There were also some stunts on horseback that I did, but I can't remember those.

I remember you falling face-first to the ground from the top of a stagecoach in one ["The Night of the Amnesiac"].

That was another one of those stunts that "coulda been" [coulda been fatal]. When the show got cancelled, the stuntmen for whom *Wild Wild West* was day-to-day work, of course, were devastated for the time being, until they went on to do other shows. But I knew that there was going to be a death comin'. I just *felt* it in my body, that someone was going to die. So I said, "It's time to move on."

Why didn't you do any on-camera stuff for the DVD, just voiceover?

'Cause I wasn't asked! If I had been asked, I would have done it. I'd have done on-camera in a heartbeat.

The cartoon opening of the show: Was it better when the girl with the knife swoons from Jim West's kiss, or when he punches her in the face?

[*Laughs*] I think it was a *lot* funnier when I punched the girl!

JAMES DARREN ON
THE TIME TUNNEL

> *[If I could time-travel,] there are so many places I would love to visit.*
> *To be a cowboy, and meet people like the Dalton brothers and Jesse James*
> *and Frank James.... I would like to have been one of them!*

It's the best of times for fans of Irwin Allen's small-screen forays into big-time fantasy-adventure: Fox Home Entertainment is continuing to give his seminal '60s series the deluxe DVDeluxe treatment, and we continue to mark the occasions by revisiting with these shows' stars. For *The Time Tunnel*, it's Mission Completed for Fox, now that the second half of its one-season (1966–67), 30-episode run has made its home video bow—and now turning back the clock to reminisce is James Darren, who starred as reluctant time traveler Dr. Tony Newman in the short-lived but still popular series.

Philadelphia-born and –raised, the former James Ercolani came to Hollywood in the mid–1950s and soon hit it big as a light leading man (in the era's *Gidget* movies et al.) and "teen idol" recording artist. Darren went from having his clothes (and even his hair!) torn at by teenybopper fans to a different type of action when *Time Tunnel* creator-producer Allen signed him and Robert Colbert to play the scientists responsible for the development of the government's Project Tic Toc—who then proceed to enter their own Time Tunnel and get lost in the swirling maze of past and future ages, often ending up on the doorstep of historic figures on the eve of historic events (the *Titanic* sinking, the Alamo attack, etc.). Darren reminisces about the show and his co-workers, and tocs about what makes *him* tic, in this timely tête-à-tête.

Do you have any idea who came up with the idea of you as the Time Tunnel *star?*

It had to be Irwin Allen's idea, it wasn't Fox. Irwin called my agent about my doing the role of Tony Newman, and my agent told me what it was, a science fiction series called *The Time Tunnel*. I had not read the script or anything, but I told him I wasn't interested in doing television and not interested in doing do a science fiction TV series. Well, they called repeatedly, and finally my agent told me that Irwin wanted to talk to me. I called his office and he set up a meeting. I went into the meeting, and by the time I left, he had talked me into doing *Time Tunnel*.

Funny!

Yeah, it was! He said, "*This* is something you have to do. I know you don't want to do this, but I think you're perfect for this role and I want you to do it," and he convinced me.

Irwin was one of the great salespersons of our time. I accepted the role because of my meeting with him.

Had you ever even heard of him before this all started?

You know, not really. I'd maybe *heard* of him, but I didn't really pay much attention to it. He was doing *Voyage to the Bottom of the Sea* and *Lost in Space* then, but they weren't shows that I would necessarily watch. So I really wasn't that familiar with Irwin Allen. But after I was doing *Time Tunnel*, then of course I watched *Voyage*—and *did* an episode of *Voyage* ["The Mechanical Man"]. And I watched *Lost in Space* because it was campy [*laughs*]. He was a great guy, I loved Irwin Allen, he was a terrific man and he was *very* good to me, and very fair. I do miss him, I'll be honest with ya, I really miss him.

From teen idol to time traveler, and beyond: James Darren tells the tale.

What was your objection to doing a TV series, and what was your objection especially to do a science fiction TV series?

Well, my head really wasn't there about doing science fiction. I might have looked at *Voyage* or looked at *Lost in Space* and figured I didn't want to deal with monsters and things like that. It was something that just didn't really appeal to me at the time. And as far as doing a TV series, at that point in my career I didn't really want to do a series, I wanted to continue doing films. But fortunately for me, I did accept the role.

When I interviewed David Hedison, the star of Voyage to the Bottom of the Sea, *he told me more or less exactly the same story you just did: He didn't want to do* Voyage *but Irwin Allen just kept after him and after him, and he finally caved.*

[*Laughs*] Well, with me, it didn't take *that* much, I just had the one meeting with Irwin and he convinced me.

Did he ever tell you why he was so set on having you in the lead?

Irwin was that kind of a person. If he thought I was the perfect Tony Newman, then he wasn't going to rest until I did it. That was it. No matter what it *was* with Irwin, whether it be casting an actor or … I don't care *what* it was: If he had his mind set that that was the way it had to be, then he would work on it until it happened. In his head, I was the perfect Tony Newman and that was the way it was gonna be.

Had you had much experience with action stuff prior to Time Tunnel? *I know about* The Guns of Navarone *[1961], but beyond that, were there other roles in which you did the kind of stuff* Time Tunnel *called for?*

My first movie *Rumble on the Docks* [1956] took place in New York, and I guess that was relatively physical. I can't really think offhand of anything else. Nothing as much as *The Time Tunnel*, no. But I enjoyed all that [action] stuff, so that would have made me *want* to do it.

Did you have to be trained how to do fistfights and swordfights and so on?

Swordfights, sure, absolutely, because I could not fence, I'd never dealt with swords. But as far as fighting was concerned, I was brought up in South Philadelphia, so I knew a little bit about that [*laughs*]!

Was it fun *doing that action stuff on* Time Tunnel*?*

I loved it, I really did. Actors love doing action stuff. I mean, *most* actors—I can't speak for every one of them. But most actors love doing their own stunts. When I did a movie called *Gunman's Walk* [1958] with Van Heflin and Tab Hunter, we had to actually herd cattle. I had ridden before, but I had not ever herded cattle before. Cutting cattle, that's a big job! And it's a big responsibility: If the horse gets spooked, you're in trouble, because if it throws you, then you're under the hooves of all the steers. So it was kind of exciting. My point is that maybe actors, including myself—*especially* myself—love to do their own stunts. When I did [the TV series] *T.J. Hooker*, God Almighty, I was doing every car stunt I possibly could, that they would *allow* me to do, 'cause I enjoyed it. It takes you back to being a kid. I think that's really where it lies: It takes you back to your childhood. Only you're playing with *big* toys now!

Your Time Tunnel *stunt double was Charles Picerni.*

Oh, Charlie was great, and a good friend of mine. I got him to do *Time Tunnel*.

You got him the job?

Oh, absolutely. He was a friend, and his brother [actor] Paul Picerni was a friend of mine from almost my Day One in California, and is still a friend to this day. Charlie and I, our looks are similar, and we're built similarly. Being the star, quote-unquote, of a show, as I was on *Time Tunnel*, you can pretty much dictate who you want to stand in for you and who you want to double you. I asked if Charlie could do it; and with Irwin, as I told you before, whatever I wanted, I would get. Within reason [*laughs*]! Charlie did double me and did a spectacular job, as usual. There was a guy named Paul Stader who was the stunt coordinator, and that's who Charlie and all the *other* stunt people had to work *with*.

When we see Doug and Tony floating around against the kaleidoscope background, is that you or stunt doubles?

Those were stunt doubles. They were hanging from wires and they had special harness belts on, with little metal pegs coming out the sides; the wires were attached to those pegs. And they would spin head over heels.[Colbert remembers it differently on page 63.]

The Hollywood Reporter *review of the first episode says it's more difficult to believe James Darren as an electronics genius with a doctor's degree than it is to believe in the Tunnel itself!*

I felt the same way! That reminds me that Irwin and I had little disagreements because my sideburns would be a little long. He'd say, "No no no no no. Scientists don't have long sideburns, they have *short* sideburns." I said, "Really? Gee, I guess I don't know many scientists...." [*Laughs*] So I had to keep my sideburns short. But what I would do is grow them longer and then have the makeup department put [some white makeup] on the bottom part of each sideburn, to make it *look* as though they had been cut. It was just an illusion. A person's skin is usually a little tanned, so when you cut your sideburns, the skin that *was* under the hair is usually lighter. We would play those little tricks on Irwin. But he was hard to get things over on; you didn't fool Irwin too many times.

What was Allen like as director on the first Time Tunnel *episode?*

He knew exactly what he was doing and exactly what he wanted. You weren't looking at somebody who was saying, "Gee, should I do this or should I do that? Let me see how it looks *this* way...." 'Cause Irwin storyboarded *every*thing. He knew every single shot he would be doing and how he wanted it to end up and *whatever*. (I learned a few things from him which I later applied to *my* directing.) He was extremely well-prepared, he was very easy to get along with, and he did an excellent job.

Think about the technical components he had to work with at that time; he did a damn good job of making everything look pretty decent. If he were living today, and had all the technical advantages that they have today in filmmaking, *Time Tunnel* could look absolutely brilliant. For back *then*, I thought he did an outstanding job.

Watching the new Fox DVDs was the first time I was seeing Time Tunnel *in a long time, and I wasn't quite sure what to expect special effects-wise. I thought they were terrific.*

Especially when you consider that that was 40 years ago. In the past 15, 20 years, we've come a looong way, and all because of the computer and other technical stuff. For what he had, I thought Irwin did a great job.

When writers were trying to dream up the next Time Tunnel *episode, did they sit down and ask themselves, "What sets and what filmclips do we have?"*

That I couldn't answer, but I'm sure Irwin was in on every single thing. I think he probably started first with the story, and then if he could take advantage of the film library at Fox, he would. We did take advantage of a lot of the film Fox had in their library, Irwin used a lot of that old footage. He was brilliant in *that* sense too.

Irwin was such a control freak—and I say that kindly—that he demanded as close as he could get to perfection, he demanded that whatever he visualized in his head be put onto that screen. And he did want to know everything that was going on—and you really didn't *do* anything without Irwin knowing it, believe me. Because it just didn't fly. Everybody behind the scenes, maybe *because* of their respect for Irwin, did an outstanding job. I have to say that Irwin held that ship together, that's for sure.

Would you talk about Robert Colbert and Lee Meriwether?

Bob was great. From Day One, we hit it off. We just were friends, there was no competition. Well, he got upset 'cause he didn't have as many lines as me sometimes [*laughs*], but I would tell him, "Do you really *care*?" He'd say, "Well, look at all this stuff you have to say." I'd say, "I tell ya what: I don't even want to *learn* it. *You* say it. *You* say it, and I'll say *this*. Take this part of my dialogue." And it was all done without any kind of animosity. We had a good time on the set, and I loved working with him. And I loved working with Lee as well. Even though we didn't have many scenes together, we *were* on the same lot, we'd get to see Lee and Whit Bissell and John Zaremba and all those people quite a bit.

How 'bout the people making the other Irwin Allen shows of that time, Lost in Space *and* Voyage? *Ever cross paths with them?*

Oh, yeah, I'd go down and visit them. Because I liked being on those sets, I'd go down there. [*Lost in Space*'s] Mark Goddard I knew, and June Lockhart I knew really well. I'd go down and visit, and then I'd go to *Voyage*, which was fun; I knew a lot of the actors there.

Were there other fun things also going on at Fox, that made you happy to be there on a day-to-day basis?

Goodbye Cool World: Tony (Darren, left) and Doug (Robert Colbert) left the Swingin' Sixties behind when they set sail on the seas of time, unable to control each new destination.

I was happy to be there because I was *working* [*laughs*]. I was happy to be there because I was doing a show that, even though it was cancelled after the first season, was *pretty* successful, and a joy to do. I loved it. I just absolutely loved doing it. Like I said, I had a great rapport with Irwin and Bob and all my co-workers and Lee, so it was a joy just to be working. That's what an actor loves to *do*, to act, to be fortunate enough to be there every day.

Incidentally [*laughs*], talking about Bob and me ... we were two of a kind in many ways. He would say, for instance, "Y'know, I think we should get phones in our dressing rooms," and I'd say, "Yeah, we *should*." But they wouldn't do it. Finally Bob and I said, "Look, we *need* phones in our dressing rooms." It didn't entail *anything*—they put a phone line to your trailer. It became just a matter of principle. So we finally, after about maybe, Christ, the 18th or 20th episode, we *finally* got our phones. Now today, we would not have to argue for that, because we have cell phones.

The fact that you had different settings in time and place every week—did that variety make the show more interesting to do?

Oh, it made it *much* more interesting to do. I mean, to be on the same set with the same characters and the same *show* basically every week would be tiring. The only thing that Bob and I got a little tired of was that line, "Where *are* we?"

At the beginning of each episode, the "Where are *we?" moment.*

Yeah. But, I mean, geez, it was such a great opportunity to do the show. I look back on it, it was just fun. When you're doing things at the present moment, it can all seem [mundane] sometimes ... you may be tired one day, you may have had a bad night the night before ... but I look back on the good fortune of doing *Time Tunnel* and I wish I could do it again. I had that experience with all three series that I did [*The Time Tunnel, T.J. Hooker, Star Trek: Deep Space Nine*], I don't look back on *any* of them and think, "My God, I'm so thrilled that that thing is over," because I just had a good time. I had an especially good time on *Time Tunnel* and also on *Star Trek: Deep Space Nine*, I loved doin' that show, that was Heaven.

In 1966, TV Guide *said you were planning to write a* Time Tunnel *script about Jack the Ripper.*

No, that's not true. As I think about it, I may have *suggested* that to Irwin, but I really can't swear to it. I didn't write a script because I don't consider myself a writer. It might have been just something that I talked about to him about, because that *was* a fascinating thing, the story of Jack the Ripper. I saw the Laird Cregar movie [*The Lodger*, 1944], I saw the Jack Palance movie [*Man in the Attic*, 1953], and even though in a sense it's kind of sick to find him fascinating, because he *was* a horrible person, it *is* an interesting story.

You wore the same clothes for pretty much the whole run of Time Tunnel. *Did that get old, or didn't you care?*

I didn't care. In fact, I *loved* that, because I hate wardrobe fittings, I really do. They're just the biggest drag. I still have my green sweater—there *were* many, but there's only one left. Once when I was at [an autograph show], there was a Japanese man who he offered me $5000 for the sweater.

Did you have it there with you?

No. But he was talking about memorabilia, and I told him that I had the sweater, and

In the future-set (1968) series, the experimental time machine, housed 800 floors below the Arizona desert, was the $7.5 billion brainchild of the show's two main characters and their colleague Ann MacGregor.

he said, "Would you sell it?" I said, "Well, what do you mean? How much?" And he said, "I don't know. What do you think it's worth?" I said, "Well, it's worth a *lot* to me, because I don't anticipate selling it." He said, "Would you sell it for $5000?" I said, "Would you *pay* $5000?" He said, "Yeah." I said I wouldn't sell it.

But he put you to the test!
    I put *him* to the test!

Well, you put each other to the test. And you're keeping the sweater instead of taking the money, just out of fondness for the show?

Yeah. I mean, I don't need $5000—what am I gonna do with it? I'd wind up spending it on something that means nothing compared to the sweater. Today, $5000, you can go to a good movie and have a great meal [*laughs*]—that's about it!

Do any Time Tunnel *episodes stand out in your mind as favorites?*

The one that I like most is the Pearl Harbor one ["The Day the Sky Fell In"], 'cause it was a very nice role for me to play, Tony Newman going back to Pearl Harbor in 1941 and meeting his dad [Linden Chiles], who was killed when Tony was seven or eight. As Tony, I try to warn him to *not* stay there, to *leave*, so that he will not have died. I try to alter history. It was just a nice role for me, so I liked that. I liked "Billy the Kid" too, because of the story. Robert Walker Jr. played Billy the Kid and he was quite good—he was a good actor, and he's still working. So those are a couple that I really had a particular love for, so to speak.

Speaking of parents, were yours still around when you were doing Time Tunnel? *Did they watch the show?*

Oh, definitely. My dad passed away in '94 and, oh yeah, he was there with me from Day One, when I did *Rumble on the Docks*. He was out here [in Hollywood] with me, he flew out with me. And my mom is *still* living, she'll be 91 soon. She goes to all the concerts I do on the East Coast. So my parents really have enjoyed what success I've had.

Did you watch Time Tunnel *every week?*

Yeah, I did, for various reasons: to see how they edited what we did, and just to see the show. Absolutely.

Did you get fan mail during the run of the show?

God, yeah. Still do. I must have answered, a day or two ago, about 250, 300 letters for photographs. And a *lot* of them were *Time Tunnel*. From *all over*—I said to my wife [Evy Norlund, once a Miss Denmark], "Look where all these things are from!" They were from all over the United States and some were from Germany, some were from South America—it was incredible. I'd say I get maybe two, three hundred letters a month, believe it or not.

Does it ever get to be a pain in the neck?

[*Pause*] Yeah, it can be a pain in the neck, but I'm thankful that they still care and remember.

And what do they remember you for?

It's either *Time Tunnel* or *T.J. Hooker* or *Star Trek*. But they know everything I've done—they'll talk about *The Guns of Navarone* or they'll talk about even *Rumble on the Docks*, which surprises me. They know everything, believe me. They'll know more than *I* know, they really do. They're pretty thorough in their investigations—they're like detectives! When they care about an actor and latch onto an actor, then they do their research. It's really great. And I respect 'em because they know their business.

I told this to Robert Colbert and I'll tell it to you: On Conan O'Brien, *Tom Hanks said* Time Tunnel *was his favorite TV show as a kid, and he'd imitate you and Colbert by doing slow-motion tumbling on his sofa.*

Tunnel travelers (Darren and Colbert, standing) and Project Tic Toc personnel (Whit Bissell, Meriwether, John Zaremba) pose for the publicity camera.

Is that right?? Oh, that's so funny, and nice to hear. Carol Burnett came down one day when we were shooting—her daughter loved *Time Tunnel*. Jayne Mansfield came down, 'cause she also loved the show, and Sugar Ray Robinson too. To know that Tom Hanks liked *Time Tunnel*, that's *really* funny, 'cause I think he's like one of the most outstanding actors, incredibly talented. He's one of the great actors, and I don't use that word loosely. Every time I see him, he just knocks me off my feet, and I say, "God Almighty, I can't believe this kid can do *this* too."

My son Jimmy [Jim Moret] is a TV news correspondent, he was the CNN anchor on the O.J. Simpson trial. Jimmy was recently with Elton John and Tim Rice—Jimmy's interviewed Elton a lot of times and Elton really likes him 'cause he knows Jimmy won't pull any fast ones on him, and shit that he doesn't want to be printed. Elton said, "I see that your dad has two CDs on the jazz chart." Tim Rice said, "Who's your dad?" and my son said, "James Darren." He said, "Oh my god—I just bought his Greatest Hits album at Tower Records!" So funny! I was in a pizza shop one day with a friend of mine, I heard this motorcycle pull up, and in walked Bruce Springsteen in his little motorcycle cap, like Brando wore in *The Wild One* [1954]—I guess he left his helmet outside. I said, "Oh, I gotta go say hi to him." I walked up to him and I said, "Hi. I don't want to interrupt you, but my name is James Darren. Just want to tell you I'm a big fan. I love all your stuff." And he said, "James Darren. I bought 'Goodbye Cruel World' in Freehold, New Jersey." Isn't that sweet? My point is, it's so nice to hear these things. And to now hear the story about Tom Hanks ... it's so nice to know that these people not only see you on television and listen to your music, but that they *enjoy* it.

Talk about the cancellation of Time Tunnel.

We were doing our last or next-to-last Season One episode, we were about to go on hiatus, and Irwin telephoned me on the set. Like I said, we had a pretty special relationship. I don't think he and *Bob* did, to be honest with you, not that it meant anything, but Irwin and I just got on well. And so he called me on the set and told me that *Time Tunnel* had been picked up for another season. And he said, "You can tell Bob and whoever else you wanna tell." I was thrilled. I told Colbert, I said, "Irwin just called me and told me that we were picked up" and blah blah blah. But then later, [it was announced that] *Time Tunnel* was being taken *off* the air.

In 1989, Irwin Allen said that The Time Tunnel *was still his favorite TV show.*

Oh, yeah, for sure. It was.

Can you guess why *it was his favorite? Because of the concept? Because it was such a smooth operation?*

I think maybe all of that. I know he loved that show. And I felt really proud, *after* of course, that he had thought enough of me to want me, absolutely and only me, to do that show.

You thought you were gonna be picked up for a second year, and you weren't, so the series ended without any resolution for Doug and Tony. Are they still traveling through time, or did they get back home again?

No, they're still out there somewhere. Oh yeah! Probably havin' a helluva time, too [*laughs*]!

How often do you watch the show? Did you use the DVD release as an excuse to watch a few?

Oh, yeah, definitely. Not only that, my grandson, ten years old, watches it all the time. I got him all the episodes, not thinking that he would like it, really, 'cause everything is so ultra-hip today that I thought *Time Tunnel* would be dated for him. But he absolutely loves it. He took it to school and he showed it to the class [*laughs*]—I don't know how many episodes they saw, but they all enjoyed it, because they had both box sets there.

I asked Robert Colbert and I'll ask you: If a show like Time Tunnel *was done today, would kids watch? With the War of 1812 and Marie Antoinette and all these people that I don't know that kids today ever* heard *of?*

Half of them never heard of Clark Gable.

Half of 'em? 99.9 percent of 'em!

Four, five years ago I was directing some shows—I won't tell you which ones—and I asked people on the set if they knew who Clark Gable was. These were younger actors. And they had no idea. So I said, "Then to ask you who Franchot Tone was, or John Garfield was, would be...."

A lost cause!

A *total* lost cause! When we did *The Time Tunnel*, I think what helped the kids watch the show was, most of the Parent Teacher Associations across the country would encourage the kids to watch the historical ones. I think if a new *Time Tunnel*–type series came along, kids today would be more interested in the future ones than the historical ones. They *would* watch the historical ones if they had a school project that would demand that they know certain things about that part of history. Not that *our Time Tunnel* was that accurate, but if a show like that was done today, it would be more accurate.

Over the years, Irwin Allen and/or Fox occasionally talked about bringing back in some form Lost in Space *and* Voyage. *Were there ever rumblings that* Time Tunnel *might get brought back?*

Not in Irwin's lifetime. If Irwin were alive today, *Time Tunnel* would be made, there's no doubt about it.

Somebody did *make a* Time Tunnel *revival pilot a coupla years ago.*

Time marches on, but has left little mark on series stars (right to left) Darren, Lee Meriwether (with her stuntwoman-daughter Lesley Aletter and granddaughter Ryan) and Colbert.

Yeah, I saw it. It was dreadful. I didn't like it. To me, they lost the entire concept of the show, and the *feel* of the show. There's a certain kind of magic to some movies—I mean, good, bad or indifferent, you can watch certain old B-movies and say, "Y'know, it's not a great movie but, man, it has some kind of magic to it." And *Time Tunnel* had that kind of thing. You can't say it was one of the greatest series ever made, but you could certainly say it had a special quality. Whatever that indefinable thing *is*, *Time Tunnel* had it.

I was born in 1958 so to me, all those Irwin Allen shows had that quality. For whatever crazy reason, I still haven't outgrown 'em.

I understand that. When I watch the show now, I try to look at it objectively and just as a show. When I can get to that point, I really enjoy the show. Instead of looking at myself or at Bob, but looking at it as just a show and a story, I really enjoy it.

If there was such a thing as time travel and you could go any place you wanted in time, what's the first *place you would go?**

Oh, jeez, there are *so* many places I would love to visit. I would love to have met Michelangelo, so I'd love to go to Italy at the time of Michelangelo and be part of his world—that would be incredible. And you know what *else* I would love to experience? The wild west. Oh, yeah, I love the west. To be a cowboy, and meet people like the Dalton brothers and Jesse James and Frank James. Even though they were kind of ... [*laughs*] ... kind of *bad characters*, some of them, it was a very intriguing time, I'm sure.

You'd be willing to take your chances and meet those outlaws?

Oh, that I'd *love* to do. I would like to have *been* one of them [*laughs*]! I wouldn't want to hurt anybody, but to hold up a bank or something, I would have participated—as long as the bank people had rubber bullets and we had real ones! And what I would like to do, more than *any*thing, is travel in space. To this day, I would like to do that. If someone said, "Mr. Darren, you have a year or two to live," and they could put me in a capsule and send me off to space and keep me living for two years, just so I could travel to unknown areas, I would like that. It would be a little lonely ... maybe they could put a blonde in there with me [*laughs*], just to keep me occupied when it got a little boring! But I would like that. There is something out *there*; no doubt about it, there is something in another solar system, *some*where there's life. And I would *love* to know what that is. I would do it *today* if I could.

The same question is asked of Robert Colbert (page 68) and Lee Meriwether (pages 188–189).

MAURY DEXTER

*I think I'm probably one of the luckiest guys in the world.
A little talent ... hopefully! ... and* **lots and lots**
of help from The Man Upstairs.

Over the years, fans of the genre films of the 1950s have devoted much ink to speed-demon moviemakers like Roger Corman, Sam Katzman and others, too often overlooking another B-movie mill where the assembly line was similarly stuck on overdrive: Regal Films, the Robert L. Lippert production company cranking out mini-budgeted features by the truckload for bottom-of-the-bill 20th Century–Fox release. Beginning in 1956, the company (later called Associated Producers Inc.) churned out dozens of low-cost features, among them Westerns, war dramas and, their most enduring releases, science fiction and horror thrillers: *Kronos, Back from the Dead, Return of the Fly, The Alligator People, Space Master X-7, The Unknown Terror, Hand of Death* and the foreign-made *Curse of the Fly, Witchcraft* and *The Last Man on Earth*, among others.

Former stage and TV actor Maury Dexter got in on the ground floor at Regal, landing a clerical job there just prior to the start of production of their first movie; he then worked his way up the Lippert ladder to become director and/or producer of nearly a score of films of his own. The list includes 1963's *House of the Damned*, a haunted house-type chiller with a cast that included actual circus freaks(!), and *The Day Mars Invaded Earth*, an eerie, low-key story of Martian retaliation against Earth's top space scientist.

Where and, if you don't mind telling me, when were you born?
I was born in Paris....

Really!
... Arkansas!

[Laughs] Oh, you got me!
In June 1927. But when I was about nine years old, we moved to California, so I'm really a Californian.

How did you get interested in acting?
I was a ham most of my young life. When the War broke out, 1941–42, I had three older brothers, and my mom was widowed—my dad was killed in an automobile accident when I was about eight years old.

Before you moved from Arkansas.

Yeah. After my brothers were all drafted when I was about 14, it was just my mom and me in the house. My mom was a great movie fan, she *loved* movies, and every chance she got, she would take me to the movies. She decided that maybe I wanted to be an actor [*laughs*], and she said, "I'm going to enroll you in a drama class." I said, "I don't wanna learn how to act, I just wanna *act*." Why go through all those classes?, I just wanted to get up and act! In those days, the Hollywood schools taught Stanislavsky—"You're an apple on a mantel and you gotta tell me how it feels to be up there" and all that stuff. But when you're 14, you say, "*I'm* not an apple, I want to be an actor!" After a couple of schools, however, I enrolled at a little theater in Hollywood called Rainbow Theater, and they did exactly what I wanted to do. George Howard, a *terrific* director there, would take newcomers an hour and a half before the regular class, sit down and go over the fine points of acting. *Then*, after a few weeks of that, he would put the newcomers in small parts in some play they were doing. In other words, you were taught the basics and then you started acting right away.

Since this place was in Hollywood, I assume it was teaching people how to get into the movies.

Right. And it succeeded, it had several alumni that went into pictures. Jimmy Lloyd—you don't know him, probably—was a good-looking young guy who must have done at least a dozen B-pictures. Murray Hamilton got picked up by one of the studios from being in a play at Rainbow, and Cyd Charisse was there singing and dancing.

Every three weeks or every month, they put on a brand new play, and the talent scouts from all the Hollywood studios were invited. Believe it or not, the majority of 'em showed up. The *reason* for that was, they were looking for actors because guys were being drafted and going into the service so fast, the studios were losing half their talent! I think I was 17 when I got myself an agent, a guy who'd come and seen a show. A week or two later, the agency called and told me to go to Columbia and interview for a part in a Three Stooges comedy. I went over there and got the part—it was two or three lines [in *Uncivil War Birds*, 1946]. A little side note here: The *very* first school that my mother took me to, when I was about 14, was for training radio actors. I was put in a little studio with a phony mike and the guy said, "Okay, read the Gettysburg Address." I got to the part, "...We are engaged in a great Civil *Waw* [Dexter says it so that it rhymes with *law*]," and the guy said, "Wait a minute, hold it! What did you say? Read that again." Again I said, "We are engaged in a great Civil Waw." He said, "No no no no no. *War*. W-a-r. 'We are engaged in a great Civil *War*.' Say *war*." Once again I said, "... a great Civil Waw." So he said, "Well, you're a smart-ass kid, obviously—" and I said, "*Wait* a minute! President Franklin Roosevelt says *waw*, and if it's good enough for *him*, it's good enough for me!" That's true, Roosevelt always said waw—and I worshipped FDR. Anyway, getting back to the point, the Three Stooges comedy was about the Civil War and the Stooges were out in front of a Southern mansion with their girls and I came running in and I yelled, "Fellows! Fellows! We're *in* it! We're in the Civil War! We're in the Civil War!" The director [Jules White] said, "Cut, cut! Hold it, hold it! You're a *Southern* boy, you don't say war, you say waw!" [*Laughs*]

That's wild!

It is, and it's the honest-to-goodness truth! That was my very first acting job in the movies. Shortly after that, I think I had just turned 18, I was doing a Rainbow Theater play—and by now, after two or three years, I was doing leads. I was doing the lead in this comedy called *Wallflower*, and one of my best buddies, Don Gordon*, who had a very small part, said to me, "I want to be extra-good tonight. My mother's very close friend is married to a Republic Studios producer, and he's coming to see me in the show." I said, "Don, I don't understand—why the hell do you have him coming when you have a small part?," and Don said this was the only night when this producer was available. We did the show; the final curtain closed; after a bit, everybody looked out to see who was left in the audience, and nobody was there. Don was waiting for this producer to come back and at least say, "I saw the show," but the man didn't bother coming back. Don was dejected, to say the least.

The cast had a ritual that after every show we would go up Hollywood Boulevard about two blocks to DuPar's on Vine Street, an all-night place where we'd get desserts and spend an hour or two. We went up there like we'd always done, I got there first and I opened the door for the remaining cast *sans* Don because he got upset and went home. As I held the door, they all went in; a man and a woman were coming *out*, so I continued to hold the door for *them*. As the man passed, he took me by the arm and he said, "Can I talk to you?" I thought, "Whoops. I've *heard* about Hollywood, but *this* is a little rare!" [*Laughs*]

He gave me his card and he said, "I'm Donald H. Brown from Republic Studios. I just saw your show and I thought you were absolutely terrific. I want you to call me Monday and come out. I'm gonna put you in a motion picture I'm doing." Just like that! I did go out to Republic, and he said he had a script that he had been sitting on for a *long* time and he didn't know what was wrong with it. But when he saw our show, a show about young people, he realized that what was wrong with his script was that it had no young people. "I'm having a juvenile lead and an ingenue lead written in," he told me. "In a couple of weeks, come back and you'll get the script and the part." That was my first big part [*One Exciting Week*, 1946]. I was 18 years old.

Your acting career didn't last long, obviously—I found credits for you in 1946, and then you're just about done!

After *One Exciting Week*, I formed the Burbank Theater Guild and I produced and directed show after show. That's how I got involved in wanting to direct. Then I went to New York in 1948 and starred in a 15-minute live show on television, about a young couple, newlyweds, and their problems. Being from the stage, it was perfect for me—I could memorize lines in ten seconds and not worry about it. I did it for about five months, then got sick of it. And *haaaated* New York, for obvious reasons, being a farm boy from California.

A little side note here: After World War II, my three brothers all came back in one piece, thank God. I got my notice when I turned 18 [in 1945] but was rejected due to a heart murmur. I think it murmured only because I was so damn nervous [*laughs*]. Then in 1950, when North Korea invaded South Korea, I was reclassified and drafted. I was 23. I was sent to basic training December the 21st. I went through basic training, I went through leadership school for OCS, I finally got to be cadre for a couple of months and then my butt was shipped to Korea. I was on the front lines for nine straight months. After I got hit in the knee by shrapnel, they put me in Special Services. Then when I came back [to the U.S.] and was waiting to be discharged, I was in Special Services at Camp Roberts in Northern California. It was my job to bring up so-called stars from Hollywood to entertain the troops on Saturday nights in the auditorium. One guy who appeared in the shows regularly, like every

---

*Not the familiar TV-movie actor Don Gordon (*The Twilight Zone, The Outer Limits, Bullitt, etc.*).

third week or so, was a comedian named Hank McCune. He had a radio show at that time and was planning on doing a TV series. I met Hank several times, and one time he said, "I understand you're getting out in a couple of weeks. Here's my card. If you need a job, call me and I'll see what I can do for you." I was grateful for him being concerned, but ... [*laughs*] ... but I didn't think this guy had much talent, frankly, and I thought to myself, "With all due respect, Hank, I think you're going to have your hands full just taking care of your*self*!"

Well, when I came back [to Hollywood] in 1952 or '53, I couldn't get arrested. I'd been gone for a couple, three years and I'd aged, and I couldn't even get an agent! I'd been home for six, eight months and things were really looking bad and money was running out when I remembered McCune's card. I called him and he said, "I'm shooting a TV series [*The Hank McCune Show*], come on over here!" I went over and, sure enough, he was doing two shows a week, doing each show in two and a half days. And on film, not live. He asked me if I wanted a job, and I said, "Ohhhh, I sure *do*!" He said, "I'm gonna write in a part for you," which he did. But after about four or five months of that, I went to him one day and I said, "Hank, I love you dearly, and I appreciate what you're doing for me, but I can't live on $80 a week." He said, "Okay, you can become my dialogue director and I'll pay you an *additional* $80, so that's 160." Well, to me that was a lot of money! I did that for about two and a half, three years, '53, '54, '55, and he also did a movie called *Wetbacks* [1956] that I had one or two lines in. I only did it because I was part of his company.

Along the line, I met Harold Knox, *The Hank McCune Show*'s production manager-first assistant, and we took a liking to each other right away. A hell of a guy and an ex-colonel in the Army. He was married to Irene Ryan—do you remember Irene Ryan?

From The Beverly Hillbillies.

Well, this was prior to *Beverly Hillbillies*, of course, when she was a well-known nightclub entertainer. Harold and "Renie" were my two favorite, closest friends. When the McCune show was cancelled, Harold went over to work for Bob Lippert, who in those days was making a lot of little pictures, small Westerns and things like that. Four or five months later, Harold called me and he asked, "Are you working?," and I told him I hadn't worked since *McCune*. He said, "I'm on a real cheap show, a five-day Western [1956's *Naked Gun*], but if you need a job, come on over and I'll put you to work." I went over—he was working on a little independent stage in West Hollywood—and he said, "I'm gonna pay you out of petty cash because there's nothing in the budget, and Lippert's got a guy named Bill Magginetti who watches every buck. I really *need* you as an assistant, and I'm gonna give you 100 bucks a week." And then he added, "Bill Magginetti is the production head of the company and he comes over every morning to see how things are going." He described Bill to me and he said, "If you're on stage and you see this guy coming in, get the hell in the back office and don't come out, 'cause I can't explain your presence here!"

One day, two or three days later, I looked up and I saw this guy that I knew must be Magginetti and I took off. The next day, I saw this guy again and I took off. We finished the movie and I was helping Harold wrap up all of the paperwork, and he said to me, "Hey, jump in the car, take all of these checks over to Lippert's offices and get Bill Magginetti to sign 'em all." I said, "I can't go over there. He doesn't know who I am." Harold said, "Tell him you're a messenger, wait for 'em and bring 'em back to me."

I went over and for the first time went into Lippert's headquarters, and soon I was sitting in Bill Magginetti's office and he was signing the checks. I didn't say a word and he never looked up at me, he just kept signing. When he was about halfway through, suddenly he asked, "How long you been working for Harold Knox?" So I said, "Hommina hommina hommina" [*laughs*]—I didn't know what to say, because no matter *what* I said, I was going to get Harold into a lot of trouble. So I said, "Harold who? I'm just a messenger, Mr. Magginetti." He said, "Awww, come on, come on. I saw you over there, I know you were doing something. And let me tell you something: I know Harold's paperwork, and the paperwork that's come across my desk, Harold Knox didn't *do*!" [*Laughs*] Bill said, "I'm not stupid, I put two and two together," and he asked again, "How long you been working for Harold?" I said, "This is the first show." He said, "No kiddin'? What are you gonna do now that the show's over?" I said, "Gee, I dunno. I guess I'll go to the unemployment office." He said, "No, I don't think so. We just signed a seven-year deal with 20th Century–Fox to make 20 pictures a year. I need a first-class assistant, and I've seen your work, so ... when do you want to go to work for me?" I said, "How 'bout ... *now*?" Absolute true story! I couldn't believe it happened.

I went to work not knowing what I was going to do exactly. He gave me an office next to his and he showed me how to do the chart of accounts and all the ropes, *everything*. I'm a fast learner, I will say, so I picked it up very quickly. Lippert had built this building brand new and there were offices for accounting, there was post-production, offices for the various producers and directors and so forth. On the third floor—the top floor—were two penthouse offices, one for Bob and one for the president of Regal Films, Ed Baumgarten.

Lippert wasn't the president?

That's an interesting story. Bob made a lot of pictures on his own [in the late 1940s and early 1950s], and a few years later he began distributing all of them to television—and it was my understanding that he never paid any residuals to writers or directors. Well, as a result of that, he was blackballed, so now he could not get an IATSE crew, a union crew. So what he did was this: The chief loan officer for the motion picture department of the Bank of America was Ed Baumgarten. Bob went to Baumgarten and said, "I'm setting up a new company. I've got a Fox deal, so I don't need any more financing. You come on over and I'm going to make you president of the company"—and I'm sure Bob offered to pay him a helluva lot more than bankers get. So Baumgarten did. That's why, on all of the Regal Films, you never saw Bob Lippert's name ever appear on *anything*. When I first heard the story [of how Lippert got around being blackballed], I thought, "Boy, that's devious as hell!" But, looking back, jeez, I've got to take my hat off to him. He knew how to operate!

Anyway, after I'd been there about a week, I was walking down the hallway on the bottom floor and I met Lippert—he was coming out of the elevator. I said, "Good morning, Mr. Lippert," he said, "Good morning!" and went a few steps further—and then I heard, "*Wait* a minute!" I turned around and looked at him and asked me who the hell I was! I said I was Maury Dexter and he said, "Yeah? What do you do? Do you work here?" I said, "Yes, sir." He said, "*Where*?" I said, "For Bill Magginetti." He said, "The hell you *do*!" and he turned and went right up the elevator. I thought, "Well, that's the end of *my* career!"

That was your very first meeting with Lippert?

That's right! A half-hour later, after walking around the block a few times, I went back into the building and Bill said, "Where've you been?," as though nothing had happened. I said, "Didn't Lippert come in here?," and Bill said, "I hired you, *I* fire you." In other words, Bill had stood up to Lippert, and I still had my job. Lippert did want to fire me, because he figured that Bill didn't need the help. We were doing 20 pictures a year, and he didn't think Bill needed any help! Anyway, that's how I met Bob Lippert and that's how I got started with the Lippert organization.

After several years of working in various capacities for budget-conscious movie mogul Robert L. Lippert, Maury Dexter (above) began producing-directing because "we got to the point where I felt it was stupid to call in producers and directors from agents and pay agency fees—I'd do it for half the price."

What were some of the first movies you recall being made while you were there?

I *don't* recall! We made so *many*, I can't even remember what the first ones were.

Do you remember being on the sets of movies like Kronos *[1957] and* She Devil *[1957] and—*

Yes, but I can't tell you anything *about* them because we were making the pictures so fast in those days that it's [now all a blur]. In fact, we seldom ever got a chance to *see* 'em when they were finished! They went right in to Fox, and Fox put 'em right into distribution. And I became pretty darn proficient. I hope I don't sound like I'm patting myself on the back, but I'm proud of a guy [*Dexter is talking about himself*] who had absolutely no background in production, doing what I did! We had as many as five movies shooting independently at the same time, all over town, and *some*body from the company had to go at least once a day and check on each of these companies because otherwise, with no supervision, they would feel like they could do what they wanted. Bill said to me, "Maury, you take the first two or three on your way to work and I'll take the others," and we did that, 1956, 1957, 1958.

Even though you didn't have anything to do with these Lippert sci-fi movies except visit the sets, can you talk a little about the guys who made them? Like Kronos' *Kurt Neumann?*

Kurt brought that project *Kronos* to us. I was on the *Kronos* set many times, but not enough to absorb anything other than the fact that everything was on schedule. Kurt was serious ... sedate ... knowledgeable ... he was a talented guy. Like many of us, he got the jobs done on time and on budget, and did some nice work, *I* thought. He also brought [the story] "The Fly" to us, having read it in *Playboy* magazine. Kurt did for us *Kronos, The Fly* [1958] and a few others. He was a "let's get the job done" type of guy and, on the occasions when I would go over and talk with him briefly in the mornings, he seemed like a very nice person to me.

Edward Bernds, director of Space Master X-7 *[1958] and* Return of the Fly *[1959]?*

I didn't know him. Now, when I say "I didn't know him," I saw him going in and out of Bob's office numerous times. He was hooked up with your friend, [producer] Bernie Glasser. I couldn't *stand* Bernie Glasser. As far as I was concerned, he was little Sammy Glick. Anyway, Bernie and Eddie Bernds were always together, Bernie always seemed to wind up producing Ed's movies, and they worked very closely together. So Ed Bernds was there, I met him, I knew who *he* was, he knew who *I* was, and there was no rapport *per se*.

The first season of Gunsmoke *[1955–56] just came out on DVD and I'm watching them, and producer-director Charles Marquis Warren's name is all over every episode. And around the same time as* Gunsmoke, *he was making crummy horror movies like* The Unknown Terror *and* Back from the Dead *[both 1957] for Lippert!*

[Producer] Bob Stabler had set up a company which included Bill [Charles Marquis] Warren. Bob came to us and said, "Bill has just written a little Western, and he'd like to direct it. Are you interested?" We read it and we said yeah. Well, their company ended up doing *several* movies for us, most of 'em Westerns.

But why was Warren, the guy behind one of the biggest Westerns on TV, also dabbling in movies for Lippert?

You just answered your own answer. Television was in its infancy. There were only a few shows that were successful, and everybody was working for peanuts on those shows. We [the Lippert organization] were paying motion picture scale on *every*thing.

Prior to becoming a producer-director, part of Dexter's Regal Films job was keeping tabs on the company's *other* producers and directors. One production he monitored was *Kronos* with George O'Hanlon (left), Barbara Lawrence and Jeff Morrow (posing with set visitor Forrest J Ackerman).

It's just so funny to me to look at the crew list at the end of every Gunsmoke, *and it's almost identical to* The Unknown Terror*'s!*

These guys [like Warren] wanted their names on a screen at a theater, not on some 13-inch television. It was that simple! They were making a little money doing what they did [television], and they were getting a little more prestige by coming over to us. We at Lippert were making second features and *yet*, we were still 20th Century–Fox. Even though the movies went out as Regal or as Associated Producers, [guys like Warren] knew that Fox was financing these movies, and they knew that somebody at Fox was looking at 'em, and they thought, "Why not let 'em look at *us*?" Part of it was ego, naturally.

How did you start moving up the ladder at Lippert?

Up in Lippert's office they would always have a production meeting on every movie before it started. There was Lippert, a production manager, the director, the producer, Bill Magginetti and myself. I had been in several meetings, maybe a half a dozen, and I never opened my mouth. I'd sit there with paperwork and listen and make notes. Bob had a very bad habit of yelling, he *loved* to yell at people. And I had a very good habit of *hating* people who yelled at me [*laughs*]—I couldn't stand people yelling when all they had to do was ask a question. Everybody including Bill and every producer, director, etc., called him *Mr. Lippert*: "Well, now, Mr. Lippert....," "Thank you, Mr. Lippert...." and so on. We were in a meeting where there was a hot and contested problem about something on a picture we were just about to start. I totally disagreed with Magginetti, the producer and the director as Lippert was fighting for something that I thought he was 100 percent right about. Which was one of the first times ever [*laughs*]! I remember this vividly, he said, "Well, I think *blah blah blah*" and there was a long pause and he looked at me for the very first time in *any* meeting and he said, "What's *your* opinion, kid?" And I said, "Well, *Bob*..." Whoops! "...*I* think that..." and so forth and so on. Lippert, who always smoked cigars, almost choked on the cigar when I said "Bob." But what I subsequently said made sense, and Lippert said, "The kid's *right*, and *I'm* right, and that's the way we're gonna do it." Well, after that, I never called him anything but Bob. From that point on, he would call me personally and say, "Hey, kid, come on up here, I got somethin' I wanna talk to you about, okay, kid? Come on up, kid" and I'd say, "Okay, *Bob*!" [*Laughs*]

When did you get your first opportunity to produce?

Well, I *almost* had an opportunity in 1958 with a picture called *I Married a Monster from Outer Space*. [Director] Gene Fowler, Jr., and [screenwriter] Lou Vittes did two or three movies for us, and one day Gene came to me and he told that he and Lou had concocted this *I Married a Monster* thing and they had a first draft. Gene asked me if I would take it to Lippert, and I said sure. But right away I *also* said, "Gene, with all due respect, [the title] is ridiculous. This is an AIP-type title. This is not a Lippert title." Gene said, "Well ... *give* it to him," and I said okay. Of course, Bob said, without even reading the script, "No, no. Tell Gene I'm not interested, and thank him very much."

I told Gene that, and then I said, "Let me tell you what I'm going to do...." I had heard that Paramount Pictures was starting to get into the second feature market—*very* slightly, but getting into it nonetheless. I said, "I'll set up an appointment at Paramount. You, Lou and I will all go over there, and let's pitch this thing." I went over with Gene and Lou and I pitched it—*I* pitched it—as the producer, Gene as the director and of course Vittes doing the screenplay. *I* pitched it and *I* got the deal. A week or two later, I went to Bob Lippert and I said, "I've got an opportunity to go to Paramount to produce a movie with Fowler and Vittes, and I'd like to get about six weeks off." And he said, "No, there's no way you're going to get out of here. There's too much to do. I love you dearly but *forget it*, it's not gonna happen." I said, "Fine. You're the boss." I went back to Gene and I said, "I can't do the picture, but I'll go back to Paramount and set *you* up as producer," and I *did* that. They made the movie, and Gene got 25 percent—I negotiated that. *I* got, I think, $500. Now, the only reason I'm telling you this is that I just recently read what Gene said about *I Married a Monster* in the interview you did with him, and not only was I not mentioned but, according to him, he did *every*thing. And it's not true. So that's my take on Mr. Fowler!

So what was your first movie as producer?

About 1960, Lippert called me in and he said, "I want to do an old classic called *The Little Shepherd of Kingdom Come*" [a 1903 novel already filmed twice, in silent days]. Bob loved remakes! He told me to read the book by John Fox and draw him up a budget. He was bypassing Magginetti. I went to Bill and told him, and Bill said, "If Bob wants you to do it, *I* want you to do it, Maury. I'm busy enough, I can't get involved." So I drew up a budget,

Gloria Talbott and "friend" in *I Married a Monster from Outer Space,* **a movie Dexter got off the ground, and had initially planned to produce.**

I did this and that, and Lippert decided that he was going to make the movie. Then he said, "Get me a strong producer in here. I want a strong 'production producer' who knows how to watch the money, because we're not gonna spend a fortune on this movie." I said, "Well, I'm the best guy in the world who knows how to protect your buck." He said, "Okay, you produce it."

And that's how you got your start as a producer, just by making that comment?

Yup, just like that. *Little Shepherd* was shot mainly on the back lot at Fox but we did all of the war stuff and so on up at Big Bear. While I was up there, I got a call from my best friend at that time Harry Spalding, the head of the writing department at Lippert. Harry said, "Maury, you're in for a shock. Lippert just fired Magginetti and he wants you to take over the reins of the whole business." I told Harry I wasn't going to do it. Bill was not only my mentor, he was a personal, close friend. Harry said, "Maury, you've *got* to. You know Lippert when he makes up his mind." I said, "You know *Dexter* when he makes up *his*! I'm not putting a nail in Bill's coffin, no *way*. Lippert fired Magginetti, let him get himself another boy."

About a week later, we came in on a Saturday from location to continue shooting at Fox on the following Monday. I didn't call Lippert even though he knew we were coming in. The next day, Sunday, he called me at home. He said, "First thing in the morning, I want you in my office." I said, "I can't be there, Bob, I'm shooting tomorrow and, as you know, I'm the first one on that set and the last one to leave. We've got a seven o'clock call, and I'm going to be on that set at seven." Now, Lippert was a guy who never got into the office 'til ten, but he said, "Okay, I'll be here at *six*, kid. Come on by here, and then you can go right to the set." I walked in at six, nobody there but just the two of us, and he said, "I want you to take over" and blah blah blah. I said, "Wait a minute. Let's get back to Magginetti." He said, "I'm not going to discuss that because that's none of your business, that's strictly between Bill and me, and I'm justified in what I did." And I said, "I don't think you *are*, Bob, because I know the story." He said, "*Listen*. You're gonna *take* the job. I *need* you on the job, there's nobody here who can do this. *Nobody* knows this operation like you do because you and Magginetti set it up and you're the backbone. So I don't care what you say, *you're* gonna take the job." I said, "I'll take it on three conditions."

He almost swallowed his cigar. I'm telling you, giving him conditions was like giving the Pope conditions! He went, "Conditions? *Conditions*?!," and he jumped out of his chair. "How *dare* you come in here and talk to me that way!" I thought he was going to have a heart attack!

I said, "Fine, Bob," and I got up and I started walking. I got to the door and he said, "Come back over here and sit down!" I sat back down and I said, "I'll take it on three conditions. *One*, and most important … if you ever yell at me the way you yelled at Magginetti, I will walk so fast you won't know what hit you. I will *never* yell at anybody, I have *never* been guilty of it, and I will *not* have anybody yell at me. There's not enough money in the world." Lippert said a few things under his breath and then he asked, "What *else*?" I said, "Number two, I want double what Magginetti was getting, because he was the most underpaid person in this operation." He *was*—he and I were the *two* most underpaid people. I said, "You got a *bookkeeper* downstairs making as much money as *we* do, and we're running the company." Lippert said, "Okay, kid. What's the third condition?" I said, "I want to continue to produce. Every few projects along the line, if I like it, I want to produce it. Apparently I'm doing a good-enough job on this one I'm on now, 'cause otherwise you wouldn't have me in here." He said, "You got it, kid." That was how I started producing.

By the way, getting fired by Bob was the best thing that ever happened to Magginetti, 'cause he went over to Desilu as a production manager. So he went from the poorhouse to the *estate* [*laughs*]—he did very well!

Dexter (with hat) behind the scenes on his first film as producer, *The Little Shepherd of Kingdom Come*. Left to right, actor Robert Dix, Dexter, actor Jimmie Rodgers, boss Robert L. Lippert, director Andrew V. McLaglen and actor Chill Wills.

So did Lippert keep his promise never to yell at you?

    After that point, in my presence, he never yelled at any single person or employee again, as long as I was with him. Well, with one exception, which I'll tell you about later. And with one exception—the *same* exception!—I never heard the man ever use profanity. I was as close to Bob as anybody for a little over ten years and I never heard him use the f-word or anything even close to that. He was a man of great integrity and he believed firmly in the product he was making. He wanted to make good, clean entertainment—he didn't want to offend anybody, he just wanted to put an honest product out there. The one exception was … well, it was on a picture I know you're going to ask me about, so I'll tell you about that later.

How did you get your start directing?

By that time we'd cut down to maybe two, three pictures a month, instead of what we *had* been doing. I was still overseeing all of that, I was still drawing budgets, still doing the paperwork, still head of the production on all those movies that we were shooting. And I was also producing on the side. The second thing I produced was a picture called *The Third Voice* [1960] with Eddie O'Brien, directed by Hubert Cornfield. That came off very well, and Fox liked it. One day after that, Bob called me in and said, "Fox is getting a little edgy. We're making too many movies, and they can't distribute them because they don't have enough A-features to go *with* 'em. They're talking about maybe doubling these pictures of ours up, putting these out as double features instead of one at a time [supporting A-pictures]. I have a feeling they want to try to get out of the contract, so what I want to do is to see if we can make these pictures any *cheaper.*" I said [*voice cracking*], "That's *impossible!* How can you make a movie for half of nothing? Right now we're at the bottom!" He said, "Well, I want to do it. Let's just call it an *experiment.* See if you can put together something for me."

We got Spalding in, and Spalding wrote a very simple little whodunit called *The High Powered Rifle* [1960]. Lippert said he wanted it made in x-amount of days. I sent the script out to about five different agents for producers and directors and they all sent it back and said, "You've got to be kidding. There's not a director in Hollywood who's going to try to direct it on that schedule." So I went to Lippert and told him what the reaction was and I said, "There's only one way to get this thing off the ground: I'll direct it." He said, "You couldn't direct traffic." I said, "Well, I couldn't produce either, but I *did.*" All he said was, "Yeah, okay. Go ahead and direct it." We made it on budget, on schedule, and it was exactly what it was supposed to be: It was a small picture on a small budget and it didn't insult anybody. But after that "experiment," the pictures went back to seven days, $100,000 budgets—our original schedule. And we got to the point where I felt it was stupid to call in producers and directors from agents and pay agency fees—I'd do it for half the price. That's how I started producing and directing most of the movies myself.

What was the budget on The High Powered Rifle, do you remember?

It was ludicrous. It was 50,000 bucks. I'm half-tempted to tell you not to print that, and I'll tell you the reason: I'm *proud* of what we did for the money but today, 45 years later when they spend $2,000,000 on a B-picture, if I say ours was $50,000 it makes it look like we were a bunch of scavengers. And we *weren't.* We used Hollywood actors and we used CinemaScope lenses. (We had to pay 5000 bucks to Fox every time we used CinemaScope lenses, because they had to pay it to Bausch & Lomb who owned 'em.) Also, we had a full union crew. There was no cheating done anywhere, it was done strictly on a Hollywood union scale.

Did you enjoy yourself, directing The High Powered Rifle?

Oh, very much. Very, very, very, very much. But, you know something? Having been an actor briefly, and having been behind the camera and so forth, I thought I was just gonna go in and direct. As I was preparing, I had the *High Powered Rifle* script at home one night and I suddenly realized that nothing had rubbed off on me. The important thing about a

Willard Parker (left) was the star of the first movie Dexter directed, *The High Powered Rifle.* **According to Dexter, the budget was so low, "it was ludicrous."**

motion picture director is not how he works with the actors so much as where the hell he puts the camera. And will it cut? So all of a sudden I started getting a little worried. I looked at one scene and I thought to myself, "Where I am going to put the camera? Where does the camera go?"

We shot the whole thing on live sets—no studio, all real homes and offices and that kind of thing. I was shooting in a nice, old-fashioned little house on Cahuenga in Hollywood—it belonged to Gary Cooper's mother. We didn't pay much [*laughs*], but she loved having film people there because her son was an actor. We were shooting in the small living room with a fireplace and I had as my cameraman Floyd Crosby, who won the Academy Award for *Tabu* [1931]. Floyd asked what I wanted him to do and I started describing what I wanted, including a shot over the shoulder of an actress who was sitting on a couch. Floyd said, "Well ... fine, Maury, but ... let me ask you a question. The sofa's against a wall. You can't put a camera back of her because you can't move the wall." In a studio, it'd be a set and you'd move the wall! So I said, "...Oh! I never *thought* about that, Floyd," and I came up with something else. That was the first time I realized that you'd better *know* the whole scene before you start shooting. Believe it or not, from that point forward I never had one single worry about how I was going to stage a scene.

What memories of getting involved on your first horror movie, House of the Damned*? Were you a horror fan?*

No. But I'm first and foremost a filmmaker. Even when I first started out, my intent was to take a script, whatever that script was, and do the best I could under the circumstances. Whether it was a Western or a whodunit or a horror film or whatever ... it didn't enter my mind that I was doing something of a certain genre, or something that I hadn't done before. It was a movie that had to be made, I enjoyed making it, sometimes I *loved* making it, and I did the very best I could with it. If it was an eerie kind of a thing, I approached it that way. If I was doing a Western, I approached it *that* way. You know what I'm saying?

But you have to have seen *horror movies and Westerns to know what the approach is, so I assume you had a fairly wide background in watching movies.*

I watched almost every movie ever made when I was a kid. But I was never drawn to any *particular* genre, I loved almost everything.

One thing I like about House of the Damned *is that, until the very end, you only see the freaks in the dark or through a screen or in extreme closeup. So even when you're seeing 'em, you're not quite sure what you're seeing.*

That's right. At one time I did love ... not horror stories, but *ghost* stories. I loved the eerie things that you never really saw and you never really could get a grip on, but they were there. Some of that may have rubbed off. But I was not a horror fan *per se*.

What was the story on that big, strange house where you shot?

Oh, "the castle"! Back around 1946, when things got scarce after I did *One Exciting Week*, I got a job as a printer in a little silk screen processing shop in West L.A. A guy named Grover Lee owned the shop, and over lunch one day he said to me, "I've got to go drop off something to friends of mine. How 'bout taking a drive with me? I want to show you something interesting." He drove up Beachwood and all around, and up some long private road that was maybe three-quarters of a mile or a mile long, and finally pulled up in front of this ... house, or whatever you call it. We walked up to the door, a big, huge wooden door—and it was riddled with bullet holes [*laughs*]! *Riddled*! And there were bullet holes all over the stucco around the door. Somebody let us in, there was an *elevator* in the house, we took it up and I got to meet these friends of his, a couple that was living there. Then they told me the story of the house....

During the War, a bunch of Vegas gangsters had moved in and taken it over and had a huge gambling setup there. Because a private road led to the house, and that was the only way to get to it, their guards could keep out anybody they *wanted* to keep out. Including the police. But one day the police decided, "Enough of this," and they went and they stormed it. The door was barricaded, but somehow they managed to get into the house—I assume that's where the bullet holes in and around the door came from. Then they went up and they ripped the place apart and made arrests. The place was so big that people were not only gambling there, but some of the dealers and other people were sleeping there! The police went into all these different rooms and tore up the furniture and tried to wreck the whole place.

That's how I found out about the place. So when Harry Spalding came to me and outlined the story of *House of the Damned* and said, "We need a castle," it dawned on me about this house. I called Grover, he called his friends who lived there and then Harry and I went

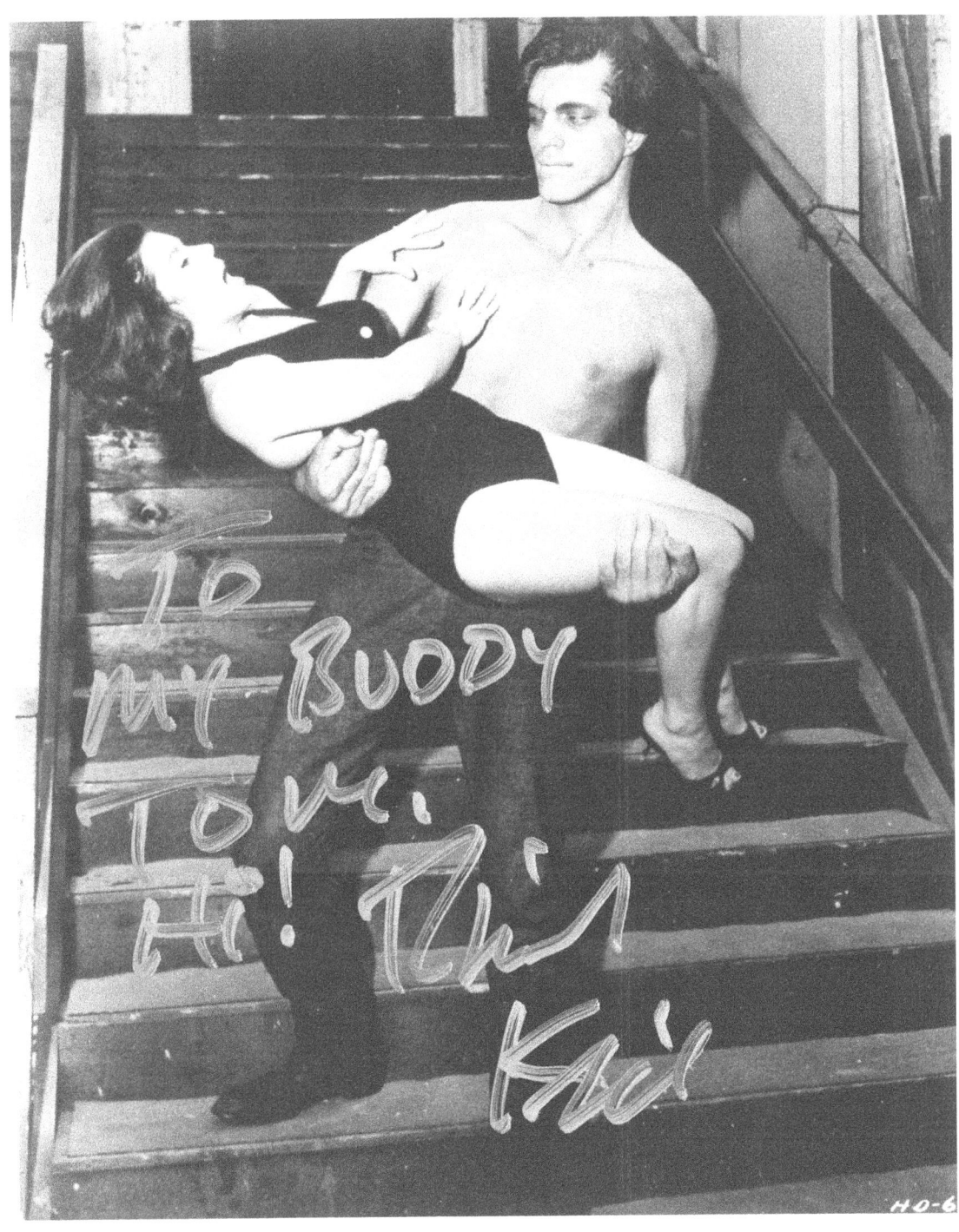

A haunted house, a gaggle of circus freaks (including Richard Kiel), a babe in a bathing suit (Erika Peters)—what more could anyone ask from a *House of the Damned*?

up and walked through it. We went through and we laid out the whole movie around that house. By the way, the bullet holes were still in the door, so we patched 'em up before we shot!

What would you pay somebody to shoot in their house for, say, a week?
It would depend on the location itself, how long we were there, what we actually needed, whether we were outside, inside, outside *and* inside, whatever. It was never cheap, but it was a heckuva lot cheaper than working in a studio.

Did you ever see the movie Freaks *[1932] that gave Harry Spalding the idea for* House of the Damned*?*
No, but I knew about it.

Was there any feeling of awkwardness at all *working with your "freaks"?*
I approach things in such a way that those things don't bother me. I don't dwell on the unfortunate. I can't *afford* to, because [*laughs*] ... because I'm so sensitive to those things, I get too involved! What I had to do was look at those people that we used—nice, wonderful, warm people!—as *actors*. That was the way I handled 'em and the way I talked to 'em, as actors, not as deformed people. I didn't go up and say, "How you *feeling* today?" [*Laughs*] No, I'd say, "Now, listen, this is the way we're going to do the next shot, and this is the reason, and this is what I want from you. I've got the camera there, and you come toward the camera and blah blah blah...."

Richard Kiel told me, "These people [the freaks] were all excited about becoming movie stars." Do you recall that attitude?
When I told them what I wanted them to do, they would go [*in an enthusiastic way*], "Oh, yeah, yeah!," so, yes, they did get real interested in what they were doing. Rather than go up and say [*in a meek way*], "Can you do *this*?" or "Can you do *that*?," I just told 'em what I needed. If they could do it, great. I had a very good rapport with those people. Of course, they only worked like one or two days. There was the little black guy [John Gilmore] whose body ended either above or just below his navel, I don't know which. I was curious but I never stared, I wouldn't dare do that! I would glance, and he'd catch me, and I'd look away! He walked using his arms and hands like legs and feet as his torso swung back and forth. And there was the little lady [Frieda Pushnik, "The Armless, Legless Girl Wonder"] who I put in a cabinet, behind a screen. That was *my* idea, I put her in the cabinet because ... what are you going to do with someone who....

Who's just a torso.
Right. They were very eager to please and they did exactly as they were asked. I wanted to get their interest, and they *were* interested in what they were doing. We had a good rapport. The little guy, by the way, wore a little turban on his head. It made him look like he had a square head.

That's what he wore in real life, and you had him also wear it in the movie?
Oh, yeah, because I thought it was great. In silhouette, it looked like a block head, it didn't look like a human form!

Did they have people there to take care of them?
The torso lady had someone there who would pick her up and carry her and so forth. The little gentleman with the swinging torso also had somebody but only to help him, say,

get in the car or whatever. He didn't need very much help, because he could move like crazy! He could take off and do a dash—literally! And he did! He said, "I'll show you what I can do" and *zzzzzip*, boy, he was *gone*! I said, "No, no, no, I want you to go *slowly*, so your torso slowly swings back and forth, and the audience won't really know what they're seeing." I never thought of them as "freaks," as unfortunate people. I looked at 'em as nice people and as actors who were doing a hell of a job for me.

And the Fat Woman and the Giant, Ayllene Gibbons and Richard Kiel?

The Fat Lady was supposed to go up the cellar stairs at the end, and she took about three steps and almost passed out. I mean, not literally, but she stopped and said she couldn't make the stairs. She *could*, but not on camera, it would take her forever. Dick Kiel, it was one of the first things he ever did. He was a great big guy who I'm sure had been stared at for most of his young life. He was a very nice, very cooperative person.

Did the owners of the house take an interest in what was going on?

Oh, yeah—owners always do! But we didn't shoot it *all* at the house. The bedroom scenes, for instance, were all shot on a stage, and also the cellar [seen at the finale]. But the hallways and just about everything else, we shot at the house. We also shot *outside* the house, of course, including the lily pond. Incidentally, in the scene where the old man is found dead in his bed, covered in cobwebs and so forth, that gentleman's name was Felix Locher. Our casting guy Freddie Roos brought him in to me, and I found him to be a very pleasant man, and I loved *his* look. And the reason I bring him up is because he told me he was Jon Hall's father!

Yes, I've seen him in a couple of movies. It looked like you could open a can on that nose of his!

You know who he reminded me of? Finlay Currie, the British actor from *Great Expectations* [1946]. I couldn't figure out how on Earth Jon Hall looked like he looked when he had a father who looked like Felix Locher [*laughs*]! We shot his scene at the house.

And the stars of the movie? Ron Foster?

Ron was a close personal friend of mine. In 1953, after I got out of the service, I decided to go back to theater. I went to Rainbow and I told them I wanted to rent the theater on x-number of weekends, and I produced and directed some plays. When I got ready to cast one called *John Loves Mary*, I auditioned Ron, who was just starting out. He wasn't bad ... but he wasn't good [*laughs*]! But he was a nice-looking, handsome guy, and I thought, "Well, the girls will like him." I worked with him and he turned out to be pretty good. Then I put him in another play and I got him started in movies for Lippert and "brought his career along." Jeez, I've known Ronnie since 1953, and he's *still* a good friend of mine.

The leading lady, Merry Anders?

Loved her. Dated her. But that had nothing with do with my casting her [in four movies]. She was a well-known actress and did far more important things than I could offer her, so my dating her for a while had nothing to do with her being in my movies. With me, the personal had nothing to do with the professional. She was a good actress, she could do almost anything, and she was one of the sweetest people that you'd ever want to meet. The other gal in it, Erika Peters—God, she was gorgeous, and in an exotic type of way. I don't know where she came from, and I don't know where she went [*laughs*]! By the way, the casting guy I mentioned a moment ago, Freddie Roos, was a near-genius. He came up with some incredible people for a lot of the Lippert movies—well, on *House of the Damned* he got us the "circus people" [the freaks]. Fred Roos later became a producer for Francis Ford Coppola and produced every movie that Coppola made [including *The Godfather Part II* and *Apocalypse Now*] for years. Still a good friend of mine.

Something else I like about House of the Damned: *It gives you the idea that Richard Crane's character, supposedly a friend of Foster and Anders, is up to no good. There's never any dialogue to that effect, there's just something about the way you presented his character that gives that impression.*

That wasn't in the screenplay but I did talk to Dick about it, I said, "I don't want a red herring here because that's corny. What I want you to do is, *don't* be overly friendly about everything. Just be kind of like a static character, and don't become too emotionally involved with the other people." So that was done intentionally. Subtly, I hope, but intentionally. Maybe *too* subtly, because I think you're the only person who ever picked it up [*laughs*]! Dick Crane was a guy we had used in a couple of things, like *The Alligator People* [1959], where I first met him, and *Surf Party* [1964]. I hired him for *House of the Damned* and that's when he and I became fast friends. We turned out to be neighbors; we lived in Studio City a few blocks from each other. He had a beautiful daughter, just entering college, and she would come over to the set and visit.

One day some time later, there was a knock on my door at home, and standing there was Dick Crane with a hat on. He said, "I hate to barge in on ya, but I gotta talk to ya, I gotta talk to *some*body...." He took off his hat, and he was bald! He had lost his hair in the time between going to sleep one night and getting up the next morning. Totally bald, and he was in shock—we were *both* kind of in shock. We must have talked for four hours, with me not being a psychologist (but trying to sound like one) explaining that the hair *had* to come back and "Don't worry about it" and so on. About ten days later he called me and said he wanted to drop by, and he did, and he had a full head of hair! Now, that sounds impossible but it's absolutely the truth. Unfortunately, though, within a few weeks or a few months, he died of a heart attack [in 1969]. So he must have been going through some terrible stress. The hair was the warning, and then after that it went downhill. When he died, it just broke my heart. Nice guy, good actor. I loved him dearly.

John Nickolaus, your d.p. on House of the Damned—*what did you like about him?*

Everything. Johnny had started out with us doing, oh, good Lord, a couple dozen pictures as a camera operator. We were about to start a picture, kind of a tough picture to do, and Harold Knox my assistant director-production manager came to me and he said, "I want to up Johnny to head cameraman." I said, "Are you out of your mind? He's an operator." Harold persisted and I said, "Okay, it's your responsibility, but ... you've got a schedule, and you've got an operator as head cameraman...!" Anyway, Johnny did it, he was terrific, and he did, oh, I can't tell you how many more movies [as d.p.] for us after that.

Seeing the "torso lady" for the first time through the screen, and the black guy in silhouette as he creeps into the bedroom—I thought those scenes were staged and photographed marvelously.

Those were my ideas. That was "the directorial touch," not a writer's touch, and I don't mean to take *any*thing away from Harry Spalding, who was terrific. Don't print this if you think it sounds egotistical, because I don't mean it that way, but I saw the movie again the other day and I was pleasantly surprised at the way I was able to set up a scene, hold the suspense and use the camera. And I *did* use that camera, moving it in on people and so on. I didn't just set it up and say, "Act!" As I watched it for the first time in 40 years, I was saying to myself, "How the hell did I *do* that when I really didn't know that much what I was doing?" [*Laughs*]

Were you satisfied with the way the movie ended? The "happy ending" where it turns out that all the "freaks" are nice people? It was so innocuous, I was a little disappointed.

Well, I thought that ending *had to be*, because when you see ... let's call 'em "unusual-looking people" ... that is sad, sad, sad on its own. Now, if the movie also made them heavies or made them even more weird, to *me* that's adding insult to injury. I think Harry and I talked about the fact that the only way it could "work" is that [the freaks] *had* to turn out to be quote-ordinary people-unquote with regards to what they were doing there. In the story, an old man [Locher] owned that house and took care of them as long as he lived because he thought of them as his "children," and then when he died unexpectedly, they were frightened to death, they had no place to go, and they *had* to try to frighten away the newcomers to the house. It's pathetic, when you think about it.

Let me add—I was a little disappointed with the ending, but I sure couldn't think of any other way it could *have ended.*

Me either. We couldn't make them bad people who were trying to kill the newcomers. We just softened it. Here are some awfully unfortunate people, and *that's* bad enough. Let them have a happy ending.

How many days of shooting on House of the Damned?

[*Laughs*] Well, if you really have to know, seven days. In fact, they were all seven-day shows.

What kind of hours do you work on a seven-day show?

Not long. Because it doesn't pay to work long hours and have time-and-a-half or double-time. We had a normal day, I would say eight to ten hours a day.

You must have had a heckuva crew.

Incredible. *Incredible.* I had a crew that I used over and over and over and over again, it was the best in the world. I had such rapport with every single member of the crew. We were family. *We were family.* That's the only way you could get things done. And let me say this again, because it's extremely important to me: On all these pictures, I worked with wonderfully professional performers who gave you everything that you wanted. Everything they *had*, they gave you. People like Willard Parker and Merry Anders and Kent Taylor and my good friend Russ Bender and on and on. We had short little schedules but I did normal coverage, and sometimes even more than normal. And I couldn't have done it if it weren't for these actors. There wasn't *one single actor* I worked with that I didn't *love*, that I didn't have *great* respect for. They were people I couldn't *wait* to get on a set with, because these were genuinely nice people. You know the term "has-been"? They used to use it a lot in Hollywood. "Oh, well ... she's a has-been," "He's a has-been." The so-called "has-beens" that I worked with were some of the most talented, experienced, nicest people in the entire film industry. And if I ever heard *any*body refer to them as has-beens, I'd do everything but hit 'em right in the mouth!

Early on in your Lippert career, you were one of the guys showing up on the sets of other people's movies and keeping an eye on things. Did you have Lippert guys checking in on you?

No, never. Bob Lippert and I had become very, very close associates. Not good friends. I'd go to his home occasionally only because I felt like I didn't want to insult him—I was asked often but I went occasionally. But we *were* close associates, and Bob was a helluva good guy to work for. He was a self-made man: He opened his first theater in San Francisco when he was 16 years old. Can you believe it? He had sold papers and he had five jobs, and he saved some money, and borrowed some more, and he used it to open up an old, broken-down relic of a theater somewhere in San Francisco. This was during the early part of the War. He ran the oldest movies that he could find, because he could pay practically nothing for the rentals. But it didn't matter, because there were people in those days who had no place to sleep. When soldiers and sailors who were on leave couldn't get a hotel room, what they'd do was pay their 25 cents to get into Bob's theater, which showed movies 24 hours, and they'd sleep all night! That's how he started, and by the time I worked with Bob he was either the third or the fourth largest theater owner in America.

Did he visit you when you were shooting?
For the most part, the only time I ever saw him on a motion picture set was if he'd come by to say hello to, say, maybe some of the actors that he knew. Generally, though, he never came on a set unless he was asked ... and I never asked him [*laughs*]! But he was always welcome! He was the kind of guy who relegated authority and then just walked away from it.

The Day Mars Invaded Earth *with Kent Taylor—what prompted Lippert to make that movie?*
About ten years before that, Fox had a very, very popular movie, a big hit called *The Day the Earth Stood Still* [1951]. Get it? *The Day the Earth Stood..., The Day Mars Invaded...? The Day, The Day, The Day* [*laughs*]—okay? I loved *Day the Earth Stood Still*, by the way, and I thought Michael Rennie, who was new in Hollywood at that time, was terrific.

So whose idea was it to make a movie with that half-alike title?
Lippert. Listen, he'd come up with *all* these titles. See, Bob was an oldtime exhibitor, and he knew that it didn't matter whether the title fit the subject so much, but if it was an *intriguing* title, it would bring people into the theaters. So he would think up what *he* called "intriguing titles" and give 'em to Harry Spalding and say, "Write a script around it." One day he came into Harry's office when I was there and he said to Harry, "I got a great title. The next movie I want you to make is called *Police Nurse*." Harry said [*sounding dubious*], "*Police Nurse*?" Lippert said, "Yeah, *Police Nurse*. It grabs ya." So Harry wrote a picture called *Police Nurse* [1963], about a nurse [Merry Anders] in a police department. We shot it. Then we found out there's no such *thing* as a police nurse! There never *has* been! So we had a motion picture out called *Police Nurse* and, like us, nobody knew the difference [*laughs*]! Lippert came up with all these titles and we shot 'em. Thank God for Harry Spalding. I still don't know how he did it, show after show.

Did you collaborate with Spalding on the screenplays at all?
He'd come into my office while he was writing and we would kick things around. But I want to take nothing away from Harry, [writing-wise] he did 99 and three-quarters percent. He and I had such a terrific rapport. Knowing our limitations, when he would start outlining his stories, he'd come to me and tell me what he needed and ask, *could* we *find* it?, is it possible to do *this*, is it possible to do *that*? We would stop everything and we'd go out and get in a car, I'd drive, and we'd drive all over trying to find what we needed location-wise. So the scripts were more or less written to the locations! Harry was a genius, writing scripts around titles, around locations and sometimes even around sets: The studio manager at Producers Studio, Johnny Loche, was an incredibly nice guy who took a liking to me and vice versa. I'd ask him, "John, what have you got standing?" and he'd say, "Come on, I've got

Dexter wanted his micro-budgeted "alien invasion" movie to have "a weird *feel* ... something a little bit different, a little eerie"—and was reasonably pleased with the results.

several things"—he had about five stages. I'm not exaggerating when I tell you that sometimes Harry would sit down and write scenes around the sets that were standing! I'd tell Johnny, "Listen, we won't be ready for a few weeks. For God's sake, don't strike these sets!" [*Laughs*]

You mentioned Kent Taylor earlier, one of the names on your list of actors who "gave it all they had."

Loved him. One of the nicest people I've ever known in my life, one of the most cooperative, easy, good, good actors I've ever worked with. We'd send him a script and he'd call and say, "Oh, I loved it! Thank you, guys! I look forward to being with you again!" Kent lived about three blocks from our office, and so he used to drop in! He didn't come in to say, "Have you got a part for me?," he just came in to visit, and we'd sit around, and we were like old friends. I loved him because he could do *anything*, he was such a good actor, and a very *thoughtful* actor.

Again on Day Mars Invaded Earth, *you shot in an actual house—this time a rather famous one!*

We shot that at Greystone, the largest home ever built in Beverly Hills [905 Loma Vista Drive]. The guy who had that house built was Edward Doheny, the oil billionaire, in 1927 or '28. It was huge ... *huge*. Fifty-five rooms! And it had four-inch slate roofing, all brought in from Wales—can you imagine? It had gold inlaid molding all around the rooms instead of the regular wood molding, it had I-don't-know-*how*-many bathrooms, and every bath faucet was gold. The ceilings were like 12-foot ceilings, it had a bowling alley, it had its own theater, there were maid's quarters where you or I could live for the rest of our lives and feel like we living on Easy Street, it had a huge swimming pool, it had French gardens. It also had a guest house that sat back up from the pool, and that's where we shot the interiors—in the movie, that's the place where Kent Taylor and his family stayed.

But you also shot inside of Greystone itself, for the scenes where Taylor goes into the main house and meets his "Martian double."

You bet. I did a movie called *Maryjane* [1968] for AIP a few years later and I also used the exterior of Greystone extensively in that.

Was anybody living there when you did Day Mars Invaded Earth?

No. By then the Doheny that the house had been built for [Edward Doheny, Jr.] was long-dead—killed right in that house, in fact. And [in 1955] his widow willed it to the city of Beverly Hills. And so, now Beverly Hills had it as a ... *what*? It couldn't be a park, it couldn't be a *this*, it couldn't be a *that*. They didn't know what to *do* with it! I had seen in it in some motion picture, but all I saw was the outside—the gate and the driveway up to the main house. I called the city of Beverly Hills and told 'em I wanted to use it as a motion picture rental, and they said okay. Harry and I went up, we walked the whole house and the guest house and the rest of the property, and I said, "I want to shoot *everything* here"—inside, outside, the gardens, everything. We didn't pay very much, maybe $2500, which was not little in those days but certainly not a lot. We shot just about the whole movie there, except for the early scene of Kent Taylor and William Mims in an office, which was shot at Producers Studio.

When you lucked into places like Greystone, weren't you in some ways better off than A-picture directors at Fox, who no matter how big the budget could not build a set as spectacular as where you were shooting?

In essence, that's true! By the way, right down the street probably a block and a half from Greystone was the Cord mansion. You're too young to remember the Cord automobile from the 1930s, incredible coupe cars, hand-tooled and very, very expensive. Mr. Cord became a multi-millionaire, and lived in the Cord mansion. Around the same time as *Day Mars Invaded Earth*, I produced a movie called *The Yellow Canary* [1963] with Pat Boone, written by Rod Serling, and we shot there extensively. Inside, in the huge foyer, there was an incredible circular staircase, I think it was three floors instead of two. A sad story: Years earlier, when the Cords' only daughter had her coming-out party, her debut, all of her college friends and lots of other people were in the foyer. The daughter appeared at the head of the stairs and she made some kind of a gesture like "Here I am!" and they all turned around ... and she got on the banister to ride the railing down. About a third of the way down, this poor girl slipped and fell and her head went right to the marble floor of the foyer, and that was the end of her, she was killed instantly. The parents were in such shock, they closed the house shortly after that and moved to Palm Springs, and the story *I* got is that they never returned. Then, years later, we were lucky enough to get in there to shoot *Yellow Canary*.

The role of the long-suffering housewife in Day Mars Invaded Earth *was so different from the tough broads that Marie Windsor usually played.*

That was the first and only time I ever worked with Marie. She had always played bar girls and heavies and she was always mean ... and I didn't *want* her in *Day Mars Invaded Earth*, truthfully. But Lippert wanted her. He came up with the names of three or four actresses he thought might work [for the role of Kent Taylor's wife]. He seldom ever did that, by the way, we generally handled it ourselves. But he suggested Marie. I don't know whether he was a friend of hers or what.

She was in a number of Lippert's early pictures, including a "biggie" for him, Little Big Horn *[1951].*

Then that's why. I never knew that. Anyway, I said, "For goodness sakes, she looks like a barroom gal to me. And she's a *big* gal." Then I thought, "Well, maybe we could do something with her hair, maybe lighten it to give her a little lighter look...." I ended up *loving* her, by the way. Like all the people I'd worked with, she was professional, she knew her lines and, boy, she was sweet, she was nice, she was warm and friendly. She was a joy.

Harry Spalding told me that Betty Beall got the part of the teenage daughter because she had a twin sister who could play her "Martian double."

Exactly. Also, she happened to be very pretty, and she wasn't a bad actress. I had to work with her on lines, but she was smart and picked things up very quickly. Kent Taylor's Martian double was Troy Melton, a favorite stuntman of mine—I used Troy on almost every movie if I needed a male stunt. He was almost Kent's identical size, and he did all the doubling work for Kent. Over-the-shoulder, down the hall and all that.

The robot device seen on the Martian surface in the opening scene—that's very much like what we're sending up to Mars these days!

That *is* what they do now, and there was talk about that at the time. I went to a special effects house in Hollywood and said, "I've got $1.75 and I want a $400 robot." Harry and I had talked about it, and Harry kind of designed something on paper, and they made it. It was just a little remote control thing, about as big as an ottoman, three by three by three — not very big. We didn't want it *too* big, because it was supposed to be on the Martian surface, so we didn't want anything enormous because it would dwarf the Martian set [*laughs*]!

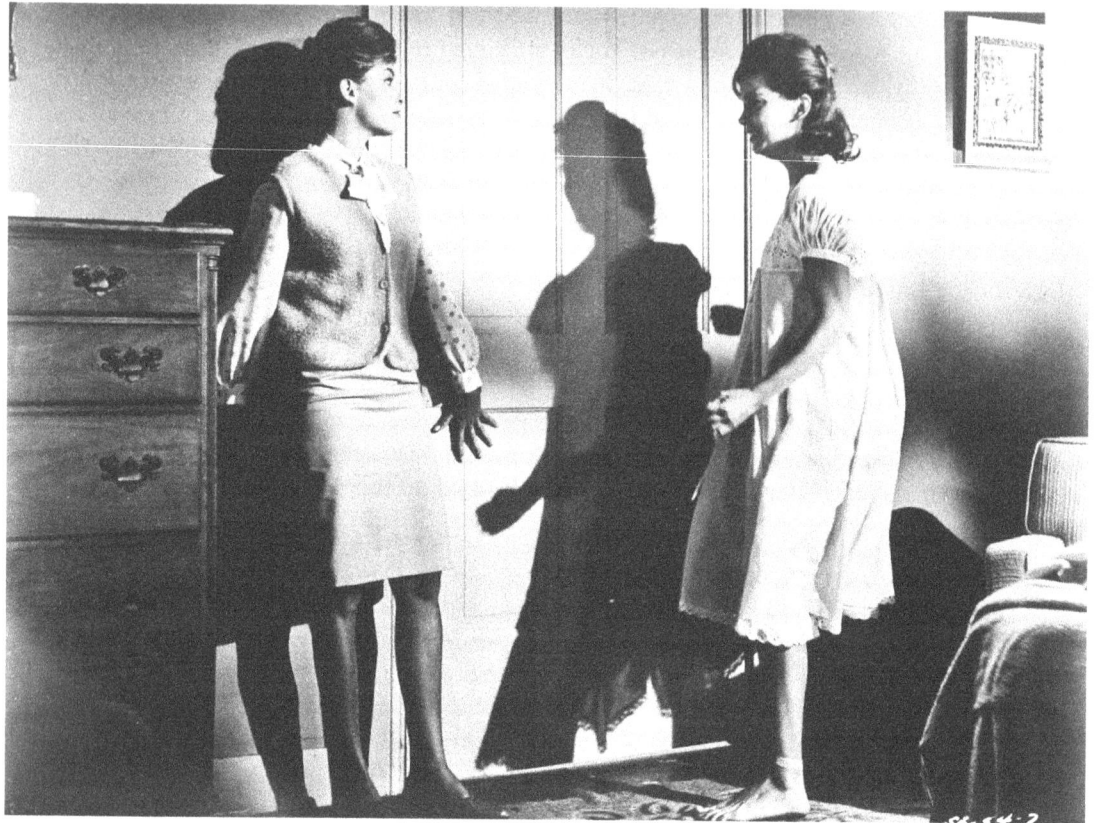

In *The Day Mars Invaded Earth*, the character of Judi is menaced by her Martian doppelganger. To save money on special effects, an actress (Betty Beall) with an identical twin sister was cast in the role(s).

I first saw Day Mars Invaded Earth *as a kid, and the ending where you see the ashes of the bodies of all the film's characters in the empty swimming pool blew me away. I remember sitting there a long time after* THE END *came up, a 12-year-old thinking, "That can't be. Movies don't* end *that way...!"*

Harry came up with that. That, to me, was the best thing about the movie. The shot of the ashes in the empty pool had to be a one-take thing. Water hadn't been in that pool for God knows how long and it was dusty and dirty and full of leaves and so forth. We put out the ashes in the shapes of the bodies, and then we had the Department of Water come up when we were ready to shoot. It was set so that the water would come on only at one end of the pool, and come on as a blast, and wash away the ashes. And we knew that if we didn't get it right the first time, then we'd have to wait for the pool to dry. We couldn't put new ashes in a pool where the tile was wet, and we knew it'd take hours and hours to dry out. So it was a one-shot thing, and we were just lucky that we got it in the one shot.

Were you satisfied with the way Day Mars *turned out?*

I was happy with it—in fact, I liked the movie very much when we were shooting it. By that point I had directed several movies, and on this one I was keenly aware of wanting to try to get ... a weird *feel*, if that's the right word. Something a little bit different, a little eerie. I tried to achieve that by the way I'd move the camera in, by the way I'd stage it. In one scene I had Kent Taylor and Bill Mims walk through the French gardens, down to the end, and talk about the [mysterious goings-on], overlooking all of Beverly Hills in the background. To me, there was something interesting about events *that* weird happening right in the heart of Beverly Hills, California.

While you were a producer-director at Lippert's company, he made a couple "genre pictures" which you did not produce or direct, Hand of Death *and* The Cabinet of Caligari.

Hand of Death is a nice story and an interesting story: In 1961 I did a picture called *The Purple Hills*, a very simple little "trek Western" with Gene Nelson, who a few years earlier had been a lead in a bunch of song-and-dance-type movies at Warner Brothers. I liked him, we got along okay, he took direction well and I had no problem with him at all. About six months later, he came to me one day. "Maury," he said, "I wanted to direct. I've been going to film school at UCLA and I want to start directing. What do I have to do to direct one of your movies?" I didn't want to tell him that *I* was directing all of 'em [*laughs*]! He said, "Keep me in mind, Maury, *please*. Do me that favor," and I said okay, thinking nothing would come of it.

Then out of the blue, a guy named Eugene Ling came out of New York with this [*Hand of Death*] script he'd written. He wanted to be a Hollywood producer. For some reason, Bob owed this guy a favor; and so Bob told him, okay, he could produce it. Well, it was a *god-awful script*. Harry took it, and I remember him saying, "Jeez, Maury, I'd have to start [rewriting] right from page one. I can't do too much with it." And I didn't want to touch it [direct it]. What happened next was very much like that other situation, *High Powered Rifle*: I sent the script out to a couple of directors' agents and they sent it back saying, "Seven days [of shooting] and *this* script?? No!" And these were directors who were doing small pictures! So I got a "brilliant" idea and I called Gene Nelson and I said, "Gene, get your butt in here, I want to talk to you." We sat down and I said, "I'm going to give you a script. I'm *not* going to give you a commitment, but I'm giving you the script to take home. Spend a couple nights looking at it. It needs a lot of work. If you can come up with some ideas of how to fix this thing, there *may* be a chance of me getting you to direct." Well, he was elated. In fact, he couldn't believe it—and I don't blame him! I mean [*laughs*], he'd been to me only a week or ten days before, almost pleading to get a job, and I told him it would be impossible! Well, the next morning, he was there at the Lippert offices before I got in, waiting for me! He had all these Mickey Mouse ideas [of how to fix the script]—but the point is that he had worked his butt off all night long to try to make it better. And he'd improved it a *little* bit—not much, but a little!

I went to Bob Lippert and I told him, "Nobody wants to direct this *Hand of Death* thing, I've struck out everywhere." Bob said, "Maury, we've *got* to do it, I've committed to this guy Ling. So you direct it." I said, "No, *I'm* not going to direct it, but I'll tell you what I *will* do: You remember Gene Nelson? He's been going to film school, and I'm going to sign him to direct because ... I'll *help* him." Bob hemmed and hawed but finally he said, "Okay, do it, kid." So that's how Gene got the job.

And did you help him out?

For several days I helped him prepare and I talked to him about cutting patterns and this and that. But I said, "Once you say *roll 'em*, I'm not there, Gene. It'll be in your pocket then. One thing you've got to promise me: If you feel like you're getting in trouble—and the key word here is *getting*, not *get*. If you start *getting* in trouble, you better call me. I'll come out. I'll be there. I won't take it away from you but I'll be there to help you." He never called me—he did the film. It wasn't a *great* film but it wasn't a great *story*. Now let me tell you what's interesting about that: He took that little film of his and—don't ask me how!—he went to MGM and he got a job directing a musical called *Hootenanny Hoot* [1963]! So help me! And then he did a couple more for MGM after that, a pair of Elvis Presley pictures! And now I'll tell you the thing that irritated me: A press release on one of those pictures included an interview with Gene that described him as an ex-dancing star and now a director. They asked him how he got started directing and he said, "Thank God for Bob Lippert! He gave me my first break. If it hadn't been for Lippert, I would not be here today." That burned me up! I thought, "The least you could do, you son of a bitch, is say, 'Maury Dexter got me the job.'" But of course, in those days Lippert's name was a little bit more important than mine!

And Cabinet of Caligari—*what do you recall about that?*

Nothing but horrific memories! Bob, as I told you, loved to do remakes, and he loved classics. I assume you've seen the old, Expressionist German film from 1919 with Conrad Veidt, *The Cabinet of Dr. Caligari*? Well, Bob wanted to do a version of that. Harry Spalding tried his best to talk Lippert out of doing it—"That was an Expressionistic picture, Bob, it had its own style. *Today*, what the hell are you gonna *do* with it?" But Bob was undeterred and he sent word out to the various agents around town that he wanted to do it and he needed a writer and a director. Then one day Bob asked me, "You know a guy by the name of Roger Kay?" I didn't. "Well, he's from Europe, and he's got great ideas for *Caligari*." To make a long story short, Bob hired this guy Kay against my wishes and against Harry's wishes. Bob brought him over here from Europe, set him up in an office, and Kay started writing an original screenplay based on *The Cabinet of Dr. Caligari*. I would go down to his office and I would ask him certain things, and he would ignore me. Well, *all* but ignore me—I'd get a grunt or a "yeah" or a "no." Finally he finished the screenplay, and Lippert had a few copies made and sent one to me. After I read it, Bob asked me what I thought, and I said, "I don't know *what* to think. I don't understand it. This has nothing to do with Dr. Caligari, this has nothing to do with a cabinet [*laughs*], it has nothing to do with the original." Bob said, "No, it's a new concept, a whole new psychological approach." I said, "Bob, it is so psychological, I don't understand it. And I'm not stupid." Harry tried to talk him out of it too, he told Bob it was ridiculous. But again Bob said, "I'm committed, we're gonna go forward," and he *did* go ahead with it. To play the lead, we got Dan O'Herlihy, who just died a week or two ago [2005]. What a nice guy he was! Just terrific. And also Glynis Johns, who I'd always loved, because I'd seen her in all those British movies that she made.

Did you have any confidence that Roger Kay would be as efficient as a Lippert director needed to be?

Well, I put one of the top production guys on *Caligari*, [production manager-assistant director] Lee Lukather, knowing he'd keep the picture on schedule no matter *what*. Now comes the story I promised I'd tell you, about the one time I ever heard Bob Lippert use profanity. The very first day *Caligari* was shooting, I was on the set over at Sam Goldwyn Studios. I was there about 8:00, 8:15, and nothing was being done. The set was lit, but the technicians were all standing around, Roger Kay the self-proclaimed genius was sitting in his chair ... and nothing was happening. I walked up to Kay and I said, "What's goin' on?" He said, "Well ... we're having a little problem." I went to Lukather and I asked, quietly, what the problem was, and he said, "Jiminy Christmas, Kay and Glynis Johns had some kind of a disagreement this morning. She rushed into her dressing room and locked the door, and now she won't come out." I said, "Oh, *really*?" Well, I walked back to Kay and I said, "Okay, what the hell is goin' *on* here?," and he went into "I told her to blah blah blah, and *she* said blah blah blah, and so *I* said...." I told him, "Listen, pal: Get off your ass, go to her dressing door, knock on the door. *You* get her on this set, or you're in a lot of trouble." And he said to me, "*You* can't tell me what to do." I said [*calmly*], "No I can't. But I know who *can*. I'll be right back!" [*Laughs*] I went to the phone and I called Bob Lippert—he lived only a few minutes from there, up in the Hills. About 15 minutes later the door opened and in came Bob with his cigar. I explained to him what happened, and I said, "I told him to get her on the set, but I have no authority here because as you know I'm not on this particular project." He said, "Okay, thank you," and he walked right over to Roger Kay and he said, "Listen, you son of a *bitch*. If you don't get off of your fat *ass* and get over there and—" Bob chewed him up and down! So [profanity-wise] the worst thing I think I ever heard him say was "son of a bitch" and "fat ass." And that was under extreme conditions, to say the least!

When *Cabinet of Caligari* came out, nobody understood it. The reviews were god-awful and Bob was so upset with this guy Kay, he coulda killed him [*laughs*]! I said, "Don't kill *him*, Bob, kill your*self*. You're the guy who put all this together!" It wasn't a very pleasant experience!

Why did you leave Lippert? Or did he stop making movies?

We did *so* many movies—I think I made about 17 or 18 there myself—that Fox finally said, "We can't *take* any more!" But Lippert and Fox had a seven-year deal, so I'm sure Fox had to pay Bob off, or *some*thing, and that Bob did okay. Bob called me and said, "We have to close down," and I said, "Okay. I need a rest anyway!" This was early '65. I did a couple pictures [abroad] and then in early 1967, a friend of mine who was head of production for AIP, Burt Topper, called and asked me to come on over to AIP and talk with them about doing some shows there. Jim Nicholson and Sam Arkoff and I sat down and we worked out a three- or four-picture deal. I was to have total autonomy; the only thing they had was final script and final cast approval. And they came up with these provocative titles, like *Maryjane* which was obviously a picture about marijuana and so on. I did four movies for them [*Maryjane*, *The Mini-Skirt Mob* and *The Young Animals*, 1968, and *Hell's Belles*, 1970], and I brought every one of them in on budget and so on.

Memories of Nicholson and Arkoff?

Nicholson was a perfect gentleman. He was an ex-film salesman, he had been in the business for a long time and he was quite intelligent. A very nice-looking gentleman, quiet-spoken, and he knew what the hell he was doing. In my opinion, he was the one responsible for AIP's success. As for Arkoff, my instincts about him turned out to be true: I never particularly cared for the type of person Arkoff was. I don't think I have to draw you a picture. After working with Lippert for ten years, I wasn't about to get involved with Arkoff. So I did all my dealings through Jim Nicholson.

Have you got any AIP "war stories"?

I really had no problem other than when I was shooting *Hell's Belles*, a "Western on motorcycles" shot out in the middle of nowhere, in the desert out of Tucson. In the early morning of the third or fourth day, I was to shoot a love scene: Near a campfire, Jeremy Slate was to crawl over to Jackie Lane and start to snuggle up and make love to her. Early that morning, when we had just arrived on the location, I looked up and I saw the production supervisor for AIP, Norman Herman, coming over to me. He said, "I've got a message for you from Sam," and he handed me a piece of paper, and it was words to the effect, "When you shoot the love scene, I want sex in it. I want to see a lot of sex." This was the late '60s and there were now [sex scenes in some movies], but not in mine—I wasn't about to get into it. The note insulted my intelligence, so I tore it up and threw it in Norman's face and told him that the next plane was leaving at 8:05 and to be *on* it. And of course I shot the scene the way I had intended to shoot it, a nice, warm, sexy but certainly not overdone sex scene.

He went back and I'm sure reported to Sam every little thing I said—which was fine. We finished the movie weeks later, and some time after that I screened a rough cut for the

In the second half of his Hollywood career, Dexter (left) worked as a television director and assistant director. He's seen here with Michael Landon and director of photography Haskell Boggs.

guys at AIP. Sam was in the back of the little room and I was in the front. The rough cut was screened, and after it was over, nobody commented on it; and I got up to walk out. Sam came down to meet me at the EXIT door. "Dexter," he said, "I've got a very important question for you." I said, "Yeah, what's that, Sam?" He said, "What do you have against *sex*?" Well, you can't print what I said. But it referred to his birth. And I walked out. That was the last time that Mr. Arkoff and I ever had a conversation together.

You didn't do much directing after that.

While I was at AIP, a great script called *The Haunting of Teresa* came our way—laid in New England, World War II setting, a wonderful suspense movie. They liked it and so we bought the script. And Jim Nicholson wanted a name in it—he thought it was too good to go out as one of their second features, so he wanted a name. Susan Hayward was my favorite actress at the time, so I personally got the script to her, and she read it and said she wouldn't touch it! At the end, a 15-year-old girl, the niece of the character I wanted Susan to play, had two and a half pages of drama, a terrific scene, and Susan said, "Maury, the only thing people will remember when this picture's over is that 15-year-old girl. Thanks but no thanks!"

I finally bought it from AIP, and then I bought a couple of other properties that I wanted to do, and I got myself so heavily financially involved in properties that I couldn't get off the ground, I just quit! The next time I went on a set, it was as an assistant director, which I had never been. That's how I met Mike Landon. My good friend Bobby Jones was first assistant on a big made-for-TV movie that Mike was directing, *It's Good to Be Alive* [1974], a picture about the black baseball player Roy Campanella. After the first week, Bobby and Mike had a falling-out. Minor, very minor, but enough to make Bobby walk. I took the show over, and I finished it, fortunately, on budget and on schedule. Mike was so impressed that he said, "I'm doing a pilot for a new series for NBC, and if it sells, I want you to be with me." He said it was a new show called *Little House on the Prairie*. I thought to myself, "You've got to be kiddin'!" [*Laughs*] Little Joe playing in a series called *Little House on the Prairie*?, there's no way that's ever going to sell! I thanked him profusely, never expecting to see or hear from this guy again. Well, they shot the pilot in January-February [1974] and in the first part of March, while I was working on a movie of the week down in Malibu, I got the word that Mike wanted me to come over right away for *Little House*! I was lucky enough to work on the very first episode of the series, and almost ten years later worked on the last. And I worked on every second one in the interim.

And you also directed a bunch of 'em.

About halfway through the run, Mike kept wanting me to direct and I didn't *want* to direct, because I'd heard horror stories about stars not paying any attention to directors because they [the stars] had all the power. But Mike insisted and I started directing, and I directed a slew of those. Then after that, he went to a series called *Highway to Heaven* and I was on *that* with him for five years; and then we did a couple of movies of the week and a couple of pilots. Then in 1991, we did a pilot called *Us*, CBS loved it and said, "Go to series right away," and Mike said, "Maury, put the crew back together!" But soon after that, Mike found out that he had cancer of the colon and it was spreading into the liver, etc., etc. After that, everybody knows what happened. When Mike died, I retired. I said, "I'll never work again," and I haven't.

And in summation, what do you want to say about the career you've had and the work you've done?

I think I'm probably one of the luckiest guys in the world. A little talent ... hopefully! ... and *lots and lots* of help from The Man Upstairs. I have never been afraid to tackle anything that's come my way. But Fate works in strange ways ... or it may be the Good Lord, who knows?: Almost every major thing that I've tried to do, like getting my properties off the ground after leaving AIP, I have never been able to get *any* of that stuff [to come to fruition]! Everything that I have enjoyed and everything that has come to me professionally has come out of the blue. What*ever* it was, I had nothing to do with promoting it!

I probably worked harder than most people in the industry, physically and mentally. I never would settle for second-best, nor would I settle for something just because we didn't have the extra two dollars to make it a little bit better. I would always somehow find a way to make it a little better. So I'm proud of what I've done with my life professionally and, looking back, I don't think I would change very much. In my mind, the main reason that I never ever really gained prominence in this business is that I would never ever lower myself, in my estimation. I wouldn't play "the Hollywood game." I had the opportunities—which I won't go into. I turned down opportunities that I knew weren't for me, the personnel wasn't for me, the type of stuff wasn't for me. I said, "Look, I'm going to go ahead and do what I'm doing. As long as I can make a living, I'm happy." And I was.

PAT FIELDER

*As a child, I had always been deeply into fantasy....
I thought that witches were real; I had to have a candle in
my bedroom at night, and all that kind of thing.*

Indie production companies crowded the exploitation movie world in the late 1950s, and in the sci-fi-horror vein one of the very best of the bunch was Levy-Gardner-Laven with their medium-budget, high-quality genre fare. An important part of their movies' appeal: Above-average scripts by the first woman writer in Hollywood ever to make a specialty out of the cinemacabre. Pat Fielder unleashed giant prehistoric mollusks on Southern California swimmers (*The Monster That Challenged the World*, 1957), dreamed up the most loathsome bloodsucker since Nosferatu (*The Vampire*, 1957), and turned the King of Vampires loose on Small-Town U.S.A. (*The Return of Dracula*, 1958). But amidst the horrors, there was also humanity: protagonists more lifelike and sympathetic than the genre norm and, most strikingly, greatly improved roles for female characters. Instead of stereotypical damsels in distress, self-reliant working women emerged from the Fielder typewriter.

The Pasadena-born Fielder continued with Levy-Gardner-Laven as writer of the jungle-set SF adventure *The Flame Barrier* (1958), the teleseries *The Rifleman* and *Law of the Plainsman* and the feature *Geronimo* (1962). Among the other 100 writing credits on her résumé are episodes of political and legal series (*Slattery's People* and *Owen Marshall, Counselor at Law*, both earning her award nominations from the Writers Guild of America), medical shows like *Dr. Kildare*, the crime drama *Baretta*, the supernatural *Time Express* and (naturally!) the "you *go*, girl!" TV milestones *Police Woman* and *Charlie's Angels*. Her one producing (and co-writing) credit was the epic-length 1981 TV movie *Goliath Awaits*, a pseudo-scientifically plausible tale in which the crew and passengers of a luxury liner that sank in 1942 are found alive in the air-filled ship on the ocean floor 40 years later.

Your first science fiction script, written in 1956, was The Monster That Challenged the World.

United Artists commissioned a horror picture from Levy-Gardner-Laven, and David Duncan wrote a script that for some reason wasn't suitable. In fact, it was about to be abandoned. Meanwhile, I was working at L-G-L as a production assistant-story editor-secretary, and was also assigned to read material that was submitted to us by agents for their clients. If I liked the screenplays or books that were submitted, I'd pass them on to Jules [Levy], Arthur [Gardner] or Arnold [Laven]. *And*, on my lunch hours, I was messing around with trying to write a domestic drama of some sort—a stage play. I can't remember the plot, but it was about a small-town family in crisis and that kind of thing.

L-G-L were also in a crisis: They didn't have the financing at the moment for another writer to take on the rewrite of Duncan's script. So Art Gardner, who I think had read a draft of what I was writing, wondered if I'd like to take a crack at it. I said *yes* ... but I wasn't all that certain I could *do* it. That was the script that became *The Monster That Challenged the World.*

Prior to writing the script of Monster, *how "into" horror or sci-fi or fantasy were you?*

As a child, I had always been deeply into fantasy and had wanted desperately to be an actress, and I'd spent endless hours creating fantasy plots with neighborhood kids. I was in plays all the time, from grammar school up through college. (However, I usually would get such terrible stage fright before a performance that I thought I'd never want to try to make a living at it!) I was *very* insecure as a child; I thought that witches were real; I had to have a candle in my bedroom at night, and all that kind of thing.

Horror movies—did those hold any interest for you when you were a kid?

I don't think I followed horror at all. I grew up seeing what I thought were great, classic movies. After all [*with a grand tone in her voice*], I was a theater arts major at UCLA, and we didn't go around and see all the schlocky pictures, oh, no, no, no [*laughs*]!

So how does somebody who didn't grow up with horror and science fiction movies write *one? How do they know what's expected of a script in that genre?*

You do some research into werewolves and the undead and all that, and read Bram Stoker's *Dracula*, and—

For my purposes here, let's stick to Monster *for the moment.*

Well, I was kind of an academic, I was interested in research. And I did see *some* sci-fi pictures that were out at the time. I saw *Them!* [1954], of course—*Them!* had been a huge hit and it served as a model for all kinds of other sci-fi films that were subsequently made.

You mean, once you got the job of writing Monster, *then you went out of your way to see movies like* Them!*?*

Yes. It's possible that we might have looked at *several* of the science fiction movies of the last few years. I also found a *Life* magazine article that David Duncan had also found, about a California desert dry lake bed that a flash flood had filled with two feet of water. Within days, there were millions of shrimp in that lake, hatched from eggs that had been dormant for centuries. So, yes, *Monster That Challenged* is far-out, but it does have some scientific fact to back it up! It took only one skip of the mind into fantasy to see how such an incident [the reappearance of a prehistoric species] could have really happened; the best science fiction *is* something that you can strongly believe could have happened. I did research into *that*, research into what was going on in the Imperial Valley where we had decided to set the story, and then at that point I just let my imagination *go*. Science fiction's a genre where you don't *have* to be really realistic, you *can* let your imagination go and you can imagine all these wonderful things happening.

And, even better, a lot of terrible things!

[*Laughs*] Exactly! I was also always interested in science and even in astronomy. As a matter of fact, at one point I thought about going into astronomy, but I was not strong in math and I figured that that would keep me from pursuing any kind of a career in it. But those were my favorite classes, science. So, working with the old Duncan script and the research I'd done, I wrote *Monster That Challenged the World* in which the prehistoric mol-

Write Fielder: Rookie screen scribe Pat became a genre M.V.P. with her scripts for the home-run hits *The Monster That Challenged the World*, *The Vampire* and *The Return of Dracula*.

lusk eggs beneath the bottom of the Salton Sea were hatching in radioactive water, and these gigantic mollusks were now proliferating at a horrifying rate in the All-American canal system of irrigation in the region. Hungry, *huge*, and beginning to attack the local population, and ultimately ... the *world* [*laughs*]!

When you wrote Monster, *were you showing L-G-L a few pages or a scene at a time, or did you present 'em with the finished product?*

Oh, I *had* to show them a scene at a time, I'm sure. I *don't* really remember, but I *must* have, because they would never have let me go through all the way to the end. And I would have needed guidance and help, I'm sure. I attacked the subject by first writing an extensive one-line outline—of course, with Levy, Gardner and Laven's help. This outline was eventually approved by them and I launched into the script, sitting at the secretary's desk in the outer office, but still placing calls for them and doing some office work as well! L-G-L were pleased with the draft of the script, sent it to UA and, amazingly, got an okay to make the picture.

Would you care to guess how long it took you to write it?

Gosh, I would say not terribly long, maybe seven, eight, ten weeks, something like that. It's the outline that's so hard, *that's* what takes the time, and working the story out. Once you get into screenplay, it *flows*—at least, it does for me. The places *I* get stuck are in the turns on the story. Of course, I had Arthur and Jules—I was in the outer office, I could very easily go in and say, "I'm stuck!" [*Laughs*] I'm sure they were extremely helpful because that's the kind of guys they were, very hands-on. But they also knew when to leave you alone and let *you* work it out. I don't remember any real, major problems. I don't remember any major problems with *any* of the [horror-sci-fi] scripts, they really did seem to flow. Part of that is from a nurturing situation where the producers have faith in the writer.

You also worked on the movie as a production assistant.

My aunt and uncle had lived in Brawley, California, for several years and so I knew the area around the Salton Sea somewhat. I mostly remembered, from when I was a kid, big bugs all over the place, and how awfully hot it was during the day. (The nights were lovely, filled with stars, so close you could almost touch them. But days were killers.) So when Arnold Laven the director went down to research the locations, he took me with him to document camera setups he was planning, look at locations and all of that. There was also an air base in the Imperial Valley, in El Centro, where they taught

Fielder poses with a model of the Kraken from *The Monster That Challenged the World.*

Army personnel the ins and outs of parachute jumping; that was another location we researched.

Did you have an air base in your script?

I honestly don't remember if the fact that the air base actually existed impacted the screenplay first off, or if it was integrated into the screenplay after we visited it. We then got farther into prepping the picture, which was tremendously exciting for me.

Did you know who would be in the picture as you were writing it?

No. Kerwin Coughlin and his associate Pat Rose, who became a good friend of mine, did the casting on several L-G-L pictures, including *Monster*. It went through normal channels: They sent out the script to the actors they thought might be right for various roles. Tim Holt was cast and it was considered a real coup since I don't think he'd done anything for a few years—he had sort of retired from movies. At the time, honestly, I didn't know who he was, I really didn't know his background until later on. Tim was a really nice guy and everybody liked him. A very gentlemanly, very nice man … down to earth. And he worked his heart out. Hans Conried was a wonderful character actor, funny and sly. And of course Audrey Dalton as the girl lab assistant-secretary was … well, you guess *who* [*laughs*]!

How did you like shooting in the desert?

It was a very physically demanding job, there were a lot of locations, and of course the *climate* in the Imperial Valley was just *so* hot that it was really a tough, tough shoot.

Heat and *humidity?*

Pretty much heat. It's dry, it's desert. God, but it was hot hot hot! I almost had heat stroke! I didn't get screen credit as a production assistant but I was there for every shot, rewriting if necessary and all of that.

When the picture began shooting, the title was The Jagged Edge.

Yes, and then it was changed by Jules, who felt that the title *The Monster That Challenged the World* was more exploitable. We were, after all, going for "the horror audience." I never really liked his title! I thought, "It's very much 'on the nose'"—and it *was* [*laughs*]! But of course it was an intriguing title for people who love those kinds of movies.

To what did The Jagged Edge *refer? That title kinda goes over my head as it relates to* Monster That Challenged the World.

There's a saying, "You're on the jagged edge of…"—well, despair, or what*ever*. I'm sure it came from that, and it might have been my title, but I'm not positive.

What memories of seeing the Monster itself?

It was very exciting, because our special effects man Augie Lohman created a fantastic creature. Cables ran from the Monster to a control panel, and I'm sure it was Augie at the controls. The operator would open the Monster's mouth and move the body itself, forward and backward and sideways. It was very effective.

Did it match what you had in mind when you wrote?

I must say, it was much worse-looking than what I had in mind when I wrote. I mean, worse in a *good* way [*laughs*]. Terrifying!

Next up was The Vampire *with John Beal.*

The Monster That Challenged the World was *very* well-received by United Artists, who then had a brainstorm that they would release it as half of a horror double-bill, and did L-

G-L have a second picture to pair it with? So that's how *The Vampire* came into being. There was a rush to get *The Vampire* ready.

Obviously on Monster *the basic idea was agreed upon before you got the job of writing, so you didn't come up with that. But did you come up with the idea for* The Vampire?

I'm not sure. It probably was me ... but maybe not! At L-G-L, we sort of sat around and had story conferences and talked about what might work as far as a suitable companion feature for *Monster That Challenged the World*. The idea came out of one of those meetings, and then I went to work. I had a great friend, a doctor, who gave me advice on the technical parts of the medical sequences—he *was* in fact a small-town doctor, like John Beal's character in *The Vampire*, so I think I based some of John's character on him. Small-town life has always appealed to me, at least in terms of drama. And horror in juxtaposition with family life is *always* intriguing. Weird people have weird experiences, but when *real* people have weird experiences, *then* I think you have true drama!

As I said, I kind of modeled John Beal's doctor character after my dear personal doctor; well, he came one day, to give us some advice on the surgical scene in the operating room. How the gloves would be handled, and this, that and the other thing. But when he wanted to correct things, they were not terribly kind to him [*laughs*], because they were in a hurry to shoot! And he wanted things done right! It all worked out, but I think it was kind of traumatic for him!

So you were a production assistant on The Vampire *too?*

Yes, always on the set as much as possible. I really began to seriously think about becoming a director at this point, but there were *no* women directors except Ida Lupino. Guys on the stage would say to me, especially later, "Well, why *don't* you become a director? Ida Lupino did." Yeah, yeah, yeah. Not possible then, and very difficult even today.

Were you around when they shot the scene of the Vampire chasing Coleen Gray down the street?

Yes, that was in Culver City. Writing that, I was influenced by the great scene in the Val Lewton film ... was it *Cat People* [1942] or *The Leopard Man* [1943]? The scene where the girl is stalked on the street at night by the big cat? A great scene!

So you did *see horror movies growing up!*

Yes, you're reminding me now—I *must* have! I thought that was one of the great scenes; in fact, I've used that scene several times in my [writing career]. It's one of those things where you've got the girl and you've got the shadows and the night and no moon, and ... you can't resist it!

John Beal seemed to me to be giving it his all in The Vampire.

He was *such* a great actor. And he had such a history behind him—he had done all kinds of things on the stage in New York, and he'd been in movies too. I remember, when they said that they were going to be able to cast him, everybody was *so* elated, because he was such a good actor. The young girl playing his daughter [Lydia Reed] also did a most interesting job. Coleen Gray and Kenneth Tobey were both good actors. Coleen became a friend of mine, she was a lovely lady. Ken Tobey, who was also in *The Thing* ... I always thought he was very cute! He had such bright red hair—he *did*, anyway. He was really a doll.

Again in The Vampire, *the female lead is a working woman—"coincidentally," a secretary-receptionist!*

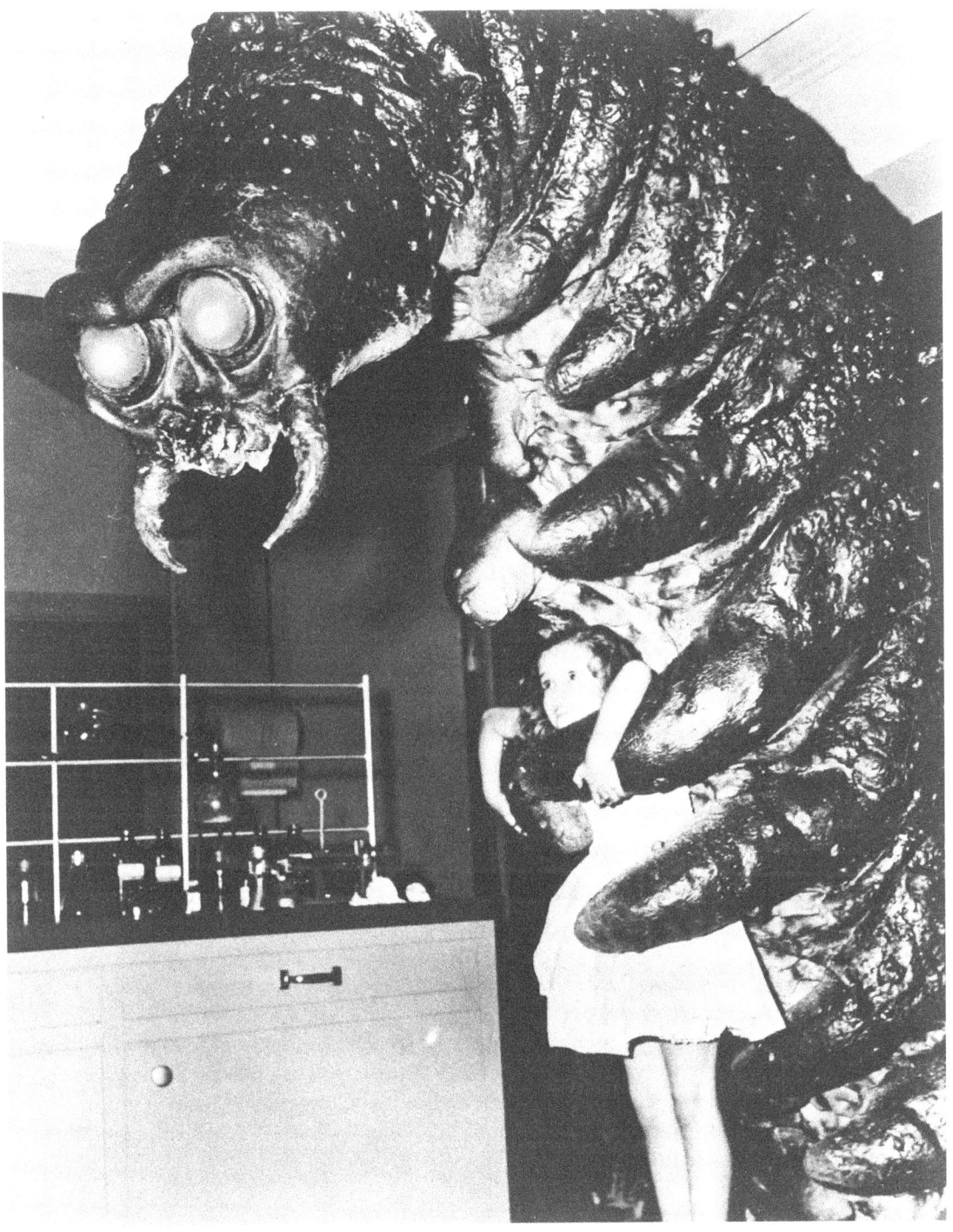

Shock-a-bye baby! Kid actress Mimi Gibson in the grip of *The Monster That Challenged the World*.

Fielder's L-G-L duties never brought her in contact with giant mollusks or vicious vampires, but in some small ways those movies' female leads were modeled on Fielder herself. Here John Beal menaces Coleen Gray in *The Vampire.*

Right, right! There were so few jobs that women held at the time—this was not an era when there were all these women scientists and various things. I tried to find a logical place to fit a woman properly into the story, and so they were not running astrophysical labs or whatever!

The two scientists played by Dabbs Greer and James Griffith in The Vampire—*a very amusing "odd couple" if ever there was one!*

I too liked their crazy relationship. I guess I have a bizarre sense of humor which I try at times to suppress, with no luck [*laughs*]! I saw *The Vampire* again a few Halloweens ago, Turner Classic Movies ran horror movies all night on Halloween, and when it got to their scenes, I thought they were really very funny. I can now look at it "detached" from having written it, which is exciting!

There's one stretch in The Vampire *where one horror or action scene leads into another, and another, without a breather. I thought that was fabulous.*

Well, good, I'm glad. That makes me happy [*laughs*]! I *love* action—I love to have a story really take off and *go*, and *never* stop. That's my theory. So you don't sit around and talk for long periods of time.

How exciting an experience was it to have a script of yours in production, and to be there?

Oh, incredibly. *Incredibly.* And everybody was so helpful and supportive. It was a great experience. I've rarely had the sense that, suddenly, everything seems to work. It's a wonderful feeling.

Gerald Fried's music really helps it to work. His scores for The Vampire *and* Return of Dracula *are two of my favorites of his.*

He wrote the music for three out of the four horrors [Fried also scored *The Flame Barrier*]. He was very young at the time, and I thought he did a great job, his music was terrific. I got to meet him, yes, he was around. L-G-L was a "family affair," *every*body was around, all the time—they were all very, very close. Arthur and Jules' strength was to draw their team in, and then they could count on them, and that was great.

Drama-wise the best scene in The Vampire *must be the one where the doctor tearfully sends his young daughter away, because he knows that the Vampire half of him will eventually kill her if he doesn't.*

I'd seen *Dr. Jekyll and Mr. Hyde*, too, the [1941] version with Spencer Tracy, and I was influenced by that.

The scene where Jekyll breaks up with his fiancée [Lana Turner] because he's afraid what Hyde might eventually do to her?

Yes. The theme of the father potentially destroying the thing he cared about most—the ultimate victim being his daughter—seemed to me a classic theme around which to build a story. It seemed to have a particular kind of horror, going back to the Greeks, to Oedipus and Medea, all the great classics.

If there was a woman regularly writing Hollywood SF movies before you, I can't think who she was. You had to have been the first.

Gosh, I don't *know* if I was the only woman writing science fiction ... I hadn't even thought about it. But ... *maybe.* Well, who else would it have *been*? Actually, because I *was* so young, *and* a woman, it was a publicity angle as well: United Artists sent me on a promotion tour when the pictures [*Monster That Challenged* and *The Vampire*] first came out. They sent me to Denver, to talk on the radio and various things. They really made a "play" to get as much exploitation as possible.

Out of the fact that a woman had written these pictures.

Right. When I checked into the Brown Palace Hotel in Denver, I was met by the UA representative there. They had sent a huge bouquet of roses to my room and, being a Pasadena girl, I felt right at home. Denver was a beautiful city. The air was soft and warm, and the people were lovely. A publicity man took me on a sightseeing tour, and it seemed strange and unexpected to be a sudden celebrity. The next day, I went to the radio studio to be interviewed, and then went back to L.A., where a different publicity man, Logan Smiley, took me to the L.A. Press Club. I was given a chance to speak to the L.A. Press Club [about becoming a screenwriter], which was really amazing. They tried to make a whole exploitation thing out of the fact that I was a young woman, just out of college, who had written these movies. There are even some pictures of me with the Monster [the giant mollusk], because it was an exploitation angle, "Beauty and the Beast," which was cute.

Incidentally, by then I was divorced, and living alone in Laurel Canyon. The LA papers did a story on me, and I asked them not to mention that I lived alone, since weirdos would call me on the phone and ask me ghoulish questions. But of course they *did* mention that I lived alone. More weirdos called, until I had to have my phone unlisted.

Can you talk individually about what Levy, Gardner and Laven were like?
  Oh, they were absolutely terrific, they were wonderful. They really were my "family," they protected me, they were so good. Jules Levy was the one who had the oddball ideas—ideas from "out in left field." He was the one who thought up wild things to do. Jules and Arnold Laven had both been script supervisors [prior to the 1951 formation of Levy-Gardner-Laven] and they had learned all aspects of set operations. Arnold wanted to be a director and so he became a director, and Jules always wanted to be a producer and so he became a producer. Arthur Gardner had been a production manager and wanted to be a producer. It was not the Hollywood scene at all, they were just really great, wonderful guys. Honest guys, and so hard-working. Their first picture was called *Without Warning!* [1952]. It was shot in black-and-white on the streets of LA, natural locations, and they made it very cheaply.

And your first time meeting and working for them was in 1952 when they made Vice Squad.
  I was just out of school, broke and out of work, and I was asked by a friend to take on a two-week typing job that she was unable to do. So I went to work for Levy-Gardner-Laven and met them for the first time and typed their script of *Vice Squad*. That was at the Goldwyn Studios. We didn't have computers then, we had to work with carbons; I was a *lousy* typist [*laughs*], and I made a mistake every time someone walked into the outer office, which was usually Jules Levy! But I did get through the script somehow, and they asked me to stay on during the shooting. Because I had learned how to diagram things as a theater arts major, Arnold Laven [director of *Vice Squad*] took me with him, to scout the local locations and roughly draw the setups that he indicated.

The sort of thing you said you later did again with him on Monster That Challenged the World.
  Right. Then we had them blueprinted, and copies were made to be distributed to the cameraman and lighting director. In the interim [between typing the *Vice Squad* script and the production of *Vice Squad*], I did general office work, delivered the script to actors like Paulette Goddard and Eddie Robinson, typed changes, etc., etc., etc.! When *Vice Squad* was being shot, I worked as a liaison with the set and generally hung around and watched whenever it was possible. By then, L-G-L had moved to Culver City, the old Selznick Studios, and we were associated with Sol Lesser Productions.
  After *Vice Squad*, which was a terrific picture, L-G-L closed up shop for a while, and I worked for a couple of other companies, in a secretarial capacity, until I rejoined L-G-L, who were now at the Hal Roach Studios. I told them I wanted to be more than a mere secretary, and had ambitions to be involved in production and to write one day.

After Monster That Challenged *and* The Vampire, *you scripted the next double-feature,* The Return of Dracula *and* The Flame Barrier.
  Since UA was so happy with the results on *Monster* and *The Vampire*, yes, they commissioned two more horror films. *The Return of Dracula* was originally titled *Curse of Dracula*, and why they changed it I don't remember. I really loved writing this script, but then I usually end up loving writing most of the scripts I write because otherwise you couldn't survive the grief and drudgery of writing them at *all* [*laughs*]. I was influenced by the original Bram Stoker story, of course—the angle about the friendship of the two girls. Thornton

Bram Stoker's novel *Dracula*, and even Alfred Hitchcock's *Shadow of a Doubt*, were Fielder's influences during *The Return of Dracula*'s writing phase. Here the incognito vampire king, loose in Anytown, U.S.A., casts a baleful eye on his "cousin" (Norma Eberhardt).

Wilder's film for Hitchcock, *Shadow of a Doubt* [1943], was my model for the script—there again, small town, ordinary people, caught up in a truly horrific situation. It was fun to create a character who was so suave, so evil ... so far from Transylvania, and right on our own back doorstep.

So you think it was your idea to set this Dracula movie in the U.S.?

I suspect it may have been. The idea of a Transylvanian vampire coming to a small town, to California, is *so* bizarre in itself that it sounds like something I would think of [*laughs*]!

And you say you read Dracula.

Oh, sure, once I knew we were going to do a Dracula-type picture. I either had a copy of *Dracula* or borrowed it from the library or bought it, and read it at that point. And of course read all kinds of other things I could find on vampires, and the undead, and transmigration into other forms, like the wolf [Dracula in wolf form] that kills the investigator played by Charlie Tannen. Incidentally, when I was a little girl, my parents went to see *Dracula* on the stage at the Pasadena Playhouse. They came home and told me the story, which utterly terrified me. Remember, I'm the one who was, and still *is*, afraid of the dark [*laughs*]! They said something that I remember to this day: That in the night, you can see the eyes of the vampire, one green, one red, coming through space and into your room! It scared me to death. No wonder I lit a candle by my bed, and almost burned the house down [*laughs*]!

Well, when you grew up, you cooked up some scary stuff yourself. Like, in Return of Dracula, *having a helpless blind girl [Virginia Vincent] become Dracula's first victim in California.*

I was once asked why I wrote that character as blind. Well, what is more horrifying than *not* to be able to see the horror that is about to engulf you?

Do you recall if any actors other than Francis Lederer were approached about the Dracula role?

I'm sure they must have been. I'm sure the casting people had meetings with Arthur and Jules, but I don't remember being in on those meetings. And I'm *not* sure that in those days I would have known who Francis Lederer *was*.

[Laughs] I'll let you in on a secret, if he hadn't been in Return of Dracula, *I'm not sure I'd know who Francis Lederer was!*

I really don't think I *did* know who he was, but once he was there, he was so perfect for it, so great! I loved Francis Lederer.

Very "ahead of its time" is your depiction of the Van Helsing equivalent in Return of Dracula *[John Wengraf] being a globe-trotting government agent. So many of your ideas were so "different"!*

Well, as I've said, I was always very interested in all this kind of stuff. When I lived in Pasadena, there was an area between the city of Pasadena and the Santa Anita Race Track called Baldwin Park, and it was *vvvery* spooky. It's an arboretum, it's got a lot of plants and lakes and an old, decrepit house of 1890 or so. Kids would go there, you'd go there on a date or something, and it was really very creepy. I wrote a short story about it, sort of a horror story, which I never got published; that was when I was in college. My husband and I met when we played in *Night Must Fall* at Pasadena City College, a great play. He played the killer and I played the lead, the woman he wanted to kill [*laughs*]. And we fell madly in love! So, you see, I had an interest in "spooky stuff" from high school, junior high school, and junior college. It all kind of weaves together in a kind of a web....

And then you were able to start coming up with new, off-the-wall ideas for horror stories yourself. Making the staking of the lady vampire a color sequence in the otherwise black-and-white Return of Dracula—*was that your idea?*

No, that was Jules' idea. The movie goes to color for a split-second when they're pounding the stake into her heart and the blood is gushing out. Jules said, "We gotta have this in color," and they did it!

Were you on hand for the shooting of that?

Yes.

The main female character, played by Norma Eberhardt—not *a secretary this time!*

No, but ... I have from time to time in my life worked as a volunteer for various organizations. So having Norma's character involved in charity events for her church made sense to me, especially in a small town. I loved that character because she was so often "putting off" her boyfriend, who was played by Ray Stricklyn. Her character really reflected "the modern woman" at that time, I thought. And Norma Eberhardt, who played her, was beautiful too, which was nice. But, yes, you're right, she was *not* a secretary!

You not only made some of the female characters in your movies working women, but also tried to make them interesting people and give them good dramatic scenes. Even some of the supporting ones, like Marjorie Stapp in Monster That Challenged the World.

I recently looked up some of these horror movies on the Internet and found fans commenting on them, and they said, "You can tell that a woman wrote this because there are all these women characters." It was interesting, it came up several times, how interesting and unusual it was to find [good roles for women] in this kind of picture. I guess it must have struck a chord with other women, because these were women who were writing these comments.

I assume you made a conscious decision to write better-than-average roles for women in these Levy-Gardner-Lavens—and, I'm sure, in some other scripts of yours?

Of course you're right. My decision to write interesting roles for women seemed a natural one. And being a woman, with ambitions of my own, I had a perfect opportunity to develop characters rather out of the mainstream. And later on, in my writing, I've often dealt with women who face huge and difficult obstacles in their lives, and have jobs and relationships common to many of us, and rarely dramatized. I've written a lot of "problem dramas" dealing with abortion and single woman parenthood, female judges, cops, doctors, psychiatrists, etc., long before this kind of characterization became popular. It's not that I go looking for this subject matter, it just seems that opportunities presented themselves, along with producers who were willing to gamble on offbeat stories.

Last and ... well, definitely *least of your four horror-sci-fis for Levy-Gardner-Levy:* The Flame Barrier.

I agree with you, I think it's the least effective of the lot. We had a greensman who said, "A tree is a tree and a rock is a rock," so they shot this jungle movie on a soundstage where there was a lot of moving-plants-around and so on. But Paul Landres, the director, did as good a job as possible with the limited budget and time constraints.

You and George Worthing Yates share screenplay credit but I got the feeling watching it that it must have been more Yates than you. Am I right?

Equally, I guess. It was done in a rush. We did as good a job as possible, but we had *no* budget, and we had to shoot it in, like, six or seven days. I mean, it was really a very, very difficult shoot.

Did Yates put pen to paper first?

He had written a script, and I then took over. I don't really remember whether I rewrote his script, or if I started out fresh, or what*ever*.

But you never worked shoulder to shoulder with him.

No, no. In these situations you generally don't work shoulder to shoulder. With my later writing partner Dick Bluel, I did, because we *were* partners. But if you're brought in to rewrite an existing script, you sort of try to start over, depending on the producer's requirements. Especially if the script has problems. I was on the set of *The Flame Barrier* a lot—it was part of my job to be sure that the dialogue was okay or make any adjustments.

In a 1958 newspaper interview, you said you were tired of "ghouls and monsters" and wanted to do something different.

I *loved* horror and science fiction, it's just that I think it had kind of run its cycle, maybe. As you know, it's all so cyclical as far as the movies are concerned. I really wanted to spread

Arthur Franz and Robert Brown battle the Blob-like creature that came from *The Flame Barrier*.

my wings, I wanted to write *other* things. And then of course Westerns were coming in. A young, unknown writer had the office next door to mine at L-G-L and he was writing the pilot for *The Rifleman*, his first assignment. His name was Sam Peckinpah. I used to work late and so did Sam, so we became great friends—a friendship that lasted several years.

You wrote for The Rifleman, *and then L-G-L's movie* Geronimo. *Which* again *had some excellent parts for women—from the leading lady to the farm woman who brings the Indians into her house for a chicken dinner.*

Well, women had not really been dealt with particularly in Westerns in that sense. And certainly not Indian women. I think this was one of the first pictures that showed a sympathetic view of the Indians—don't you think so?

There were a few in the 1950s, like Broken Arrow *[1950], but* Geronimo *was certainly another notable early one.*

I loved *Geronimo*, and I wish I could have gone even further with it. But we had to adhere to certain action. The true story of the Indians and the reservations is really a tragic story. The Indians weren't treated fairly. They were caged, in that sense, put on reservations and forced to be farmers, and I felt a great deal of sympathy for that.

And, again, I'm sure, a lot of research before you wrote your script.

Of course! I remember Jules being elated that he and Arthur had been able to acquire the title *Geronimo* from the MPAA Registration Service, and asking me if I knew anything about the famous Indian rebel. Of course I *didn't*, but I said I'd begin research and I could learn. I wrote a *very* long one-line outline and finally got approval to write the screenplay. Once I finished it and UA was happy with it, we got a commitment to shoot it. This time it was agreed that I would be the dialogue director and go with the company to location to Durango, Mexico. Again I traveled with [director] Arnold Laven to scout the locations and draw his camera setups as well as adjust what dialogue was necessary, coach the actors, etc. We were on location, counting pre-production time, for about three to four months.

You left L-G-L around that time, and started to freelance.

I felt a need to expand my horizons and move away from "the family" [the Levy-Gardner-Laven "family"]. And so, yes, I did begin to freelance. There was a great freelance market for television at that time, something that doesn't exist today. I began by writing Westerns and then moved into all the current episodic market—medical, legal, cop shows, psychiatric shows, all that kind of thing. I had an office at MGM for a while, working on their shows, then moved to Universal where I was given an office near Richard Bluel, who had recently been a producer at Warner Brothers and was trying his hand at freelance television writing. Richard and I became friends and ultimately writing partners. We wrote many TV episodes at that time and finally the mini-series *Goliath Awaits*.

Whose idea was Goliath Awaits?

The idea was originally Richard's, who came up with it about 20 years earlier. It started out as a one-page pitch idea that he had co-written with a producer, Hugh Benson. Hugh went to CBS and got them to agree to have a story written by Dick and me, on the basis of that one page. But in order to write a story, we had to do *all* this research, because we didn't even know whether the premise was actually possible—the survivors of a 1942 luxury liner sinking, still alive at the bottom of the ocean in the air-filled ship 40 years later. If you were going to do pure science fiction, you would just make it up, but we wanted it to feel *real*. It took us weeks and weeks and weeks of research—

Of course!

[*Laughs*] With permission from the Department of Defense, we traveled to Panama City, Florida, to the Navy's Oceanic Study Center, and spent three or four days there. The guys in the "think tank" there were *wonderful*. We came in with this *impossible* premise, and we told them what we wanted to do with it, and they would say, "We'll think about it. Come back tomorrow." Then we'd come back the next day and they would have *solved* it! There was only one problem: After three or four days, they said, "You realize you can't have the divers in the rescue party from the surface take their oxygen masks off aboard the ocean liner." I said, "They can't take their *masks* off? How's the hero gonna kiss the girl??" So we worked out all those transferal-of-air ideas, which was very complicated, but *accurate*, and could have been done. It was all very exciting stuff.

CBS agreed that Richard and I could write the script, but they wanted a three-hour script. Then when we were deep into it, they said, no, they would only fund *two* hours. Now, we couldn't tell the story in two hours, we couldn't tell it in *three* hours, so we decided that we would write it in two parts, two hours and two hours. On our own we wrote the extra hour, and then we got a commitment from Channel 13, a local station out here that was being very audacious and trying to break the prime-time stranglehold the networks had.

You shot on board the Queen Mary *in Long Beach. What was that like?*

Very interesting. The Queen Mary—God, it's amazing it's still floating, because it looked to me like it was gonna *sink* when we were there! There was water all over the lowest level! It was a very difficult shoot, but I thought it looked great—don't *you* think so? You could have never, never, never duplicated that in a studio. We made the pool area into a hydroponic garden, which we had found out was possible; we researched all this stuff and then we put it in the script. A society *could* live down there at the bottom of the ocean! We had a Brit as a director, Kevin Connor, and he did a great job. And it had a very good cast. I thought Christopher Lee was wonderful, and so was Jean Marsh.

As associate producer, what did your extra duties entail?

We were shooting in various locations, and I had technical responsibilities as well as [doing some] rewriting. The wonderful thing about having a writer on a set is that the writer can make a decision that will save thousands of dollars, by cutting a scene or making a transition of some sort, that they [the crew] may not *think* of in the heat of production. But most companies want the writer to go away during production; they're always very nervous that the writer is going to say, "Oh, you're not shooting my script the way I wrote it, and I hate you!" [*Laughs*] But in a good situation, the writer is *extremely* valuable because he or she can make these cuts and can come up with alternate ideas. Incidentally, it was supposed to be "Produced by Richard Bluel and Pat Fielder and Hugh Benson"—the three of us. But at the last minute, the powers-that-be decided they didn't want *that* many names on the screen. You ought to look at the credits of modern TV movies and series; *nowadays* there are 10 or 12 producers on every show [*laughs*]! But at that time, we were told, "We don't want a proliferation of names," and so I caved and agreed to an associate producer credit, I'm sorry to say!

How did Goliath Awaits *do ratings-wise?*

We *creamed* everybody. The night of Part One, the first two hours, we had the highest ratings of all the competing shows. We were a sensation! We were very proud of that. Then the next week they ran the *next* two hours, and again we beat everybody and got even higher ratings. And then of course it's been rerun for years.

And you continued to work in TV with Richard Bluel after that.

Yes. But by 1987 the TV market had changed dramatically and Richard and I, weary of always starting over, decided to pre-

Fielder was recently honored by Women in Film as one of the 25 women to have contributed most to the art of television writing in the past quarter-century.

95-years-young Arthur Gardner, the actor (*All Quiet on the Western Front*) turned indie filmmaker, with Fielder at their recent lunch-reunion.

pare a slate of six theatrical films to be shot in Europe, and written and co-produced by us. We traveled to Europe on several different occasions to raise money for the productions. However, Richard died en route on one of our trips, in 1992, and we were never able to bring the projects to fruition.

Wrapping up with, again, the old Levy-Gardner-Laven sci-fi and horror flicks ... have you kept in touch with anyone from the old days there?

Well, Arthur Gardner. He's 95—can you believe that? You know, it's funny, he called me again just recently because he'd talked to you, and he invited me to lunch. We went to a little luncheon place, and we got to talking about the past and *I began to cry* [*laughs*]. I couldn't control my emotions. I felt *so* touched by seeing him, and recalling the past and everything. I felt like such a *fool*, because there we were near Rodeo Drive, in one of these posh little restaurants, and there I was, sitting there wiping my eyes and wanting to hold his hand and everything!

What current activities?

In later years, although I've continued to write, I focused recently on two novels and, yes, one of them is in the horror genre. Around 1988 I made a trip to Greece and I found the island of Rhodes, and an idea for a horror story came to me. When I came back, I told Dick Bluel about it, and we decided to develop a horror screenplay. We were going to shoot it among our group of European pictures, but that didn't happen. Recently I decided it might make an interesting novel, and I've just finished it, and I'm hoping that I can get it published. Dick and I also wrote a screenplay, *Tokyo Rose*, based on the life of Iva Toguri, innocently convicted of treason in World War II, from a book by Rex Gunn, and that's currently under option. I'm going to be a co-producer on that. It's strange, Tom, when you think how *one moment* of fate—that two-week job—changed my life around.

The two-week job typing Vice Squad.

Exactly, which I typed so badly [*laughs*]! And you had to erase all those carbon copies, too, it was horrible! Anyway, it's the most amazing thing, because I would have never conceivably thought that I could earn a living as a writer, it was nothing that I would even *dream* of. But that typing job led to writing *Monster That Challenged the World*, and then to so much more. The moral has to be: Never turn down a two-week job. Trust in fate. You have no idea *where*, to what wonderful place, it will lead you!

RICHARD GORDON ON *SVENGALI* (1954)

Quite frankly, I was afraid to come up against Robert Newton alone. He was a big, strapping guy, known for his violent outbursts, and I wasn't about to risk being beaten up by him. I thought if I brought a private detective with me, it would give me some measure of protection.

He first cast his "evil eye" on movie audiences in the early days of film: Svengali, the roguish villain of George du Maurier's 1894 novel *Trilby*. From all around the world came numerous silent renditions of the story of the "crazy scarecrow" of a musician-hypnotist who discovers in the Latin Quarter of 1890s Paris a beautiful young model whom he turns into a great singer. But even with his mesmeric power, he cannot make her love him.

In 1931, after the advent of sound, Hollywood produced a highly effective John Barrymore–starring version (*Svengali*) highlighted by the Great Profile's alternately comical/sinister portrayal of the notorious title character. In 1954, George Minter of England's Renown Pictures and writer-director Noel Langley decided to bring a second sound *Svengali* version to the screen, this time in color, and top-lining character star Robert Newton—a notorious character in his own *real-life* right. Peripherally involved with the production an ocean away was Manhattan-based motion picture distributor Richard Gordon, who here recalls the series of bizarre events, from astrologic to alcoholic, that ensued....

In the early 1950s, I established my office in the old General Motors building at 57th Street and Broadway in New York City. I was active primarily as a producer's rep for companies such as Renown Pictures in England and other European producers, to get their films distributed in the United States. As time went on, I was also asked by various [overseas] producers to negotiate for Hollywood actors to appear in their films in order to make the films more salable in the U.S. For George Minter of Renown Pictures, I sent Wayne Morris to London to star in Terence Fisher's *The Gelignite Gang* [U.S. title, *The Dynamiters*, 1956] and William Bendix to co-star in Robert Siodmak's *The Rough and the Smooth* [U.S. title, *Portrait of a Sinner*, 1959].

In 1954, George Minter and Noel Langley decided to remake *Svengali* for Renown. Minter and Langley had known each other for many years. Langley had been in Hollywood where he worked for MGM, and had writing credits on such films as *Maytime* [1937], *The Wizard of Oz* [1939], *The Prisoner of Zenda* [1952] and *Knights of the Round Table* [1953]. He was also the co-author with Robert Morley of a play called *Edward, My Son* which had a huge success in London and on Broadway. When MGM bought the movie rights but assigned someone else to do the film script, Langley had a falling-out with them and returned to England, where he set up a production unit with George Minter. Their joint ventures included *Tom Brown's Schooldays* [1951], *Scrooge* [U.S. title, *A Christmas Carol*, 1951], *The Pickwick Papers* [1954] and *Our Girl Friday* [U.S. title, *The Adventures of Sadie*, 1954].

Then they conceived the idea to make *Svengali*, in color. George informed me that he had arranged with 20th Century–Fox to borrow Hildegarde Neff to play Trilby. She was then in Hollywood, under contract to the studio. Her agent was Martin Jurow in New York, who just died a couple of weeks ago [February 12, 2004]. I met with Jurow at his office. I didn't have to negotiate any terms; that had already been settled. I was asked only to complete the paperwork with Fox, arrange the payment of Neff's salary, her transportation to and from England, etc. Later I got to know her well when, after the completion of *Svengali*, she came to New York and starred on Broadway in Cole Porter's *Silk Stockings*, the musical version of *Ninotchka* [1939].

Robert Newton was to play Svengali. He had appeared as Dr. Arnold in Minter's *Tom Brown's Schooldays*—more of a cameo role than a leading part. But George had had a good experience with him and liked him.

What did you think of the casting of Newton as Svengali?

Newton was a fine actor. He was very flamboyant and I thought he would probably make a very effective Svengali. He had starred with James Mason in *Odd Man Out* [1947], played Bill Sikes in David Lean's production of *Oliver Twist* [1948] and was known in America. I was very concerned about how he would behave during the making of *Svengali* but it was not my business and I had nothing to do with it.

Why do you say you were concerned?

Because Newton had by then acquired a terrible reputation as a drunkard, a troublemaker, and for being unreliable. In fact, producers were having difficulties getting insurance on him and he was having trouble finding work in England. He had married ... an English girl, I think, and moved to Hollywood, where they had a child. However, he had done well for Minter in *Tom Brown's Schooldays* although, as I said before, it was really just a cameo role for which I guess he was employed only for three or four days. So it was not as much of a risk as hiring Newton to star in *Svengali*.

And the deal with Newton?

I had nothing to do with that, it was all arranged by George Minter, who had hit it off very well with him during *Tom Brown's Schooldays*. Newton came back to London and brought his wife and son.

Donald Wolfit received a BAFTA Best Actor nomination for his performance as the mad mesmerist in the 1955 film version of *Svengali*.

After *Svengali* had been in production for about two weeks, I was woken up one morning at six A.M. in my apartment in New York by a telephone call from Minter in London, who informed me that Newton had defected from the film. Apparently he had developed a crush on Hildegarde Neff but she absolutely detested him and couldn't stand him [*laughs*]. She thought he was repulsive. So Newton began to play what he thought were funny jokes on her. She told me later of an instance where, when they were about to film a romantic closeup, he bit into a bunch of raw garlic in his dressing room before coming on the set. She nearly got sick and it disrupted the production. And so on and so forth.

Maybe it was because of Newton's crush on Neff, I don't know, but his wife suddenly decided to return to Hollywood while the film was in production. That apparently set Newton off. He fell off the wagon with a resounding thud, and the next thing that happened was that he was photographed by the newspapers in a London nightclub, roaring drunk and causing a major disturbance. When they threw him out, it turned out he was wearing pajamas under his coat [*laughs*]. It was in all the London newspapers the next day and that's when George called to say that Newton did not show up at the studios—and when they went to look for him, they found out that he had boarded a plane for America. George wanted me to intercept him in New York and see what I could do with him. George suggested that I go out to the airport—Kennedy Airport, which was called Idlewild at the time—and try to catch him. We agreed that I would take a private detective with me, but we missed Newton because he simply changed planes and continued to Los Angeles immediately. So I never got to meet him or even talk to him.

Why did you bring along a detective?

Because we wanted to serve Newton with a summons for breach of contract, damages and everything else. Also, quite frankly, I was afraid to come up against Newton alone. He was a big, strapping guy, known for his violent outbursts, and I wasn't about to risk being beaten up by him at the airport [*laughs*]. I thought if I brought a private detective with me, it would give me *some* measure of protection. I got him from the classified pages of the New York telephone directory because it was all on such short notice. I only remember vaguely now that he was a young guy who seemed to know his business and quite relished the idea of taking on such a job. It never happened, though, because Newton had already left for Los Angeles by the time we got out to the airport. I telephoned my brother Alex out in Los Angeles, to see if *he* could catch him out there. Alex and a local sheriff tried to serve Newton with a warrant, but he managed to elude them by donning a disguise and taking a further plane to *Australia* [*laughs*], where he remained while he was starring in a television series called *Long John Silver*.

How much did Newton's "defection" set George Minter back?

It cost George a considerable amount of money. The insurance policy which George had been able to take out on Newton in connection with *Svengali* specifically excluded problems resulting from alcohol or drinking on Newton's part, so the insurance company claimed that they were not liable.

What was Minter's next move?

The problem was that everything which was shot with Newton had to be re-shot with another actor. Hildegarde Neff had only been made available by Fox for a total period of ten weeks, and they expected her back in Hollywood at the end of it to start another film. I went to Martin Jurow to try and get it extended, because George was talking about shut-

Svengali was one of several Renown Pictures on which New York–based Richard Gordon was involved. Here at the London premiere of Renown's *Scrooge* (a.k.a. *A Christmas Carol*, 1951) are, from right to left, George Minter, head of Renown's London studios, Gordon and Renown sales staff members Leonard Hope and Henry Taggett.

ting down *Svengali* until he could recast it. But Fox was not cooperative, and said, "No, we need her back for another project. She has to return by the cut-off date."

Donald Wolfit stepped in to play Svengali.

That's right. George succeeded in getting Wolfit, who had appeared in The *Pickwick Papers* and was well-known as a classical stage actor. Wolfit wasn't really any kind of a film name although he had made a few films in between his stage roles. But he was sufficiently trained as an actor so that he could step into a role almost overnight and absorb it. So the picture went on with Hildegarde Neff and Donald Wolfit.

Made very quickly, I'm sure!

Very quickly, yes. Incidentally, sharp-eyed viewers will be able to detect several long shots of Newton in the finished film which Noel Langley did not re-shoot, in particular a ballroom sequence where Svengali plays the piano with wild abandon.

Were you again involved on the distribution end?

Yes, I was, which was true of all George Minter's English productions. I had released *Tom Brown's Schooldays* and *A Christmas Carol* through United Artists, and licensed *The Adventures of Sadie* to 20th Century–Fox. I was able to make a deal with Metro-Goldwyn-Mayer to distribute *Svengali* in the United States and Canada. MGM decided that, because it was a British film, co-starring Wolfit and Neff, it should be released as an art house pic-

Wolfit's Svengali could get Hildegarde Neff's Trilby to sing—but *no one* could get her to come to the movie's New York premiere!

ture, which I thought was totally wrong considering its subject matter and the nature of the film. But they decided to open it in an art house in New York City, expecting to get some very good reviews that would help it down the line, and so it was booked to open at the Trans-Lux Theater on Lexington Avenue at 52nd Street. The Trans-Luxes had a policy that any new film would always open on a Saturday and they scheduled the premiere for Saturday, September 26, 1955. By this time, Hildegarde Neff had come to New York to prepare for her starring role in the stage musical *Silk Stockings*, and she agreed to help promote the movie. But she was very much influenced in almost any decision by her astrologer, Carroll Righter, the "Astrologer to the Stars," whom she always consulted. She had this in common with Marlene Dietrich, with whom she was on very close and intimate terms—Dietrich never made a movie without consulting Carroll Righter. So Neff, unbeknownst to me, consulted Righter about the prospects for *Svengali*, and I was told by her that Righter had said, "Unless the picture opens on a Thursday, it's going to be a disaster." [*Laughs*] I was then faced with the daunting prospect of first informing George Minter that I couldn't get Neff to the theater unless they changed their opening date to a Thursday, and then going to Harry Brandt, the head of Trans-Lux theater chain, to see if he would agree. And of course

Harry Brandt politely and firmly threw me out of his office, saying, "I don't want to know!" And Hildegarde Neff refused to promote the film at all. *Maybe* it was an excuse because I think she was having a hard time preparing for *Silk Stockings*, which was due to open in Philadelphia before moving to Broadway. Anyway, the end of the story is that *Svengali* opened on a Saturday, was not well-reviewed, and had no real success in distribution until it came into its own in the United States much later, when MGM put it on television. Neff blamed its failure on their refusal [to open on a Thursday].

What did you think of the movie?
   Being a movie buff, and having seen and admired the John Barrymore *Svengali* of 1931, I thought it was not a very good remake. The Barrymore film was far more effective and he was a much better Svengali than Donald Wolfit. But it was very colorful—it had a sort of Moulin Rouge-type of background—and I really expected it to do better. Maybe it *would* have done better ... with Robert Newton.

Is that Neff we hear singing in the movie?
   No, George Minter engaged a very famous opera singer, Elisabeth Schwarzkopf, to dub Neff's singing voice. This added immeasurably to the realism of the concert scenes.

I recently got a-hold of Neff's autobiography and I see that she skips right past Svengali—*doesn't mention it at all.*
   I'm sure she omitted it because it was an unhappy experience with Robert Newton and just didn't want to go into it.

Wolfit and Neff—what did you think of their performances?
   I thought Neff was pretty good, considering she was a German actress with a heavy accent, and then was shown to sing through the voice of Elisabeth Schwarzkopf, who had no accent at all. I thought Wolfit was rather hammy and overdid it. Well, for that matter, so did John Barrymore, but Wolfit did not have Barrymore's finesse. Mind you, I was a great admirer of Wolfit as a stage actor, having seen him in several Shakespearean plays, particularly as King Lear. I think it was the best performance of Lear that I ever saw; it had become Wolfit's signature piece when he was touring with his repertory company all over England, doing Shakespearean plays in which his wife, Rosalind Iden, was always the leading lady. I saw *King Lear* on the stage again later with Ralph Richardson and on another occasion with Laurence Olivier, and I have to say that I remember Wolfit as the best of all those I'd seen. It was a stunning performance in the theater.
   When Hildegarde Neff came to New York to do *Silk Stockings*, we became good friends. She invited me to come to Philadelphia for the opening night. It was quite a spectacular affair. Harold Arlen, the famous composer, was in Philadelphia at the same time with his show *House of Flowers* starring Pearl Bailey that was also being readied for Broadway. Arlen at that time was in some sort of relationship with Marlene Dietrich, and she was there, helping him with his production. And because of the close friendship between Dietrich and Neff, Dietrich showed up at Neff's post-premiere party, in a suite at the Warwick Hotel, which was the one and only occasion on which I actually got to meet Marlene Dietrich and to be able to sit down and talk to her. That was a great thrill for me—very exciting.

Any memories of anything else Neff told you about the shooting of Svengali, *or just the garlic?*
   At this stage of my life, I remember only the garlic incident, and her general revulsion towards Newton, who she thought was coarse and unfeeling, and not interested in anything

or anyone except himself. She did not acknowledge to me that there was any kind of a romantic interest in her on Newton's part—*that* was something I heard about from George Minter. But she definitely was not happy with the whole setup! As for Newton, Minter finally served him with a summons in Australia and Newton declared bankruptcy. Shortly after that, he appeared in Mike Todd's *Around the World in 80 Days* [1956], which was his last movie. He died shortly thereafter at the age of 50.

Speaking of *Svengali*, what surprises me is that nobody has ever turned the story into a Broadway stage musical show. When you think about productions like *Phantom of the Opera*, it would seem to me that *Svengali*, which is about a girl who becomes a fabulous international opera singer, would be an obvious subject for somebody like Andrew Lloyd Webber. And since it was written by George Du Maurier, of course it's public domain as it was published in the last century. Well [*laughs*], now *two* centuries ago!

RON HARPER ON
PLANET OF THE APES

> *Our* Planet of the Apes *stories degenerated into*
> *"*The Fugitive *with Fur." I think that's one of the things that*
> *curtailed what should have been a longer run.*

The *Planet of the Apes* saga was brought to the screen over the course of five profitable feature films (1968–73), and then 20th Century–Fox was in a quandary: The full-circle story had been told and yet a fan base, and a potential for further profit, still existed. One solution was for the tales of far-future ape-human conflict to move to a new medium, television. So confident was Fox in the new series that they didn't even monkey with a pilot: *Planet of the Apes* went directly into production with Ron Harper and James Naughton as Alan Virdon and Pete Burke, 1980 astronauts whose unscheduled trip through the time barrier lands them in 3085 California, now a primitive wilderness where apes are the masters and humans their slaves. Joining Harper and Naughton in the cast was Roddy McDowall, a carryover from the movies, as the sympathetic chimpanzee Galen who goes on the lam with his new human friends and helps them avoid capture by gorilla pursuers.

A combination of factors resulted in a shockingly short run, as discussed and dissected here by star Harper, who says he knew even before the ax fell that the small-screen series would *not* have Apes fans going bananas. A native of Turtle Creek, Pennsylvania, the blonde, 6'1" Harper did some early acting while attending Princeton and subsequently tackled some of his first professional jobs on the New York stage and television. *Apes* was his fifth TV series as a regular; he has since starred on soap operas, guested on episodic TV, traveled *backwards* in time for the 1970s Saturday morning SF series *Land of the Lost* and, in more recent years, played supporting parts in the movies *The Odd Couple II* and *Pearl Harbor*, and the genre flicks *Venomous* (killed by a mutant snake) and *Glass Trap* (killed by a giant ant!).

How did you land the leading role in the Planet of the Apes *TV series?*

I was living in New York at the time, and I got a call from an agent on the West Coast who said that the producers of *Planet of the Apes* were interested in having me come and test for it. I was then about to get married, for the first time, to my sweetheart, [actress] Sally Stark, who I'd been crazy about for a couple of years. I'd proposed to her a couple times and she said, "Are you kidding? Get outta here!"; then she asked *me* a couple of times [*laughs*], and I said, "Hey, what *is* this? I do the asking!" Finally we came to an agreement and decided we were going to get married in June 1974.

Fox wanted me to fly out and test on a Friday. The wedding, which had already been planned for three months, was going to take place in a little church in Riverhead, New York, where she grew up, the following day, Saturday! I knew I could just barely do it—I would of course miss the wedding rehearsal dinner, but that didn't bother me. But I emphasized to the producers, through my agent, that I had to be finished on Friday because I had to get *out* of there Friday night because I was getting married early Saturday morning. With trepidation, I kissed Sally goodbye and I got on the plane and I went out and I did the test.

Had they already told you what you'd be doing in the test, so that you could prepare?

Yes, they had sent me the test material, which I had looked over and worked on. I did the test and I got out of there in time to get on a plane at six o'clock at night. The plane took off and it was out about 45 minutes when the pilot's voice came over the intercom saying, "We've encountered an engine problem and we're going to have to turn back." "Oh, Christ," I said to myself, "open the door and let me jump out, because I'm dead. If I'm not there tomorrow, I'm dead!"—Sally had about ten cousins who were really big, tough guys! The plane turned around and came back to L.A. and I made some frantic calls to her. The problem with the plane was fixed and we got back on, and I did manage to get back to New York, to Long Island, I think about 4:30 in the morning—it was *that* late, almost dawn.

How did you feel you'd done on the test?

I was very hyped-up because I thought I had done a fairly good test, and *Planet of the Apes* looked like it was going to be an interesting project. I knew that Fox had done five movies that had been very successful. And this series was a pre-sold series—there was no pilot, it would be going right into production, which was pretty unusual. I was a little bit tired at my wedding, but I remembered the vows—we had written our own vows and memorized them. We had a wonderful wedding and the reception was great.

Did you get to go on a honeymoon, or did the possibility of a Planet of the Apes *part screw things up?*

We were going to Europe for our honeymoon—we planned to spend a week in Majorca relaxing, just forgetting *every*thing, and then a week in Ireland because she was half-Irish. We were in Majorca for a couple of days when I got a phone call from my agent saying, "They need you to come back. They want to test you again. And they want to lighten your hair." I said, "Tell 'em I'd be *glad* to do it, but I'm on my honeymoon...!" After it went back and forth for about two days, I was told that it was really important that I come back because they wanted to start [shooting on the series] in about two weeks—*very* quickly. They were willing to fly me back, and I stipulated, "*And* my bride. I'm not gonna leave her here alone!" They agreed to everything—"Okay, fly them *both* back, first-class, put 'em up in a hotel. We just need to get him back here!" Once I got back to Fox, they lightened my hair and I tested again—I was still testing for the part, [up against] five or six other guys. Then I got on a plane, my young bride and I, and we went back to New York. We were there two or three days when I found out Fox wanted me—I had the part. But now they wanted me to test opposite some *other* guys so that they could figure out who they wanted to get for the part of Pete Burke! So I had to fly *back* to L.A. [*laughs*], and test with about six guys who were vying for the part of Pete. Jim Naughton was one of them—I think it was his second audition for the part. Then I flew *back* to New York [*laughs*], and within a week I was told, "They're ready to start shooting, you've got to come back." So I said, "Hey, Sally, listen, good luck with your married life. I'll be out in California!"

Was she working at the time?

Yes, she was on a soap. So I went back and we started shooting immediately. That's how fast it all happened. Sometimes things happen like that and sometimes they take forever—sometimes it'll be months before you hear anything. This went bang bang bang. It was a harried but very exciting time.

What was the first episode you shot?

It was "The Good Seeds."

Which was not the first episode to air.

That's correct. They did that deliberately, and they were very smart about it. Before they would shoot the first episode to reach the air ["Escape from Tomorrow," in which Alan and Pete's spacecraft crashes in the ape-dominated futureworld], they wanted me and Jim to be comfortable and experienced, and they wanted everything running smoothly. So we shot "The Good Seeds" and then another episode, maybe "The Gladiator," and I think the third one we shot was "Escape from Tomorrow." The thinking was, "Ron and Jim will be better, they'll know their way around, they'll know each other. It'll be an easier and a smoother production." By the way, the spaceship in that first episode, where we crash on the planet—that was left over from the first *Apes* movie. We used a *lot* of the stuff from the movies. I think our uniforms were from the original movies too.

When you started on the series, how familiar were you with the movies? Had you seen any of them?

The first one. I had not seen the other ones.

Working for the first time in an Apes *episode—how did you like the experience?*

I liked "The Good Seeds"—I liked it a lot. It was warm, and it was not terribly violent. In it, I was living with a farm family of apes and teaching them about modern farming methods, particularly the young son who said, "Oh, we don't use the good seeds [kernels of corn] for planting because that's silly, that's wasteful"; I told him, "You're wrong, the good seeds make the best crops." But once the series was on the air, we were told that the network [CBS] wanted more action. "All the sentimental, warm, folksy stuff is great," the network told the studio, "but ... that ain't *Planet of the Apes*. Get those apes out there with the guns and

The uncertain life of an actor: Ron Harper unexpectedly found himself cutting short his honeymoon in order to grapple with 31st-century apes at 20th Century–Fox.

have 'em start shootin' some people and fightin'. Get some action goin'. Forget that sentimental crap!" [*Laughs*]

Going into it, you thought it would be a successful series and a good opportunity, correct?
Without a doubt. The five *Apes* movies had made millions and millions of dollars. It was my fifth series, after *87th Precinct* and *Wendy and Me* with George Burns and Connie Stevens and *The Jean Arthur Show* and *Garrison's Gorillas*, which was a *great* series.

I was only a kid when that ran, but I loved it. I still remember being crushed when it was cancelled!
You know why it went off? There was a wave running through Congress of "Too much violence on television." A Senator [John] Pastore was leading the charge, saying, "The violence on TV is ruining our youth, and the worst offender is that there *Garrison's Gorillas*." We were a war series, I figured we were safe [*laughs*] — people *were* shooting at other people during the Second World War! Our share never fell below a 32, which was a good share. But they said the violence was very bad. Things have changed, boy!

Talk about your Apes *co-stars Roddy McDowall and James Naughton.*
Roddy McDowall was a wonderful gentleman, and an excellent actor. And, God, such patience, such endurance! He had to come to work at 3:30 in the morning because it took three hours for the makeup people to put those appliances on his face. He couldn't sleep while they put the appliances on, so he listened to classical music. He was a sweet guy and a bright guy, and I found him very interesting. He even had a sense of humor. At one point he gave me a tall director's chair, and it had my name on the back of it: It said **RIN HOOPER** [*laughs*]. He said, "Oh, I'm sorry — did I misplace a few letters?" I said, "Well, it's really *Ron*, but ... Rin is close enough. And it's really *Harper*...." Then he laughed and he brought out the *real* covering for it, and it said **RON HARPER** [*laughs*]. I still have it!

TV Guide *said that McDowall was rumored to be getting $25,000 an episode, which I assume in 1974 was quite a good salary.*
It would have been an *excellent* salary in those days. I don't know where they got that figure but if they *didn't* pay him that, they really *should* have! But in those days, [TV salaries] weren't that much. Whatever he got paid, I'm sure it was not nearly enough for the amount of work that he did. I mean, consider his reputation, his body of work ... and consider what he *endured*, which was three hours of makeup every morning. I don't want to tell you for publication what *I* made but, at the time, for me, it *was* a lot of money, because it was more than I had been making in the theater in New York. There I was getting like 150 a week.

And James Naughton?
He was married and had a very nice wife and two little kids. One of my most vivid memories of him: We were on location on the back ranch at 20th Century, shooting something around a lake, and he was on one side of the lake and I was on the other. Suddenly he started singing with this *beautiful* baritone voice. I said, "Jim — I'm surprised — where'd *that* come from?" He was an excellent singer! Years later he won a Tony, Best Actor in a Musical, for *City of Angels* [the 1989–92 Broadway musical comedy].

The character Jim played, Pete Burke, did not like being on a planet *with* the apes, he didn't like what was going on at all. He would be dragged into the various adventures against his will, which makes for a very good comic relief part; one "hero" and one guy who's reluctant and being comic about it makes for a very nice combination. Some people felt that, if the part of Burke had been played with a little bit *more* humor, the combination of a hero and a "reluctant hero" on the series would have been a *better* combination.

All the ape actors—what challenges did you see them facing on a day-on-day basis?

Those poor sons of.... [*Laughs*] It was a three-hour job, putting appliances on those guys. The makeup people had to glue those on individually and hold them and set them. *And*, they were all different—there was not *one* ape mask, they were all different faces, so that each character had a distinct, characteristic personality. It got to be like 120 degrees underneath those masks, particularly out on location at the 20th Century–Fox Ranch in Malibu. Poor Roddy! After about two or three episodes, his face looked like raw hamburger. Raw, red hamburger. They had to give him like two weeks off, to let his skin breathe and come back to normal again. I don't know how those ape actors could stand it. They would eat with very long spoons, to get the food way back there [into their real mouths]. Roddy had a long cigarette holder, so he could smoke his cigarette all the way back.

And not a lot of 'em got to do much real acting through all those appliances and hair.

It was difficult for some of them, ones who were not that experienced, to do certain things. For instance, the exaggerated mouth movements that were necessary if they wanted to get their mouth appliance to open wider. Some of the ape actors, you'd hardly see their ape mouths move while they were speaking. Roddy of course was the best one because he'd had much more experience, because of all the movies he did. He used his mouth and his *eyes*, and you could see the different expressions. Some of the other actors had to really strain to try and get a different expression.

On *Planet of the Apes*, Harper played a 1980 astronaut time-transported, along with fellow spaceman James Naughton, to a gorilla-ruled futureworld. Roddy McDowall (left) as a considerate chimpanzee helped the fugitives stay one step ahead of their persecutors.

Ron Stein is a name you'll see a lot in the show's credits. He was a very good stuntman and I became very fond of him. He doubled me a little bit, before they got a different double who looked like me. In one of the episodes ["The Legacy"], I jumped down off of a window ledge and I was supposed to fight with a gorilla. Ron, who was dressed and made-up as an ape and standing nearby, came over to me and suggested a couple of moves that he said would probably "sell" as possibly capable of incapacitating a gorilla. I said, "That's *very* good!," and he thanked me. This was at a time when they had not yet selected a head stunt person, so I called Stan Hough, our producer, who's gone now, and I said, "You know something? Ron Stein is an *excellent* stuntman." I was saying that not only because of that incident, but because I saw some of his other work. I told Stan, "You ought to make him the head stunt person, because he knows what he's doing. He's smart and he's got the experience. And he presents it [to the actors] in such a way that it's very easy to accept it. Which is very good for a leader." So they made him the head stunt person. And he was a wonderful guy. By the way, it was kind of funny: I thought the gorillas [I'd be playing opposite] would be *big* but when we did the show, it seemed to me the gorillas were very short. But then I realized, most of our *stuntmen* were short [*laughs*], and so they couldn't *do* anything about it!

A favorite episode?

"The Horse Race," in which I competed in a race against an ape. I knew how to ride pretty well because, years earlier, I'd worked on a ranch out in South Dakota for one summer. The other ape was played by a stuntman, a guy who had been a regular, and he really could *ride*. I said, "Jesus, where'd you learn to ride like that?," and he said, "That's my *bag*, baby!" I don't know if he was a jockey or not, but he was an *excellent* horseman. There's one scene where you can see that I'm riding full-out and he's riding next to me, and he starts hitting me with his whip, and then I grab the whip—it's an old, standard thing in Westerns, where you take the whip out of the other rider's hand and smack him back with it. He worked with me on that, and we were even able to keep the horses going at a pretty good clip as we carried this off. And the stuntmen *hated* horses. They said, "They're dumb animals, and they're heavy, and you can't predict them and you can't really control them!" So ... they hated horses! I had three stuntmen working on that episode, doubling me. Two of them broke a leg, and one wrenched his ankle or his knee so badly he was incapacitated for the rest of the shoot. All three injuries involved the horses.

Who was your regular stuntman?

Glenn Wilder doubled me, particularly on very difficult stunts, or intricate ones. I had at least two others: One was the son of the actor John Ireland and he was a very good double, he had blond hair and looked like me a little. And there was one other young guy.

Do you remember the two other regulars on the show, Mark Lenard [Gen. Urko] and Booth Colman [Zaius]?

Not very well, though I was very fond of 'em. Mark was wonderful ... *he's* gone now, too. But I didn't get to know the [actors who played] gorillas very much at all. They were there three hours before me, and at night I'd be gone while they were still getting out of makeup. I remember one time when I was riding back from location in the van, and I said to a guy who was also getting a ride back, "Hi, I'm Ron. What's your name?" He said [*after a pause*], "...Ron." I said, "...What? ...Who? ...Are you...?" He said, "Ron *Stein*," and I said, "Oh, for Christ's sake!"

Somebody you'd been working with day in and day out!

Yeah! So, you see, I had no idea what my [co-workers] looked like, because *some* of 'em I never saw out of their makeup. Booth Colman's another one that I don't remember seeing *out* of makeup for the entire series. I see him a lot now at autograph shows. He goes to a *lot* of the shows, and I've sat with him a couple of times. He's very active with that, I think he's got a nice little second career going!

Where was Planet of the Apes *shot?*

Apart from the studio? Generally on the 20th Century–Fox Ranch out in Malibu. At that time, they had maybe 50, 75 acres. It was a good location because there were no telephone poles or anything, so it looked "natural." The original sets from the *Apes* movies were still up at the Ranch, so of course we took advantage of that. Then another favorite spot was north of Malibu, on the Pacific Coast—the episode with the hang glider ["Up Above the World So High"] and the shark episode ["Tomorrow's Tide"] were shot over there. Do you remember the scene in "Tomorrow's Tide" where James and I swim under flaming water trying to spear fish? We shot that in a pond on the back lot at CBS in Studio City, where they shot *Gunsmoke* and a lot of things. The flames were coming up from gas pipes. The director Don McDougall had me walking into the water ... and walking into the water ...

With most of his co-stars buried under ape makeup, Harper sometimes wasn't sure who he was playing opposite. Director Don Weis seems to know.

getting closer and closer to the flames. When I was about 20 feet from the flames, Don said, "Go out further, Ron." So I went out another 15 feet and asked, "Okay?" He said, "Go a little further." Finally I'm practically *touching* the flames—which didn't *bother* me, but I knew that if I *did* get burnt, it would interfere with their production schedule [*laughs*]! I said, "For Christ's sake, I'm almost in the flames! What do you want to do, *toast* me, or *what*?" Don said, "Okay, that's far enough, Ron, back down!"—and he laughed. He said, "I wanted to see how far you'd go!" Don McDougall—I liked him!

What do you remember about shooting the underwater scenes in that same episode?
We shot that off Catalina Island, in about 35 feet of water. Jim and I put on face masks, and we had mouthpieces in our mouths, and there were air tanks for us, and two stuntmen took us down to the bottom, about 35 feet. To help us stay down, they'd also put lead weights in those rags that we wore, and we would grab a-hold of some seaweed or some rocks. They'd get the camera in position, and this really phony-looking mechanical shark [*laughs*], and when the shot was all lined up, [the stuntmen] would rip off our masks and take out our mouthpieces and get out of the shot, and then we would swim around acting for about a minute at the most, and then come up to the surface. We kept repeating that all day long. The important thing that you have to remember when you're doing scenes like that is, you don't puff out your cheeks, you keep your face looking the way it would on the surface [*laughs*]!

Did your show use a lot of sets made for other *TV shows or Fox movies?*
There's one that took place in a castle ["The Legacy"].

A castle right in the middle of what was supposed *to be Oakland, California—that was very strange!*
Again, I enjoyed that episode, because it was a kind of an *acting* thing with Zina Bethune and the little boy [Jackie Earle Haley] playing her son. They were supposed to be symbolic of my character's wife and son on Earth, back in 1980. Anyway, that castle set was left over from a Mel Brooks movie, *Young Frankenstein* [1974]. It was going to be torn down, so Stan Hough, who was a hands-on producer, asked, "*When* do you have to tear it down?" They said, "Next week." He said, "All right, we're gonna shoot it." [*Laughs*] So we shot it *that* week! To save money, they tried everything they could do! Do you remember the episodes set in the wrecked city with the huge piles of rubble?

I was very impressed by those sets. On a TV show budget, I thought they looked great.
You know *why*? We shot that on the back lot of MGM, when they were tearing it down!

Oh, that's brilliant!
MGM had that beautiful back lot—the back lot where we shot *Garrison's Gorillas*, by the way. But in 1974, MGM sold it off, and now they were destroying those city street sets. So, of course, 20th Century-Fox jumped in and said, "Hey! You mind if we use those rubble-strewn streets?," and we did. Those streets became our "destroyed cities." So, yes, it did look authentic—because it *was* real!

Any guest stars stand out in your mind?
Royal Dano, who was in "Escape from Tomorrow," I always admired because somewhere along the line I'd seen him play Abe Lincoln—and he *looked* like Abe Lincoln! He was gaunt and everything, and I always thought of him as Abe [*laughs*]. Beverly Garland ["The Interrogation"] has a hotel out here, and that's where they have celebrity autograph

shows two or three times a year. She was on my first series, too, *87th Precinct*, as a guest star. William Smith was in "The Gladiator" and, boy, was *he* well-built. I'm still friends with him—in fact, I've become *better* friends with him in the last five or ten years. He's an interesting guy because he's such a weightlifter with those arms and that chest, but he's also very bright. He speaks, I think, five languages. Isn't that amazing? And a nice guy.

Sondra Locke ["The Cure"] I liked. That was an episode where there was a disease sweeping a village and everybody was contaminated, and she was nursing some of them through it. I have to tell you something: After acting with her in a couple of scenes, there was something *so feminine* about her that I could picture myself easily falling for her. So I can see why Clint [Eastwood] was interested! She's one of those women who exudes femininity, and you just become so attracted to that.

Some of the 14 episodes are, in my opinion, just "The Fugitive *with Fur," but a number of 'em are interesting and feature some surprises. What did you think of the writing?*

Remember I told you that, soon after the beginning, they wanted to go for much more action than the dramatic, "real" stuff? As a matter of fact, one of the associate producers talked to me at one point about "The Good Seeds" and about my *voice*. As an actor, you don't think about your voice when you're trying to do good acting, you just do what you're

Steering clear of gorilla aggressors got complicated when Harper's character became caught up in the lives of future humans.

In his first series role, Harper (right) brought law and order to 1960s television co-starring in *87th Precinct* with Norman Fell (left), Gregory Walcott and, seated, Robert Lansing.

feeling and you try to get that feeling across. He said, about my voice, "You're a *very* good actor, and you did that sentimental scene with the young boy *so* beautifully. But ... we would like you to use [*Harper starts talking in an extremely low voice*] your deeper voice, your masculine, he-man voice." I said, "Really?," and he said, "Yeah, we want that deep-chest voice." And I thought to myself, "Oh, Christ...." [*Laughs*] "Here they go again!"

Now, to answer your question about the writing ... here's the thing: Moments like that one in "The Good Seeds" were what I really enjoyed. "The Good Seeds," the one with Zina Bethune and her little boy, *those* moments. *Garrison's Gorillas* was a lot of action too, but on that show we also had breaks in there where we [Harper's "Lt. Garrison" and his commandos] talked with each other, and the audience could see some humanity. But CBS wanted more action in *Planet of the Apes,* so your statement about "*The Fugitive* with Fur" is exactly right. After a while, in every episode, one of us, Roddy, James or me, would get captured by the apes and the other two would rescue him. We took turns. Whose turn is it to get captured?, is it Roddy, me or Jim? And I thought, "This is getting to be monotonous." This was a science fiction thing and we could have gone anywhere in the world we wanted with our imaginations. I wished we were doing something more interesting than capture-rescue, capture-rescue. If you get a chance, look at *Land of the Lost*, a series I did after *Planet of the Apes*—it just came out on DVD. In their stories, they used some of the old myths, like the Medusa, and the Flying Dutchman. Those were much more interesting than some of our *Planet of the Apes* stories once they degenerated into "*The Fugitive* with Fur." I think that's one of the things that curtailed what should have been a longer run.

The series started out with your character several times mentioning the wife and kid he left behind in 1980, and also determined to find a computer and some advanced humans and somehow trying to get back *to 1980. But after just a couple episodes, I don't know if any of that was ever mentioned again.*

I agree with you that we needed [some continuing story arc]—because, obviously, the way we ended up going was not very successful. I mean ... 14 episodes, y'know [*laughs*]? But somebody up there was thinking, "Let's not get into the homey, dramatic, heartwarming stuff. Forget the wife and the kid, go out and fight a few gorillas!" If a show does that kind of thing often enough, people will think, "This is gettin' boring." Early on, Alan Virdon did carry around a computer disc [that contained flight information about their space voyage] and he thought that, if he could get it to a computer, that might give him an idea how to travel *back* through time. By the third or fourth episode, one day I said, "I can't find the computer disc [prop]," and they said, "Never mind, we're not gonna use it any more!" [*Laughs*]

Alan and Pete, in my opinion, needed to have a goal, *like the Fugitive did—he had to find the One-Armed Man. The goal for Alan and Pete should* not *have been, every week, to be able to hike over hill and dale and stay out of the way of the gorillas!*

Exactly, there had to be something more than capture-rescue. I think, had the series gone on, as they intended it to, they may have brought in some more imaginative writers.

With parallels to the days of slavery, Planet of the Apes *could have "said" something. Do you think that would have been a good idea, or no?*

Yeah, I *do* think so. I wanted it to be a little bit deeper than it was.

There were toys and trading cards connected with the series, yes?

Oh, God, a lot of them. They expected to sell a lot of merchandise off of this series. About ten years ago, when my daughter Nicole was five or six, we were in a museum here in Los Angeles, and they had a display of memorabilia, of "Americana." And there was a lunchbox from *Planet of the Apes* with my picture on it! She looked in the case and said [*in a high voice*], "Daddy! Look! There's your lunch bucket! You're in the museum!" [*Laughs*] I thought, "Maybe someday I'll be in the Smithsonian!"

Did you have a chance to do any promoting of the show?

No. I did a lot of interviews for the show, but there wasn't time to go out on the road. I would have done *anything* they'd asked me to do, but [the show didn't last]. Everybody expected it to be a big hit, everybody expected it to go five years, and then....

Your reaction when you found out it was being cancelled? Were you surprised?

I had seen the writing on the wall. About three or four episodes before the end, I'd realized, "This is a boring series." It had become what you and I just talked about, "*The Fugitive* with Fur." "Whose turn is it to get captured?"; "Not *me*, I did it *last* week!"

The 2001 Tim Burton Planet of the Apes—*did you see it?*

I thought it was crappy. My daughter and I went to see it, and I kept falling asleep. And that ending! I didn't understand it, so I asked my daughter, and she didn't understand it either. I later read an article that said about 65 percent of movie critics could not figure out the ending.

I left the theater annoyed, because the ending was so senseless.

I don't blame you. It *didn't* make any sense.

It wasn't bad enough that we went to see this sucky movie, it was like the movie also gave us a big raspberry on the way out!

Exactly!

A couple of your more recent genre movies have been for director Fred Olen Ray.

I'm very, very fond of Fred. When I did the first one for him, *Venomous* [2002], I'd just had an operation on my right shoulder for a rotator cuff, and my right arm was still mending from that. Well, Fred was unbelievably solicitous. In one scene, I was working on an old barn and I was supposed to be picking up some two-by-fours, and [because of Harper's operation] Fred told me to use my left arm instead of my right. Well, in order to make it *possible* for me to use my left arm, he had to change all the lights, change the camera direction, he went to a lot of trouble so that I wouldn't have to use my right arm. And he told everybody, "*Nobody* get near Ron's right shoulder."

Vowing to continue "as long as anyone still asks me," Harper has been more recently seen in the sci-fi action films *Venomous* **and** *Glass Trap.*

which was very solicitous of him. Then he called me again and the next one was called *Glass Trap* [2005]. I went and I did it, and again he shot it very well. We were shooting on Father's Day and his wife and his two sons came in with a Happy Father's Day cake, and he was very, very touched. I'm very fond of Fred and I think he does excellent work, and he's very loyal to some of us "more mature" actors who are not being sought after [as much as in earlier years]. He's wonderful with actors.

Right now, what future plans have you got?

I recently did a movie called *Touched* [2005], another independent film. This one's a drama, very well-written by a guy named Timothy Scott Bogart. It stars Jenna Elfman and it's got some pretty good actors in it, like Bruce Davison. It's an interesting dramatic story about a guy who sees his little boy killed in an automobile accident, and goes into a coma, and when he comes *out* of the coma, he has lost his sense of touch—he can't feel anything. I play a doctor in it. Something else I've been doing lately is a lot of interviews and commentaries for my series going to DVD. I just did one for a movie I did called *The Soldier* [1982]. I wasn't the major actor in it, but ... I don't think they could find anybody else [*laughs*]! And I did an on-camera interview for the *Land of the Lost* DVD, and that turned out well. So at this stage, it's whatever comes up that I want to do, and that *they* want me to do. I came into this profession because I loved acting more than anything. And still do—except for Nicole. And I will continue doing that as long as anyone still asks me.

CHARLES HERBERT

For some reason, science fiction and horror movies have never been [appealing] to me. Maybe it's because of all the work I did in 'em!

A giant robot, a human-fly, a fly-human and 13, count 'em, 13 ghosts were loose on the sets of Charles Herbert's various genre films; who would have suspected that a grim scenario was also brewing *behind* the scenes? Herbert's career as a kid actor was great while it lasted but, too typically for pint-sized performers, it was the recipe for trouble later in life. He survived encounters with the title characters in *The Colossus of New York* and *The Fly* (both 1958), William Castle's *13 Ghosts* (1960) and even with Blackbeard (in Bert I. Gordon's *The Boy and the Pirates*, 1960), *plus* a pass through the Hollywood gristmill; and now, with the hope that what ultimately happened to him won't happen to others, he tells his tale...

According to the books, you were born in Culver City on December 23, 1948.
   The books are accurate.

Did you have any other family members in the movie-TV business?
   [*Laughs*] Absolutely not! They didn't know anything about the business at all. I just happened to be riding on a bus one day, and a gentleman who was a talent agent in Hollywood, named Cosmo Morgan, saw me talking with my mother, and must have thought I was cute or something. He gave me his card—which I immediately tried to give to the bus driver! I must have known something even then [*laughs*]. That's basically how it started.

What was the first job that you landed?
   I was four years old and I did *Half Pint Panel*, which was a TV show back in ... probably 1952. The first movie I did was one that Desi Arnaz and Lucille Ball did together, *The Long, Long Trailer* [1954]. I went in with like 40 kids and they picked *me* [to play a role]—and then they cut me out of the movie! That was my first experience! I should have known that this *meant* something! You can see that I'm taking a negative tone, but I'm just being honest.

At what point does your memory of these things begin?
   In all honesty, I have a unique memory. I can tell you what clothes I was wearing 35 years ago ... but I can't tell you what I had for *dinner* last night. I guess it's a semi-photographic memory. From the time that a person can *have* a memory, I remember almost *every*thing.

Oh, fabulous.
　Not necessarily [*laughs*]! Not necessarily!

Being a kid actor ... it wasn't *all autographs and sunglasses, was it?*
　No. And I have an obligation.... [*Pause*] I know that you want to talk with me about my work in science fiction movies, and that's just fine, but there's an obligation I have to ['50s kid actor] Paul Petersen and an issue that I must address. I won't dominate the interview with this, but I wouldn't be able to look myself in the mirror if I didn't at least address the issue of the child actor situation.

I've got a dozen questions for you about that.
　I want you to understand something: It's not about *me*. Whatever I "lost" as a child actor, I'll never get back. But there are child actors working today that I need to speak my piece for. I understand that's not why you've called, but I was hoping that you at least were familiar with that, because it's an issue that is very significant.

Like I said, I've got a whole bunch of questions along those lines and I was hoping you *would be willing to talk about it!*
　It's not something I *want* to do, because it's not a pleasant situation for me. But it's something I will *have* to do—okay? Shoot.

With all those TV shows, and all those movies, was there much room in your life for school and other activities?
　Education for the child actor is non-existent. The law states that you, the child actor, must do three hours of schoolwork [a day] while you're working in the studio. They have a schoolteacher who comes in and you're supposed to go to school for three hours. Now, in those days, that schoolteacher was not even certified. The people they were using were retired schoolteachers who needed the job. You [the child actor] would sit there with the schoolteacher for a little while, say 20 minutes, but if they needed you out on the set, they would come in and say, "Look, we need Charlie." The schoolteacher would say, "He's got another half-hour to go, I can't let him go." And the schoolteacher would then be told, "Well, that's fine. The person who replaces you will let him go."

And when you weren't *in a movie, I assume you went to school like every other kid.*
　I went to *public* schools. My parents made that mistake, without malice—they were not too familiar [with the problems that child actors face]. Most kid actors went to schools for kid actors. *I* went to Melrose, Fairfax High, Bancroft, all regular public schools. That was a major mistake because after a while, with me being in all those movies and over 50 TV shows, I got to be very well-known. So it was very uncomfortable for me to be in that atmosphere. I made up the story that I had a twin brother—that it wasn't me they were seeing in movies and on TV, it was my twin brother the actor. I *tried* to get away with that, anyway. And when I got an acting job and I had to ask my [public school] teachers to give homework to me, so I could bring it in to the studio teacher, they were very resistant. It was extra work that they had to do, and they resented that. Now, there were some great studio teachers, I'm not saying they all were bad—Lillian Barkley comes to mind. And I had some great teachers in my *public* schools. But I also had some who resented the fact that they had to put in extra time to give Charlie extra homework to take to the studio, and they wouldn't do it.

Did this bother you at the time?

Actually, *at the time* it was no big deal for *me* because I was always under the impression, "I don't need an education. I'm gonna be an actor for my whole life. Who needs an education?" Well, guess what? It didn't work out that way. I needed an education, and I didn't *have* one.

I've always figured that had to be one of the pitfalls of being a kid actor: You get your schooling in dribs and drabs, there are probably lots of distractions—and then when you're older, everybody's got a leg-up on you.

Believe me, it's like starting a mile run one lap behind everybody else. I want you to understand something: I have had a lot of dysfunctional areas in my life, and for a while I blamed it all on being a child actor. It took me a long time to realize that if, for example, you walk under a tree and you get hit on the head by a branch eight, nine times in a row, the tenth time you gotta take responsibility for walking under that same tree. I *knew* what the problems were after a while, and I didn't correct 'em. So now I don't blame everything in my life on [the acting career], I don't look at each of my problems and say, "Well, *this* is because I was a child actor, *that* is because I was a child actor." I take my share of responsibility.

I was in a unique situation: My father was sick, he had a heart condition, so he never worked a day in his life. My mother had to take care of my father. And they were much older, they had me when they were 40. The parents [of a kid actor] have an obligation: One of them has to be at the studio eight hours a day *with* you, they have to help you read lines and study and stuff like that. But I was the only one getting a paycheck in my family, out of my father, my mother and myself. (My brother and sister were much older.) Mine was the only paycheck that ever came in. This is what *upsets* me, and is a good example of Hollywood's indifference to child actors: They [the studio bosses] stood back and watched a family of an adult male, an adult female and a child for 15 years, and the only paycheck that ever came into that family was from the child. There was a time when it was an adult male, an adult female and a *four-year-old* child, and the only paycheck was from the child. And no one said, "Hey ... what's goin' *on* here?"

Because they didn't care what's going on here.

That's exactly right. And, see, when you talk about what you lost, I lost a lot more than the financial things. Financial things are way down the list for me. The way that it's set up in Hollywood is, I did 50 TV shows, the 20 movies, the commercials, *all* of that stuff ... and when I turned 21, zero was put away in the bank for me. It was not that way for *every* [kid actor]: If you signed a long-term contract, like for instance if you did *Lassie* or *The Donna Reed Show* or something, they put away like five percent for you. But if you were not on a long-term contract, *all* of the money you earned for the movies, for *all* the TV things, went to your guardians, and your guardians could do with it whatever they saw fit.

What "gets" me is, Hollywood's attitude is, "We got a child actor here, and he's working three months on this movie. How much do we want to make sure that he *has* when he turns 21?" And the answer that they've come up with is *zero*. Now, am I saying I should have had one *hundred* percent? No. The parents deserve at least 50 percent, because it's like a job for them too. *Some*body had to be with me in the studio, plus they had to run lines with me at night. So they put in their time too. But it should *not* be 100 percent for the guardian and zero for the child. There was $1700 in my trust fund when I turned 21 and, believe me, I

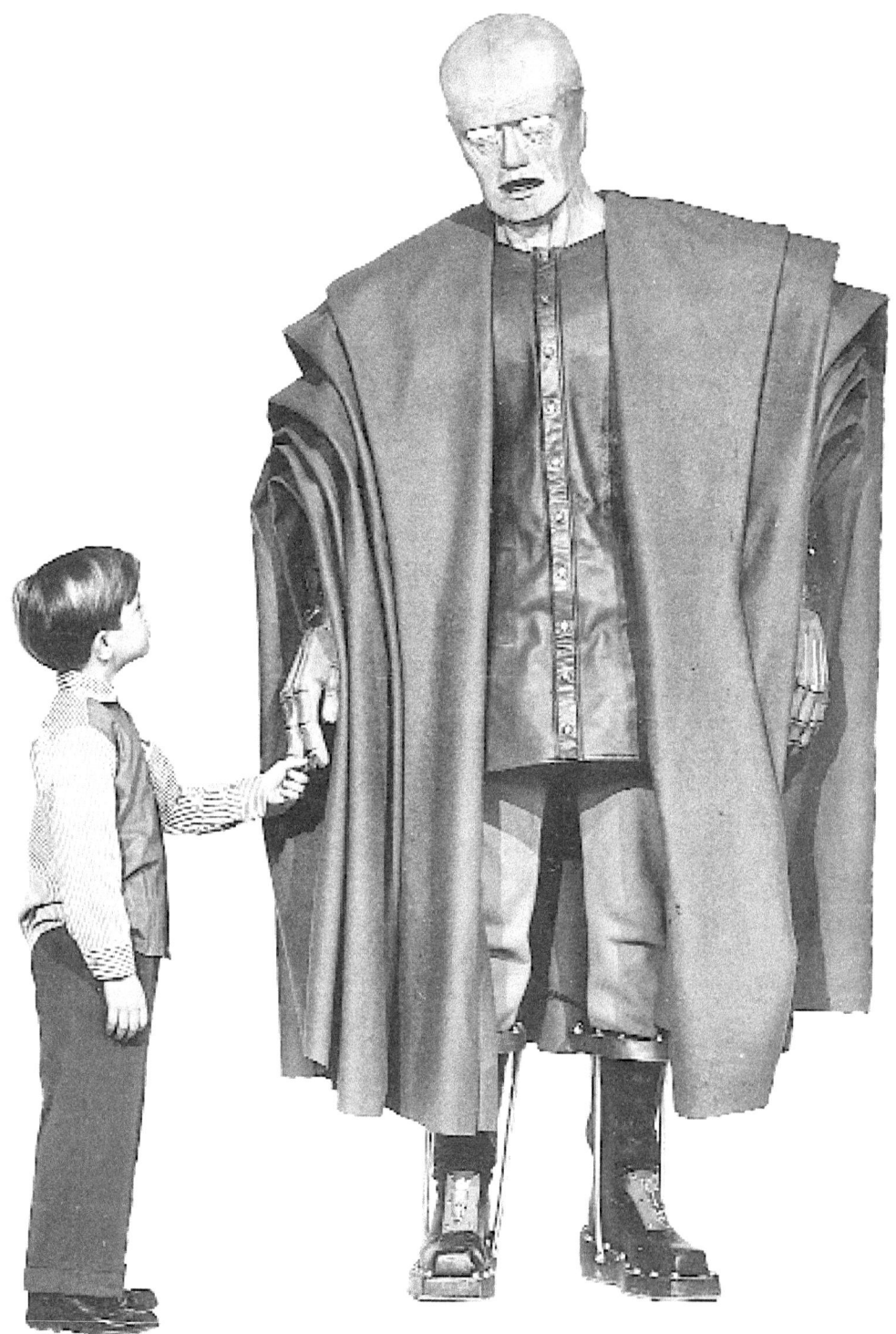

The helmet of the Colossus of New York had to be removed, to show nine-year-old Charles Herbert there was a person (Ed Wolff) inside, before their scenes were shot.

made well over $50,000, I'm sure. I don't *know*, because all I ever did was sign the checks. It's just a good example of the abuse.

It's not the *money*—I never will look back and say, "Boy, if I had all that money...." because I would have probably [blown it]. So that's not an issue. There are a lot more important things that you lose. But that's a good example. And I know ... I *know* that when I make that statement, when I tell a person that after all those years of working I had *zero*, I know that after I hang up the phone or I walk away from the person, they think, "Well, now, wait a minute. That's not possible. It can't be possible that he could work for three months on *Houseboat* [1958] and make $25,000, and when he turned 21 he got *zero* out of that." *That's* the number—zero.

Well, 1700 in your trust fund.

Okay, right. Only a kid who was on a long-term contract makes out, but even *then* it's only like five percent. Paul Petersen is doing everything he can to try to alleviate these things. He's just a marvelous person. [Petersen addresses these issues on his website, www.paulpetersen.com]

The first sci-fi movie you made was The Colossus of New York.

With Ross Martin. I've seen it on TV numerous times. They had a big, huge guy [Ed Wolff] who played the Colossus. I was scared a little bit, because the guy was like eight, nine feet tall. They had to take his helmet off so I could see there was a real person inside. Actually, they took his helmet off because I kicked him in the knee [*laughs*]!

You did that when you were nine years old. Nine isn't old enough to know not to be scared of a "robot" on a movie set?

As soon as he took off his helmet and I could see that he was not a real giant, I wasn't scared. But, yes, they had to familiarize me with the fact that this was not a real giant.

Were you kidding me, or did you actually kick him?

Yes, I was kidding, I did not kick him. Listen, I was cute but I wasn't stupid—the guy was eight feet tall, I'm not gonna kick him. Or if I *was*, I was gonna kick him in between ... *you* know ... that area there [*laughs*]!

Any memory of some of the people in the cast?

Ross Martin, who played my father, was just a wonderful person. I don't remember my "mother" in that, Mala Powers, very much, but Ross Martin was an extremely nice man. And anybody who is in that category [a well-known actor] who is nice to the children is a nice person. 'Cause I worked with some who were *not*, like Doris Day. I worked with her for three months [on *Please Don't Eat the Daisies*, 1960], she never said two words to us kids. Alan Ladd [*The Man in the Net*, 1959] never, never spoke. I think they were actually jealous ... resentful ... of children. If dogs could talk back, they wouldn't have talked to a dog either. But then there were people like David Niven [also in *Please Don't Eat the Daisies*], who was nice as could be. There were actors who would not allow children to get closeups in a scene—the closeups had to be on *them*. People like Sophia Loren and Cary Grant [the stars of *Houseboat*], David Niven, they would rather the child got the closeup. That's the kind of people they were.

Did you like movies when you were growing up?

I gotta be honest: I'm a big movie fan, I always *have* been, but I've never been a big science fiction fan. It's the only category of movies I'm *not* a fan of. I know this is gonna make some of your readers unhappy, but I gotta tell the truth. I love comedies, I love dramas, action ... but I've never been a huge sci-fi fan. For some reason, science fiction and horror movies have never been [appealing] to me. Maybe it's because of all the work I did in 'em!

With all your credits, after a while, did you even have to audition for movies any more?
To answer that question, I gotta jump ahead to a movie I did called *13 Ghosts*. William Castle, who I'm sure you're aware of, called and wanted me to do *13 Ghosts*. That was the movie where you had to wear special glasses—like 3-D glasses—in order to see the ghosts. Castle wanted me to do it, but I had an obligation to do something else. So Castle told my agent that if I would do the movie, he would give me star billing. Star billing didn't mean anything to *me*, I didn't know any difference. And also in the movie, billed below me, were going to be Donald Woods, Martin Milner, Rosemary DeCamp, Margaret Hamilton who played in *The Wizard of Oz* [1939], a number of well-known people. So I did the movie and I was the star of the movie. So I not only didn't have to audition, but I got a bonus by just doing the movie.

The star billing was your bonus.
Yeah. As I've been saying, children and animals are not big favorites with movie stars. Certain people were not friendly on that *13 Ghosts* set, and later on I realized that it was because I had the star billing. Like it was something I had any control over—I didn't even *know*, 'til years later!

The Fly—*what memories of that one?*
I have a lot. Like *13 Ghosts*, which was recently remade, *The Fly* has *also* been remade—and they didn't call me [*laughs*]! In *The Fly* I worked with Vincent Price, and I should have mentioned *him* in the same category with Sophia Loren and Cary Grant. One of the nicest people you could possibly imagine. Extremely.

Can you give me an example of Vincent Price being nice?
People like that, I can't give you specific examples, but the impression they make on you stays with you forever. 'Cause [working on a set] is intimidating for a child. I didn't come from a wealthy family, or from a family that lived that type of lifestyle. When I walked in and saw people like that, it could be very intimidating. But some, like Price, went out of their way, they made sure you understood they were *glad* you were there. And I was good [acting-wise]—I knew my lines, because I have that semi-photographic memory I told you about. They called me One-Take Charlie. And that was important. When you're doing a scene and you make a mistake, it doesn't matter whether it was a significant line or *not*, they have to do it over. So they appreciate having a child who's not gonna make mistakes. I didn't make many mistakes.

That should have taken some *of the pressure off you.*
It did. I was never, never intimidated. I had one 26-line speech in a *Donna Reed Show*, and I got it in one take. Incidentally, I'll tell you one thing you don't want to hear from a director. You could do a scene, and it could be great, everything could seem to go perfect, and the one thing you don't want to hear from the director is, "Cut, that's perfect, that's *absolutely* perfect"—'cause it's gonna be followed by, "Let's do one more." If he says, "Cut," then that was *it*, but if he says, "Great, perfect, wonderful!," the next thing out of his mouth is going to be, "Let's do another one." [*Laughs*] I'll always remember that!

In The Fly, *David Hedison and Patricia Owens were your parents.*

Not *David* Hedison, *Al* Hedison ... who later changed his name to David Hedison. I could never quite figure that out—he went from Al Hedison to *David* Hedison. Is that *better* [*laughs*]? In those days, didn't guys normally change their name to ... you know ... to Rock? Or Tab? But, no, he went from Al to Dave. Go figure [*laughs*]! To answer your question, both he and Patricia Owens were very nice.

And the director, Kurt Neumann?

A very difficult person to get along with, because he was a European who was very demanding. I didn't have a problem with him that I can remember, but he had that reputation. Remember, though, Vincent Price was in that movie, and he was such a wonderful person, everybody *loved* Vincent Price. So Kurt Neumann was probably less demanding on that movie than any place else, 'cause there was no way you could do a movie and be *around* somebody like Vincent Price and be rude or anything like that. Vincent Price just rubbed off on you, he was so wonderful.

Herbert puts his co-star in *The Fly*, Vincent Price, on his short list of grown-up actors who were considerate to kid actors on movie-TV sets.

The Fly *was a biggie, box office-wise.*

The Fly at that time was a *very* big movie. I went to the Fairfax Theater to see it in the movies, and I very seldom ever went to see any of my own movies. But when *The Fly* came out, I went with some of the kids who knew that I was an actor. There's a scene in there where my mom [Owens] and the housekeeper [Kathleen Freeman] and I are searching for the white-headed fly, and they kept shouting, "Where'd he go? Where'd he go?" And I, as a wiseguy kid in the back of the theater, got up and said, "He went out to get a ham sandwich"—which is not a good thing to say in a Jewish neighborhood! The usher came in and he was going to throw me out of the theater! My friends were all screamin' at him, "You can't throw him out—that's him on the screen!" But he threw me out of the theater!

I've also got to tell ya, *The Fly* was a movie that I actually got scared at. When Patricia Owens pulled that cloth off of Al Hedison's head and revealed that ugly fly head, that really did scare me. And also the famous scene at the end where the fly with the Al Hedison head is in the spider web yelling, "Help me, help me, help meeee!"—that's stayed with me forever. Back in those days, the very few people who *did* know I was an actor, when they were kidding me they'd go, "Help me, help me, help meeee!"

This kid actor career—it turned into problems later in your life, needless to say. But at the time, when you were on the sets of these movies, were you enjoying yourself?

The only time that I really felt comfortable was when I was working. Most of the time I was glad to be there, it was enjoyable. I'm a big sports fan so I got along with the grip guys and the crew, and I always brought my [baseball] glove to work. So, yeah, I enjoyed being there. And because I was good with my lines, I never was scared. I did five *Playhouse 90*s [and other live broadcasts], and I did *The Reluctant Dragon*, which was live theater. I also did a Jell-O commercial with Johnny Carson, and I've got to tell you what kind of person *he* was. We were doing this and it was live, he was doing his lines, I was doing my lines, and I *made a mistake*. I said a line about three, four lines ahead of where I *shoulda* said it. When I realized what I'd done, I looked him straight in the eye and I was panicked—"Oh my God, what did I just do?" He looked back at me, and I had a feeling that *with* that look, he was telling me, "Don't worry, just follow what I do. It's gonna be out of order but it's gonna be okay." He got all that across with a look.

It was live so they didn't yell *cut*, we had to continue on. He said another line.... I said another line ... him ... me ... and, somehow, he got me through it. And if you *saw* the commercial, you could not tell anything had gone wrong. When it was over, he pulled me aside and he said, "You did a great job. Did you know what I was tryin' to tell you?" I said, "Yes, Mr. Carson, I did." So he was *also* a very wonderful person.

You played the son of William Lundigan on his TV series Men Into Space.

I was supposed to work three, four days, something like that, and they were going to pay me $750 for the *week*. But we got it all done in one day, so I ended up getting $750 for one *day*. And that's the only thing I remember about *Men Into Space* [*laughs*]!

You also got top billing in Bert I. Gordon's The Boy and the Pirates.

I have wonderful memories of that too. We did that for a number of weeks, it took a long time. I was in practically every scene, playing a modern Massachusetts kid who's interested in the history of pirates, and then gets transported back in time by a genie to pirate days. I don't know how successful it was, but it was very enjoyable, a lot of fun to do. *Boy and the Pirates* wasn't a *Houseboat*, but it was great.

Why? Because of the kind of part you played?

That, and the fact that I worked with people I liked. Susan Gordon and I were very close friends, and Bert Gordon was a terrific person. Murvyn Vye played Blackbeard, and Timothy Carey played Morgan the Pirate. Do you know who Timothy Carey is? He, on that movie, probably scared me more than the Colossus of New York [*laughs*]! But he was a nice man, and he always tried to make you feel, "I'm not really crazy," and you would say, "Okay." And then he would walk away and you'd go, "He's *crazy*!" He was a scary man.

Again, can you give me a for-instance?

It was just his eyes—those *eyes*! He'd look at me and I would run behind my mother. And I had to catch up to her, because she was tryin' to find somebody *else* to hide behind [*laughs*]! His eyes, and the way he talked—all the time, he just seemed *angry*, and out of control. But after a while, it didn't bother me. He wasn't somebody who was different off-screen—he was crazy on- *and* off-screen.

And you liked Susan Gordon?

She and I were real close friends. I went to Fairfax and she went to Hamilton, but we socialized, and we did a lot of work together. We went on publicity tours, a lot of different things, and she's just a great person. I'm looking forward to seeing her again at Monster Bash in June [2006].

When Bert I. Gordon first announced Boy and the Pirates, *he said it was budgeted at over a million dollars.*

You keep saying Bert *I.* Gordon—is it necessary to always say I.?

He always used the middle initial in the screen credits. Maybe he liked to be called Mr. B.I.G.

Well, there you go! He let *me* call him Bert.

Well, you let me call you *Charlie.*

So *far* [*laughs*]! I don't know if he really planned to spend a million dollars on it—you have to talk to Mr. B.I.G. about that. The pirate ship stuff was shot on a set, and the beach was ... the beach was.... [*Pause*] Oh, I remember where it was—it was near the ocean [*laughs*]. That's the best I can do! Near the water!

Pint-sized hero Herbert and his gal pal Susan Gordon in the fantasy-adventure *The Boy and the Pirates.* In recent years, the pair has reunited at monster movie conventions.

And, finally, 13 Ghosts.

That was a very interesting movie to do, because it was the first movie, and you can correct me if I'm wrong.... No, *don't* correct me if I'm wrong [*laughs*]. *13 Ghosts* was the first movie where they gave out special glasses that enabled you to see certain things on the screen. In other words, you couldn't see the ghosts without these glasses. That was a big thing. I never realized 'til later on that those glasses were very collectible, and valuable. I sold two to a guy at an autograph show for two dollars apiece, and found out from another guy that *he* was getting *50* dollars for 'em! In that one, I worked for William Castle, one of the biggest horror producers of all time—*House on Haunted Hill* and [1958] *The Tingler* [1959] and so on. I didn't have an awful lot of contact with him—which can be a positive thing, because there were different types of directors. There were a lot of directors, some very successful, who basically just rolled the camera and let the actors act. They didn't do a lot of demanding. He seemed to be that type. And a very gracious person, a nice person.

The cast?

Donald Woods and Rosemary DeCamp were really nice people. And Jo Morrow—I guess you could say, if I had any crushes, then I had a crush on *her*, because she was such a pretty woman. Such a wonderful person, and so *pretty*. There *were* [actresses] like that, who were not pretentious. Donna Reed. She was a beautiful woman ... but you could *talk* to her. She was a *nice person*. Jo Morrow was like that too.

Martin Milner was someone I thought *might* have resented the fact that I had star billing, but I don't know this for a fact so maybe I shouldn't even have said it. But *this* child, on *13 Ghosts*, was doing what he was *told*. I had nobody ask me, "Do you want to be the *star?*," nobody asked me if I wanted to *do* a movie, nobody asked me *anything*. I did what I was told to do, like all child actors do. To resent the child for *anything* is absurd.

What a bastardly thing to do, to give a hard time to a kid who's already under a lot of pressure.

That's right, exactly. I'm not gonna mention names, but there was a very, very successful child actor who at the time could not read or write. He had the kind of memory where they would tell him his lines and he would remember them. But he could barely read or write. You'd say, "Well, how is that possible if you have teachers there who are supposed to be educating this child?" Well, very simple: They were not there to educate him, they were there to get a paycheck. He never *went* to public school, because he did a series and he was constantly at the studio school, which was the only education that he had. He's doing great *now*, by the way.

13 Ghosts—scary when you saw it?

I did go see *13 Ghosts* and we had the glasses. It was very scary. But *The Fly* was *the* scary one, the one that I will always remember, when she took off the cloth over his head. That was one ugly person.

The acting ... did it ever start to "get old," or could you have stuck with it longer if the offers had kept coming in?

The hardest transition is to go from being a child actor, to an adult actor. Because as a child, in all honesty, you don't have to act. You're cued, you remember lines. But for an *adult*, it's different.

Herbert feels that at least one of the other actors in *13 Ghosts* resented his (Herbert's) star billing.

Are you saying that you couldn't do it?

No, I'm not saying that. But I'd been working for 15 years and now they wanted me to study acting. "What do you mean, 'study acting'? I've been *doin'* it for 15 years!" I didn't realize, yes, you *have* to study acting if you want to be a successful *adult* actor. Because as a child, I sometimes just read my lines on the way to the studio, and I could remember 'em. I had *some* dramatic scenes—like when I played a blind boy on a *Science Fiction Theatre* ["The Miracle Hour"], for instance. Basically, though, I was just being a kid, being natural. That was the key word, *natural*. But as an adult actor, yes you have to be natural, but you also have to know how to act.

Once I got out of acting, once I reached the point where they didn't call me any more, I was happy. I didn't want to *do* it. "Great. You don't want *me*, I don't want *you*. Now I can do whatever I want to do." Unfortunately, I then turned around and realized, "Let's see. I don't have an education. I don't have any money. I have no skills.... What the hell *am* I gonna do?" Years later I tried to get *back* into acting, and I found something out. The one thing you need as an actor, to be successful, is: You have to have an identity. In other words, you have to be able to look in the mirror and *see* somebody, you have to be able to see a *person*. I kept looking in the mirror and all I saw was a mustache and hair ... I had no *identity*. And that's the biggest thing that I'd lost, because my identity was one week I was David in *Donna Reed*, one week I was Roberto in *Houseboat* ... *that* was my identity. Charles had *no* identity. If you have no identity when they ask you to act ... you can't *act*. Because you need an identity to become a character. You can't just slip yourself into a role and say, "Okay, I'm *this* guy or *that* guy," you have to have somebody to slip *in* there. I had no one. I *did* try to get back in [return to acting] after a while, and it was worthless, absolutely worthless. I didn't realize 'til later on in my life, when some things happened, when I established an identity, that I did have the ability to do it back then. That I had a natural talent that never goes away. It was something I was born with, so I don't pat myself on the back for having it. I was *born* with an ability to do certain things, like an athlete. But, see, as an athlete, you can just go on the field, and maybe sometimes you don't produce as much as you should, but you'll be able to produce. The abilities and gifts that *I* had, you have to have an identity to perform those, and it took me many, many years, 'til I was out of the business for years, to realize I had that.

Do you ever watch your movies nowadays?

I watch *Houseboat* if it's on, because it has such great memories. Working on *Houseboat* with Cary Grant and Sophia Loren was the most special thing in my whole career. Otherwise ... not really, no.

Do you have a family of your own now?

No, I don't, I've never been married.

If you had to show one of your movies to somebody, which would it be?

Houseboat.

How readily do you admit to having been *an actor, when you're with people who start talking about TV and movies?*

Never. Well, very seldom. If I tell anybody about it, then it's someone I like a lot, someone I feel close to. One of the reasons is—as you can see, obviously—if I'm going to talk about it, it takes a *long time* [*laughs*]! Thank God I'm not on the clock! It's an injustice to just hit-and-run when I talk about that subject, because there's an obligation that I have, because of what I went through, and because of what kids are still going through. The laws haven't changed. [Hollywood] is still abusing children *now*.

What's the worst thing you can lose in your entire life? There are health issues, I understand that, but the *worst* thing a person can lose is your identity. You form *who you are* as a child. When you're growing up, Tom Weaver is becoming who Tom Weaver will be as an adult. If you don't have an identity 'til you're 17 or 18 years old, you're 18 years behind everybody else. And I think the identity is the most important thing a human being *has*, because it's who he or she *is*. If you can't sit in a group of people and feel that you're a person, if you can't feel that Charlie is there with Tom and Bill and Frank and Doug, if you just look at other people, and you look at yourself and you say, "Well, I'm just *here*...," then... [*trails off*]

It's hard to explain, I understand that. But an identity is what you form as a child, and if your identity keeps changing every week, if one week you're Roberto on the screen and the next week you're Fred and the next week you're Tom Sawyer, it's hard to know *who Charlie is*. It's okay as a child because people look at the screen and say, "Okay, he's Fred" or "Okay, he's Tom Sawyer." But when you're an adult, people don't know who the hell you are—you don't walk around with your credits. They want to know who Charlie is. And I didn't know.

Wow. I never heard it put that way before.

Again, I'm not trying to get on a soapbox. I made mistakes in my life, I had a very difficult life. Things are wonderful for me now. But to look back and say, "I blame *everything* on the child acting days...." [*Pause*] Well, I can blame a *lot* on that; the thing is, I knew after a while that that was the problem, and if I didn't make the adjustment, then it's *my* fault.

What has made your life wonderful again in recent years?

I'm now in a situation where I've got a wonderful job, and ... uh ... uh ... uh ... I'm ... uh.... [*Pause*] Well, okay: After 39 years of spending my life on drugs, I'm clean. I'm clean for 14 months now [October 2005].

Congratulations.

Well, it's not a "congratulations" thing ... I *appreciate* that, but the thing is, I spent 39 years consistently doing drugs, and I try to explain to people when I talk about it that there's a difference between quitting doing drugs and *stopping* doing drugs. I was 55 years old when I stopped. I didn't quit, I *stopped*. In other words, I *couldn't* do it any more. I didn't have the satisfaction of "I made a decision to quit"—the decision was made *for* me. I'm grateful that I don't do it any more, but there's a difference, and that's why I tell people that you want to *quit* doing drugs, you don't want to just *stop*.

JIMMY LYDON ON
ROCKY JONES, SPACE RANGER

> *The* Rocky Jones *shows were not ... how can I say this kindly? ... they were not pearls in any department whatsoever. Not in the writing or in the production values or in anything else.*

In the early 1950s, long before the phrase "space race" was coined to denote the *not*-so-friendly U.S.–U.S.S.R. competition to be the first to conquer space, there was a very different type of space race on TV soundstages: casts and crews working against the clock to produce, on tight schedules and budgets, kiddie-oriented adventure series like *Tom Corbett, Space Cadet* and *Space Patrol* (both live shows), among others.

Amidst all the juvenile space jetsam, the made-on-film *Rocky Jones, Space Ranger* stood out because of its better-than-average special effects and the serial-style heroics of stars Richard Crane (as the baseball-capped Rocky) and Scotty Beckett (as co-pilot Winky), patrolling the universe in their spaceship the *Orbit Jet* on behalf of the Alliance of United Worlds. Midway through the series' short run, however, Beckett was ejected from the *Orbit Jet* and replaced in the boyish-sidekick slot by a thirty-ish actor struggling to get his Hollywood career back on track after a lengthy stint in a live New York-based soap opera: long-time juvenile lead Jimmy Lydon.

After the New York soap opera The First Hundred Years, *what prompted your move back to the West Coast, and how did you get the* Rocky Jones *job?*

The move back to the West Coast was very simple. We were the very first ones to ever do a soap opera on television, and at the outset nobody knew if one *could* be done. Six people memorizing 26, 28 pages of drivel every day, 52 weeks a year—and yet we did it. But it was so tough that, after a year and a half, once every month or so, [co-star] Bob Armstrong and I would go up to Benton and Bowles, the agency, and we'd go in to see the head man and say, "We *quit!*" And he'd say, "Come on, fellas, relax now. You know you can't quit. Go back and behave yourselves!" It got to be a running gag with us all! But Bob and I would have *loved* to quit, and when finally the sponsor Procter & Gamble dropped the series after 390 shows, we were *so* glad. They dropped it the end of June, and I left for California with my wife Betty Lou the very next day [*laughs*]!

In Hollywood, if you don't work in motion pictures for a year or so, everybody thinks you're *dead*. I'd been out of the Hollywood scene for a year and a half, and so I had to be reintroduced again somehow or other. And so my agent of many years Danny Winkler began to check around and he came up with a feature and a couple of other things, and a year later the *Rocky Jones* series. And that was that. It was *work*.

*You replaced Scotty Beckett as Rocky's sidekick. You must have known Beckett, you'd done a couple pictures together [*Gasoline Alley *and* Corky of Gasoline Alley, *both 1951]. What were your impressions of him when you worked with him?*

Well, Scotty Beckett was a very bad young man. First of all, he was a very bad loser. Some people play cards on the set to wile away the time between shots, while the crew is lighting and everything else; well, Scotty Beckett played gin rummy and games like that, and when he lost he didn't *pay* anybody. Therefore, he got a very bad rep. Then he began to drink, and all sorts of things that were not conducive to working every day in a very quick series where you need to memorize lots of dialogue. I don't mean to bumrap a guy who's dead, but I don't mind with Scotty. I made those *Gasoline Alley* films with him, he played Corky and I played the other kid, Skeezix, and even then, he was a very bad boy. What happened to him was very sad. I don't know if you know what happened....

Jimmy Lydon (right) with Sally Mansfield and Richard Crane in an episode of *Rocky Jones, Space Ranger.* **Lydon was hired to play Rocky's (Crane) sidekick as a replacement for Scotty Beckett (1929–1968), who was booted off the show because of his drinking and other peccadilloes.**

I've heard a couple different versions. I'd love to hear what you *know.*

Scotty went to Las Vegas during some time off and he wrote several checks for the five or six hundred dollars which he'd lost in the gambling casinos up there. Then he came back to Hollywood and stopped payment on the checks. So "the boys," if you know what I mean by "the boys," came to Los Angeles and said, "Mr. Beckett, you shouldn't *do* that. That's a legitimate debt and you owe us. Now, pay the debt." And he didn't do it. About a month later, they found him in a motel on Sepulveda Boulevard, drunk, out of his *mind* with booze, the motel had been robbed of $11 and he had $11 in his pocket. He'd been set up, obviously, but he was taken to court. But he got out of *that*. He took his wife and absconded to Mexico, where he wrote more bad checks, and just got out of Mexico before they could throw him in the jail *there*. One thing led to another, and finally he was in a terrible crash, and he was paralyzed, and got around in a wheelchair. But from the injury, he *died* when he was fairly young. He was 38 years old. So that was Scotty Beckett, poor man.

And when the Rocky Jones *people dumped Beckett at some point in his colorful career—*

When they got rid of him, I happened to be around, looking to go to work again, and away we went.

When you came onto the show, did you get the impression that Beckett was missed by anybody there?

No, not in the least. This is a very serious and professional business, and if you don't behave yourself, they have plenty of ways to get rid of you. Because when you don't behave yourself, you're costing them *money*. That's the one thing you *cannot* do.

Your character was Biffen Cardoza, an alien, an exchange visitor from the planet Herculon, and yet you played it like the boy next door. Is that what they asked for?

They asked for a kind of bouncing juvenile semi-leading man type of relief from Rocky Jones, who was very serious. They wanted a contrast between those two characters, Rocky who was straight-laced and the kid I played, who was a little bit flighty and fun. That's what we did.

Did you feel you were too old for this boyish role?

It played all right, because Dick Crane was a little bit older than I was. He was a lovely fella and I was very fond of him. *Rocky Jones* was when I met him for the first time.

What did you like about him?

Oh, everything. I also knew his wife, and he had a couple of daughters, and he was just a fine, fine gentleman, a hard-working, professional fella. Years later Dick and I formed a company, Film Trend, as partners, and we ran it out of Allied Artists down on Sunset Boulevard for almost a year. We tried and tried, but we couldn't get arrested making industrial films, and so we abandoned the company finally.

Sally Mansfield, who played Vena?

Very pretty, very bouncy and ... how do I say it?—*alive*. An interesting young leading lady.

The kid, Robert Lyden—no relation, I'm sure.

You're right, he wasn't any relation. He spelled his name in the German manner, L-y-d-e-n, and my name is pure Irish. I have no memory of working with him. But that's [understandable], because we worked very rapidly.

Captures, rescues and escapes were a big part of the kiddie-appeal series. In this shot, Mansfield is helped out of a bind by (from left) Crane, Lydon and their boy sidekick Robert Lyden.

And do you recall any of the producers?

Just Arthur Pierson, who was also a Writers Guild member and a good rewrite man when we were trouble. He could come on the set and rewrite an upcoming scene as we were *doing* a scene, and then we'd pick up the pages for the scene which he'd just rewritten and go and shoot it! And the director, Holly Morse, was a wonderful guy. I'd known him when he used to be an *assistant* director, and then I also knew him when he married [actress] Sally

Eilers. He was her last husband, and they were a very nice couple. Holly was a great big, tall man—he must have been about six-foot-five. A very gentle fellow, and lots of fun. And you *have* to have fun when you're doing those things so quickly. We had some moments that were kind of fun for everybody, and then Holly would say, laughing, "Okay, fellas, c'mon, we gotta get this thing shot!," and we'd go back to work again.

So there was *a little bit of time for fooling around.*

Oh, yes, there *had* to be, because otherwise it'd drive you crazy. Because the *Rocky Jones* shows were not ... how can I say this kindly?... they were not pearls in any department whatsoever. Not in the writing or in the production values or in anything else.

I am able to see them for what they are, but at the same time, I think they're a little better than a 1954 kid show needed to be.

Well, as I say, we were all professionals and we tried very hard with whatever material we had and whatever budgets we had. You tried your best, every time out. We call that professionalism, and we were all professionals in those days. As a director [in more recent years], I've had times when my leading man would arrive on the set and not know the words. I don't consider that professionalism.

You're listed in the credits of every episode as James *Lydon. Were you trying to put "Jimmy" behind you?*

I really didn't have anything to do with [James appearing on-screen]. I've always been known as Jimmy, but I guess the *Rocky Jones* people who put the names on the screen decided that after a certain age you shouldn't be a juvenile any more, you should be a grown-up, and they decided I'd be James. But nobody's ever *called* me James [*laughs*].

Do you recall where you shot Rocky Jones?

Yes, at a studio down from MGM in Culver City, the Hal Roach Studios. They had about four soundstages and a little bit of a lot, and on *Rocky Jones* everything was shot there at Roach, we never went on location. Incidentally, at the time, I had a kind of Spanish house, a big old place way up in the woods above Glendale. It was in the back of this very private kind of street that went up a hill, and once a week I had to put the garbage out down in the front. It's hard to explain the layout to you, but suffice to say that [on foot] it was quite a haul to take the garbage down to the street, so I used to *drive* it down in my car, in the trunk. And about once a month, I'd *forget* it was in the trunk and I'd wind up at Hal Roach Studios with the garbage still in the trunk. The crew used to laugh like hell. My car got a little "flowery" sometimes during the summer [*laughs*].

At the time you were doing Rocky Jones, *did you picture kids being your only audience?*

Y'know, I never even thought about it. It wasn't my department.

Did you ever watch it?

No.

How quickly did you have to work?

We would do, I'd say, 13 to 15 pages a day. In certain master takes, we would run two minutes, sometimes two and a half minutes. Two or three pages of dialogue in one master take, and then they'd bounce in for a couple of close-ups here and there. If anybody made a mistake, we'd keep right on going until we got to the end of the scene, 'cause they could bounce in for a close-up where we made a mistake. (We wouldn't make mistakes purposely

Mansfield, Lyden and Lydon catch some sun. Or moon? Actually, probably neither!

in order to get a close-up ... that'd be kind of cheap.) We *had* to do it that way, because we didn't have that much time. We'd do 13, 14 pages in one day, and sometimes 65, 70 different camera set-ups a day.

You once told me that you got tired of the aftermath of starring in the Henry Aldrich series— people calling out "Hen-reee! Henry Aldrich!" at you for years afterwards. Were you concerned that a long-enough run on Rocky Jones *might turn into a similar situation?*

Again, I never thought of it. I don't mean to be cold and blasé about this business which I love dearly, but to us it was a *job*. Like you'd make a Ford Motor Company vehicle on a production line, that's the way we made film. Once we finished a thing, it was finished, it was over, and you went on to the next one, and the next one, and the next one, hopefully. And if you were lucky, you could continue as I did for 62 years, in front and *back* of the camera.

Did kids ever recognize you in public as "Biff"?

Not that I can remember, although in recent times I've been to a couple of oldtime movie conventions, one in Seattle and one in Newark, New Jersey, and there I met fans like you: fans of *Rocky Jones* and fans of other things I've done. They're very interesting folks and very nice. They're not—forgive me for saying this, but they're not autograph hounds, if you know what I mean. Those people are very rude and sometimes very callous, and almost mean.

Actors put to the test: For series regulars Mansfield, Crane, Lydon and Lyden, the production pace of *Rocky Jones* meant shooting 13 to 15 script pages a day. The old lady with the slingshot is character actress Ida Moore.

I long ago stopped asking my interviewees for autographs, because some autograph hounds can be so loathsome that I want nothing in common with them.

    Please understand, I don't mind *your* people, because that's a different thing. Your people are aficionados of films, and they're fun, and they know more about your life than *you* do. That's very interesting to me, and I enjoy that. But an autograph hound is an autograph hound, a whole different cat. To show you what it's like for us, I remember one time I was dancing with my wife at the Mocambo, the nightclub out here. (I don't like nightclubs, but *she* did.) Anyway, I was on the dance floor with my wife, and suddenly someone grabbed me by the shoulder, wheeled me around and said, "Can I see your teeth?" Now, I didn't know *what* the hell *that* meant [*laughs*]! But that's what they'll do to you!

    When I was a kid actor in the theater in New York, on matinee days we used to have lunch in the Woolworth's 5 & 10 right on Times Square. The wonderful lady there, a grandmotherly type named Emma O'Rourke, loved the theater kids, and Sidney Lumet and I were the two leading juveniles in New York. And I mean *juveniles*—12, 13, 14 years old. We did a couple plays together and we were her favorites. We were such favorites that we'd go in there and we would have lunch for 79 cents, including the tip, which was five or ten cents, and she would give us a scoop of ice cream that wasn't on the bill.

Now, I go to Hollywood and I'm a "star," whatever the hell that means. We weren't really stars, *you* know what a star is. A star is someone who not only gets top billing like we did in little B pictures and things, but a star is somebody who *brings people into the box office*. And we *never* did, we just got star billing on a bunch of little things, and that's *not* a star. But the public doesn't know that, they think we're *all* stars. At one point I had to go back east to be the godfather of my second-oldest brother's first daughter, and this was at a time when the Henry Aldrich series was very popular throughout the country. One day I went into New York City to see a couple of old friends, and while I was there I wanted to try and see Emma O'Rourke. I went downstairs in the 5 & 10 and it got to be a little buzzy and exciting [because people were recognizing Lydon], and a manager came over and I asked, "Where's Emma O'Rourke?" He said, "She doesn't work here any more, she works at Toffenetti's restaurant," which was at Broadway and 43rd Street. I said, "Thanks very much" and he said, "Get outta here before the riot!" I hurried out and I ran down the street and I went into Toffenetti's. The manager came over and I asked for Emma O'Rourke, and he said, "Right in the kitchen there. She's in charge of the salad department."

I didn't know Toffenetti's, and as I ran into the kitchen, I didn't notice that the whole wall between the kitchen and the public was all glass, so customers could see the food being fixed. Well, Emma came over and she gave me a big hug, and it was all grand. I was facing her and *she* was facing the glass wall. All of a sudden, her eyes started getting bigger and bigger and I said, "Emma, what's the matter?" and she said, "Turn around." I turned around, and there must have been 100 people at the wall! The manager came in and he said, "They're going to break the glass, you gotta get out of here!" I said a quick goodbye to Emma and gave her a hug, and the manager took me to the garbage elevator—the kind of elevator that comes right up through the sidewalk! I came up with the garbage cans and jumped into a cab and got away [*laughs*]! *That's* something that we [actors] can't avoid, but of course it doesn't happen to me, *thank God*, any more—it hasn't happened in many years.

There were lots of fistfights in the Rocky Jones *episodes. Did you enjoy doing fight scenes?*

Well, to answer that, I've got to go back a long ways. The very first big picture I made in California was called *Tom Brown's School Days* [1940], from the British novel written by Thomas Hughes in the 1800s. It was about English public schoolchildren, I played Tom Brown in it and Freddie Bartholomew, who *should* have played Tom Brown, played East. We shot this picture for three and a half months. In one scene, after being out at night (which was against the school's rules), Tom Brown had to climb up the side of this tower, kind of a castle-like tower, and then climb through a window to get into the dorm. The cameraman was a guy I knew 'cause I was under contract to RKO and he was one of the favorite cameramen there, Nick Musuraca. While I was sitting around waiting to do the scene, he came over and said, "Jim, you think you can climb that thing?" I was 16 and very athletic and very slight—I was almost six feet tall and didn't weigh over 118 pounds. So I said, "Yeah, sure. Why? What's the problem?" He said, "If you climb it now, I can check the lighting." So I climbed up some tied-together sheets and into the second story window. Only the front of the building looked legitimate, the back was a fake, and so once I got in the window, I went down a ladder that was in the back.

Now, I need to mention that *Tom Brown's School Days* was set in the 1700s or 1800s and we wore top hats, swallow-tailed coats and congress gaiters—period costumes. And when I got down to the bottom of the ladder, there was a guy standing there, just about my size, and exactly the same wardrobe! He said, "Hey, Jim ... you gonna climb the tower in the shot?" I said, "Gee, I don't know. Why?" He said, "Well, I'm the stuntman, and if you climb it, I'm gonna lose my job and I'm gonna break your legs!" He didn't mean it, he laughed, and I laughed, and I said, "Then, no, of course not!" And that's how I began to admire stuntmen for what they do. All the fights we had on *Rocky Jones*, we did opposite stuntmen—stuntmen would be the heavies and we'd fight with them. And the first thing I would do, before a fight scene, was go to the stuntman and say, "You're the expert, tell me what you want me to do," and I would listen. They would take very good care of you, to make sure you looked very strong in the scene, and to make sure that you can "beat them up" without hurting *them* and without hurting *you*. That's how we did the fights. The stuntmen were wonderful, and all my life I've admired them.

How much were you paid for being one of the stars of Rocky Jones?

Not a helluva lot. We shot 'em in three days so maybe $1500 for the three days. I really don't know now.

And no regrets when you found out it was cancelled.

No, no. That's part of the business. We have no control over that. And every time [a series ends], we always swear undying friendship with our fellow players and everyone else, and sometimes we never see them again [*laughs*]. But Dick Crane and I, we did remain friends.

Have you or your kids or grandkids ever watched Rocky Jones *in the years since?*

Never. I haven't even looked at the *Rocky Jones* DVDs you sent me [*laughs*]. I *thank* you for them ... but I don't know what I'm going to *do* with them! Maybe my grandchildren will look at them someday. And, really, I don't *remember* any of 'em [any individual episodes]. I don't mean to sound blasé because we tried very hard every time we got involved with something, no matter *what* the budget was. If it was a big budget, we had lots of time, but if it was a little budget, like *Rocky Jones*, we worked harder and quicker. But once a show was over and they said "Cut! Print! That's *it* for this series," we forgot about it the next day. We *had* to. You can't keep all that stuff in your mind.

These days, you're retired.

I'm in *forced* retirement: At the end of 1999, when I was president of Pegasus Productions, an independent company on the Fox lot, we were thinking about putting together a feature, and so I called the insurers. These companies insure two stars and the director against illness, accident or death for the length of work on a feature. They turned me down, saying it was

Lydon in the early days of his acting-producing-directing career (1937-99), which he contentedly calls his "62 years in a candy store."

because I, at 76 years of age, was too great a risk. No insurance meant I couldn't work so I dissolved the company, packed up my belongings (scripts I own, etc., etc.) and moved off the lot.

I'm very fortunate, I have a lovely home and guest house and pool and spa on two acres in Bonita, and Betty Lou and I are quite comfortable. I'm not filthy rich but I'll never be poor. Our two children, both girls, are doing very well. The older one is a teacher in Albuquerque, New Mexico. The younger is a former businesswoman, now a housewife with two girls; she and her husband are multi-multi-millionaires in England. They have more money than we have, and are as happy as we are. So I'm very blessed. First to be able to work for 62 years in a candy store! Second, to be successful on both sides of the camera. So we are comfortable ... well off ... well cared for by gardeners, housekeeper, pool man and handyman. But I miss our business and I shall for as long as the time I have left on this planet.

As a former Space Ranger, do you take any interest in the space race and NASA?

I don't think I take much more interest than everyone else does. But in my case, maybe a *little* more, because I'm a pilot. I learned to fly before the Second World War—I wanted to be in the Naval Air Corps. So as a pilot, I'm always concerned with anything in the air and in space, and with the modern things that we have today which are so marvelous. I used to own a Beech Bonanza at one time, and I had a lot of fun with that airplane. At this point I haven't flown by myself for two years, but my license is still good.

Since you're a pilot, my last question is: If you'd ever been offered a chance to go into space, would you have taken it?

Oh, I think so, yes, depending on how old our children were and how well financially we were at that moment. If I had enough money to see the family through for a year or two, yeah, I'd take a crack at space.

Even today?

Oh, sure, "even today." I'm not gonna be 84 until the end of this month [May 2007], and I get around pretty good for an 83-year-old guy!

LEE MERIWETHER ON *4D MAN* AND *BATMAN*

> *I was a big moviegoer [as a kid]. And, as for horror and science fiction ... I adored them.*

Being offered the chance to co-star in *4D Man* in 1958 was a pivotal moment in the early acting career of Lee Meriwether, primarily because it was her first feature film after several years of TV work—but also because the former Miss America is, believe it or not, a lifelong horror and science fiction movie fan. Eight years later, she made fantasy film history when she became the first big-screen Catwoman.

Born in Los Angeles and raised in Phoenix, the daughter of an accountant, Meriwether was attending City College of San Francisco in 1954 when a fraternity entered her in the Miss San Francisco pageant. The green-eyed teenager quickly went from Miss San Francisco, to Miss California, to winning the Miss America title on the first telecast of the Atlantic City pageant.

Following the end of her one-year reign, Meriwether continued appearing on TV and even landed a regular stint on NBC's early-morning *The Today Show*. In 1958 came the offer of a *4D Man* leading role from the moviemakers at the Valley Forge Film Studios in Chester Springs, Pennsylvania. Robert Lansing starred as Dr. Scott Nelson, a research scientist who develops the power to go in and out of a "fourth-dimensional state" and pass intangibly through solid objects, without realizing that each feat causes rapid aging; now mentally unbalanced, he begins killing others for their "life energy" which restores his own. In her film debut, Lee, then 23, played Lansing's research lab assistant and girlfriend.

When the popular ABC-TV series *Batman* spawned a big-screen movie in 1966, Meriwether found herself following in some very distinctive paw prints: taking over the role of Catwoman from the series' Julie Newmar. She got right into the spirit of campy fun in her dual role as Catwoman (in that unforgettable, "painted-on" catsuit) and as Comrade Kitanya Irena Tantanya Karenska Alisov (Miss Kitka for short), Gotham City correspondent for *The Moscow Bugle*; the team of Catwoman, The Joker (Cesar Romero), The Penguin (Burgess Meredith) and The Riddler (Frank Gorshin) nearly spelled cat-astrophe from Gotham City's resident crimefighters Batman and Robin (Adam West and Burt Ward). Meriwether had her second Bat-experience guesting on the series itself (a 1967 two-parter with Victor Buono as the nefarious King Tut).

In 1958 when you did 4D Man, *your Miss America victory was four years behind you and you were working on New York TV.*

Yes, and I had gotten married in 1958 to [actor] Frank Aletter—we were living in his apartment in New York, on East 75th. While I was Miss America, and afterwards, I did some TV. And I was using my scholarship money from the Miss America pageant to study theater in New York. I studied with Lee Strasberg and Curt Conway and Lonny Chapman.

Were you still on The Today Show *around the time of* 4D Man?

No, I had finished by then. I went on *The Today Show* right after I crowned Sharon Kay Ritchie "Miss America 1956," and I was on *The Today Show* the tail end of '55 and all of '56—I was their first on-air Women's Editor. I also did a few of the *Philco TV Playhouse* shows in New York, I did a *Men of Annapolis* at Annapolis, and I went out to the West Coast and did a couple of *Matinee Theater*s. But *4D Man* was my first movie, so I was very excited about it.

Were you a movie fan growing up? Did you like horror and/or science fiction movies at all?

I was a big moviegoer. And, as for horror and science fiction, *yes*—I *adored* them [*laughs*]. My favorite movie in that genre was *Invasion of the Body Snatchers* [1956]—oh, I just loved that! Later I got to finally meet Kevin McCarthy, and that was a treat. My *favorite* movie was *13 Rue Madeleine* [1946] with James Cagney.

And favorite stars at that time?

I loved *any* movie with Richard Widmark in it, and I loved Don "Red" Barry and Turhan Bey. Those were my three favorite actors. When I was young I saw everything that I could of theirs, and several times *over* if I had enough money from pulling weeds in the garden. They were the best actors in their particular fields: Of all of the B-Westerns stars, Don "Red" Barry was the best actor. Turhan Bey was the best actor in those Universal swashbucklers. And then starting in the late '40s-early '50s, Richard Widmark was a wonderful actor. They were all outstanding performers. I appreciated [good] acting, obviously, at a very young age [*laughs*]! I'm kinda proud of that.

How did the 4D Man *people come to choose you, do you recall?*

No, and I don't recall reading for the part or anything. I think I was just asked to do the movie. I don't remember any angst about, "Oh, golly, I wonder if I got the part," so I'm sure that it came through my agent and I got the role.

And you were looking forward to it because it was *a movie.*

Oh, yes! *And* because it was science fiction—I loved science fiction. When I was a little girl, my mother would take us to matinees every Saturday at the Strand Theater in Phoenix, Arizona, and one of the first movies of that type that we saw was *The Wolf Man* [1941] with Lon Chaney, Jr. As Lon Chaney changed into the Wolf Man, my younger brother Don crawled across me to get to my mother, to sit on her lap. And she proceeded to tell both of us exactly how it was done.

During the movie?

Yes! And she pretty much hit the nail on the head, she said, "They put a little bit of hair on his face, then they film a little more, then they put a little *more* hair on and they film a little more. He's not really changing into a werewolf." She told us in order to ease Don's horrible angst. And probably mine! I think that took care of any fear I had of [scary] movies. I was always appreciative of that, but … it was like, "Aw, shucks, maybe she *shouldn't* have done that," [*laughs*], 'cause knowing that took away all the fun that my friends always seemed to have in scary movies. While they were having fun being scared, I would just sit there and analyze, "Well, now, how did they slit that guy's throat...?"—that sort of thing!

What were your initial impressions of the people who made 4D Man*?*
The organization was a religious organization, and they had made religious films. Then, to get more money to continue on with *that* work, they decided to make two science fiction movies. They made *The Blob* [1958], and it was successful enough to generate enough money for them to continue with their religious work. Then I guess they needed more money, so they decided to do *4D Man*.

Did you find them to be friendly?
Oh, yes, very, very friendly, both the director "Shorty" Yeaworth and the producer Jack Harris. Very nice. We [cast members "imported" for the movie] were put up in different homes. If I'm remembering right, I stayed in the home of "Shorty" and his wife Jean. *Someone's* home, anyway—I know we were not in a hotel. Bob Lansing was there with his wife Emily [actress Emily McLaughlin from *General Hospital*], and they had their new little baby, Bobby Lansing, Jr. I babysat with Bobby a couple of times while they were able to go and have dinner some place and go into town.

Did everything go smoothly?
No, I know they had problems. The first day of filming, they started with a prayer, and I think were very respectful of each other and all. As it progressed and things went wrong, I saw problems. The energy that sustained them seemed to diminish a little bit....

When things would go wrong.
Yes. I felt that maybe they were just not able to go *back* to that energy, or that belief that stimulated their involvement. I saw it sort of deteriorating and it made me sad. Bob helped a great deal with some of the directing difficulties: "Listen, let's just do *this*, let's just rehearse it and rehearse it until we get something that will work." And he relieved "Shorty," I think. I don't mean that Bob relieved him of his *job* [*laughs*], no, but a couple of times Bob relieved "Shorty" of the burden that was kind of pressing him down. Bob was able to do that, and do that in a gentlemanly way, just to help "Shorty."

"Shorty" halfway admitted that to me. He said that Lansing was "as helpful and concerned as could be." The exact opposite of The Blob*'s Steve McQueen, who "Shorty" said was very difficult!*
Oh, yeah, Bob was terrific, he really was, and I liked him a lot. I did two movies with him, *4D Man* and *Namu, the Killer Whale* [1966], and a couple of TV shows. We remained very close friends and family friends. We'd all spent birthdays and Christmases and things like that together.

When they were casting 4D Man, *Yeaworth and Harris were trying to decide between Robert Lansing and Jason Robards.*
I have never heard that! Jason Robards certainly was a good actor, and he probably would have been wonderful.

Robert Lansing told an interviewer that when he was first approached, the 4D Man was not the main character in the movie, his brother *was. Lansing said he talked "Shorty" into making the 4D Man the star before he took the role. Does that sound like a Robert Lansing move to you?*

Lee Meriwether wore her real-life wedding gown in a *4D Man* restaurant scene.

Bob was very cognizant of the way Hollywood works, and the way one becomes a star. So I think that probably *was* what happened.

Lansing once told an interviewer he was "pretty hammy" in 4D Man.
  Oh, now that's interesting. No, I never would think he was *hammy* ... he just went into a heightened state of being mentally deranged. I always *believed* what he did. So, no, I didn't find him hammy. If I'd seen that, I might have said something to Emily [*laughs*]! Also, consider how quickly it was shot, *and* that he was injured.

Injured?
  By a blank from one of the guns, when the policemen in the movie were shooting at him. This was on one of our locations ... night-for-night shooting. They thought they *might* get around to shooting a scene of Jimmy Congdon and me, so we were brought along just in case, but it was mostly going to be Bob working, running away from the police in the rain, and there were going to be policemen shooting at him and there were going to be a lot of extras. At one point, Bob came out of a building through a door onto a little porch area as he was escaping, and the police were shooting at him. He jerked to one side, and held his face, and started to run away—they were still shooting. He finished out the scene, and then he said, "Uh ... gang, I think I'm hurt." So they looked, and the side of his face

near his eye had been hit with wadding, or *some*thing, fired by one of the guns. They took him immediately to the hospital, and Bob came back with the most *wonderful* story—it was just fabulous.

Dean Newman, who did the makeup, had designed an old age makeup for Bob, because in the movie any time Bob passed through any barrier, he got older and older and older. And so in this scene where he was running away from the police, Bob had this old age makeup on. He didn't touch the makeup until he got to the hospital, where that late at night only one doctor and a couple of nurses were on duty. Bob said he thought this doctor was from the Middle East somewhere, and his knowledge of moviemaking was nil. This doctor didn't know *any*thing except, here's this "old man" coming in, and all of a sudden tearing at his skin [*laughs*]—pulling it off! The doctor started yelling at Bob, "No, no! Don't! Don't *do* that!" Bob said, "No, it's makeup, it's makeup," and *still* the doctor couldn't really comprehend what it was that Bob was doing, and he

According to Meriwether, Robert Lansing's old man makeup was realistic enough to create an incident inside a hospital during *4D Man* production.

literally tried to grab Bob's hands away from his face. Part of the latex came off, and the doctor *screamed*. Bob said, "Please, look, look, look. I'm not old, I'm an actor, I'm an actor," over and over again, and finally it got through to the poor doctor. But the doctor had nearly collapsed, he almost fainted. He admitted that to Bob later, he said, "When I saw you doing that, I almost fainted. The blood just raced out of my head!" [*Laughs*]

Speaking of injuries, did you allow yourself to be hit in the face playing tetherball in the playground scene, or was that an accident?

Oh, no, that was an accident.

You took it well!

Thanks [*laughs*]! The ball actually did hit me—and that hurt! Try and keep laughing while you're really hurting! Oh, my nose has taken *so* many jolts! It's so crooked, you have no idea!

All from movies and TV mishaps, or real life?

The "original" was when I was 16, I was tickling a boy and he jumped, and he caught me with his elbow right underneath my nose. That did the major damage. Then, I guess, the tetherball; and then I was hit in the face with a basketball. And I hit my*self* with a tennis racket. That's hard to do [*laughs*]—try and think about how I did that.

I can't imagine!

I have no idea either! Oh, remember the bedroom scene where I'm in bed and Bob is standing over me and I'm frightened of him and finally I jump out of bed and run away? I hit my head on the camera as I passed it on one of the takes! I did that the first time, I guess, and then they readjusted the camera angle [so she could pass]. Then when I faint at the sight of Bob standing outside the door of the house, my "slow-motion fall" was one of the hardest things I ever had to do! The first couple times we did the shot, I fell as if I had really fainted, and they said, "She went right out of the shot!" The camera operator couldn't "hold" me, he couldn't tilt [the camera] down fast enough. So I had to fall in slow-motion so he could follow me to the floor with the camera!

Robert Strauss, who played your slimy colleague at the research center—what memories of him?
    He was fun. I *wish* that I had had a chance to talk to him at length, because I imagine he had great stories to tell about his career. But he came in and was gone very shortly. Have you talked to Jimmy Congdon? He was a charming, witty gentleman to watch as an actor. And he was always surprising you. The fall down the stairs that he does in one scene—he hadn't *done* that before the actual take. We thought he'd fallen for real, and he said, "No, no, no"—he'd planned it all.

So he rehearsed it without the fall, and then fell when the camera was rolling?
    Yes! And I marveled at him as an actor in that night scene in the rain I told you about. It was a difficult shooting sequence that we had to do, with them pouring water on us, and I think he had to do the scene several times. He really was very good, he kept his head while all around were going crazy. The last time I saw Jimmy was when he did a *Barnaby Jones* with me. It was funny, he was married to Mary Fickett years and years ago—they're not married now—and I was the gal who replaced Mary Fickett on *All My Children*. The world goes around and around! And, oh!, Edgar Stehli, he was charming, ab-so-lute-ly charming. Do you know the feeling, when you're watching a play, and someone comes on stage, and you just go, "Aaaaah, yeah...."—you relax, because he's *so* in command of what he's doing? You think, "This is the *man*, this is the *character*, this is the *real person*." That's what Edgar Stehli presented, the minute he walked on the set. I don't think I actually had any words *with* him in *4D Man* but I remember watching him work a couple of scenes and thinking that he was extremely good playing the controlling, sneaky boss, but *appearing* to be so nice and so genuine and all. He was an awfully good actor.
    Dean Newman, who did the makeup, also played a doctor in the show—they gave him a role as Bob's first victim. Then as the gate guard they had Guy Raymond, who was then a New York actor. A dear, sweet man. Guy later came out here to Los Angeles and then we got to really know each other. I worked with his wife Ann Morgan Guilbert on *The New Andy Griffith Show*, she played my sister. Guy has passed away but she's still with us and still working. By the way, on *4D Man*, somehow Guy's soundtrack must have been ruined, because that is "Shorty"'s voice as the gate guard. Guy had a very distinctive voice, and when I saw *4D Man* I went, "Oh, for Heaven's sake..." because I knew it wasn't his voice. And then I realized: "Wait a minute ... that's 'Shorty'!"

And Patty Duke as a little girl killed by the 4D Man.
    Little Patty Duke! It's so funny [*laughs*], I *still* think she fibbed about her age at the time! I told her that once, and she said, "*I was nine!*" [*Laughs*] I said, "Okay, all right, all right!" *4D Man* was just before she did *The Miracle Worker* [as young Helen Keller] on Broadway.

I was always surprised that Lansing kills her in the movie.
    [*Whispers*] Yes! Well, they were doing a [takeoff] on the scene of the Frankenstein Monster and the little girl [in the 1931 *Frankenstein*]—that's what *I* figured. Somebody, I've for-

gotten now who, said, "Oh, we shouldn't have the 4D Man kill the girl," and I said, "But he's a monster, he kills people, he can't help it. He doesn't want to but he *has* to, or he's going to die. It makes him more poignant."

In an old interview, you talked about "Shorty" doing something startling in the scene where you're kissing Robert Lansing, and you're actually holding a gun and getting ready to shoot him.

Yes—*he* discharged a gun [*laughs*]! He was in that enclosed set with us, and from about two feet away from Bob and me, he discharged a gun loaded with a blank, at the same moment that *I* was supposed to be firing at Bob. He must have read a book about directing that said, "Startle the actors, you'll get something wonderful!" Well [*laughs*], what he *got* was the wonderful spray of saliva that you see on the screen between Bob and me as we jumped apart when the gun went off!

For a little company in Middle-of-Nowhere, Pennsylvania, that usually did religious movies, I think they went the extra mile and then *some. I really think* 4D Man's *"a cut above."*

I do too. I mean, heavens, it was the first time that they had ever done any kind of [special effects] frame by frame. Nowadays it's just digital and the special effects guys can do it standing on their heads, but in those days the shots of Bob's hand and the shadow on the object going through it and coming out had to be painted on frame by frame. I thought it was fabulous.

In the woods of Pennsylvania, what was there to do *when you weren't working?*

[*Laughs*] There didn't seem to be much *time* to do much of any going-places or doing-things. We would work long hours and, at the end of the day, my memory is that we just all went to bed! Then there was the time we lost our cook. My memory fails me as to what happened to him, but the possibility that the man had a drinking problem comes to mind. So I had to—well, we *all* had to chip in and help cook meals [*laughs*], so that we would have some food! There weren't any restaurants nearby where we could go all together, so we all ate communally in the kitchen of the building where we did some of the shooting.

Was it a union picture?

I think it was, because I think I remember having to join SAG to do the movie.

Both "Shorty" and Jack Harris have said that 4D Man *was a better picture than* The Blob. *What would you say to that?*

That's interesting that they would say that. I think they had learned a great deal on *The Blob*; on that picture, they "went to film school." "Shorty" had done religious films beforehand—

And then, with The Blob, *he and Harris went to "sci-fi feature film school," let's say.*

Yes! Also, *4D Man* had a good script, and it was easier for audiences to swallow the plot of *4D Man*. As a result, it did well and it was accepted, because it was in the realm of possibility. *The Blob* was ... well.... [*Laughs*] At least it didn't do anything to destroy Steve McQueen's career! Incidentally, I traveled around with Jack Harris when *4D Man* was released, we did a publicity tour down into the South. I remember going to Atlanta, and [at the Underground Atlanta mall] going to see that diorama of the Civil War.

You just re-watched the movie, so—what do you think of it in 2005? Do you think it holds up?

Yes, I really do! I was really rather amazed at my performance! I thought, "Why, for heaven's sake ... I wasn't half-bad!" There were line deliveries that I thought, "Hey ... that's pretty good!" [*Laughs*] And as I watched the movie, a lot came back to me. You know the scene where Jimmy Congdon first arrives at the research center and I say to him, "I'm the good fairy who passed you through the gate." Well, in one take, just as I said "fairy," a fly landed on my nose [*laughs*]! I would give *anything* for that piece of film, but I'm sure it's gone. We were all in hysterics, we laughed and laughed. After that, trying to get back to acting the way we were supposed to in the scene was very hard! I also saw that I wore my own clothes in the movie—I forgot all about that. Remember the scene in the restaurant where Jimmy and I dance, and he puts his hand on my back and then takes it away because my dress is backless? That's my wedding gown, shortened to be used at a later date, and it *was*—it was used in *4D Man*! I hated the swimsuit I wore in the scene with Bob and Jimmy in the park. In that scene, I wore a swimsuit, Jimmy wore a bathing suit, but Bob was fully dressed. Bob refused to wear a bathing suit—he even wore a jacket! I don't know why he refused to wear a bathing suit, because he didn't have a bad figure at all. But he just felt self-conscious about ... *some*thing, I guess.

Oh, and I found a mistake in the film! Whenever Bob was in the fourth dimension, you heard that "oooo-wooo-oooo-wooo" sound. Well, in the scene in the rain where he's running from the police, at one point that sound is on, but he grabs one of the metal bars of a railing to swing underneath. His hands *should* have passed right through it. Good heavens, I've seen the movie several times, but never caught that before!

Was the experience of making 4D Man *better or worse than you thought it would be?*

I didn't have any expectations, I just couldn't wait to do a movie! It was a wonderful experience, even though I felt the spiritual quality of the work being done by some of the crew seemed to deteriorate as things went wrong. Toward the end, they pulled themselves together, and then the spirit became revitalized. If you drew a graph, it started up high, and went down—dipped—and then went back up again.

Since 4D Man *was your first movie, you* must *remember where you saw yourself on the big screen for the first time...?*

Oh, dear.

[Laughs] Or maybe you don't!

Isn't that something? It had to have been some little movie theater in New York. That's so funny, the fact that I can't remember. I do remember that at some point later on, Bob Lansing went back to New York for something and *4D Man* was on television, it was on the *Million Dollar Movie* on Channel 9 in New York. *Million Dollar Movie* played the same movie twice a day, seven days a week—*the same movie!* Bob was so funny, he said, "Oh, Lee, our careers went downhill when the movie first came out. Can you imagine what's gonna happen with it on seven days a week?" [*Laughs*]

He joked about it, but I think both he and I were ... I know *I* was ... I was *proud* of that first effort. I really was. It was a good joke, Bob saying, "What's going to happen to our careers with it on seven days a week?," but I *know* we were both proud of *4D Man*.

You were a regular on the TV series The Time Tunnel *with James Darren and Robert Colbert in 1966–67. Elsewhere in this book, I ask Darren [page 89] and Colbert [page 68] to name the first couple places they'd go if there was such a thing as a Time Tunnel. Where would you go?*

I'd like to go once into the past and once into the future. When my mother was about 80, I suddenly thought, "I should be asking her family questions that I don't know the answers to." I asked her, "How did you meet Daddy?" and she said, "I picked him up in a movie house!" I would love to go back to that day, or maybe even before: In Portland, Oregon, she went to the movies every Thursday, right after work, and saw the movies, which changed every week. And she noticed this handsome man who was *also* in the theater every Thursday. He always sat in the same seat, so each Thursday she moved a little closer, and finally she was within eye contact of him. He noticed her, and then they left at the same time the *next* time, and she said, "Do you come here often?" [*laughs*]—you know *that* line! She "picked him up," that's how it all started, and I'd love to go back and see all of that.

Then I'd love to go into the future and be present when my granddaughter Ryan Oldham [now 13 years old] graduates from college. I don't know when that will be; *hopefully* I'll still be around for *real*, but in order to be sure, I'd like to take the trip now!

For Baby Boomers, I think your claim to fame is always going to be Catwoman—would you agree?

I guess! A lot of people even remember the name "Miss Kitka," but not what it stands for [*laughs*]. I've been asked, "Do *you* still remember what it stands for?"—and I do! Some people tell me that Catwoman's my claim to fame, but others, believe it or not, remember me from *The Today Show*. Some people remember Miss America. Some people remember *Barnaby Jones*. And then, for some, yes, it's Catwoman. It's a rather *strange* career [*laughs*]. And the role of Catwoman is one that I do share with several other ladies. I was not the first to play Catwoman, although I *was* the first one to do it in the movies.

How familiar were you with Batman when growing up?

Very! Of course I remember the comic book; in fact, I believe that I had copies of *several* issues. I had a great comic book collection which, unfortunately, didn't make the trip from Phoenix, Arizona, to San Francisco—I think I had some #1s of different comic books, and they would be worth a lllllot of money these days! Oh, dear! I loved *Captain Marvel* and *Superman* too. These were "reading materials" for me—actually, that was how I *learned* to read, to tell you the truth.

So it didn't take the Batman *TV series to make you aware of Batman.*

Oh, no, no. I *loved* the show, incidentally. But when I went in for the audition, to play the role, I had not seen Catwoman on the show yet. Either the first Catwoman episodes [with Julie Newmar in the role] hadn't aired yet, or I had missed them.

Anyway, my agent heard about the *Batman* movie and got an audition for me, and I was very excited about going in to

In the 1966 Batman, Miss Kitka (Meriwether) is also the villainous vixen Catwoman. Batman was a bit slow picking up on their striking resemblance.

read for it. Then my enthusiasm lessened when I heard that there were going to be at least 200 women contending for the role! When I went to the 20th Century–Fox studios to try out for it, there were at least 20 women waiting outside the producer's office, and they were all voluptuous and gorgeous. I thought to myself, "Well, Lee, don't count on *this*!" I suppose that's a good way to go into something, to not *expect* it, and not to want it too much. Truthfully, the only reason I really wanted the role was because I knew my girls Kyle and Lesley would be *so* excited, because they loved the show. I let them watch *Batman* because it was such fun, a lot of laughs.

Finally it was my turn to go in and read for it. Les Martinson the director was there, and Charles Fitzsimons, Maureen O'Hara's brother, who was the associate producer, and Bill Dozier, the producer—I have in my mind that there were about three or four people there. Well, because I had heard that there were so many women "up" for it, and because so many of the ones I had seen were gorgeous, I knew I had to do *some*thing so that they would remember me. Thank heavens I've had a lot of cats in my life: I just started being a cat almost immediately. I curled up in the chair that they provided for me—luckily it was roomy enough that I *could*—and while I was reading the role, I licked my hand, and I did some purring, and I did some kneading on my own lap like my cats used to do. And as I left, I thought, "Well, at least I gave it a shot, and did *some*thing." Well, within days, I got a call saying I was chosen—and the following day I was *working*. Time-wise, they were up against it. I had heard that they were filming on the day that I was auditioning.

Do you happen to remember who else was up for the role?

No. I don't think I knew any of the women in the outer office, because I would have *talked* to them. Incidentally, when I got the role, my daughters were just ecstatic. They came on the set with me one time, when we were on location, and had a great time.

Why didn't Julie Newmar play the part?

I don't know, but there've been any number of reasons put out. I have heard that she had injured her back, I've heard that she had already signed to do *another* movie ... I heard at one time that she wanted more money [*laughs*]. *That* I doubt very much. But I never did really find out, and I never asked her. I could have, I suppose. Maybe if there's another memorabilia show where we're all together, I'll ask her.

So you have met her through the years?

Oh, yes, yes, and I like her a lot. And in 2004 I finally got to meet Eartha Kitt [who also played Catwoman on the TV series]. For the TV Land Awards, they had the three of us together, Eartha, Julie Newmar and me, and that was fun.

How did you prepare to play Catwoman? Did they show you Julie Newmar episodes?

They liked what I did in the audition, and they didn't want me to vary from that. They also liked my attempt at a Russian accent. They did show me a clip from the show of Julie playing Catwoman, maybe a five-minute clip. But without sound! Just so I could see the way she moved. I said [*Meriwether gasps*], "Oh, golly...!" Julie was a dancer, and when I saw the way she moved, I was a little intimidated. They said, "We just wanted you to have a flavor of it, that's all," and I said, "Well ... I'll *try*!" Actually, I *had* taken dance lessons and ballet lessons when I was in New York, and I had been taking dance classes here in Los Angeles as a regular in Betty Garrett's dance class, that she gave to members of Theatre West. That was our actors' workshop, and we both still belong to it; in fact, she and I are currently appearing in the musical *Nunsense*, written and directed by Dan Goggin. So, yes, I *was* limber enough to handle the moves required of Catwoman. They certainly did have me in some strange positions in that outfit. The outfit was *not* the most comfortable.

Did you have much experience in comedy in those days?

Yes, thanks to Theatre West. To play a *Batman* villain, you have to be *so* serious, and believe everything you do. It's tricky playing that kind of farce. That's why I could never understand why people didn't just *heap* accolades on Adam West and Burt Ward [Batman and Robin], because they both were so good. As Robin, Burt had to mimic what Adam was doing, that's what he was expected to do, and he was very earnest and played it to the hilt. Adam had the more difficult role, of course. Oh, dear, those lines! For him to say them, and to be "believable"—it was such a fine line he had to walk! And he did it with such conviction and style.

I'm sure no performance quite like that was ever given in all the years of movies and TV preceding Batman.

The former Miss America went from catwalks to Catwoman, playing the arch-villainess and also her alter ego, *Moscow Bugle* **correspondent Kitka (here cuddling with Adam West as millionaire playboy Bruce Wayne).**

Well, *all* of us had to play it that way: Burgess Meredith [The Penguin], who played two characters as I did, and Frank Gorshin [The Riddler] and Cesar Romero [The Joker]. They were so *into* it, and they were enjoying themselves tremendously. They *loved* it, *loved* it. *Loved* doing it.

And the Batman *people must have loved* them, *to keep bringing them back so many times.*

Oh, absolutely.

Talk about the costume ordeal. How was that made for you?

You know, I have absolutely no memory of how I got into it. I have wracked my brain trying to remember, and I can't. Someone has said that they were positive there was a zipper. I have *no* memory of a zipper in that costume. It's *possible*—I had to get into it *somehow*—but I just don't know where it was. If the zipper was under my arm, you'd think you'd see it. You'd think you'd see it down my back. But I just don't remember getting in and out of it.

I would stay in it all day—and not drink a lot of liquids, obviously. It was very uncomfortable in the heat. In the air conditioning, it wasn't bad, it was fine, but outside ... oh dear! And I somehow got *sunburned* through it, because it was made of some kind of metallic material and there was some stretch in it—but not *much*. There's the old expression "tighter than my own skin"—well, you can *sit* in your skin [*laughs*], and I couldn't really sit very comfortably in *that*. But, oh, wouldn't it be fun if I could have that costume today. And I'd give anything if I could fit *into* it [*laughs*]!

And your Catwoman makeup? Those kooky eyebrows?

Loved 'em. The guy who did my makeup was Bruce Hutchinson, who just finished I-don't-know-*how*-many-years on *Frasier*.

You had no hesitation at all about taking the part? You'd have a weird costume, have to give an over-the-top performance, do a crazy accent, play comedy—were you ready for all of this?

It's funny, I had no trepidation about doing the role. It just was such fun. Luckily, I'd had Theatre West, the actors' workshop that I've belonged to since 1961, which afforded me constant "exercise," if you will, in performing. Still to this day, I'm playing roles there that TV and movie folks just wouldn't cast me as—for example, an ancient mother, a drunk, a singing-dancing nun. How fortunate I am to have Theatre West, because, over the years, I've been able to do *so* many things that I'd never get a chance to do on film.

How often have you been an evil character on TV and in movies?

Oh, maybe three, four times. Usually I play characters who've "got a good heart," who are "nice," that kind of thing. But I once played a crook on [the TV series] *The F.B.I.*, an embezzler—but she was in an iron lung when they caught her, so there was a *little* bit of redeeming quality [*laughs*]! I was a killer on [the TV series] *Murder, She Wrote*, and I was vicious there. I even tried to kill Angela Lansbury! Those kinds of parts are *always* fun to play.

Once you started shooting Batman, *what was the atmosphere on the set? Different from the average film or TV show?*

When she landed the Catwoman role, Meriwether (pictured with Cesar Romero as The Joker) says, "My daughters were just ecstatic."

Because of the short shooting schedule, the atmosphere was "We've got to get this out!," "Time is money!"—and you *felt* the crunch. I think there were a couple of times when they maybe got behind, and then there was worry or concern. I think they only *had* 18 days to film it, it was a really short schedule. To make this movie, they had a little bit of time between the end of the shooting of the first season of *Batman* and the start of the shooting of the second season. They had just that length of time to do it. The prep time and the back end time were also very short.

How did the director Leslie Martinson cope with this stress? I've been told that, when things went wrong, he was a guy who could get kind of ... emotional!

At one point they couldn't figure out how to film something, and I know he went off into a corner and was *very* upset. I guess he just needed time away, to re-think the scene, the

Meriwether collected comic books as a kid ("That was how I learned to read") and in the '60s watched the *Batman* series. She's one of us. (Left to right, Burt "Robin" Ward, Frank "The Riddler" Gorshin, Meriwether.)

mechanics of the scene—I think it was a case of a camera not fitting where he *wanted* it to fit, and he wanted to get a certain angle that he couldn't get. But he came up with *something*. I think Adam was able to help him there.

On a personal level, Adam West and Burt Ward?

Oh, great fun. I didn't get to work with Burt much at all—in fact, *did* I have any scene with him? Oh, just at the end when I'm captured aboard the submarine. Whenever I talked to him he seemed pleasant, and *eager*, and just having a ball. Adam was so witty—he still *is*. He's truly very funny. And he's an actor who takes his work seriously. I remember that he wanted it to go smoothly for me, because he knew that I was thrown into it literally at the last minute. Cesar Romero knew that as well, and he too was just incredible. He helped me tremendously. My first day was on the submarine, and he saw me being probably quite nervous [*laughs*], and he just was so nice and so understanding. *They* [Romero, Meredith, Gorshin] had all played their roles before, and I hadn't, and Cesar knew that. He was helpful. Encouraging. That was his forte, he'd always been like that. And for years afterwards, too. We did a lot of charity things together, he was always volunteering for different organizations. He was super.

Frank Gorshin?

I loved watching him work. He was always working on his character, always off on the side running lines with himself, working out how he would do something. It was a wonderful lesson, seeing him go off to the side, and not being intrusive with his work. He was a working actor, trying different things. He would try different things in *scenes*, too: "I'm gonna try *this*," "Would it be okay if I tried *that*?" Same thing with Burgess, Burgess would try different things, and they were all wonderful. For instance, toward the end of the movie, in the Penguin's submarine, when things are starting to go wrong, the Penguin's cigarette is now drooping in its holder, which was just delicious—and that was not in the script. They were constantly thinking of things and helping out. It was wonderful to watch them all. Burgess, by the way, was a wonderful human being, very dear, and we had a lot of fun together. *All* of the fellows were really terrific. We had a very nice working relationship and they were lovely to be with. And, oh, professional—oh, heavens! They *always* knew their lines, they always were "right there." I have no memory of *any* scene going on into a Take Four, a Take Five—it *never* got there. Thanks for taking me back to that time. I do miss those three gentlemen so much.

That Russian accent of Miss Kitka's—were you doing that for the first time, or had you done it before?

Oh, I'd never done it before. Thank heavens for watching movies when I was growin' up [*laughs*]—I often heard actors playing Russian characters in movies, *and* on television, and I'm lucky that I have a relatively good ear. I'm currently doing a New York accent in *Nunsense*, so right now I'm being [*now speaking with the accent*] "very, very New Yawk. Oh, *shoo*-wa [sure]!" We're about to venture out on a mini-tour with this musical.

What locations did you go on for Batman*?*

We had a couple of locations. We went to Santa Barbara for one location, which was the pier, and then we went out to the 20th Century–Fox Ranch, which was where they had the pool and the submarine. That's where they shot all the exteriors of the submarine, including the big fight on top. There was a big cyc of the sky behind it.

Which of those two locations did your daughters visit you on?

They came to the Ranch. But the *really* big day for them was coming on the Batcave soundstage. On a day when I wasn't working, I brought them over and they were there as a scene was shot on the Batcave set. Of course I watched them and made sure that they weren't getting into any kind of mischief. When we made *Batman* [April-May 1966], Lesley was two and a half and Kyle six. The girls were overjoyed.

You were at the Batman *world premiere. What was that like?*

Good heavens, they had major, major crowds—*so* exciting! I remember being out on a platform in front of lots and lots of people—the crowds were incredible. I had to be in the

Catwoman costume outdoors, and then evening gown *in*doors. For some reason, I can remember only Burgess and Cesar and me, I can't remember Adam and Burt being there. Although they *had* to have been, I just can't imagine Adam and Burt not being there. *Unless* they were working. Those fellows were working *all* the time on weekends—they were going out and making appearances at big, big fairs and things like that—and I hope they were making money hand over fist!

Your reaction to the movie when you first saw it?

The reaction I remember: I was so *big*, up there on the screen! I guess I just wasn't prepared to see myself that big! Partly it was because I was so close to the screen—they took us down closer than I normally sit in a movie. I would normally sit toward the back, but at the premiere they had us way down front, and I remember thinking, "Oh, my gosh, my face is so *big*!" That was rough to take! Incidentally, I saw it again recently, they had a showing here in Los Angeles at a moderate-size theater where they play art films a lot. I was asked if I would come, and I did get there in time to see it, and [*laughs*] ... I was very pleasantly surprised. I thought it was really good. And this time I wasn't thrown by it—but I'm sure that

Meriwether's other memorable television roles include regular stints on *The Time Tunnel*, *Barnaby Jones* (Emmy and Golden Globe nominations for her performance as the daughter-in-law and assistant of homespun sleuth Buddy Ebsen), *The Munsters Today* (as Lily Munster) and the New York–based daytime drama *All My Children*.

was because I was able to sit back where I wanted to sit! And with a box of popcorn. It was fun and I enjoyed it, I really did.

The A&E series Biography *once devoted an episode to Catwoman, and some of the "experts," the talking heads, said you were very "wholesome" as Catwoman.*

I know! When they said that, I thought, "Isn't that interesting...!"

Actually, your Catwoman is kinda ruthless compared to Julie Newmar's. Yours has no crush on Batman, she just wants to rob and kill—and you still came across as wholesome to those talking heads!

That's right, even when Kitka was dating Bruce Wayne, it was all just to get him to be the lure for Batman.

Maybe the talking heads were so used to seeing you play "wholesome" that they ascribe wholesomeness to all your characters—even when that's not part of the character at all.

[*Self-mockingly*] Maybe enough of my "goodness" showed through!

When Julie Newmar left the Batman *series, why did they bring in Eartha Kitt instead of you as the new Catwoman?*

Well, I couldn't have done it if they *had* asked me, because I think I was doing the TV series *Time Tunnel* by then. I thought Eartha was fabulous!

Much as I like the way the Batman *TV series presented Catwoman, Joker, Penguin and Riddler ... I have to admit, I find King Tut funnier than* any *of 'em!*

Victor Buono was *adorable.* And, interestingly, pessimistic about his life. We were in two episodes of the *Batman* TV series together ["King Tut's Coup" and "Batman's Waterloo"], Victor as King Tut and me as a girl he kidnaps because he thinks she's Cleopatra, and one day when we were just sitting around, waiting for a scene to be filmed, he said, "Oh, Lee, I'm not gonna live past ... oh ... probably 31." I said, *"What?!* Stop that! Bite your tongue!," and he said [*in a resigned voice*], "No, no, it's true...." And he did die very young—although he made it past 31 [he died at 43]. I had no idea he was so young when we did *Batman* [29 to Meriwether's 31], he seemed older. Sometimes babies are born "old souls"—they just look older, and continue to do so as children, and all their lives they just have a mature look to 'em. So I bet he probably had that from childhood. Lee J. Cobb was the same way, he had "an old face." When he did the movie *Anna and the King of Siam* [1946], the original *The King and I,* and he played the Kralahome, I think he was not much more than 30.

Victor Buono—when he wasn't talking about dying at 31, what was he like?

A very serious actor. Again, there was not much time to talk between scenes. It was [*Meriwether starts snapping her fingers*], *"Come* on. We gotta get this, we gotta get this. Up and at 'em!," so Victor and I didn't spend all that much time talking to each other. He was certainly pleasant on the set, never a tantrum or anything like that, very patient. And so pessimistic about his life.

There've been a number of Catwomen on the big screen in recent years—can you rate all *the other Catwomen?*

They were fabulous, all of them. Julie Newmar was just *so* statuesque, and moved like a cat. When I eventually saw her *do* the role—

With *sound!*

[*Laughs*] Yes, with sound and *every*thing! When I eventually saw her, I thought she was so slinky. And very mysterious: You never knew what she was *thinking,* or what she was about to *do.* She captured that aspect of the persona of some cats—certainly a couple that I had as a youngster. You just nnnnever know whether certain cats are gonna slip away ... or if they're gonna *pounceonyou* [*laughs*]!

Eartha had the best meow and purr. She has that earthy singer's "vocalese," and it was so "right," and made her kitty purrr-fect. Super! And she moved well—she had a feline quality about her that was really wonderful.

Michelle Pfeiffer [*Batman Returns,* 1992] was outstanding. Her acting was magnificent, and she brought several different nuances to the role. There were also a couple of additions to her character which were unique. I don't think she lucked out on her *costume,* but ... it was different [*laughs*]. It *made sense,* though—they showed how the costume came about, which I liked. I liked the costume for what it was because *she* [Pfeiffer's character] made it, it was homemade, and still looked great. And, of course, her figure—well, fuhgeddabout [*laughs*]! Aaaarrrggghhh, she was terrific!

Halle Berry [*Catwoman,* 2004]—oh ho, you *go,* girl! How marvelous to have *that* explanation of the character, and to be the *lead* character. She didn't have to contend with Batman and Robin, she had fun allll by herself! And with the wonders of all the digital things that they can *do* nowadays, her Catwoman was able to run along the walls and pounce down.

Of course, she was fabulous with that incredible figure, and she used her sultry sexiness to the fullest.

Did you see these movies because Catwoman was in them, or have you seen all *the Batman movies?*

Actually, I've seen them *all*, yes. I'm a *fan*.

It's so much fun to talk to an interviewee who seems like she might be as "trapped in adolescence" movie-wise as I am. "Adult-olescents," I think they call us.

Oh, sure! I love movies, I'm an addict—I even love the coming attractions! I missed, though, the first ten minutes of the latest one, *Batman Begins* [2005], and so I have to go back and catch it from the beginning. And I can't wait. You *see?*, I really *am* an addict. You know, I've been thinking while we talked … there are five of us Catwomen, all of us different. I wish that there was some way to put us all *together* in a movie. Not as Catwoman, but just women. It would be *such* fun!

LAURIE MITCHELL

*Who else do you know who's taken a bubble bath
in a coffee can? Just me [laughs]!*

For fans of 1950s science fiction schlock, it has endured as one of that decade's all-time great campfests: *Queen of Outer Space*, the loopy, serio-comic tale of a motley rocket crew that crash-lands on Venus and finds it to be entirely populated by mini-skirted, ray-gun-packin' glamazons, most recognizably Zsa Zsa Gabor as a leggy scientist, and most formidably Laurie Mitchell as the masked and ruthlessly cruel title character, "Yllana, the Queen of Outer Space." Scripted by SF master Charles Beaumont, it's a color-CinemaScope trashterpiece of interstellar proportions—and just one of several fantasy films on the résumé of Mitchell, who was also reduced to the size of a doll in the same-year (1958) *Attack of the Puppet People*, and who made a return voyage into space to play a lunar maiden in the similarly surreal *Missile to the Moon* (1958).

Born in New York City and raised in the East Bronx, Mitchell (real name: Mickey Koren) moved with her family to California while in her teens. Acting school led to stage roles and then to movie assignments, beginning with *20000 Leagues Under the Sea* (her 1954 film debut) and followed by *Girls in Prison*, *The Monolith Monsters*, the Bowery Boys' *Fighting Trouble* and many more. Long-retired and now the wife of a medical salesman, she has recently been "rediscovered" by her fans and has begun making the celebrity expo and autograph show rounds.

Your first movie was also your first science fiction movie, Disney's 20000 Leagues Under the Sea.*

In the scene at the beginning of the movie where you first see Kirk Douglas walking down the muddy street, Gloria Pall and I are walking with him. We're two ... supposedly ... hookers [*laughs*]! That was my introduction to show biz! It was a nothing part but, I tell you, to be working with one of the most important, top actors of that time, the handsome, talented Kirk Douglas, was such a thrill for me. It was unbelievable for a first-timer. That scene was shot on the Universal back lot, and when it got to be lunchtime he said, "Are you hungry? Let's go to the commissary and we'll have lunch, okay?" So we did. We took something that looked like a golf cart, only it was dressed up like a submarine, and we went to the commissary.

A golf cart that looked like a submarine was how he got around on the lot?

Yes! The whole *thing* didn't look like a submarine, just the front of it—it had like the "nose" of a submarine. It was very cute. We went to the commissary in it, and the people

---

*The title on-screen, on the video box and in the Internet Movie database is "20000 Leagues..." (with no comma).

In one day, Laurie Mitchell (center) launched her movie career, *and* lunched with Kirk Douglas—during the making of *20000 Leagues Under the Sea*.

walking down the street who saw us were going, "*Ha-ha-ha,* look at that!" It was a joy for me. It was a joy for me to be with him, period. We talked a little about each other's background. He told me his parents came from Russia, and that they were very poor. I told him *my* folks also came from a small village in Russia, and spoke of their hardships. Then we drifted on to other subjects. He said, "You're not only pretty, but a very sweet person." I said, "Thank you!," and we drove back to the set. And that was that. We finished the scene, said our goodbyes and left. I felt great. This was such a great guy, a beautiful, good-looking man and a very fine man. Days later, there was a knock on the door of our apartment on Crescent Heights—I got a delivery of some yellow roses and a note, THANKS FOR THE LOVELY CONSIDERATION AND CONVERSATION WE HAD AT LUNCHTIME. KIRK. I almost cried from joy. That was really, really nice.

Speaking of *20000 Leagues*, I also remember how thrilled I was to have had Tony Curtis' dressing room. Incidentally, he was not inside the dressing room [*laughs*]! He wasn't working then, so they let me use it—that's where the wardrobe mistress changed me. It was all mirrored, very gorgeous, just like *he* was. I was like a kid, looking *around,* looking at his *clothes*...! I was quite impressed, and I said to myself, "*Some*day, I'm going to have this ... *some*day I will!" It was a great thrill for a young kid to have Tony Curtis' dressing room. Little did I know that I'd be working with him in the future in *Some Like It Hot* [1959], another classic. So *20000 Leagues* was fun, a great experience. For a young kid, all of this was a thrill.

Prior to this—as a kid growing up in New York—did you like movies?

Very much. Also live stage shows, which my sister Fran, six years older, took me to on Saturday afternoons; since our parents worked, on Saturdays she was in charge of me. Well, needless to say, Broadway was our beat! Usually we'd see performers of her choice at the Paramount Theater, like Frank Sinatra, whom everybody loved. We would sit through three shows. "Mickey," Fran would say to me, "if you watch the show with me one more time, we'll go to the Automat and I'll buy you anything you want to eat."

You could stay three times, they wouldn't kick everybody out between shows?

Oh, no, they loved having all the young girls screaming at him! And the idea of going to the Automat sounded really wonderful, so I would agree. So I screamed along with all the other young girls as Ol' Blue Eyes performed. One day at the Automat, Fran and I were finishing our pie when two gentlemen approached our table with i.d.s from a radio station, WOR, and asked if I would be interested in taking part in a publicity stunt for them. All I had to do was wear a negligee (not too revealing!), lie on a chaise lounge and be carried on it by two men down Broadway in New York City. I had long brown hair and pretty brown eyes which they told me was a plus. I don't remember what the schtick was, I don't remember what they schlepped me down Broadway *for*, but obviously it was a publicity thing for some WOR program. It was a kick doing that, it really was, and a photograph of me being carried on that chaise lounge appeared in *Look* magazine and that helped sell a lot of copies of that issue, which was amazing to me. Can you imagine what this felt like for a young lady? This was absolutely thrilling for me, and it started the beat in my heart for show biz.

Step two: My dad fell in love with California after seeing a movie called *The Jolson Story* [1946]. He drove out with some friends and bought a little house, called my beautiful mom and said, "Adele, we're moving to California." My mom thought he was out of his mind! How can you give up an apartment in the East Bronx, friends, business? But my dad did it. After I finished high school, we moved. My dad was absolutely thrilled to get out of New York City. After a few months of living out here, we met some family who had a son that they wanted me to meet. The son, Larry White, came over to the house, and he was absolutely gorgeous, and we started to date. He also came from New York—he was a magician and a trumpet player. He was really a terrific guy. We got married at the Roosevelt Hotel in Hollywood, which is now a landmark. This man apparently and obviously saw something in me, and he said, "You know what? I think I need to send you to dramatic school. Let's see what happens." He sent me to Ben Bard's Acting School, and I performed several plays on stage. I even did, believe it or not, fair Helena in *A Midsummer Night's Dream*. Can you believe a girl from the Bronx doing Shakespeare [*laughs*]? Well, I did it!

I was doing a play one evening, I *think* it was at Ben Bard's, and after it was over, a very distinguished, handsome gentleman approached me backstage. He said he was an agent for actors, Sam Armstrong. He thought my performance was great and he wanted to sign me as a client for six months; "Then we'll see how it goes." What a wonderful human being he was. Throughout my show business career, he never left me. Unfortunately, he left *us* [died in 1974]. I still love him. Once he signed me, we started with the one with Kirk Douglas, *20000 Leagues Under the Sea*. It was a nothing part but, I tell you, it was the thrill of my life, because Kirk Douglas was such a gorgeous, gorgeous, lovely, lovely gentleman. The *perfect* gentleman.

In your next science fiction film, you had one of the leading roles: Attack of the Puppet People.

Not knowing at first what it was all about, of course I was *curious*. I found *Puppet People* to be very interesting—in fact, it was an absolute blast. Who else do you know who's taken a bubble bath in a coffee can? Just me [*laughs*]! It was shot at an independent studio, and I was so intrigued by the way the camera went all the way up to the ceiling and shot down at us from there to make us appear to be little tiny people. They put me in that coffee can, and in a giant tube—we [John Agar, Ken Miller *et al.*] were playing people who had been miniaturized by a crazy dollmaker [John Hoyt] who was lonely and wanted to keep all of us for himself. There was also a giant phone that we used to try to call the police, battling to pick up the receiver and shouting to be heard. It was very, very interesting, how they did all that.

Is it tough to act in science fiction movies, where you're playing characters who are having experiences that no one has ever really experienced?

The director [Bert I. Gordon] would explain to us what was going on, and why he put the camera way up high to make us all look tiny and so on, and that helped. And the props were very well-made. It seemed to me, when I was looking at them, and when I was getting *into* them [*laughs*], that they looked realistic, that it looked like a normal coffee can. Except that it was gigantic! Incidentally, when the director first told me about the bubble bath scene, I thought, "My gosh—this might be a nude scene!," to which I would have said, "Absolutely *no*!" But he told me, "Don't worry, you're going to wear a bathing suit."

What memories of some of the other people involved?
They were very nice to work with, they really were. Nobody was jealous, we all were friendly with each other. Ken Miller was nice and friendly, and John Agar was all right. As far as the other people ... they were okay too, but I really can't say much about any of them as far as being *terribly* friendly. We did our business and we said "Good night" to each other at the end of each day, and that was all. On some productions, people stick together and kid around, but on *Puppet People*, I don't know why, but....

Well, maybe it was just a question of having to work so fast, there was no time for kidding around.
You know, you might be right. Budget budget budget, and let's shoot it in four hours [*laughs*]. They worry about money money money. We all giggled and laughed, but overall it

Splish-splash! A bubble bath in a coffee can (observed by June Kenney and Marlene Willis) was one of Mitchell's memorable moments on the *Attack of the Puppet People* set.

turned out to be a very effective little picture. We all thought, "Oh, gee, what a silly thing," but some people really thought *Puppet People* was good!

For a little company like AIP, it was an ambitious picture.
Yeah! I think back and I go, "Gee, that was not only a B, but a *double* B movie," but people really like it. So many people have said to me, "Gee, I remember that movie, that was great!"

Bert I. Gordon?
He was friendly enough, but not to the extent that, say, Mr. Bernds [*Queen of Outer Space* director Edward Bernds] was. He was an angel, that Mr. Bernds. Bert I. Gordon was certainly more friendly than *some* directors. Some directors are, "Do your business, and thanks a lot, and *goodbye!*" [*laughs*]—some of them are like that! But I didn't find Bert Gordon unkind, nor did I see him banging his head against the wall because somebody didn't remember their lines—I didn't find that at all.

How much would you be paid for playing in a B movie like that in those days?
For that movie, it could have been scale, for all I know.

Would you go see all the movies you acted in?
Oh, sure. Absolutely! I saw *Puppet People* again just recently, because some very kind gentleman up north in Oregon sent me a video of it. I looked at it and saw myself and said, "Look at me. What a cute kid I was!" [*laughs*], and I enjoyed it again. It was corny, but ... okay!

Next, "the biggie"—you played the title role in Queen of Outer Space.
Sam, my agent, sent me out to Allied Artists to see this beautiful, God-love-him man, Mr. Ben Schwalb [producer of *Queen of Outer Space*]. What a sweetheart he was! Sam sent me out to see about playing [*imitates Zsa Zsa Gabor*] the "vicked kveen." That was quite an interesting production, let me tell you!

You'd already acted in one of Schwalb's Bowery Boys movies.
Maybe I met him then, I don't remember. But this time it was obviously a much better meeting. I went in and met him and whoever else, probably the writers or whoever I had to meet then. Mr. Schwalb was a darling, a real sweetheart, and I'll tell you why as we go on.

Did you have to audition for the part?
I recall reading a few pages of it, and I left, and then a few days later Sam called me and said, "Laurie, you have the part." Then two hours of makeup with Emile LaVigne, the makeup man, God rest his soul, doing a plaster of Paris....

Oh, a life mask!
Oy! I had to sit there 'til it was hard, and then he took it off. It was horrible, but it had to be done. I still have the mask—it's in the closet, wrapped in clear plastic. It's cruddy now, it's aging like me [*laughs*], but I still have it! Then there were the days when he had to make my face up to look burned, for the scenes where the vicked kveen is unmasked. Putty and black-and-blues marks and everything, to make it look like my face was eaten up by radiation. Emile, the darling, he should rest in peace, he'd put the makeup on me right on the set. Zsa Zsa was always, always late, so Emile would say to me, "Laurie, as long as we're waiting, I might as well do this nice and slow with you." It could take two and a half hours to put the makeup on, the ugly stuff. He was wonderful to me, and so were the wardrobe

Mitchell's short meeting and script reading for the movie's producer and director convinced them to coronate her Queen of Outer Space.

mistress and ... well, *every*body was just so wonderful. [Wardrobe supervisor] Irene Caine, she was divine. Any little thing that bothered her, if I had (say) a crease in my outfit, she was right there. She was just an angel.

Could you speak clearly enough through the mask that they had no problem recording you, or did you dub it later?

I don't believe I had to dub it. My voice came through pretty good, I thought.

The first time Emile LaVigne put the makeup on you, and you saw it going on gradually, was it an unpleasant experience, or interesting?

Very scary! "Oh, Emile....," "Oh, *God*....," "Oh, jeez, God forbid!" I remember saying that, "God forbid"—God forbid there should be a person like this. Watching it go on ... it could cause nightmares! Emile would say, "Don't worry. I'll get it off," and every day, he used cold cream, or ... what*ever* he got it off with. Oh, God, they took so many pictures. They would be right there with their cameras, every day. They sent me so many pictures—of this ugly person [*laughs*]!

And what memories of Zsa Zsa?

When it came to Zsa Zsa, she wanted *this*, she wanted *that*, she wanted glitter in her costumes—she wanted certain things which were very, very expensive. An actress she wasn't, but in those days she had some sort of name, and so they wanted her for the picture. She used to yell—she'd want a certain color hair, she didn't want the *other* girls to have the *same* color hair and so on. Later, on *Some Like It Hot*, directed by Billy Wilder, Marilyn [Monroe] didn't want any of the other girls to have the same color hair as her.

You had the same color hair as Zsa Zsa in the movie. Well, you had to, she impersonates you at one point.

Hers was just a little lighter.

Did you wear a wig?

No, that was my hair. My hair is blonde.

Didn't you tell me a minute ago that you were brown-haired?

When I was younger. Also, I should mention, I used a lower voice as the kveen, because I had to be in command and give orders and sound believable. I don't know where it came from, but it was quite low!

Ed Bernds—my first-ever interviewee—told me he went to Western Costume with Zsa Zsa and, when she got demanding, he found a phone and called Ben Schwalb and got after him to dump her!

She was very demanding, about clothes, about everything. And *he*, Mr. Bernds, was the sweetest man, he was such an angel—*every*body said that about him. Zsa Zsa couldn't remember her lines, and she used to yell out to the dialogue director [Herman Rotsten], "Herman! Vot is the goddamned line?" She could never remember, so finally they got her a teleprompter!

Did Bernds' patience ever seem to wear thin with her?

Yes, but he was *such* a patient man. I remember seeing him hold his head and go [*Mitchell makes a combination groan-sigh sound*]. But he was just a very sweet man: "All right, let's do another take," "*Another* take" and on and on. It was just like Billy Wilder with Marilyn: "Okay, Marilyn, darlingk ... Take 22!"

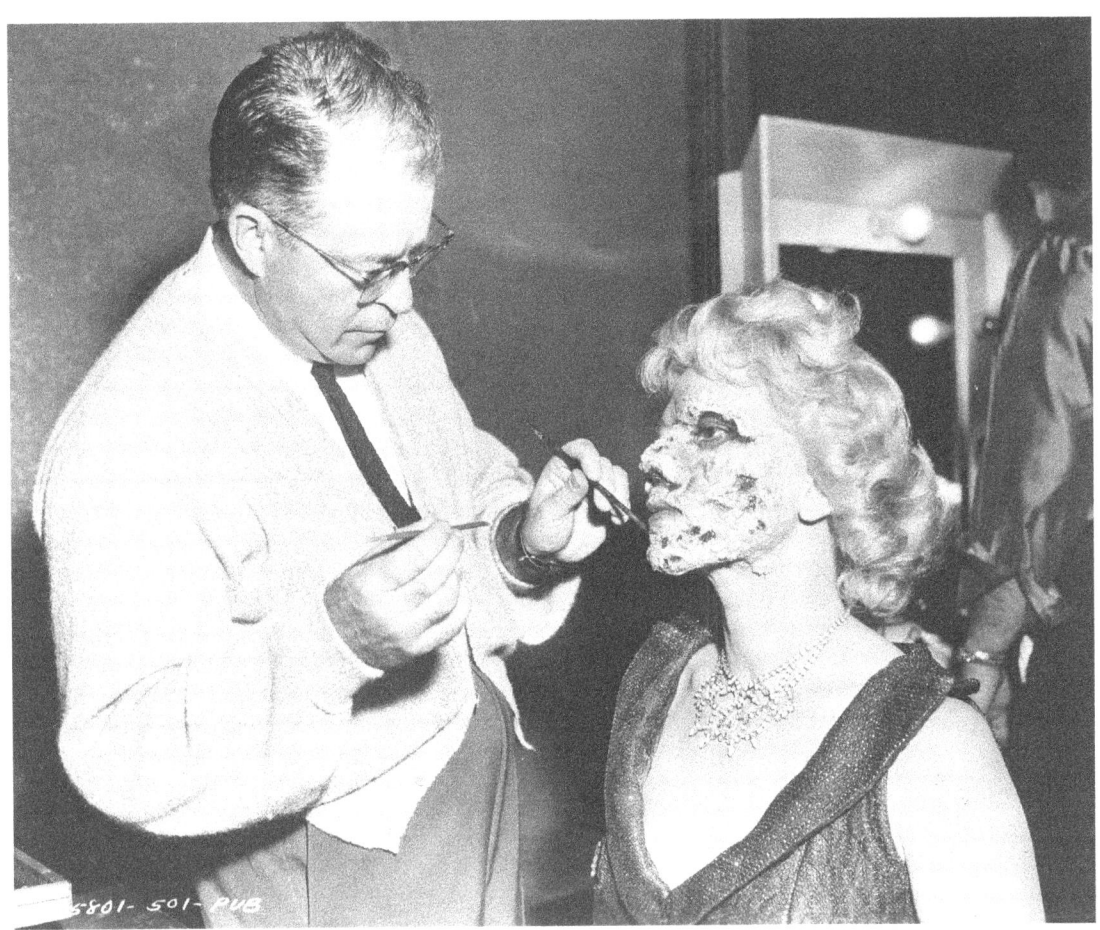

Outer Space makeup man Emile LaVigne transforms Mitchell into the burn-faced Queen Yllana. "Watching it go on ... it could cause nightmares!" she says today.

Early on, when you heard that Queen of Outer Space *was going to be color and CinemaScope, did that give you the feeling, before you knew better, that it was going to be a bigger picture than it was?*

No, I didn't think it was going to be a big picture at *all* [*laughs*]! And at the beginning I really thought it was not gonna do too well, because I felt that *she* was not doing such a great job. I remember the guys on the set—the people in charge of the lights, the carpenters, all the people who try so hard. They were saying things like [*in an exasperated voice*], "Oh, shoot!," "Oh, *this*" and "Oh, *that*" during the hard hours they were putting in. "Oh, this is *never* gonna go." Under their breath. Big sighs and big groans and comments like "Oh, jeez...."

All in reaction to Zsa Zsa being Zsa Zsa.

Yeah. All the behind-the-scenes people were doing that as Zsa Zsa went into Take 4 and Take 5 and Take 6. You have to have compassion, and I'm one who has great compassion, 'cause I was born in July, I'm a Moonchild, and I feel great compassion for people. I still remember all their remarks.

Ed Bernds told me that he could tell that Zsa Zsa "didn't like the competition"—all the younger, beautiful girls in the movie.

That's what I remember too, I certainly do. A self-centered person, that's all.

For you, *what was it like to be on a set with so many other beautiful women?*

I didn't think anything of it, it didn't bother me. 'Cause I'm a warm person. I was never on an ego trip, I was never like, "Listen, *I'm* the leading lady"—I never felt that way. I was just glad that they were working. And *I* was glad to be working!

Halfway through the making of the movie, Ben Schwalb went into the hospital for ulcers. Do you think Zsa Zsa gave him his ulcers?

I wouldn't be surprised [*laughs*]! The poor man!

Didn't anyone think it was ridiculous for a woman on Venus [Zsa Zsa's character] to have a Hungarian accent?

That *is* food for thought, isn't it? Where the hell *did* she come from? The Hungarian part of Venus? Well, maybe the Earth Hungarians took her and dropped her off there [*laughs*]! As for the other people in it, Eric Fleming was ... okay. He was cordial enough, but he wasn't particularly *warm*. I think he was wrapped up in something within him*self*, and I don't know what it was. Maybe he had problems within himself. Some actors are [*in an enthusiastic voice*], "Hi! How *are* ya? What's goin' on?" Eric was [*in a cold, businesslike voice*], "...Good morning." And that was *it*.

The Queen is so gaga over Eric Fleming's character, and as I watch the movie I think, "What does she see in this *lump?"*

He *was* very standoffish. A few years later, he was doing a movie in Peru and he was in a canoe that capsized, and he drowned. Terrible. Now, Patrick Waltz, another one of the leading men in the movie, was a sweetheart. He married the dearest little Lisa Davis, who was *also* in the movie. They married, and Lisa was such a sweetheart, adorable, adorable girl. They were a darling couple, and he died so young, of a heart attack. That was a tragedy. I ran into her several years ago, after he passed away. I was taking my sister to a doctor in Beverly Hills, and I looked up, and she was the nurse. I went, "...Lisa?" She went, "...Laurie??" We hugged each other, and I said, "Oh, I am so, so sorry," and she said, "So am I." A beautiful girl.

While making 20000 Leagues, *you told yourself that someday you'd have a Tony Curtis-level dressing room. What was your dressing room like on* Queen of Outer Space?

[*Laughs*] I had a *very* nice dressing room. But not all-mirrors!

Is it always you in the mask, or did you have a double?

It was always me.

Even at the end, when the kveen is inside the Beta Disintegrator as it's sparking and smoking?

Always me, yes, I was in the sparks and the smoke! One take. When it was over, the cast and the crew applauded, and I went, "Yyyyyyay!" [*Laughs*] I was so thrilled! They'd said, "Do it in one take," and I did, and they all applauded. When we finished the picture, I don't remember if we were a week late or *two* weeks late. By then, Ben was in the hospital and somebody called him, it must have been Ed, and he told Ben, "Laurie picked up the picture" [helped keep production moving along]. And Ben said, "Give her $850 more, because she is such an angel." It was Ed who told me that that's what Ben said. In those days, $850 was a lot of money, and I was *so* thrilled!

Earth astronaut Eric Fleming knows he can kiss tomorrow goodbye if he refuses to lock lips with Mitchell as the radiation-ravaged ruler.

And part of the reason Queen of Outer Space *took so long to shoot was Zsa Zsa not knowing her lines?*

Oh, absolutely. Well, they knew going into it that they were going to have a problem with her. She wanted *this*, she wanted *that*. Rubirosa [playboy Porfirio Rubirosa] was her boyfriend at the time—"Rrrrubirrrosa" she would call him. He would call her on the phone in her dressing room and she'd speak to him either in Italian or German—not Hungarian. And not English, that's for sure [*laughs*]! He sent her a case of the tiny bottles of champagne, which she shared with me. Zsa Zsa would say to me, in the morning, in the makeup room, "Oh, vot a shame they stuck a mask on such a beautiful face!"

Do you think she was sincere?

I don't think she was sincere. No. Not at all. Sometimes at the end of the day, when the mask and the makeup was off, and I was putting regular [beauty] makeup *on*, she'd go, "Vhere you goingk?" I'd say, "I'm going to meet my husband and get a bite to eat," and she'd say again, "You really *are* pretty, aren't you?" I'd say, "Oh, thank you"—but I'd be thinking to myself, "B.s.!" [*Laughs*] Incidentally, the gossip column of the *Los Angeles Times* said that she and I had a feud—which we never did. Why would she give me champagne, if we were feuding? They wrote that I was jealous of her, or that she was jealous of me, but it was baloney. Then, I would say ten years ago, I ran into her in Europe. I was at Heathrow Airport in England, and lo and behold, who was beside me but Zsa Zsa. I said, "Hello, Zsa Zsa, it's Laurie." She said [*distantly*], "Oh ... hello." I asked, "Do you know who I am?" and she said, "No, I do not." I said, "I did *Queen of Outer Space* with you. Queen Yllana."

She said [*still distant*], "That's nice.... Oh, I am so terribly upset. They vill not let me put my dog sitting next to me in the plane. They vant to put him with the luggage. He vill die! He vill die!" I said, "No he won't die. I'm sure everything will be fine," but she was furious: "I am going to make a big fuss over this! I vant him to sit next to me! Don't they know who I *am*?" "Yes, Zsa Zsa, they know who you are...." "I am never going on this airline again!" "All right. See ya. Bye!" [*Laughs*]

A lot of the stuff that goes on in Queen of Outer Space *is meant to be funny. Is it funny when it tries to be?*

No. But, what the heck, it sold. I don't know whether or not it made money, but I hope it did. And I enjoyed being Yllana, Queen of Outer Space.

I've interviewed two or three people who worked in Missile to the Moon, *and nobody remembers doing it!*

All I remember is that big spider coming at me in the cave. Today they'd do it with a computer, but in those days they had a guy up high

A closer look at Mitchell in makeup.

Mitchell to the moon: Between takes on *Missile to the Moon*, the actress (lower right), other lunar lovelies and Earthman Tommy Cook take a coffee and *Variety*-reading break.

handling the so-called "special effects," moving the legs of the spider like a puppet on strings. Target would make a fortune selling a spider like that for Halloween today [*laughs*]! Last Halloween I saw my nephew Scott making a big spider out of chicken wire, and I swear it looked exactly like the one that ate me up in *Missile to the Moon*! Leslie Parrish was a darling and very friendly and fun to be with, and a very pretty, pretty girl. As far as the other actors, I can't tell you much about them because I don't *remember* much else.

The most famous movie you were in—by far—would be Some Like It Hot.

Let me tell you something: The most thrilling experience of my show business career was that movie. It started out to be a three-week job, and I was so excited to get the part. Three weeks wound up three months, because of Marilyn—she was pregnant, she was always late, she didn't show up at all, all kinds of problems. And whether she showed up or *not*, we would get paid for the day. I met the most wonderful women, the finest women [the actresses who played the other girls in the band], and, I tell you, that was marvelous. I was so thrilled to be in this movie with Marilyn and Jack Lemmon. Jack was a darling, a darling. He schlepped around with all of us, he took us everywhere. Tony Curtis was kind of ... okay ... but we all loved Jack, he was just an angel.

Those eyebrows! Those legs! Those butts (on the soundstage floor)! Mitchell goes from a smoke break to a *smmmokin'* pose.

Why'd you give up on the acting?

I don't know what happened. When I married my husband Ron, a medical salesman, in 1978, he was traveling all over the country going to children's burn centers and trying to save a lot of kids with a certain product. I was going with him as his model: I would wear a leotard and he would put this product on me to show nurses how to use it, for burn victims. Then I stopped doing that, stopped going all over the country with him, and then *he* got out of that—

I'm sorry—you got away from my question. Why did you stop *acting?*

Because I was going around the country with *him*. I think he just wanted me to *be* with him—he's just a jealous cat [*laughs*]. I was pretty, and skinny. And now I'm neither!

Everybody who remembers you, remembers you for Queen of Outer Space. *How often do* you *watch the movie?*

Not often. But it was shown a lot over the years and, as I said before, it's amazing how many people saw it and are interested in it and are interested in sci-fi. I cannot believe the people who go to these sci-fi conventions and they want your autograph and they surround you. Me, little me! They go, "Laurie Mitchell! Can I have your autograph?" I'm absolutely amazed, and it just thrills me! It's like the paparazzi or something, *crowding* you! I recently went to a reunion of [veteran actors] at a place in Studio City called the Sportsmen's Lodge and at one point I went to the ladies room, and when I came out, [*Mitchell holds up her hand*] I swear to God, I came out and here were all these people gathered about, "Please sign this," "Please sign that," "Please, may I have your autograph?" Now I have a little bit of an inkling how these big *stars* must feel, wherever they go! A couple of the people who were coming at me at Sportsmen's Lodge couldn't even speak English! At first I wasn't sure what was going on, I was going, "Me? Me?," but then I realized that it *was* me whose autograph they all wanted. It was really so nice and it made me feel so good. Like I was a kid again.

Mitchell ruled Venus in *Queen of Outer Space* **and now, unmasked, reigns at autograph shows. Here she is at the 2007 Monster Bash with** *Puppet People* **co-star Kenny Miller.**

TANDRA QUINN

In the '50s, I did manage to slip into a few B-movies—
B for Bad [laughs]—starting with **Mesa of Lost Women.**

Literally, it looms 600 feet above Mexico's "Desert of Death"; figuratively, it towers over most of the other contenders for Worst '50s Sci-Fi Film. It's *Mesa of Lost Women*, the notoriously nonsensical shoestring saga of a spider-obsessed mad scientist, Dr. Aranya (Jackie Coogan), whose "master race" experiments in a Zarpa Mesa cave laboratory have resulted in an eight-foot spider, a slave crew of arachnid women (actresses bewigged with black-dyed mops), leering dwarfs, and his one perfect creation: The delicious but deadly Tarantella, a superwoman who, Aranya boasts, "possesses the capacities and instincts of the giant spider!"

Perhaps part of the reason this drecky exercise in dream-like delirium has lagged behind in Worst Film coverage is that, until now, almost nothing was known about the making of the movie outside of the fact that writer-director Herbert Tevos' original 1951 version proved to be unreleasable, and that director Ron Ormond was hired the following year to do the necessary fix-up work. Now coming forward to dispel the clouds of mystery is the one survivor among the key participants, Tarantella herself, '50s actress and pinup model Tandra Quinn. She may have been mute in her two fright flicks, *Mesa* and *The Neanderthal Man* (also 1953), but has plenty to say now (not much of it good!) about her days of neverlasting stardom...

I grew up seeing The Neanderthal Man *on TV, and you played a deaf-mute in it.*

In *Neanderthal Man* I was supposed to be deaf and dumb, and I communicated by "signing." There was a lady on the set who taught us how to do the signing.

Then later I saw Mesa of Lost Women *and again you didn't speak, and I said to myself, "That settles it, she must have been deaf and dumb in real life!"*

[*Laughs*] Yeah, they cut my tongue out at birth! You thought I was actually deaf and dumb? How funny! That's kind of ironic, 'cause when I was just 11 or 12, screen-testing at 20th Century–Fox, the sound man came over to my mother and told her, "This girl has the most remarkable voice, one of those 'special voices' that the microphone just loves. It comes over pure and perfect." And all my life I've had people tell me that, over the phone, I have a very compelling voice. Well, that and five dollars will get me a cup of coffee at Starbucks [*laughs*]! But, yes, I had an exceptional voice, and yet never did I have a decent speaking part in a movie. I would have *loved* to.

How did you get the part of Tarantella in Mesa of Lost Women?

Through Herbert Tevos—it was his enchilada. He was the director and the writer and of course was the one who developed the part of Tarantella. I was still living at home in L.A. with my parents when *Mesa* came along, and I've been trying to recall how I got involved or how I met Tevos, but it doesn't come back to me. I remember taking the bus on a long, long trip to go up to the ranch house in Encino or Sherman Oaks where Tevos was living. He was a German director and he used to brag how he directed Marlene Dietrich in *The Blue Angel* [1930] and molded her into the star she became.

As I'm sure you know by now, he didn't direct Dietrich in Blue Angel *or anything else. I think* Mesa *was his only movie.*

I guess he also gave the *Mesa* producers a big line on his background, about how he directed Dietrich and Erich von Stroheim and how he was one of the greats in Germany. He had a very heavy accent so I'm sure he *was* from Germany, but just what he *did* over there I don't know. Tevos was a real character. He tried to be my Svengali, my mentor, and kinda dominate every one of my moves. He wanted to make this exotic character out of me and he came up with the screen name "Tandra Nova" for me. That was too heavy a label to put on me, it sounded like a Russian ballet dancer or something—how embarrassing and ridiculous. It also made me think of the old prizefighter, *Lou* Nova! I said, "Oh, come *on*. I'll take Tandra—I'm not crazy about it but I'll take it. But you can keep the Nova!"

So who came up with Quinn as a last name instead?

I "borrowed" that from Joan Quinn, a lovely dancer with whom I went to the Grace Bowman School of Drama and Dance when I was 10 or 11; I was much younger than she was, and I used to watch and admire her because she was so graceful. A lot of "young hopefuls" were there at Grace Bowman's, Mala Powers and Connie Laird and several girls who ended up on TV, I can't remember their names. Speaking of Tevos, I also remember going with him to a record store and getting the music for me to dance to in the *Mesa* movie. Some time after that, when he and I were at a party at somebody else's home, there was a little stage there in the house and Tevos wanted me to get up on the stage and dance to the music. He suggested it, and all the other people there started clapping, so I didn't have much choice [*laughs*]!

For him to have brought along the record, he must have had this planned.

Tandra Quinn received special "Introducing..." billing in the hair-raisingly horrid Mesa of Lost Women.

Quinn agrees whole-heartedly with any and all critics and Worst Films fans who have cast stones at her performance as the sexy, self-regenerating spider woman Tarantella (Photofest).

Oh, sure. He was trying to re-form my personality, he wanted me to be more outward. I was kind of just a sheltered, quiet kid, and he tried to bring me out of my shell, make me more sexy and brazen.

How much older than you was he?

He was an old duck, probably 50 or 55. Being 18 or whatever I was, that seemed reeeally old to me at the time!

So you were a teenager when you did all three of your movies?

Yep. I look older 'cause I was rode hard and put away wet [*laughs*]! Oh, on one occasion, Tevos just about wanted to kill me: He had a party there at his house and I didn't drink, I never cared about alcohol, I'm an ice cream and cake and cookies person. We were all in the yard and I was sitting in a big wooden chair and Tevos kept filling up everybody's glass with champagne or some kind of wine. I didn't want to be rude so I'd let him fill my glass, and when he wasn't looking I'd pour it on the lawn. Well, the next morning, all the grass around the chair was dead [*laughs*]! "You wasted my champagne!"—oh, he just went crazy, he was furious. He probably spent his last buck on that bottle of wine!

His last buck? I thought you said he had a ranch house.

[*Laughs*] Oh, no, he lived in a little guest house in the back of somebody *else's* house. I guess the owners let him stay there to oversee things or take care of the grounds while they were abroad or something. Evidently he was livin' pretty cheap.

Who owned the property?

I have no idea, I don't think I ever met 'em.

So he was like the 1950s Kato Kaelin!

Yeah, I guess so! Tevos was real serious, I don't think he ever laughed, I never saw him laugh. One of these directors consumed with his art, real grim. When he spoke, it was like Herr General Herbert Von Tevos, giving orders [*laughs*]!

Why did you go up there so often? Did you actually think he'd be able to help you with your career?

Like I say, he was trying to act like my guru or Svengali, trying to mold me into one of his protégés, I guess. "I did it for Marlene Dietrich, I can do it for you!" It was up to him to do some of the casting for *Mesa* and so he had Leif Erickson over to the guest house one afternoon. Tevos was trying—rather, *ordering* Leif to do one of the parts and Leif turned him down; I guess Leif didn't think the movie was up to his standards. And Tevos became furious! Leif showed class, he tried to bow out courteously and gently, but Tevos hit the ceiling and threw him out! [*With German accent:*] "You wait! You wait! You'll be sorry! You'll be sorry someday, when I am at the top of the ladder and *you* are nobody! You'll come *crrrawling* to me for a *bit* part!" Oh, he just went nuts, but Leif kept his cool. He was one nice guy, that Leif Erickson.

Reportedly when Tevos shot the movie, it was called Tarantula.

Could have been. I remember I couldn't get from where I lived with my parents, clear out to where they were making the movie, every day; it was too far and I didn't have a car. So I looked for a place to stay close to the studio. Somehow or other I found out about a lady who was looking for a roommate and I moved into her nice house out in Tarzana. She was very nice and we got along fine, and I was there when we made the movie. She was a friend of the actor John Carroll, and she and I had some good times out at his ranch. And

When she starred in *Mesa*, **Quinn was a teen still living at home with her parents; she says she looks older** "because I was rode hard and put away wet!"

[during the shooting of *Mesa*], I'd go out to eat all the time with the gang—Paula Hill [billed as *Mary* Hill in *Mesa*], Tevos, different members of the cast. The very finest grog and grub establishments in the Valley. Tevos drank only Courvoisier; it had to be Courvoisier, it had to be the best, because he had this image of himself, this persona that he was a real upperclass, famous German director and he had to do all the right things. In *his* mind, he was to be looked upon as someone you should feel honored to go out and drink Courvoisier with. No Budweiser beer for him [*laughs*]!

Your extended dance scene in the cantina is your "big moment" in Mesa.
You don't call that dancing, do you [*laughs*]? I'd taken dance lessons when I was younger, but I was never that great. So I just made it up as I went along.

The dance struck me as imitation–Rita Hayworth.
That's funny you mention her, 'cause a little later, I wanted to take dancing lessons, so I went out to Rita Hayworth's father Eduardo Cansino's dance studio. His wife was the receptionist and she gave me the price and everything, signed me up, and then I went in to meet Mr. Cansino. And, dumb me, after my interview with him I came out and I said to her, "Oh, your husband is so fascinating." Well, what I *meant* was, his accent was fascinating and his suaveness was fascinating. I was just a young kid and he was quite old so I cer-

Mesa's hotcha highlight is Quinn's dance in a Mexican cantina.

tainly didn't mean it in any other way, but she thought I had designs on him and she wouldn't let me come take the lessons [*laughs*]! She cut me off *real* quick! I was so stupid back then, I never thought before I spoke.

On Mesa, *did you have a choreographer or any*body *to help you with that dance?*

[*Scornfully*] No, a choreographer was not in the budget, so I bluffed it. I had to do my own dance, I had to design my own costume, my own makeup, my own hair and everything else.

How'd you feel when you were doing the dance?

I was born to be an actress, I guess I'm just a ham, so I enjoyed every bit of it. But I should tell you that, physically, I think I was not well when I was making that *Mesa* movie, I was sick all the time. I was a compulsive eater, ice cream and sweets. I used to live on chocolate bars!

Oh, that reminds me: One morning before Tevos started shooting, I was at a drive-in [diner] across the street from the studio, having a milkshake or something—I didn't drink coffee then. And I noticed that, sitting right *by* me was the guy who always played Japanese villains in the movies, the real mean one. I can't think of his name but it seemed like he was in every single World War II Pacific Theater movie, always playing the evil butcher. I looked at him and recognized him and remembered that I hated him in all those movies and—again, I didn't think before I spoke—I said, "Oh, I *hate* you!" [*Laughs*] He looked at me kind of weird but then he laughed and he said, "*Thank* you, miss. I appreciate that. The more you hate me, the better I like it!" He knew that my "hating" him meant that he was doing his job and that he was a good actor!

The other stars of Mesa—*what were they like?*
Robert Knapp [*Mesa*'s leading man] was one sweet guy. Very popular with some of the girls on the set, but no monkey business for him. I'm sure his lovely wife appreciated that! And the little guy who played the kidnapped scientist, the actor who looked like Elmer Fudd, what was his name? Harmon Stevens! He looked like Elmer Fudd, just exactly! Wore the little derby hat, and had that little nose, and that grin. A cross between Mr. Magoo and Elmer Fudd! But he was really nice.

I like the scene before the credits where the guy is standing there minding his own business, and you [as Tarantella] appear and start kissing him....
[*Laughs*] Allan Nixon was married to Marie Wilson. Kind of strange, real quiet, but I'm sure many thought of *me* as strange too! He was a good-looking kid, but didn't have much chance to display his acting talent in *Mesa* because he didn't have much of a part.

And the leading lady Paula Hill?
[*Sighs*] In the scene when they board the airplane, she wore this suit that some costume designer had made for her. It was real pretty, a soft cashmere wool-type suit, and I just loved it and so I asked her, could she get *me* one too? She said, "That'll be $110." But that was okay because I wanted one, I really loved that suit. So I got an exact copy of it.

If you remember the movie, the plane crashed and her suit got all messed up and dirty. Well, for some reason, later on they had to film that scene over and they didn't know what to do about her suit, and she mentioned that I had one just like it. So they asked me, "Can we borrow your suit?," and I said sure. You know me—I didn't think to say, "Yeah, but give me a deposit first"; I had no business brains in those days at all. I don't even think I got *paid* for doin' the movie! Anyway, she took my suit and wore it when they did the plane scene a second time. Afterwards I kept asking for it back, asking what happened to it. I never found out what happened to it, nobody could give me an answer. I never got it back.

Well, who except her *would have a motive to keep it?*
Yeah, I kinda think she kept it. She knew I was an easy mark.

What were your measurements back in your Mesa *days?*
Well, I always *lied* about them, but I was probably 37-27-35. And I was about 5' 5½".

In most of your scenes where you're not the center of attention, you're off on the sidelines just glaring angrily at the other people.
Oh, really? Hmmm. Maybe that's just my ornery face [*laughs*]!

How much direction did you get?
None.

Did Tevos seem to know what he was doing?
That's hard to say. Basically he was pretty intelligent, because I remember he had a friend who was a nuclear physicist who used to come over to the guest house when I was up there, and we'd have lunch, and they would talk nuclear science and so forth, which went right over my head. So he seemed like he was a pretty smart guy. But on the other hand,

Mesa leads Robert Knapp and Paula Hill are helpless in the clutches of Quinn and dwarf John George. Notice the mop wigs on the background Spider Women (Photofest).

the [*Mesa* producers] said he didn't know what he was doing on that set. So ... who knows? It was kind of sad ... he thought of himself as such a great director....

One time during the making of *Mesa*, Tevos and I went to this big restaurant out in the Valley, Sportsmen's Lodge maybe. For some reason, foreigners seemed to be attracted to me more than American guys. I found out recently that my heritage is Romanian—vampires [*laughs*]! I guess that's why I'm tuned-in with Europeans. Anyway, Tevos and I were at this restaurant and we ordered and he was always being the Svengali, telling me how I had to act and walk and this and that. And then he said, more like an order [*with a German accent*], "I would like you to marry me." It was such a shock to me that, instead of being nice and saying something nice, I didn't know what to say, so I got up and walked out [*laughs*]. Which *wasn't* very nice!

Was he a good-looking older guy at least?

Oh, no, no. Hell, I'd have married him if he was [*laughs*]! No, he was smaller than me, and rather homely. I guess he drifted off into the Old German Directors' Graveyard, I don't know *where* he went [*laughs*]!

The fans of Mesa of Lost Women *have never been quite sure: Did Tevos finish the movie or not? When you said goodbye to everybody at the end of that first go-round, did you have the feeling the movie was done, or not?*

Starring in a no-budget picture like *Mesa* entailed a mess-a extra responsibilities for Quinn (doing her own costume, hair, makeup, etc.).

I had the feeling it was done. They had like a party, a *showing*—they ran it some place, I can't remember where, and everybody came, including my mother and dad. I'm pretty sure that was at the end of the shooting that Tevos did, and that Tevos was there, but I *could* be wrong. My brain gets hazy about things as long ago as that.

Many months after Mesa *wrapped, maybe a year, suddenly it was back in production again, and with a different director.*

Yeah, Ron Ormond took over, and they changed the thing around. Shot additional scenes, and kinda "improved" it.

Did Ormond shoot at the same place that Tevos did?

No, but I just cannot remember where *either* place was. When we did the second "version," I went back and forth to the studio from my apartment on Ozeta Terrace in Hollywood, which was where I was living at that point. Most everything was filmed the first time around; the guys making the second "version" didn't add too much. One thing I remember is that I did the café dance in the Tevos one, and with Ormond we added some footage where, at the end of the dance, somebody *shoots* me. I danced in the first version and died in the second version. If you'll notice, my hair is longer in the second version. It grew real fast during that dance [*laughs*]! And got a little darker, because I put some black dye on it for the second.

What was the "blood" in that scene? Chocolate?

I don't remember. If it *was* chocolate, I would have licked it off [*laughs*]! I was a chocoholic! Oh, and I just got another "flashback": When we were doing the Ormond version, I went to a doctor because of a low thyroid or something, and he gave me Dexedrine pills, which are amphetamines. I took a couple of them, and they made me so hyper and made me feel so horrible that I didn't *want* any more! So I had these Dexedrine pills that I didn't want and on the *Mesa* set where there were a bunch of people milling around, I mentioned it. All of a sudden [*in a babbling voice*], "Oh, can *we* have 'em? Can *we* have 'em??" [*laughs*]—everybody was clamoring at me and coming to get my Dexedrine pills. I think that was the most popularity I had in the movie business [*laughs*]!

What was Ron Ormond like?

I can't say too much, I didn't know him that well, but he had a few weird friends. They were having some kind of arguments, probably about money; it usually *is*.

June Ormond, Ron's widow, said in an interview that the other spider girls with the crazy hairdos were wearing mops *made up into wigs.*

And you ask why *Mesa* didn't win an Academy Award [*laughs*]? Oh, that's hilarious, they couldn't even afford wigs! Incidentally, after the movie was made, I started going out with my future husband, and we went to Laguna Beach and we were in a bar down there when some guy came up to me and he said, "Hey, I saw you in that movie, you were *good*!" I said, "What movie?," and it was *Mesa*. I couldn't believe it! How would he remember?, how would he recognize me? That was a year or so after.

And your memory is that you didn't get paid for Mesa of Lost Women.

Really, I don't remember. I went through anguish in those days, I guess because my physical condition was affecting my brain. I was living on ice cream and candy, and I still have a problem with ice cream. I have to buy it every time I go to the store, and I fight with myself 'til it's gone! Later on, I became a nutrition expert and was redeemed [*laughs*]. Oh, it's true, it's true! If I hadn't gotten into nutrition, I'd be dead, the way I was eating and taking care of myself.

Did you see Mesa of Lost Women *when it played in theaters?*
   No, I never saw it originally, I didn't even know where it played. *Years* after we did it, my sister taped it off TV and sent it to me. When I saw the dance scene again ... well [*laughs*], we could have done better, but at the time, as I mentioned, I was lucky to even be functioning because I wasn't too well. When you [look back at your own movies], you think, "Oh, had things been different, I could have done better things, and I could have gone somewhere." Actually, my movie career was like a miscarriage after the first month of pregnancy: A little bit of spark ignited, and then it died. In other words ... it was kinda depressing. I *know* that, had I not been burned as a child and had I had a different circumstance early on, *maybe* things would have been different [career-wise]. I don't *know*, I'm just saying "maybe." Of course, I could have stepped out in front of a truck and got killed, too [*laughs*]! But I know I could have had a career in films. Nowadays I wouldn't *want* one. I don't like the garbage they make now.

How did you get burned as a child?
   When I was around two and a half years old, we were living in downtown Los Angeles, on Union Street. The guy who owned the place, which was maybe five units, was Mr. Baxter, a multi-multi-millionaire even in those days; he owned much of Los Angeles' real estate. He had his office in the back, and my mother worked in his office and he rented us the apartment in the front for like $15 a month. We had this faulty heater in there, a five dollar item, and Mr. Baxter had had three warnings from the City Health Department to replace it. But I guess five dollars was just too much for this multi-millionaire to part with. This heater had no guard on it, the flames just shot out. One night, my mother was working in the office and my dad was in the dining room; even though I was two, I remember he was combing his hair. I had a little flannel nightgown on and I had a paper doll in my hand, and I wanted to warm up the paper doll so I stuck her in the heater. And a flame went from the paper doll, up the sleeve of my nightgown—and in those days, they didn't have that non-flammable material that they use now. I went up in flames. My dad ran in and wrapped me in a rug and rolled me onto the couch. I remember the siren of the ambulance coming....
   I was horribly burned. The flames fused my neck to my chest, there was no division. So I was all crusted or scabbed, clear down my whole chest. They worked on me every day, taking off that crust; I remember the pain. It took several doctors or nurses to hold me down. I was screaming, because it was excruciating—the pain was torture! I still remember, even though it happened when I was just two and a half. Nowadays they have hyperbaric machines to put you in and everything they need to heal you, but back then they had *nothing*. After several days of this, at a point when I was not doing well, the doctor came in and told my parents, "She can't last more than 12 days. You can go ahead and start making funeral preparations." Great, huh?
   Anyhow, I survived, and they took me home, and it wasn't too long after that that I slipped in the bathtub and hit my head on the faucet or something, and I was back in the hospital with *that* [*laughs*]! Somebody up there ... or somebody *down* there ... didn't like me and was tryin' to get rid of me! But I was luckier than this little girl who lived in another apartment place where we lived, a beautiful little girl with golden curls. We used to play together, and one day her mother gave us each an orange. She wanted her orange with a hole punched in it so she could suck the juice out of it, but not *me*, I wanted mine cut in

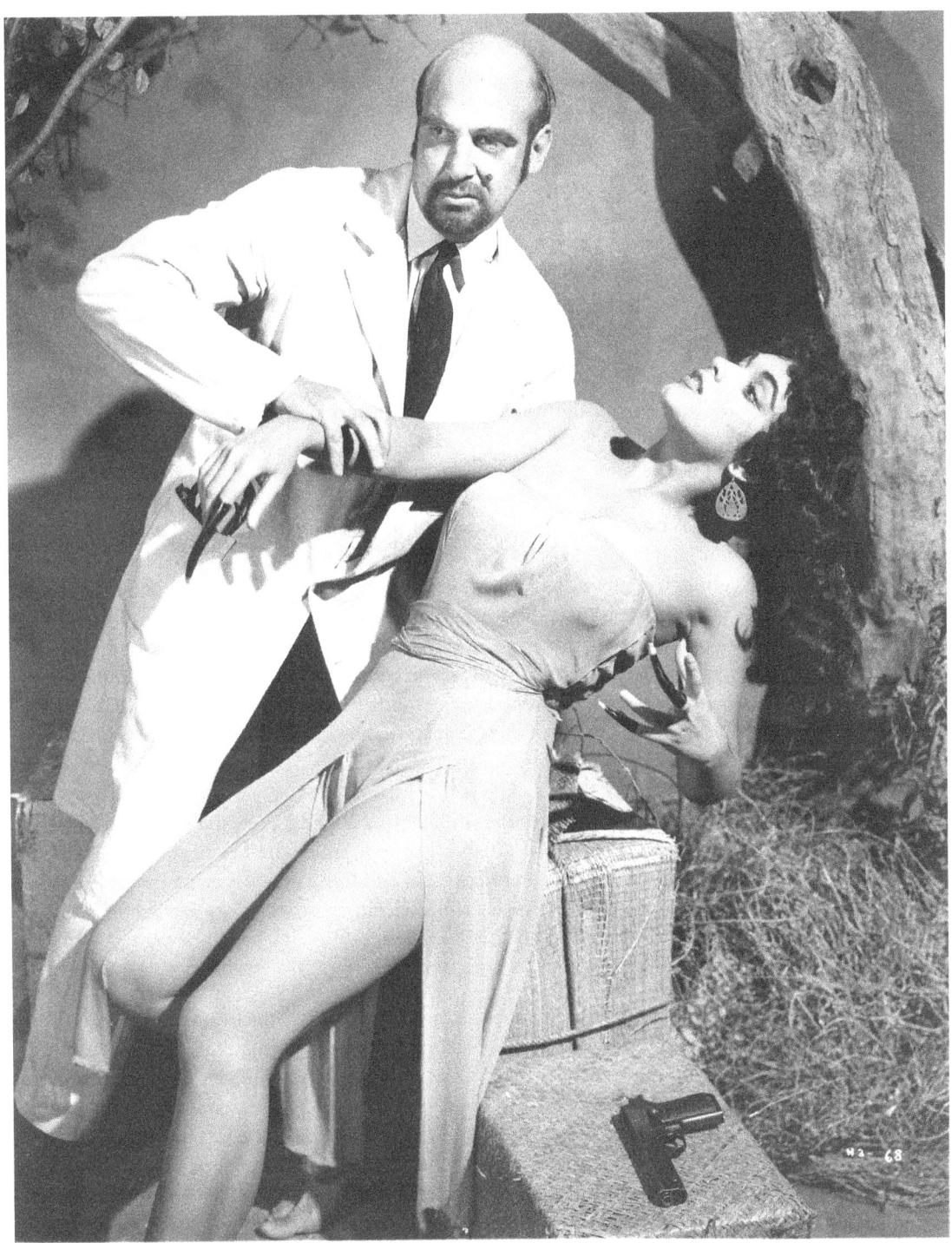

When Ron Ormond added footage to *Mesa*, Quinn was re-hired and Jackie Coogan (above) brought in to play a new character, Dr. Aranya, the insect world's answer to Dr. Moreau (Photofest).

half so I could pull out the orange sections. We played for a while, and then my mother said to me, "Come on, come to the store with me." We walked to the store, and by the time we came home there was an ambulance in the front. It was for Merle. She had her mouth on that orange, and the skin had arsenic on it. Some of it got into her system and it was too much for her. They rushed her to the hospital, but she died.

You did *have it rough.*
At the apartment place where Merle died, I remember my dad killing rats the size of small dogs—L.A. in those days had a terrible rat problem. I didn't grow up like Paris Hilton, that's for sure! But my mother had it even rougher, she had *such* a struggle in her early life that she didn't want me to have to go through what *she* went through. She never had a family or money or anything; she lived with 28 foster families....

Twenty-eight?!
When she was born, her mother died giving birth to her, and the father was so in love with the mother that it just shattered him and he died a short time later—heartbreak. And the sisters and brothers all blamed *her* for killing the mother, which is totally ridiculous but they *did*. (They were ... a bit evil.) Nobody would take her home from the hospital, so the nurses there had to take care of her until she could be placed with a foster family. She had one real nice German man who took her in as a foster child, maybe he adopted her, but then he married this horrible woman who used to lock her out and who would lie about her and everything else. *That* didn't work, so she went to another home, and it just went on and on like that—you know how those situations are. Finally one of her brothers contacted her and brought her to her sisters, and she lived with her sisters, who treated her like Cinderella, a maid: Made her do all the work and everything, wouldn't buy her any clothes and just were very, very cruel to her. So she ran away, and slept in the park, and had a terrible time. Even the churches wouldn't let her come in, they slammed the doors in her face, if she wasn't their religion. It was almost uncanny the way she survived.

Finally she got a job at 13 and worked until she was 16, and at 16 she went on the road selling magazines. And she stayed *good* all through that time, she never got corrupted or anything. This was back east, in Philadelphia, in Baltimore. Then she came out to Denver selling magazines and met my dad, who was an electrician-lineman. They moved on to California because he figured he could get better work there.

And that's where you were born?
In the throes of the Depression, in an L.A. charity hospital, my beautiful mother gave birth to an average-looking baby—me, little Derline Jeanette Smith. Early on, Mother must have said, "This kid is going to escape the traumas of *my* childhood of abandonment, abuse, poverty. I'll work hard to see that she has a good life—and what better way than to become a successful Hollywood actress?" So it began with the ol' baby beauty contest routine. Looking at old pictures, a beauty I wasn't, but I did make it as the #1 Perfect Baby in America as declared by the Chiropractors Association after a nationwide search. And with all the publicity, photo shoots, silver cup and all, Mom was obviously bitten by the show biz bug. There was no stopping her now: I was in for dramatic lessons, Meglin Kiddies (the most famous dance studio for little kids), the whole bit. Even violin lessons! Evidently I had a problem with coordination: I couldn't make the violin work, couldn't make the feet go "out, back, down." The Meglin coach broke the news to Mom that she shouldn't waste her money on dancing lessons but as for the dramatic lessons I showed promise.

As a child I did mostly fashion modeling and plays put on at my acting schools. I signed with a child actor agent, Lola Moore, who sent me on an audition for the part of Velvet Brown in *National Velvet* [1944]. Liz [Elizabeth Taylor] was there in her smart little lavender blue suit—she was a vision. The part called for a pretty English girl of about 12 and, above all, an experienced equestrienne. Well, here's this beautiful child [Taylor] from England who frequently rode horses with Anthony Eden ... and then there *I* was, not so beautiful, in a cotton dress, who rode a mule once [*laughs*]!

Did you have any *luck getting movie parts as a kid?*

No, not too much, because I was very introverted and shy—I didn't seem to have enough oom-pah-pah. You have to be very much an extrovert when you're a child star and I just didn't have it. Mother tried hard to get me in the movies; in fact, she forced me so much that I turned the other way, I didn't want to do it.

What movies were *you in?*

The first thing they put me in was *Week-end at the Waldorf* [1945]. I was one of about six schoolgirls taking a tour of New York City and looking at the Waldorf-Astoria, but it ended up on the cutting room floor. I did a lot of testing and everything, but soon a problem with my face started to come into play. When I was about 14, Mom tried to get me the part of Catana in 20th Century–Fox's *Captain from Castile* [1947] because she had known Ty Power while living next door to a lodge in Bishop where he vacationed. He was very sweet to both my mother and me, so she wrote him, sent him my picture, and he did set up the interview at Fox. I tested there, but I appeared much too young, so they signed a beautiful unknown by the name of Jean Peters who was perfect for the part. However, 20th did sign me to a seven-year contract with a drop option which they exercised because Ivan Kahn said from his easy chair in a screening room, as he looked at footage of me, "She has something wrong with her face ... a shadow appears on one side ... I can't use her."

"There's something wrong with her face," a disdainful talent executive said of young Quinn.

He was watching your screen test?

Yes, and the screen tests they gave you for long-term contracts were very exploratory, they're almost like X-rays, they photograph you from every angle, top and bottom and sideways and every other way. Mother and I were sitting in the screening room and Kahn made that remark, "There's something wrong with her face...." He thought it was out of kilter, not symmetrical.

And that was a result of that burn when you were a baby.
[*Long pause*] Yup. The burns caused irreversible damage to facial bone development, which was now proving detrimental to my pursuit of a film career. "There's something wrong with her face"—that made an indelible impression on my mind, it just threw me into a low self-esteem [situation], because it happened over and over again. So 20th Century–Fox dropped me, and we were all very depressed. My mother was in denial, she said it had nothing to do with the face—

But you heard Kahn say it was the face.
Yes I did, but she was in denial. Then, too, there were the burns on my right chest. You can really see it in the *Mesa* movie because I wear that low-cut thing, you can see kind of an odd look to the skin there. It wasn't *real* obvious, but moviemakers strove for perfection in those days and actresses had to have a perfect look. *Nowadays* you look at some of 'em, and they are far from perfect.

But you half-heartedly kept plugging away.
After I finished school, I resumed the acting pursuit along with various modeling jobs but the rejection I experienced along the way caused me to withdraw. I just wasn't tough enough. I let down my dear agent Maurine Oliver. She'd call me for an interview and I would play sick. Other interviews, sometimes I just wouldn't show. Howard Hawks called me and asked to meet with me. I said I'd call him back but didn't. He or his wife, I can't remember which it was, called again, but I never returned the call. I had a real mental block.

I was probably the only girl ever to stand up the big shot Howard Hughes! He probably saw my picture in a '50s models magazine and he had a Hollywood photographer by the name of Paul Hesse arrange an appointment for me to come to his studio and pose. Somehow I found out that Hughes would also be there, hiding behind a curtain to "check me over," making sure I was "mole-less," "scar-less," 100 percent blemish free of face and body so I would qualify to join his "harem." So I stood "H.H." up. I had some good people who encouraged me—Mel Ferrer, Andre di Dienes [Marilyn Monroe's photographer], even Mickey Rooney. And then in the '50s, of course, I did manage to slip into a few B-movies—B for Bad [*laughs*]—starting with *Mesa of Lost Women*. But the rejections—too many. I wasn't emotionally strong enough to forge on.

Just before you did the re-shoots on Mesa of Lost Women, *you appeared in the low-budget,* Problem Girls.
I'm pretty sure I got that through Maurine Oliver, my agent, such a sweet lady. By this time I was no longer living at home, I had a little apartment up in Hollywood, I think it was all of $75 a month. I can remember Maurine picking me up there. The way she drove, the wheels didn't touch the road, it was life-threatening! There wasn't much traffic then, so she would tear down Sunset Boulevard. I just closed my eyes and prayed!

Problem Girls *was shot in an actual house, correct?*
Yes, some big house in L.A., I forget what street it was on. Jimmy Seay [playing a villain] had a yellow MG, one of those little English cars, and we'd buzz all over town in that. And he was really nice. Since I didn't have any transportation, a lot of times he would come pick me up and take me where I had to go.

Marriage, motherhood and the pain of too many rejections made Quinn decide to turn her back on show biz.

Was he on the make, or just a nice guy?

Just a really nice guy. I don't know if he was married or not, but he was quite a bit older than I was, and he was a gentleman. Mara Corday [playing a pyromaniac] was real sweet, real nice to me, she took me home after work a couple of times—she had a nice convertible. She was a top pinup model and appeared in a lot of magazines. She was in it, Ross Elliott (another real nice guy) as the good guy, Beverly Garland as the floozy, Helen Walker as the other villain....

Helen Walker had starred in some major-studio pictures—

Yeah, she did *Murder My Sweet* [1944].

I think she was a drinker.

Duuuuh! [*Laughs*] She may have been drinking through the whole shoot. And cuss everybody out? My *God*! They'd say, "Miss Walker, we need you here," and she'd tell 'em to go you-know-what themselves! "I'll come when I'm goddamn *ready*. Shut up! Leave me alone!" A real caustic mouth. But she could be nice.

To you girls?

Real nice. I guess she kinda figured she'd come down a little bit in the world here, and she didn't owe them [the filmmakers] anything. She was about the only name in the movie so she had the power over everybody, 'cause she was somebody and we were all a bunch of nobodies.

The "bad girls" in Problem Girls *weren't really so bad.*

By today's standards, they'd be considered *nice* girls [*laughs*]! By the way, somebody who was at the house during *Problem Girls* was Beverly Garland's husband, the actor Richard Garland. He was nice, but Beverly said, "I'm gonna divorce him," and I couldn't understand why. I asked, "Why are you gonna get a divorce? He seems so nice," and she said, "He's in my way, he's hampering my career."

The director was a guy who, in the silent days, made some famous pictures in Germany. He was no Herbert Tevos, he actually did *make 'em!*

Now there was a character right out of the old European theater! E.A. Dupont wanted me to go out with him one night, and so we went to a restaurant-bar up in Hollywood and he started telling me how he thought I was "different," how I was the only one who had promise, that I had all this hidden talent. He also told me all these experiences he'd had and how he was a big director in Germany. He was okay, he was nice, he didn't try to get fresh or anything, and I just had a nice evening with him. He was probably quite talented ... but you couldn't tell that from *Problem Girls* [*laughs*]!

He was also an agent. Maybe he was *sincere, just interested in your talent.*

Really? I can't picture him being an agent, he was not much of a winning personality [*laughs*]! But he was very complimentary to me, Dupont. Incidentally, they made two versions of *Problem Girls*, and one was for Europe where ... [*pause*] ... where in the shower I was topless.

In the European version, in the scene where you were strung up in the shower by the mean matron [Eileen Stevens], you were topless? Did you have a problem with that?

Well, obviously no [*laughs*]. I'd done a lot of pinup modeling and stuff, so I wasn't too concerned with that.

Were you the only one they asked to do something like that?

I really don't know. In those days I was kind of catatonic, like a zombie. I'd had somewhat of a breakdown, you might say. I really just went through the motions of life, but I really didn't actually know what I was doing. I wasn't in too good of a shape. Then I met my husband, who was a lot older than I was. I owe him my life, he got me all straightened out, restored my self-esteem and everything. I married him in '54.

But before you did that, you were in The Neanderthal Man, *made by the same producers who made* Problem Girls.

Yeah, [Jack] Pollexfen and [Aubrey] Wisberg, so that's how that happened. It was shot at some studio they rented [Eagle Lion Studios]. Richard Crane, who played the lead, was nice and we were good friends on the set. It annoyed him that he had to wear mascara [as part of his makeup], he didn't like the idea of wearing mascara. And as I mentioned, in order for me to play a deaf-mute, they had a professional there who taught some of us signing. When you're young, you pick up things very fast, but I'm sure I made a lot of mistakes. I bet nobody noticed.

Only deaf people noticed!

[*Laughs*] Right, deaf people out in the audience, asking each other, "What the heck is she *saying*?"

A second mute role followed when Quinn, playing a deaf-and-dumb servant, ran afoul of mad professor Robert Shayne in *The Neanderthal Man* **(Photofest).**

In the movie we see a series of snapshots of you transforming into a cave woman.

They added the big eyebrows and everything else right onto the snapshots. I didn't get made-up as a monster, oh no no no no.

That mighta been fun!

Well, I dunno.... No, I think *not* [*laughs*]. I don't want to be made uglier, I'm ugly enough!

Not back then and not now! What did you think of Neanderthal Man *when you saw it?*

It was a little boring in some of the long periods of talk. Too much talk, not enough action.

You used a different screen name in Neanderthal Man, *Jeanette Quinn, but you're so recognizable, all the fans have always known that was you.*

I'd already "borrowed" Quinn for *Mesa* and I liked it, so I kept it, and Jeanette is my real middle name. My mother could sing like Jeanette MacDonald and so named me after her.

Why was Neanderthal Man *your last movie? Did you stop looking for parts?*

When I was 19, I met my future husband Herbert, and we got married when I was 21. He was a builder in the Beverly Hills and Brentwood area. The way we met was, he was interested in photography and he financed a photography studio for a couple of photographers on the Sunset Strip. There he saw me on a calendar that I'd posed for; it was for Navajo Freight Lines and I'd love to have a copy of that calendar, I've never seen it. Anyway, he liked my looks and he wanted to meet me and he called me. I came up on the bus to meet him, and away we went. He was a lot older than me, 20-some years older, but we got along real good and got married and had two children.

And once you started having kids, that was the end of the movies?

Yeah, we went off on other tangents, tried to do other types of projects. And there was a lot of traveling—to the South Pacific, New Zealand, Australia, Tasmania, Tahiti, Samoa, all over the place!

And in recent years, one of your passions has been ... gold mining??

My husband and I were always interested in treasure hunting, and in 1979 I got interested in gold mining. Herbert never showed any interest in that at all; he was interested in old foreign cars, and he was a tennis buff. In fact, he taught a lot of the movie stars. Henry Fonda, Walter Pidgeon, Gary Cooper ... the studios would send them over to learn tennis from him. He died in 1995.

There's gold in them thar hills—the Arizona hills, that is—and treasure hunter Quinn, seen here in a 2006 photo, plans to return and find it.

Where did you first get interested in gold mining?

It was in Vegas that I got bitten by the "gold bug." I worked hard at it, learned a lot. Moved to Arizona for better mining opportunities, then to Texas to work for a gold mining associate. I plan to go back to Arizona to develop a small mine I have between Phoenix and Kingman—that is, if I can live long enough! But I've developed a little bit of the [Unsinkable] Molly Brown attitude, something I needed way back when.

If you were a young person today who wanted to be an actress, you would think twice?

I wouldn't play some parts, I'd be selective.

But you had a topless scene in Problem Girls*!*

I'm referring more to all this gore and stuff. I just don't think I would like to do that. You're too young to know but, back in the days when I was acting, it was a *totally* different world. Every movie they made had a moral fiber to it, the white hats always won, crime didn't pay and everything was "the way it was *supposed* to be."

Are you aware that you have a lot of fans from Mesa of Lost Women*?*

I'm starting to realize that, though it *is* hard for me to believe there's anyone out there who has noticed the ever-so-tiny ripple I made so many years ago! At a big half-price bookstore in Dallas, I would always visit the video section, and one day there was *Mesa of Lost Women*. I picked it up and said to myself, "I guess I'll buy one." I went to check out, with that and some books too, and I pointed to myself on the cover and said to the cashier, "I guess I'll buy this 'cause this is me." He looked at me and said, "Oh, you're *kidding*!" and he started calling over all his co-workers. It was real embarrassing! They got another copy of *Mesa* and asked me to autograph it for them, and I wrote "Tandra Quinn" on there. That was kinda funny, them treating me like a real celebrity, and here it was just some corny old movie!

By the way, at the end of this article, tell your readers, "This story is *not over*." There's going to be a sequel, and that sequel is going to be the most exciting gold find in Arizona. You have no idea how much gold is at this mine ... and neither do I [*laughs*]. I already promised the first nugget to Stephen B. Whatley, a painter whose work is in collections worldwide, including the BBC and the Royal Collection of Queen Elizabeth II; he's got 30 paintings in the Tower of London! He really touched my heart with a cartoon tribute. But I promise *you* the second nugget—you, a painter with words of tribute to sometimes-forgotten Hollywood starlets!

WILLIAM REYNOLDS

The story [of Cult of the Cobra*] was kinda preposterous,
but the acting paid it off and made it more believable.
Unlike, say,* Land Unknown, *whose premise was logical ...
interesting ... and the body of it became preposterous!*

In the 1960s and '70s, actor William Reynolds had his longest-running success with ABC-TV's hit *The F.B.I.*; ultra-clean-cut, business-suited and cool as a couple of cold-case files, he and star Efrem Zimbalist, Jr., cracked more criminal operations than smiles on the true-case-based Sunday night series. At other points in his career, however, Reynolds was confronted by threats a great deal more fanciful: A Burmese snake woman in Manhattan on a mission of murder in *Cult of the Cobra* (1955), a T. Rex, pterodactyl and other prehistoric predators in *The Land Unknown* (1957), and the living disembodied head of an ancient warlock in *The Thing That Couldn't Die* (1958). The jewel in the crown of his genre roles, however, was the *Twilight Zone* episode "The Purple Testament" (1960), a Rod Serling-scripted World War II story in which Reynolds' tormented Lt. Fitzgerald is an officer able to see death (represented by an eerie white light) in the faces of soldiers not long for this world.

The son of an economics professor and an aviatrix, William De Clercq Regnolds was born in Los Angeles and got his first taste of far-out adventure as an avid young fan of radio series (particularly *The Shadow* and *Jack Armstrong*) and Saturday-afternoon-matinee serials. As a teenager, he worked in radio, in "little theater" and even on the sound-stages of Paramount, where at 18 he debuted in the turn-of-the-century drama *Carrie* (released in 1952). Reynolds spent most of the 1950s as a contract player at Universal, co-starring in the aforementioned thrillers—two of which, *The Land Unknown* and *Cult of the Cobra*, will be included in the upcoming DVD release *The Classic Sci-Fi Ultimate Collection, Volume 2*.

My first picture was for director William Wyler: I played Laurence Olivier's son in *Carrie*. That was my entrée to the business. Just prior to that, I'd been under contract at Paramount, I was one of the "contract kids," and they had what they called the Fishbowl [a room where actors would enact scenes, watched from outside by producers, etc., through one-way glass], and I guess Wyler had seen me there. In the Fishbowl we would also do scenes with other actors who were just coming through Paramount. Since they were the ones being auditioned, we [the Paramount contract players] would have our backs to the glass as we did the scenes, in order to feature *them*. A lot of people came through there, one of whom was the gal who became my wife, Molly Sinclair."

You were still a teenager at the time, yes?

I was 18. I was a pretty irresponsible kind of individual while I was at Paramount, and eventually they said, "This kid is sorta out of bounds," so they didn't exercise the option. But by the time I was let go, Wyler had seen me and wanted me for *Carrie*, so two weeks after the option had not been exercised, I reported to work for Wyler. Incidentally, I called him *Mr.* Wyler. (Olivier called him *Willy!*) I went from *Carrie* to *Dear Brat* [1951], which was the last of the *Dear Wife-Dear Ruth* movies. Back to back I was in those two movies, both for Paramount, and I made three times as much as I would have had they exercised my option!

What do you mean when you say you were "pretty irresponsible" at Paramount?

I met Molly at Paramount, and two weeks later we were married. We eloped to Las Vegas, I was 18 and she was 18, and the way Paramount heard about it was, they received a telephone call from Molly's mother saying, "Who is this 'Bill Reynolds'?"—Molly must have mentioned to her that she was going out with me, and when we didn't come in from the date, she called Paramount. Well, that's not the way a studio likes one of the people they're grooming to *do* things [*laughs*]. So they didn't think that was very grown-up or responsible. Also, I'd come in to Paramount on a previous occasion after I'd had some teeth extracted, and I was still under the influence of sodium pentothal, and I insisted on telling everybody, Bill Meiklejohn [executive in charge of casting and talent] and all the people in the talent department, what a great talent was going to waste. At that point, I still hadn't gotten a picture assignment, and I guess I was frustrated. But I was very young—Jesus, 18 years old. I think back on my kids when *they* were 18, and the idea that they were marriageable blows my mind! I *wasn't* mature enough to marry but I happened to have found an incredible woman who stood by me, who was the love of my life. We were married until she passed away from cancer in 1992. So I did many very stupid, immature things in those days ... but I don't think that's particularly surprising [*laughs*].

One of your next movies was MGM's No Questions Asked *[1951] in which you were dressed as a woman.*

That's true, yes [*laughs*]! Robbing a theater in drag, me and Bill Phipps, who played the other "lady." The reasons that I did it: number one, I wanted to work, *that* was the main reason. But also, I knew I'd love the moment when I took off the wig and so on, and then spoke for the first time with a basso voice ... it'd be a little startling. Those are the things that actors *live* for. I did an episode of *Bronco* over at Warner

William Reynolds turned to acting as a career partly because of his boyhood love of oldtime radio shows and movie serials.

Brothers when I was under contract there, and the reason I did the *Bronco* was because the character had a disfigured side to his face, and I wanted to "pay it off" with a turn-into-camera. But it got tipped off, shown too soon. The director is a director, but only in name, they don't set it up and they're not selective about how it's cut. And it got screwed up.

Bill Phipps told me he got a kick out of doing No Questions Asked, *being on the set dressed as a woman, but said he wasn't sure you were enjoying it as much as he was.*

It was fun, it was dress-up time. I might have been 19, I was rather young and callow, and I guess I probably could get away with it a little bit better than Bill. Which is another way of saying I was *prettier* [*laughs*]!

How did you land a contract at Universal?

By the time I'd finished *The Desert Fox* [1951] at Fox, Universal had been wanting me to be under contract there for some time. We'd discussed it, and Meyer Mishkin, my agent, set it up. I finished *Desert Fox* and, almost the same day, I went and signed my contract at the Universal gate, and went on location for *The Cimarron Kid* [1951] with Audie Murphy. As a matter of fact, after having played Rommel's son in *The Desert Fox*, I still had a crew cut when I did *Cimarron Kid*.

What was it like to be a young actor at Universal in the early '50s?

It was great. It was a unique circumstance, and it'll never happen again.

Did you go through all the training that most of the young contractees did in those days?

I'd been under contract to Paramount, so I came into Universal with a few more credentials [than other young contractees]. And with a *little* higher salary. A lot of 'em came in at 75 bucks a week, and I was 200 or maybe 250 as I recall, which put me pretty high on the totem pole. This was for 40 weeks a year. Salaries were prorated, because if you only worked 40 weeks a year, the other 12 weeks you couldn't afford to live. So you prorated it. A lot of the movies Universal made were for what they used to call "sticks release." There were rural release organizations for which Universal provided a lot of stuff. In earlier days, most of the Universal serials were done for them, and they were big hits. And when I was there, Universal had the Ma and Pa Kettle movies with Marjorie Main and Percy Kilbride and Francis the Talking Mule with Donald O'Connor. I did *Francis Goes to West Point* [1952].

Is that something you'd want me to give you a copy of?

Ummm ... not particularly [*laughs*]! But I think that Donald O'Connor was one of the most talented people I ever worked with. He was really an exceptional actor in many respects. I couldn't *look* at him, because he was a beat off. Maybe it's a dancer thing or something, but he would absolutely crack me up: With his eyes, he'd respond to something one beat or two beats before or after it *should* be responded to.

What was your attitude once Universal started assigning you to horror and science fiction movies? Nobody was in more of 'em [three] in the '50s than you were.

I did pretty much what Universal asked me to do. We didn't exactly have script approval [*laughs*]! You did what you were told, that was part of the deal. You either did it or went on suspension, which nobody could afford to do. Well, actually, *Cult of the Cobra* was a pretty good product, for what it was at the time.

Even as a kid, it struck me what a serendipitous cast Cult of the Cobra *had: None of its male stars had drawing power in 1955, but ten years later all of them, including you, would have their own TV series.*

That's true. Actually, strangely enough, most of us were also in the Army at about the same time. Dick Long was with the Armed Forces Radio Service during the Korean War, in Japan, and he came back when I was just going *in*. He contacted the commanding officer of the Armed Forces Radio Service and told him I was coming over. I finished my basic training at Fort Ord, and then I got on the troop ship the U.S.S. *General William Weigel* and I was on my way to Hokkaido, the northernmost island in Japan—the First Cavalry Division. But instead I was told to see a Major Raleigh in Tokyo, and I ended up "Army Sgt. Bill Reynolds, Far East Network, Tokyo"—that was my on-air "signature," at station breaks and before the news and stuff like that. A year and a half later, I was back at Universal and doing *Cult of the Cobra* with Dick Long. And several years after *that*, that *Cult* group, Dick Long and Jack Kelly and I, all went on to have TV series at Warner Brothers [Long on *77 Sunset Strip* and *Bourbon Street Beat*, Kelly on *Maverick* and Reynolds on *The Gallant Men*].

Faith Domergue, who played the snake woman—what memories of her?

I have more respect for her now, having watched *Cult of the Cobra* again recently, because I think she did very well with what she had to work with. The role was very limiting in terms of what she could do emotionally. She had a much harder job than I gave her credit for when we were doing it.

She hadn't done that many movies at that point. She'd been a Howard Hughes discovery and under contract to him for years without making *many movies.*

That was his m.o. On *Cult of the Cobra* she was kinda quiet, she wasn't "one of the group." We were contract kids, kidding each other and stuff like that, and she wasn't really part of the group. So I didn't really see too much *of* her other than the scenes that I did with her. I only really had one big scene with her, confronting her with my suspicions that she is the killer, and I don't think that it was paid off very well. I don't know whether it was *my* fault or the cutter's fault or *whoever*, but my character's reason for being suspicious wasn't particularly well articulated by the movie. I wasn't terribly pleased with what I was doing when I saw it the first time—and I see now why I wasn't! It wasn't that I did a bad job, I was okay for what it was.

Well, I'd blame that more on the writing.

And also, it was a very hard job for the director. I mean, you can only pay off so-many characters. The characters played by Dick and Marshall Thompson were pretty well articulated, and even David Janssen's. *Mine* wasn't. I was kind of a wise guy, kind of the cynical one, I guess. But then, you never know; at the time you're *doing* it, you never know where things are gonna fit. The director concentrated on the two most important characters, Dick's and Marshall's. Actually, the thing had an accomplished cast, much better than the other two [*The Land Unknown* and *The Thing That Couldn't Die*]. All the actors were very good and experienced.

The Cult *storyline itself—what do you think?*

The story was kinda preposterous, but the acting paid it off and made it more believable. *Unlike*, say, *Land Unknown*, whose premise was logical ... interesting ... and the body of it became preposterous [*laughs*]!

Cult *was an early credit in the directing career of Francis D. Lyon.*

I don't recall much interaction with him. But then, he was kind of a herder more than a director. When you've got a cast this size doing things, you didn't really have much of a

Sssssslain by the ssssssnake woman, Reynolds is examined by Richard Long (left) and Walter Coy of the NYPD in *Cult of the Cobra*.

relationship with the director. But under the studio system, most directors had limited authority. There were some who did have authority, for instance, Douglas Sirk, a very important director. At Universal, he may have been one of the very few who really had much autonomy in terms of what he could do, and a final cut, which most other directors did not have. I'm not sure that Lyon had a final cut on *Cult of the Cobra*. Directors were primarily responsible for getting the words and action on film on time. They exercised control by cutting in the camera—in other words, selective coverage. They could do *that*, they weren't totally impotent [*laughs*]. They could do *that* much before the cutters got it.

If there's one thing I've learned in all my interviews with actors from these movies, it's that—contrary to what you'll read about their directors—most of the time, they were primarily traffic cops.

Yeah. So much for the auteur theory!

Cult of the Cobra *is about the curse placed on the five GIs ... and, except for you, in real life none of the actors got to be old men.*

Dick Long, David Janssen, Jack Kelly, Jimmy Dobson ... yeah, that's true. I'm 75, and [*laughs*] I'm still kickin' around! Dick had a heart condition that he knew about, and he knew that he had limited time. Not that he *talked* about it particularly, but ... I mean, I understand that he prepared his own funeral. That's a little macabre, at least fatalistic, but he was aware that he had limited time.

What do you remember about venturing into The Land Unknown?

My understanding was that, when they started out to make that one, it was a more ambitious project [than it ended up being]. But I don't know when they made the decision to go with the B-team instead of big names. I'm sure it was an economic decision.

The director Virgil Vogel told me that too much of the money went into making the monsters. All of a sudden, they didn't have enough money left to make the movie the way they'd planned!

The mechanical monster in the lake makes me think of all the stories I heard about *Jaws* [1975], how they couldn't get the shark to work.

What difficulties do you remember with the lake monster?

Well, just that I don't think it paid off for the money that they spent on it. It *was* a very ambitious thing, it moved its flippers and did all kinds of stuff, but my understanding was that it cost a *ton* of money. That was one of the reasons why Universal made the adjustments [downgrading the movie], in order to accommodate the budget. I never got to see the T. Rex in action. When we were doing scenes where we'd be looking at the T. Rex or shooting our pistols at it, they'd give us an eye line, a mark to look at and shoot at. Ours was an awfully big T. Rex [*laughs*]. In real life the biggest ones were supposed to be 16 feet high, something like that, but the one in the movie looked to be about 35 feet high! I don't think the scale was really appropriate, but ... it worked, in its time. *Today* all of those things could be done so much more [effectively], and cheaper. Imagine, you wouldn't have to spend all that money on that mechanical monster in the lake, and it would *all* be so much better and so much more real-looking.

Working with Jock Mahoney?

"The best big stuntman" was his reputation in the business. Physically, he was somethin' else; I mean, we'd be walkin' down the street, let's say to the commissary to lunch, and we'd be talking, and he'd vault over a Volkswagen! He was a startling athlete who could do that with no running start or anything; he could put one hand on the roof and go right over. Just out of exuberance, or just to see if he could do it, or ... whatever. And *The Land Unknown* took on *that* aspect, it became the physical things and the running through the bushes and the swimming in the lake and all that kind of stuff. It became an action film more than it probably was originally intended to be. After a while, Jocko wasn't coming across as the scientist that the character was supposed to be.

You forget he's even supposed to be a scientist.

Yes, that wasn't part of Jocko's persona. He was very, very popular. In the early '50s he did a Western TV series, *The Range Rider*, which was a huge success. Then in 1955 or '56, when he and I were traveling to the Virgin Islands to do *Away All Boats* for Universal, we had an overnight layover in Houston, and we roomed together at the Rice Hotel. And once we got in the room, there were nothing but telephone calls! In Texas, *The Range Rider* was

Lost in inexplicable Antarctic fog, Navy lieutenant Reynolds manages to make a safe landing in the very *un*safe *Land Unknown*. Pictured: Reynolds (in helicopter), Phil Harvey (left), Shawn Smith, Jock Mahoney.

a big, big show, and once people found out that Jock Mahoney was there, the phone just kept ringing, calls from fans who wanted to talk to him. I finally had to call the desk and say, "Listen, no more calls, I want to get some sleep!"

A lot of the stuff that Jocko and I did in *Land Unknown* was physical stuff, running and swimming. At one point in the shooting, he and I ran and dove in the lake and swam across. In the movie *as edited*, they just used a small cut where we're getting out of the water, but we shot it as a long traveling shot, both of us running through the jungle and then diving into this lake and swimming. Jocko, as I say, was the best big stuntman in the business, a great athlete, and of course he took off with this racing dive. And I did too. As we swam across this lake, he looked over and expected to see me in his wake, but I used to be quite a good swimmer and so I was right next to him. And so he picked up his tempo—and I picked up *mine*. We ended up full-out swimming right to the end. As we pulled ourselves up out of the water, he had the first line of dialogue, and he was sitting there and he went [*Reynolds tries to speak but only gulps and pants and gasps*]—he couldn't say his line. Then he looked at me and he said, "...You bastard!" [*Laughs*]

Because you'd made him swim faster than he'd intended to.

That's exactly right, we were in a sprint at the end. And I was very pleased that I finally was able to extend him a little bit!

Can you describe the soundstage jungle set you shot on?

That was on the Process Stage, Universal's biggest soundstage, and everything was in there: They had the jungle and the lake and the cave exterior, at the end of the lake, and the cave interior. Then they had all these funny-looking prehistoric "plants" that, in the movie, Shawn Smith kept getting in front of, and being grabbed! The "fog" in the jungle they produced by burning oil; it's heavy so it stays down close to the floor. We used to use "fog" like that in *every*thing, the war pictures and all that stuff. You try not to breathe it more than you have to. The director was Virgil Vogel, and I guess he did all he could do [within the budget and schedule]. I later did a bunch of *F.B.I.*s with him. He was a very workmanlike director, he had a nice sense of humor, and he related well to all the actors. The good directors have a nice sensibility about them. On shows where time is of some consequence, the temperament of the directors is probably the most important asset—or liabil-

As witnessed by Shawn Smith (right) on the *Land Unknown* set, athletic Reynolds (behind) gave stuntman-turned-actor Jock Mahoney (front) unexpected competition in the swimming department. "You bastard!"

ity!—they might have. Virg was very affable, and he listened. If you had a question or something, he was very helpful. He was a good traffic cop [*laughs*]!

When I talk to other Universal contract players, some—Julie Adams and Lori Nelson, for instance—tell me they kind of gritted their teeth when assigned to sci-fi movies.

Well, when you're a contract player, you're really not accountable for the material. All you're trying to do is make the situation as real as you can, and you suspend your own sense of reality. You could drive yourself nuts with the illogic of some of the things that you're doing [*laughs*]. I mean, in *The Land Unknown*, Henry Brandon plays a scientist who's been in that prehistoric jungle so long, he's gone a little mad and looks like a caveman, and he won't give us a push-pull tube, from the wreck of *his* helicopter, that we need to make *our* helicopter work again and get out of there. How illogical is it that we never say to the guy, "Hey, Charlie, we got room in our helicopter. Give us the push-pull tube and we'll take you outta here!" I don't recall that as being part of the dialogue!

No, that was never on the table, for whatever weird reason!

When you're in a situation like that in a movie, you suspend reality and just attempt to make it as real as possible, and make the words sound cogent and ... *interesting*, I guess. We could have done much better in that arena [*laughs*]! But let me say this about Phil Harvey and the character he played. Phil had the most thankless and unsympathetic part in the picture, obviously: breaking the push-pull tube, running down the batteries making those futile Mayday calls—

Every mistake that's made in the movie, he makes. The script doesn't split 'em up among all the characters!

[*Laughs*] Yeah! But maybe the most real moment in the film was when he threatened the Henry Brandon character with the torch, saying, "Tell us where we can find your wrecked helicopter!" And my character momentarily agreed with him, because it was so logical. I think that if there *was* any time in the film where anybody behaved in a way that was logical, that was *it*. Phil's part may have been thankless or unsympathetic but, hey, he acted like a real person.

Those three pictures [*Cult, Land Unknown, The Thing That Couldn't Die*] are kind of a chronology of the way that Universal used its contract players. In *Cult of the Cobra*, they had Dick Long and David Janssen and Jack Kelly and Kathy Hughes and me, all contract players. And then later on, when the list of contract players got smaller, in *The Land Unknown*, I guess I was the only term contract player. And, again, I was the only one in *Thing That Couldn't Die*. In the 1950s, the studios couldn't own their own theaters and control the product like they used to, so [the number of contract players dwindled]. For example, when I was at Paramount, *every*body was under contract. They had like 100 people under contract ... not just the kids in the Golden Circle [up-and-coming young actors and actresses], but character actors too. The studio system could support that kind of thing when they were able to control the exhibition of the product that they made. In those days, they *had* to make x-number of pictures a year in order to be able to supply their theaters. Even though Universal didn't own the theaters themselves, they were the main providers for several releasing organizations, particularly in the rural Midwest and throughout. And the budgets of Universal pictures were geared [toward the amount of exhibition Universal knew they would get]. For instance, I *know* that they had an artificial top for Audie Murphy pictures, like three-quarters of a million. (Maybe that wasn't the figure, but it was *about* there.) That's one of the rea-

According to Reynolds (top), the T. Rex, king of dinosaurs, got even more king-sized in the paleontologically incorrect *The Land Unknown* with Jock Mahoney (holding gun) and Phil Harvey.

sons why I'd bet *The Land Unknown* was made in black-and-white instead of color, after all that money that they spent on the mechanical dinosaur in the lake, and the set, and so on.

Because Universal knew that if the cost of making it exceeded a certain dollar amount, that was coming right out of profit.

That's correct. And when you have Jock Mahoney and Shawn Smith and Bill Reynolds heading the cast, you know that you didn't have a lot of star power there [*laughs*]! But Universal was a great studio, for what it was, and as I say, it's something that'll never happen again. We made an awful lot of product for very little money.

"Very little money" describes two Universals you did back-to-back for director Will Cowan, The Big Beat *[1958] and* Thing That Couldn't Die—*the only two movies where you get top billing.*

By the time we did those, most of the contract players were gone. I think I might have been the last contract player at Universal. All of a sudden Universal had all this RKO product to distribute [after RKO hit hard times], and they didn't have much of a need any more for programmer-type things on the level of *Thing That Couldn't Die* and *The Big Beat*. I did both of them in a month. *The Big Beat* was interesting because it had some top doo-wop performers. Musical short subjects were Will Cowan's background, he knew how to do things economically and quickly, and he was very good.

And Thing That Couldn't Die *specifically?*

That was one whose premise was pretty preposterous. My first recollection of *Thing* is that big, silly-looking talisman that Carolyn Kearney wore in it. I put it around her neck, and it pulled her off-balance [*laughs*]. It was grotesque, with the anchor and the fleur-de-lis and all that kind of stuff. It looked like a Marine's tattoo! The audience probably looked at it and said, "What the hell is *that*?" When a picture has the kind of premise that *Thing That Couldn't Die* had, you don't need props like that!

What do you remember about your castmates?

Robin Hughes [the disembodied living head] was a Shakespearean actor, and a good one, and I think he probably did as well as he could. Andra Martin and I had just done *The Big Beat*. She had a lot of ability and she was a great gal, I liked her. She later went over to Warner Brothers and she was a contract player there. Carolyn Kearney just recently passed away [2005]. Just before she passed, I did an autograph show at the Beverly Garland Hotel in Studio City, and all the celebrities there had worked on *The Twilight Zone*. It's the only autograph show I've ever done and probably the only one I will *ever* do [*laughs*]—I'm not much into hawkin' pictures for 20 bucks. But I did it because I wanted to see some of the people that I'd worked with, and Carolyn was there, and I talked to her briefly. She was such a nice person, and very good in *Thing That Couldn't Die*, very young and fresh. Most of the Universal contract people would have been a little too hard around the edges to carry off this totally unsophisticated character, but she *did* it, you kinda believed her.

The best line in that picture was spoken by Charlie Horvath, who played the big, dumb handyman. In the movie, when they dig up the copper box that turns out to have the disembodied head in it, Charlie hoisted it up on his shoulder and said [*in a dumb-guy voice*], "I bet I could carry *two* of 'em!" [*Laughs*] He was playing Lennie in *Of Mice and Men*, of course—and well. I believed him probably more than any of the other characters!

He could be a great heavy.

He was a tough, tough man. He was an ex-Marine, and he didn't feel physical pain. I've seen cigarettes starting to burn the flesh of his fingers, and somebody else would have to knock the cigarette out of his hand! As I mentioned earlier, on the way to the Virgin Islands to make *Away All Boats*, we had an overnight layover in Houston and stayed at the Rice Hotel. Horvath was with us, Charlie McGraw was with us, we were all on a bus going down to the hotel from the airport, and Horvath stuck his head out the bus window and he yelled as loud as he could [*Reynolds imitates Horvath imitating McGraw*], "My name is Charlie McGraw and I can whip any Texan who ever lived, and I'm stayin' at the Rice Hotel!" Poor Charlie McGraw was pleading, "Stop it! Come on, stop that!" He understood the ramifications, obviously [*laughs*], but Horvath kept it up all the way to the Rice Hotel! And when McGraw got there, he went right to the desk and he told the clerk [*softly, surreptitiously*], "My name is Charlie McGraw—and you never *heard* of me! And if anybody asks, I'm not *stayin'* here!" That was ol' Charlie Horvath.

Did you think the scenes of the body-less head and the headless body were effective?

Even then, I suppose they could have done things, production-wise, that might have been a little bit more real-looking. Another thing that I noticed, watching the movie recently, was that they wrapped everything [very abruptly]. The picture was going along at a steady pace, but all of a sudden, from the point where Carolyn put the head on the body to **THE END**, it took about two minutes. You could tell it was a case of "Okay, let's wrap it up, fellas! Let's get the heck out of here!" [*Laughs*]

What other thoughts occurred to you as you watched it?

When you're workin' fast, there are a lot of times when you would like another take. But you could only go so far given the constraints. With more time and attention, of course you could make a better product. I mean, *all* of 'em; every one of those pictures could have been a better product.

What was Universal like in 1958, when things were slow and all the contract players gone? It must have been in rocky shape.

Oh, it *was*! And I think everybody knew it was over, when Universal just stopped renewing contracts. A lot of the actors went over to Warner Brothers, including me. Actually, when I left Universal in '58, I did a series for Jack Webb, I played Pete Kelly in *Pete Kelly's Blues*, adapted from the movie *Pete Kelly's Blues* [1955], but it was on the air only 13 weeks. I went from there over to Warner Brothers. Jack Kelly was there, Dick Long was there—there were a bunch of "transplants" [*laughs*]! Of course, Warners had like 16 hours a week of TV series on the air, so they *needed* contract people. I did the *Bronco*s and *Maverick*s and *Cheyenne*s.

How did you feel during your last days at Universal, after being there so long?

Okay. Looking forward to other things. It was pretty obvious that nothing was going to happen at Universal for a while.

Were you familiar with The Twilight Zone *before you starred in "The Purple Testament"?*

I'd seen it, and there was a lot of talk around town about it. And of course Rod Serling was respected by all of the actors and directors in town. So, yeah, it was a primo job. I remember that I got the part in "Purple Testament" as a consequence of another actor, Dean Stockwell, turning it down, and that the director Dick Bare then suggested me. I'd worked with Dick at Warner Brothers and done the pilot for the MGM TV series *The Islanders* with him. I was elated when I got "Purple Testament." It was a go, like, the next day.

Doing the "Van Helsing bit," Reynolds (with cross) returns *The Thing That Couldn't Die* (Robin Hughes) to his grave.

The day after you got the part, you were working?

I believe it *was* the next day, yes. And as you know, I had a lot of words [dialogue]. Rod Serling was great. He was hands-on on the set and kinda gagged around with [co-star] Dick York and me, keepin' people loose. But he was a pretty intense guy. His narrations were indicative of the kind of intensity he projected. A chain-smoker, a very creative and dynamic kind of guy, obviously, and remarkably prolific.

In an old interview of yours, you called Richard Bare a "crazy man."

Maybe "crazy man" was a little much, because he was a really nice guy. But also a no-nonsense type, not looking for esoteric things. He started out making short subjects at Warner Brothers, the Joe McDoakes *Behind the Eight Ball* comedies, in the '40s, and he ended up directing *Green Acres* [the 1965–71 TV series]. And all the *Twilight Zone*s he did were also very good. So he could deal with a lot of different subject matter, obviously.

After "The Purple Testament," Dick and I were in Jamaica doing background shots for *The Islanders*—shots of running through a jungle and swimming in a lagoon and landing the Grumman Goose [seaplane] in various places, to intercut with the stuff that we would do on the MGM back lot. We were flying back to the United States on the 12th of February 1960, the day that "The Purple Testament" was scheduled to run. We were in level flight, I don't know how high, maybe 1000 feet, and everything was cool, and I guess the pilot switched from one gas tank to the other—and the engines stopped. All of a sudden there was silence, except the sound of diving toward the water, which we could see through the open cockpit door. The Grumman Goose is not terribly airworthy absent power.

How many people on board?

Five—the pilot [Howard Smith], me, Bare, cameraman George Schmidt and an assistant cameraman, Glen [Kirkpatrick]. We had time to buckle up, and I presume the pilot was trying to get some kind of a glide angle so he could land belly-up. Apparently he succeeded, and the Goose split right in the middle. One moment I was buckled in my seat and the next, I was *still* in my seat, but I was spinning around underwater—I had been thrown clear of the fuselage. I could see light above me, sunlight, so I unbuckled and swam up to the surface, a few miles off the coast of Jamaica. The point of my telling this story, as related to *The Twilight Zone*, is the fact that back in Hollywood, [the *TZ* people] heard a news flash that our plane had crashed and they didn't know whether I had survived. I guess they were sensitive to the fact that I had a daughter who was a year and a half, and a two-*week*-old baby, and a wife, and they knew that it would have been a little macabre to show "The Purple Testament," an episode in which I see my own death, on the day that I had perhaps died in a plane crash. So out of respect for the feelings of my family, instead of taking advantage of what had happened, they took the show off the air that night. Even though all the literature still says that "The Purple Testament" was shown initially on February 12, it was *not*. I've forgotten when they *did* show it, I guess a couple, three weeks later or something, after they'd found out I was still alive. I thought that was just super, and out of kind of respect for *them*, I went to that *Twilight Zone* autograph convention that I mentioned earlier.

In TV today, though, what happened to me might have been advertised [exploited]; "Is he *alive*??" They'd make it a reality show [*laughs*]!

What happened to the other people in the plane?

*Every*body broke bones from the impact, which kinda gutted out the ship. My legs were cut up and my right ankle was broken, along with several ribs. And George, the cameraman, bled to death. The assistant cameraman, Glen, was cut across the eyebrows. You could see that his eyes were still intact, but he couldn't see because of the blood. Also, he was holding onto the back of his seat, as a life preserver-type of thing [*laughs*]. I don't mean to laugh, that's not amusing, except that the seat had no buoyancy, and as soon as he let it go, it sunk like a rock! I helped him over to the pontoon which was still afloat, and he held on there. Dick, a gutsy guy, was sitting in his seat, and I guess he couldn't really swim because both of his legs were broken, so he was paddling backstroke. I used my pants as flotation—tied off the legs and then scooped air into them. That was a water safety thing that one learns. I *was* concerned about whether to leave my underwear on or not, whether that white would attract sharks. Between being a Boy Scout-type and a swimmer in school, I was probably better equipped to handle this than the others ... but not a shark!

Richard Bare once said in an interview that at one point as you two were attempting to swim to shore, he mentioned that "The Purple Testament" was going to be on TV that night—and called out to you, "Bill, please don't *look at me!"*

I don't remember him saying that, but he's certainly capable of it and, knowing Bare, he probably *did*! I don't know whether this is appropriate for your story, but at the little hospital in Annotto Bay, this woman in a flower dress stitched my hand. My left hand was pretty much like raw meat, and [*laughs*] she was stitching it up like a seamstress, like she was stitching up a dress! And their medication was cognac and morphine [*laughs*]. Also, they taped up my ribs, but apparently they had flipped my X-rays, because when I got back to the States and went to a doctor, he said, "They taped up the wrong side!" [*Laughs*] So much for medicine down there, but they were marvelous, friendly, great people!

In my opinion, your performance in "Purple Testament" is one of the best jobs I've seen you do.

Well, I think it is too, because it's the best material I've ever had. Incidentally, my favorite sci-fi show is *Dead Like Me* [the recent Showtime series], I really like it, and there's a similarity in a sense. In "Purple Testament," I was my own Reaper, seeing my own death; and the total context of that show was subjective, I was living this thing and it was happening to *me*. But *Dead Like Me* has this *ob*jective aspect: *Those* Reapers are already dead, and they live with the people that they're reaping, before and after their deaths. This objectivity, this distance leaves so much room for interesting stuff. I thought that was a brilliant show, and one of the best ensemble casts; every character was just beautiful. It was a show that I would not miss, I was a *huge* fan.

Your best-known TV series was of course The F.B.I., *which you joined at the beginning of the third season in 1967.*

After playing characters in a few episodes during the first coupla years, I replaced [actor] Steve Brooks as "the young agent," and I did 153 subsequently.

Did you enjoy doing all the extracurricular things you did for The F.B.I.*?*

Oh, very much. I was really *into* it. I went back to Quantico [the F.B.I. Academy], and I went to various F.B.I. offices during the summertime, and of course met Mr. Hoover, who was a "potentate" kinda fella. I remember that his desk was elevated—or at least you got the *feeling* it was. Doing *The F.B.I.* was quite an experience. I was, and still am, quite sympathetic with them as people and as an organization.

It looks like you did your last acting in a 1978 episode of Jack Webb's Project U.F.O.

I realized at that time I wasn't gonna get an awful lot of work, and I had a daughter in Stanford, and expenses go on. I was on the Screen Actors Guild board of directors with a guy by the name of Dennis Cross, who I had worked with as an actor. Dennis was also the head of policy holder services for a medical malpractice insurance company. Well, he got me on board, and I was doing that kind of a job for almost eight years. I ended up as underwriting manager, as manager for policy holder services, as manager for research and development—I guess I had a flair for it. My father was an economics professor, but I don't know if it was anything genetic [*laughs*]! It was a long way from being an actor, except as respects relating to people. Acting has a reputation of being frivolous, but it's anything *but*. The profession of acting requires a great deal of discipline, and *that* kind of discipline [can be applied to] almost any other kind of activity. An actor became president of the United States, and did a pretty good job of it!

Do you ever miss the acting?

I love to act. But, I should tell you, I don't know if I ever would have been an actor if it weren't for the electronic aspect of it. As a kid, I fell in love with radio shows, *The Shadow* in particular. "The *Shad*-ow knowwwws...!" [*Laughs*] Then I

Watching his mirror reflection supernaturally light up, Reynolds realizes his hours are numbered in "The Purple Testament."

Co-starring with Efram Zimbalist, Jr. (center), and Philip Abbott in television's *The F.B.I.* made Reynolds (left) "quite sympathetic" with the real-life agents and organization.

would spend all day every Saturday in the movies—it cost a dime then—watching serials and stuff. And I always wanted to do that [act in radio and/or movies]. Although I've done many plays over the years, I'm not classically trained or particularly stage-trained as in repertory theater. But I don't know if acting would have been my life's work absent the fact that I could use more introspective values in performing. I like the reality that one has available to him because of the electronic aspects. "The electronics" supplies the other part of the equation: The camera can see what's happening *inside*, and that allows the actor to just do what he would *do* in a situation—

And not *have to act for the two guys in the back row.*

Right, not having to project, which is a distortion. As I was saying, my generation grew up on the great radio shows and the serials. On Saturdays, the kids in the movie theater audiences were there for the serials; it didn't *matter* what the feature was. If it was a Western, then it was fine, but the features were just tangential to the serials that were playing. I'm talking about going to the movies during the war, when the serials had a lot of patriotic-type comic book characters like Captain America. It all started for me with the radio and the serials.

BETTA ST. JOHN

> *I'd always felt that when [when my career began going downhill], I* **would** *leave. Because there's nothing sadder to see than [a veteran actor] coming in for small parts.... It's like seeing a wonderful boxer past his prime, a dancer past her prime. "Oh,* **stop,** *while people still have good memories of you!"*

What do Tarzan, musical theater and Richard Rodgers have in common? *Two* things, actually: A $10 million-plus Broadway adaptation of Disney's animated *Tarzan*, opening at the Richard Rodgers Theatre next May [2006], and—more pertinently here—actress Betta St. John, who appeared in two of the Great White Way's greatest hits of the 1940s, Rodgers' (and Oscar Hammerstein's) *Carousel* and *South Pacific*, before playing the female leads (opposite "Ape Man" Gordon Scott) in *Tarzan and the Lost Safari* (1957) and *Tarzan the Magnificent* (1960).

Born in Hawthorne, California, St. John was an extra and bit player in films of the late 1930s and early '40s as a kid (using her real name, Betty Striegler) until opportunity knocked (an offer to join the Rodgers & Hammerstein "family"). She parlayed her stage success into Hollywood and English movie roles, among them the major-studio productions *Dream Wife* with Cary Grant and the Biblical epic *The Robe* (both 1953); the Tarzans; and indies like *Horror Hotel* (a.k.a. *The City of the Dead*, 1960) with Christopher Lee and *Corridors of Blood* (1962) with Boris Karloff and Lee. Long-retired, she now divides her time between homes in California and England.

When I was a kid seeing you in movies, I always thought you were British.
  To American ears, sometimes I do sound a bit British. But I never fooled the British for a moment. They know I'm not from *there*, but they're not quite sure *where* I'm from, because I don't sound quite American to them either. I'm not a person who switches accents easily, so I probably sounded quite American at the beginning over here in America, and then sounded a *little* bit more British [after living in England]. And I never successfully became one or the other completely [*laughs*]. After I had lived in England just under a year, doing *South Pacific*, I came back to America to do *The Robe*, and on that picture the attitude about the actors was, "The Romans are going to speak with the British accent, but the more ordinary people must sound more American." They kept coming back to me, all the time, "Sound more American! Sound more American!," which, again, I didn't find all that easy to do. I didn't think I *had* a British accent at that time, but *they* seemed to think so [*laughs*]!

How did you get into the acting?

At the time when I was quite young, many mothers liked to send their daughters to dancing school and send them to take lessons and so on. Those were the days of Shirley Temple. Probably my mother was more ambitious for me than I realized. I started with theatrical schools on Saturday, dancing, singing, all the bits you do at quite an early age. In those days (and, I suppose, *still*), if studios need children, they call the theatrical schools. I was seven or eight when I first got my Social Security number [*laughs*]! I was in, oh, I don't remember, but maybe seven or eight films during the young childhood age, just because the studios said, "Well, we need so-many kids, so come along for..."—this, that and the other.

Mostly extra work, I assume.

I never played parts. The nearest I came to playing a part was in a lovely classic movie called *Destry Rides Again* [1939] with Marlene Dietrich [as Frenchy, a dance hall girl of the wild west]. I was taken to meet her, for her approval. She was in her dance hall outfit, with gold glitter in her hair—I suppose my eyes popped out, I thought that was reeeally rather marvelous. The sequence is at the very end of the film, where you see me sitting in the back of a moving wagon reprising Dietrich's "Little Joe, the Wrangler" number. That was the only time I've ever sung full-strength in a movie myself, with my own voice, with *no* inhibitions at all, reprising "Little Joe," which was *her* song throughout the film. That was my only claim to fame in those early years [*laughs*]. So, as to my "acting start," I kind of just rolled into it because, heavens, it was a *lot* more fun than going to school. I'm ashamed to say I never really got to the point of saying, "Oh, [an actress] is what I must *be* in my life, this is what I want to *do*." It was wonderful, and I just went along with it. I've been such a fortunate person, more than I ever deserved: Life just "unrolled" for me. I kind of floated along, and one thing happened after another. But I think I probably would have been much better for it, if I'd actually had to say, "*Do* I want to do this [act]? Am I going to really *do* everything that's required? Do I have the talent?" I think people who have to struggle more have much more to offer.

What other movies did you do in your childhood?

In *Jane Eyre* [1944], I was one of the orphan kids. That was one of Liz Taylor's first pictures. In two Shirley Temple pictures whose names escape me right now, I again played orphans—I *always* played orphans, very popular in Hollywood at that time! I did actually miss doing *The Wizard of Oz* [1939] only because my family had planned probably the only vacation it ever took, a trip up to Alaska, which was a pretty big trip in those days. The call came in for me to go for *Wizard of Oz*, a small part as of course one of the kids, and I can remember great discussion with the family, "Do we cancel the vacation?" So I wasn't in *The Wizard of Oz* though I should have been. Oh, and I did one picture with Merle Oberon. I can only remember that one because she was *so* gracious with the children and, at the end of our few days of filming, she had sent in an ice cream cake. That's what I remember: Not the name of the movie, but the ice cream cake [*laughs*]!

And then your "real" career started on the stage in New York.

Oh, yes. When I was 15, the Theater Guild, who already had [stage productions of] *Oklahoma!* and *Carousel* on in New York, came out to the West Coast to do some auditioning and casting, because they were looking for replacements—actors and actresses for various companies. My dance teacher, quite famous in her time, Queenie Smith, said to me, "You're too young now [to get a job with the Theater Guild], but it would be a good expe-

Among Betta St. John's childhood roles was a bit in the Western *Destry Rides Again*, as a child (lower left) belting out "Little Joe, the Wrangler."

rience to dance for them. Later on, this might be important to you." So I went along, and whatever I did obviously impressed them enough, because they came straight back and asked if I would go to New York, where they would put me into either *Oklahoma!* or *Carousel*, whichever one had the first opening. There I was, a sophomore in high school, 15, and [*laughs*] faced with the choice of, "Do you want to go back to school, or do you want to go to New York?" At the same audition was Howard Keel—he was Harry Keel in those days—and we went on the train to New York together, and Mother with me, obviously. In New York, of course, a whole *world* opened up to me, a world I didn't even know existed, because I came from a very *un*sophisticated background and I was so wet behind the ears. It was *wonderful*.

When I got to New York, the Theater Guild people realized that if they put me in one of the shows before I was 16, they'd have to conform with the child labor rules, where I had to be out of the theater by a certain time and all that bit. Since I was going to be 16 in about three or four months, they told me to just stay in New York and spend that time waiting 'til I was 16; they gave me some teachers to go to, primarily dancing teachers. Then on my sixteenth birthday they put me in the chorus of *Carousel*. I was kind of disappointed, because

I so *loved Oklahoma!* I'd never *seen* a New York show, and I obviously went to see both shows right away when I got to New York, and I just fell in love with *Oklahoma!*—I *so* wanted to be in it. But the first opening came in *Carousel*. So on my birthday they put me into *Carousel*, which was absolutely fabulous.

What did you do in New York, to fill the days as you waited to turn 16?

The Theater Guild in those days had an elegant oldtime house on 53rd Street which they used as their headquarters, with a beautiful circular staircase and all. Mother and I had an apartment on the West Side but I spent a lot of time around that 53rd Street area, because, between using the rehearsal rooms at the Theater Guild, I'd go next door and spend quite a bit of time in the Museum of Modern Art. The Museum of Modern Art was where, downstairs, they showed silent films, and there I saw all sorts of things I didn't even know existed.

And your mom was in New York with you.

In the early days, yes she was, and she stayed with me right until I went on tour with *Carousel*. I was in the chorus of *Carousel* for six months, and when Bambi Lynn, who played Louise, the daughter, left, there was an open audition for people within the company, and they chose *me* to play the part. Oh, the adrenaline rush, when I got the part! Dick Rodgers really was always lovely to me. He had Irving Berlin come and see my "opening night," my first night as Louise, and he brought Berlin back to meet me afterwards. I was impressed then, but I would have been *more* impressed now [*laughs*]. Life was just so absolutely wonderful, wonderful. Then when we went on tour, I was either 17 or maybe 18. Tours in those days were quite a commitment, quite a long time—and *fun*, too.

I toured quite a long time, two years maybe, and I lost a lot of weight—I think Mother was rather appalled when she saw me! It was quite a strenuous role. And at a certain point, I really thought the time had come to leave. I went back to New York with no plans, and just went in with a roommate that I'd roomed with before. And *again*—this is where luck is just so unbelievable for me—*South Pacific* unfolded, suddenly there was *South Pacific* to be done. I guess it came out in the general chat that the role of Liat was open for casting, I went and auditioned, and Dick Rodgers said, "We're very happy with you for Liat." But *then* he said, "We're not gonna say yes, because it does depend upon who we select to play Bloody Mary. The two of you have to be mother and daughter." I can't remember how long it took, but

Happy Birthday, Sweet 16: St. John got her Broadway break in the Rodgers & Hammerstein production *Carousel*, making her first appearance in the show the day she turned 16.

eventually I was given that part in *South Pacific*. A few years ago, in 1999, in New York, there was a fiftieth anniversary reunion of *South Pacific*, and I found that none of the other principals were left, I'm the only one left. Hearing all the other kids who were in the thing saying how thrilled they were [to be part of it], I thought, "Aww, I didn't get the thrill of thinking, 'How wonderful I'm doing this,'" because for me the opportunity just *came*. Things came so easily! I *enjoyed* every moment, but it wasn't the great thing in my life that it was for the other people who were all talking at the reunion, and when I heard them, I thought, "I never had sufficient appreciation for what I was *doing* at the time...!"

Who did play Bloody Mary?

Juanita Hall. Superb she was in the role, and we worked very well together. It always bothered me that she was quite short, and I had grown rather tall by then. Long-legged, I'd become 5' 5". But it worked wonderfully well, and doing *South Pacific* became my claim to fame. That was my launch pad.

I had a boyfriend at the time, Erik Kristen, and, through his letters, I'd enjoyed *his* experience of doing *Oklahoma!* in London—I thought, "I'd just *love* the experience of doing *South Pacific* in London." So I asked Dick Rodgers [about going to London with *South Pacific*], and he said, "We can't promise, it depends on British Actors Equity. You realize you'll get about a third or a quarter of the salary you're making now?" But I said I'd love the experience if it could be organized. Sure enough, it *was* organized, so it was Mary Martin and myself—we were the only two from the New York company who went over. That's where I met my future husband Peter Grant, who was in the show playing Joe Cable. He was English, a tenor, and *South Pacific* was his first West End show. I fell for London and for Peter, and I fell for his family, and for the lifestyle, and ... that was it. We married in '52, about a year after we met.

St. John first went to England to appear in the West End production of Broadway's Pulitzer Prize–winning *South Pacific*. Her tenor leading man (Peter Grant) became her husband.

Soon you played your first grown-up movie part, a royal Middle Eastern girl, in Dream Wife.

Hollywood and its typecasting mind! When the film *Dream Wife* came, with Cary Grant and Deborah Kerr, my name was still very fresh from doing Liat in *South Pacific*, and the part in the film was a very Liat-kind of part. So MGM contacted me and I tested for it in London and they *gave* me the part and brought me back to do *Dream Wife*. Meanwhile, Peter and I had *finally*

Landing her first grown-up film role in the Cary Grant vehicle *Dream Wife*, St. John played a Middle Eastern princess—and even got special "And Introducing" billing on-screen.

come to the decision that we *would* get married, and had the banns called in church ... and then we *both* got cold feet. So we agreed I'd go to Hollywood and do *Dream Wife* first, and if we still felt the same way about each other after I finished, after we'd been apart for a while, then we'd go ahead and get married. And that's exactly what happened. We had a registry office wedding, we didn't bother with anything fancy, but it was wonderful and fun and it felt right and it turned out to *be* right. Which *again* ... is more good luck than good management. Who of us know, when we take that step, if we're making the right decision?

After Dream Wife *and marriage, then* The Robe *came along.*

Dream Wife came first, and then immediately afterwards a film called *All the Brothers Were Valiant* [1953], also MGM, Stewart Granger, Ann Blyth and Robert Taylor—a charming man. That was a film location in Jamaica, and that was fun. Then *The Robe* came right on top of that. It was a good experience. Henry Koster the director was a charming man, and a very good man to work with. Again, I always felt my life was in the hands of my director, because ... because I *needed* a good director [*laughs*]!

If you were in all these big stage musicals, how come the books say that's not you singing in The Robe*?*

In *Carousel* I sang in the chorus, but other than that, I never sang on stage. In movies, the only time I wasn't dubbed was when I was in *Destry Rides Again* [*laughs*]. In Hollywood, they did these things so cleverly. I did sing it in my way *for* them, and then these very talented people listen to what you've done and then make it better. A couple singers have made careers of doing this. I forget the girl's name who did my singing in *The Robe*—

According to the books, Carol Richards.

Yes! Good for you! Richard Burton [star of *The Robe*] was a legit actor who in those days really felt he was only in Hollywood for the money, but it was a lovely experience working with him. *The Robe* was the first CinemaScope film, and people in the industry thought, "This is gonna change all of Hollywood" and that it would be the new thing. Everybody in *The Robe* was so madly impressed that they *were* in it, and you got this kind of "holier than thou" feeling that "We're all so fortunate to be *part* of this" and "We're doing groundbreaking work." Another thing I loved about it was, we had a wonderful photographer called Leon Shamroy—very gruff man, but an excellent photographer. As I said, everyone was feeling so holier-than-thou being on the picture, and I *loved* him because he'd walk in and say, "Good morning, for Christ's sake!" [*Laughs*] He kinda brought it down to earth!

I look at your list of movies and it goes from these MGM pictures and The Robe *and all this wonderful stuff ... all of a sudden, overnight, to people like Sam Katzman and William Castle. Several steps down the ladder. How did that happen?*

This was 1953–54, and television was arriving. When I started at MGM, the soundstages were mostly quite busy, but by the time we finished *Dream Wife*, there were less and less things happening. By the time I went back for *All the Brothers Were Valiant*, your footsteps echoed and there weren't many people around. The films were closing down! The people in the business, at that time, didn't know if it was the end of films as we knew them. Films were dying. The studios weren't putting people under contract, they didn't know *what* to do, they didn't know whether to jump with television or whether television was a flash in the pan. It was a panic time! It was a strange thing to live through.

So that's when you started working in "smaller" pictures.

Well, there wasn't much to choose from. What else *did* I do at that time? Oh, *The Student Prince* [1954] was done then and I did a small part in that. Incidentally, *Seven Brides for Seven Brothers* [1954] was during that period, and that was a film I turned down. Not that I wouldn't have liked to have done it in a *way*, because the moment I read the script I thought, "Oh, this is going to be a great film," but there wasn't a part in it for me—I would have been, obviously, just one of the girls, and I thought, "Well ... why am I doing this at *this* point?" So I turned it down. Oh, and *Rear Window* [1954]. Alfred Hitchcock asked me to do it, he said, "Take the script and read it. I'd like you to do the part of Miss Torso." [*Laughs*] I took the script home, and Miss Torso did not have one word of dialogue! Also, I had kind of an old-fashioned husband (even though he was in the business), and I thought, "I don't want to do *this*, this isn't my style." But I also thought, "Oh, how cruel..."—I knew it was going to be a wonderful film, and I was missing

Glamour photos of St. John were taken for RKO owner Howard Hughes' perusal before he would give the okay to cast her in his studio's *Dangerous Mission* (1954)—in which she played an American Indian. "Hollywood logic!" the actress laughs today.

a chance to work with Hitchcock! I wrote him a very nice letter, or I *tried* to, expressing my regrets and telling him I would have adored working with him, but I just couldn't see myself as Miss Torso! I didn't ever regret not *being* Miss Torso but I did regret not being part of such a great film!

Working for people like Katzman and Castle after you'd been at the big studios—what was that like?

I kind of enjoyed it. Bill Castle [director of *The Law vs. Billy the Kid* and *The Saracen Blade*, both 1954] was lovely to work with, one of the directors that I felt very happy with. It was a faster shooting schedule, and you didn't get all the pampering and spoiling you did [on bigger pictures]. I think it must be what people get nowadays when making an independent film—much more of a feeling that you're involved, you understand what the whole thing is about, you're not just a puppet that dances on a string. With a fast shooting schedule, you got the *feel* of a film. I think *Dream Wife* was, what?, eight weeks. Going from an eight-week picture to one done in ten days, suddenly you're much more under pressure, but in a way I kind of *liked* it. When I started doing television, it too had much more of a "real" feel to it, from beginning to end and you knew your cast and you saw it developing and you got a feeling of the rhythm happening. A big studio production, sure it's fun, you're spoiled and everything else, *but* ... I kind of liked the feeling of the smaller productions. Another film I did was called *The Naked Dawn* [1955]—*that* I enjoyed because, *again*, they said, "We've got a shooting schedule of ten days, but we're going to take a week where we *rehearse*." Well, wwwwonderful!, because to me, rehearsing is the greatest part *of* it. This is where you see it taking shape and you find out what it's about and you find the rhythm in it. Being a bigger part of something small was almost more enjoyable than being a smaller part of something big.

What memories of Tarzan and the Lost Safari, *of landing that part?*

At that time, Hollywood really had dried up. My husband Peter was over here in the U.S., and he hadn't been working—and there's nothing worse for a marriage than one working and one not, especially if it's the wife working. He was becoming known as Mr. St. John, and *that* doesn't do your marriage any good either. So after *Naked Dawn*, I thought, "Well, there's nothing else been presented to me right now on the horizon," and at that time the stage musical *Kismet* was leaving New York to go to London. There was a perfect part in it for Peter, the part of the caliph, which Richard Kiley played in New York—and the only cast member *not* going over was Richard Kiley. We were very keen for Peter to be in London so he could audition for that. Well, soon after getting back there, he did get *Kismet*, and I did the Tarzan picture.

But do you remember how you got the role?

I had a bit of a name, and I guess somebody sent me the script and asked, "Do you want to do it?" I certainly didn't test for it or anything, not in those days. I had one baby who was six or seven months old at the time, and by that point you need to get your morale back again. I had nothing better to *do*, let's say! But it was also good fun, because I shared a car with [co-star] Yolande Donlan, a *funny* lady, has a wonderful sense of humor. We both lived in the same area of London, so they sent a car for us in the morning, and there's nothing better, in a British winter, than to be able to go into a warm studio and do a Tarzan film—it was absolutely marvelous! That one was done totally inside, we didn't do *any* location work. It was Elstree, a nice, warm, comfortable place to spend part of your winter. And, you know, something not taken too seriously; I think everybody just had a good, fun romp with that. That was Wilfrid Hyde-White in there too, wasn't it? [*Gasps*] Well, no *wonder* it was a fun company, because *he* was a delightfully funny man. And, as I mentioned, Yolande was marvelous. She did quite a bit of writing in those days, and the production people were a little bit afraid because they heard that she was writing [about the experience]. *Did* she ever write about it?

Yes, a series of articles for London's Daily Express.

Yolande had a great way of seeing the funny side of *everything*. She was taking notes and writing various bits about the filming of it, and I think I can guarantee you that what she wrote would have made very entertaining reading.

How familiar were you with Tarzan movies?

I don't think I went to films all that often, but I loved the jungle pictures that Dorothy Lamour used to do in the '30s. At that time, as a kid, I just fell in love with the sarong and jungles and diving into water [*laughs*]. I think I've always had an affinity for those kind of parts, actually—even before *South Pacific* came along. Then *Tarzan* came along, and that was "jungly." I think some of it hearkens back to the time of enjoying those films when I was a child. It was just a wonderful way to get paid [*laughs*]!

Was Gordon Scott a good Tarzan?

Physically, yes. He wasn't an actor, but again, it's kind of an unbelievable character you've got to play anyway, isn't it? So nobody really expected him to do much on *that* side. He *looked* right, and the action shots were good. But I haven't seen too many Tarzans to compare. In fact, have I seen *any* to compare? No, I'm not sure that I have. So I don't know

Most of *Tarzan and the Lost Safari* took place on a soundstage jungle set complete with river, Ape Man (Gordon Scott)—and crocodile.

who I could look back upon and say, "Aaah, but then *this* Tarzan...." As a matter of fact, outside of the *wonderful* film which came out some years ago ... what was it? ... the British-made film which was based more on the book....

Greystoke *[1984]?*

Greystoke, yes! That, I thought, was a magnificent film, but of course that wasn't a Tarzan film in the way in which we think of the old ones. But "my" Tarzan picture was fun and, yes, Gordon Scott was fine to get on with. Robert Beatty was a lovely actor. A Canadian, a nice person, good actor. George Coulouris—lovely again. Great, funny person. The British have a great sense of humor. He was, what?, Russian-English or something, wasn't he? But, again, a super person to work with, good actor. You were involved with such good people that it made these a joy to do.

The director was an American, H. Bruce Humberstone.

Bruce Humberstone was an old-style Hollywood director, one who came out of the time when everything was churned out like it was a factory. And, honestly, he was such a funny, "typical American" type over there. I think this sums him up: The script girl is the one who has to make certain that all the backgrounds match and that the cigarettes that actors are holding are burned down to the same point from shot to shot, everything like that, and one day she mentioned that something in the background wasn't going to match from one shot to the next. "Oh," Bruce Humberstone scoffed, "a rock's a rock and a tree's a tree!" [*Laughs*] And of course that became the tone of the picture; after that, we didn't take *anything* too seriously. If *he* wasn't too worried about matching the shots, we could all kind of take the same tone: "Let's enjoy it!"

An actress named Eve Brent, who played in a Tarzan movie directed by Humberstone, told me he was grouchy and gruff—and that he had wanted his girlfriend to play that part!

I really don't remember him too well, because as a company, with Yolande and Wilfrid Hyde-White, we had a close-knit thing, and he was just kind of *there*. Not on the sidelines but, quite honestly, he was very much a technical man who just kept the whole thing rolling. I mean, that was all, and you didn't look for any input from him. And didn't *get* much [*laughs*]. He was an efficient factory floor manager—which isn't a good thing to say. Is he still alive? No? Okay. But, you know, he was efficient, he was one of the Hollywood guys with the attitude of "it's a job, get the thing done on time, get it done on budget," and that was all I think he was concerned about. That's why we loved the line that became our catchphrase, "Oh, a rock's a rock and a tree's a tree, don't worry about it." I don't think he bothered us, I don't remember any tantrums or anything.

Was the interior jungle set as large and impressive as it looks on-screen?

Oh, yeah. It was one big set, the whole thing was done on one sound stage, including this lake or river or whatever it was. They had one shot which was *great* fun, I got to dive in this water and the crocodile was chasing me. *That* kind of filming was *so* much fun.

And the crocodile...?

It wasn't a real one—but it still makes you swim fast [*laughs*]!

Were there any animals on the set?

Only Cheetah. I wasn't involved too much with him, Gordon Scott was, so I didn't get to know Cheetah too well. I do remember that the makeup girl had to put black pancake onto Cheetah's behind [*laughs*], because of course a bare behind picks up the light. Without that black pancake, the only thing you would see when you looked at Cheetah was this bare behind that all chimps have.

You and your whole party were captured by natives a couple of times.

Again, just great fun in those days, because you'd get to see natives running around and villages set alight. You become like children acting out: You remember when you used to play cowboys and Indians, and now you're getting to do it and you're getting paid for it!

Tarzan the Magnificent *was a whole different barrel of monkeys, being shot in Kenya.*

It *was*. We had a good director on it [Robert Day], it was a happy company, and of course it's always fun to go on location. Doing it in authentic settings is that much better than doing it on a back lot or doing it in the studio. I don't suppose the storyline had much more to offer than others, but it was escapist fun: The villains are really villainous and the good people are good, and you know where you stand! I think I was switched, I think I was initially supposed to play ["the good girl"], and then suddenly Robert Day said to me, "We've decided we want you to play the more villainous girl." I said [*casually*], "Okay!" [*Laughs*] Because, again, I was happy, I felt comfortable, I felt safe with him, so ... sure. Not that I was very villainous in it, I don't think. I did see it once, and I thought, "Why wasn't I *more* villainous?"

The casting switch was made before you went on location and started making the movie.
Oh, yes, yes, I knew before I went out.

What was the trip like?
That was a wonderful time. We stayed near Lake Naivasha. I wasn't politically terribly aware in those days, but the white farmers that we did get to meet, they had lived through the Mau Mau uprising of about three years before, and when you heard the stories of what these people had survived, it was quite an eye-opener. But there was something terribly magical about Kenya ... something very stimulating, very exciting. The physical geography of the place became ... not unreal, but ... another *dimension*? One recent film that's captured the magic, a wonderful film, is *Nowhere in Africa* [2001], the German-made film [and 2003 Best Foreign Language Film Oscar winner]. People do find that there's something *about* the place that hooks you. So it was very exciting *being* there. But this is how naïve I was at the time: We were by this lake, and one day when I wasn't called on set, they were filming on the other side of the lake. I decided to take a rowboat and row across to where they were filming. When I got over there, *oh!*, people were *really* annoyed, and I found out why: There were hippopotamus in the lake, and of course they *have* been known to rise and tip over boats. And movie companies don't like to lose actors, because that's very expensive [*laughs*]!

The jungles of Kenya provided the more authentic backgrounds for *Tarzan the Magnificent*, a trek adventure in which a treacherous St. John falls for baddie Jock Mahoney.

You stayed in a hotel?
It was not a hotel as such, it was more or less an inn with separate cottages. Of course, we filmed all *over*. We were in a small plane, just a few of us, going to a location, and suddenly the pilot said, "Look down below." I looked down and it was like a cloud underneath. He said, "That's a cloud of locusts. We're gonna go a little higher, because if we get these into the engine, it can bring a plane down." Kinds of things like this were fascinating to be concerned with. Location work is fun.

Even working outdoors in places like that?
Well ... not always! I don't know if they still do it the same way, but in those days, they would use the sun as a light source. Being blue-eyed, I had great trouble not squinting, because the light bothered my eyes. You would try all sorts of tricks, hoping that when the time came for your closeup with the sun straight at you, you could look without your eyes

watering or without squinting. So, yes, you had those technical problems, and from an acting standpoint, quite honestly, it wasn't nearly as satisfying as working indoors. But of course [working outdoors in the actual location] is *fun*, because you could pretend you *were* who you were pretending to be, in the real circumstances. You know, we're all children at heart [*laughs*], and we enjoy that side of it.

Gordon Scott on that picture—how did Tarzan enjoy being in a real *jungle this time?*

Oh, I think we *all* enjoyed it. I never had deep heart-to-hearts with Scott, we did our job, we didn't socialize particularly. Jock Mahoney was the bad guy so I got to see a little bit more of him because we had more scenes together. He arrived after we started filming, and I think the first feeling was that maybe we didn't like each other too much. At first, he kind of seemed like a Hollywood actor to me, but then I found he was an "all right" guy. He *was* kind of Hollywood [*laughs*], but once you broke down through that, he was okay! Once out on the road going to a location somewhere, we got a flat tire. Well, it was Jock Mahoney and one other actor, they went out, they whipped off that tire before the driver even knew what was happening, got the spare on, got us on the road, it was a real American can-do thing. Which is great, that appeals to me, and I think I liked him far better after that.

Among the British character actors this time, Lionel Jeffries.

Again, charming, delightful. The British character actors ... besides being so good at their jobs, they have the lovely British perspective on life. We did work with the two tribes, Kikuyu and Masai, and Lionel Jeffries being a very funny man, he had this wonderful way with them. Whenever we were in the crowds of natives, and children especially, they just responded to him. A British comedian, or maybe a comedian of any type, is the international language. Half the time I'm sure the natives weren't sure exactly what was happening or what they were supposed to do *but* they clustered around him, he always made it light and bright and fun and *they* loved it. He was a delight, an absolute delight.

Any dangerous experiences at all on that picture?

I didn't know how they planned to shoot the part where the character I played got eaten by the lion, I'd never talked to Bob Day about that. If I'd been more sensible, I would have said, "Look, how do you plan to do this?" [*Laughs*] Obviously they must have known somebody who kept lions that they could use, tame lions, and they did. Bob Day and I, and I forget who else, we were invited over for drinks to the house of the lady who had a lioness, because they were negotiating to use her lioness. It was a very strange feeling, walking up the patio steps and finding Elsa the lioness sprawled out on the side of the top step, and kind of having to walk by her [*laughs*]! I remember thinking, "Well, I *guess* this is all right or we wouldn't *be* here now!" The lady who owned Elsa was very much my size and shape, so they dressed her in my clothes and used her as the double for me. When it came time to shoot the scene, they took great care, even though this *was* a pet lion. Everybody who wasn't actually involved had to stay in cars, so I couldn't even get to watch it while they were filming it. When she was doing it, it was like a game: She would pretend to be hiding and the lion would come and jump and pounce. That's how the filming went, *I was told*, because I couldn't actually watch it.

You could step over the lioness on the patio but you couldn't be around when it was in a shot?

[*Laughs*] No! Isn't that surprising? The insurance people probably didn't realize that we *had* already been over there to her house on a social basis. If you're doing something dangerous during filming, then the company's responsible. Let's face it, money is all that they're concerned about, isn't it? I suppose that's what it was: During filming, they would take extra precautions. Even then, when the lion jumped and was playing with the lady, she got quite a bad scratch down her arm, just because ... well, it's like playing with a cat. Then we heard, by the end of the filming, before we left, that Elsa could now no longer be left around on her property because it had turned and made off with her pet baboon; she and her husband had other animals on the property, and the lioness had taken one of the other pets. So, after that, they weren't allowing Elsa to lounge around on their front steps any longer. It makes you realize that you've always got to be cautious. Even though it *is* a pet, or has been brought up that way, it can turn. *She* [the lion's owner] was lovely, and it worked out wonderfully well for the film that she matched me so well. Obviously I did the closeups and the scream, but any shot that showed both my character and the actual animal itself was only done with her.

Robert Day — what other memories?

A director I felt very comfortable with. I think I first worked with him in maybe a couple of TV films, or....

You and he did the Boris Karloff movie Corridors of Blood, *which we're going to get into in a minute.*

Yes, yes! I mentioned before that you find directors that you like working with; well, I suppose directors are the same way and they find actors *they* like working with. I just always felt very comfortable with him because, if I was nervous about something or couldn't seem to get it, he would say, "Okay, we'll do it another way." I was always happy to work with him because I felt very comfortable and safe with him.

Parts of Tarzan the Magnificent *were shot in England, Robert Day told me.*

Of course it was. We did our locations in Kenya, but all the interiors were done on a soundstage. For the scene where we're wading through the swamp, they kept the water warm, and had a bit of cork floating on the top, to make it look like mud. It was all quite pleasant [*laughs*]!

Corridors of Blood *with Karloff — what do you recall about that one?*

Boris Karloff, absolutely charming. *Lovely.* But, you see, I never saw horror films — I still don't to this day, I just don't *like* them. So I'd never really seen Boris Karloff in very much. However, we really didn't think we were making a horror film, because *Corridors of Blood* was

St. John models the latest London fashion (19th century London, that is) in *Corridors of Blood*, a unique blend of horror and medical history.

based on a true story. I didn't have any scenes anyway in any of the grisly parts of it, and (again) I always, for right or wrong, probably for wrong, only concern myself with what I was doing. All my scenes were "domestic" ones with Boris Karloff. I remember one day Bob Day said to me, "Make it sound more English," because I was playing Boris Karloff's niece, and of course Boris Karloff was English. Well, *that* finished me completely [*laughs*]!

And Karloff off-stage?

Very professional. You venerated him as an older, established actor. I don't know if it was "those days" or if it was just me, but whenever I worked with older, more established people, I'd give them the respect ... but you don't get on a friendly, pally-pally basis, I find. Or even *attempt* to. So I don't remember much more than doing the job. Francis Matthews was another one that I worked with quite a bit in various things. I'm delighted to hear that he's still going and still working. I always enjoyed working with Francis, another "matey" person to work with. I think in some ways I've always felt more at home with British people.

Did you go to see your movies in the old days?

I saw *some* of them. I recently heard an interview with John Malkovich on the radio, and he was asked that same sort of question, and he said exactly what I feel: Your eye focuses on the defects. I could take in everything happening if I wasn't in the scene. Wonderful. I

Francis Matthews (left) played St. John's cousin-boyfriend (!) in *Corridors of Blood* with Boris Karloff (dying in this climactic scene).

could enjoy it. Unfortunately, anything you're *in*, you focus on your*self*. You home in on what *you're* doing, at the expense of what's happening around you. But everyone does: Your hairdresser only sees the hair, the makeup people only see the makeup, the costume people only see the costumes, they don't *see* anything else. *The Robe* didn't disturb me too much, but most things I did really disturbed me. I think in a way I would have been far better off never to have gone to rushes as well, because you suddenly realize that, for example, you blink more than you ever knew you did. Whether ignorance would be bliss or not, I don't know, but you *do* home in on the flaws. And that, I find, is inhibiting the next day.

So you went to your early films thinking that you would *enjoy them, and found out you didn't, and you stopped after a while?*

I went to films I thought I wouldn't be too embarrassed about. *High Tide at Noon* [1957] is one film that I think I came out *not* feeling too embarrassed. Maybe the *only* film [*laughs*]!

The yellow journalist in me wants to ask—name a film that you came out of feeling very *embarrassed!*

Umm ... *Horror Hotel*. I didn't want to *do* it, I really felt "I hate horror films," I didn't want to be part of it. I had the feeling, "You're going downhill, you might as well get out of the business...." Which is a *wrong, wrong* feeling; if ever you're doing an acting job, you should always give it your *very*, very best. But I kind of went into it, I suppose, with a poor attitude. When I saw it, I thought, "Gee, it's building a *wonderful* atmosphere." There *was* a wonderful atmosphere about the film, especially the beginning—until I came on! I didn't seem to know what had gone before. When *my* part arrived, I didn't seem to have a clue what film I was in or what had happened or what it was about! If it had been impressed upon me, "*This* is what has preceded, *this* is the *feeling*...," I think I would have swung *into* it. To me, it wasn't like I was even in the same *show*! Well, that's the way *I* looked at it, homing in on the great flaw *there*, which just made me shudder and curl up and want to crawl into a hole and pull it in after me. So that was really the time when I thought, "I'm not gonna look at anything more, because it's just too depressing to me."

And the solution for this, for a performer, is...?

If only one could have a chance to rehearse and get the feeling of what's gone before and walk through it, just to get the overall feeling. I'm amazed that films come out as well as they do, when as an actor you're brought in for your five days or ten days or two days or whatever. It might be quite a big part, but you're still brought in with*out* any feeling of how it has been growing. The director should have the overall vision and, one hopes, he would try to impart it to people. You can read a script, but that doesn't always give you the feeling of how it's been developing before you get there.

I was just about to ask, did you read your scripts from start to finish, or did you just read your parts on some of these movies?

I did read from start to finish, yes, but I certainly didn't seem to home in as I should have on the general thing. And, of course, oftentimes you do rely upon directors. But some directors direct and some directors don't.

Do you still have your scripts?

I never kept scripts. We always brought them home for the children for drawing pads [*laughs*]. That's the way it was, with *all* actors. *Your* script, *anybody's* script—"The kids need more drawing paper!" So they all disappeared!

Any recollection of working with Christopher Lee in Horror Hotel?

I've worked with him quite a bit, too, in various things. Liked him very much and always enjoyed working with him. *Very* intellectual, very with-it, a very interesting person. But horror films had been kind of the poor man's [specialty]. I saw him in something new not too long ago. Good actors *keep* going, and they should!

Your leading man was a real-life pop singer named Dennis Lotis.

I guess the only reason I was in *Horror Hotel* was, they thought I had some name value for the U.K. market. And Dennis the same. You can always kinda see when people are ... a bit misplaced [*laughs*]! *Horror Hotel* was shot on a pretty tight schedule, too, because I don't remember it being more than a few *days* that I was involved. The whole town was on a stage.

Around 1960, you made your last movie. Why did you drop out?

I had three children by then [the early 1960s]. Also, I must tell you, I'd done *High Tide at Noon*, which was the one film which I really felt so good about—it was the English submission for the Cannes Film Festival. I was pregnant all during the film, and that was something I had to keep hidden because I wanted to do that part so badly that I didn't admit I was pregnant before I started. Which was a bit naughty, but I thought I could *almost* get through the film. Of course, the film ran over-schedule a little bit.... [*Laughs*] So I had done that earlier, and I felt that was kind of a high point for me satisfaction-wise, the role I played and the film type and everything. *Then* these other films I did because they were jobs that came along. I really felt very strongly, especially after my third child, that I was headed downhill as far as career and what I was being offered. And by that time I had quite come to terms that I didn't have the kind of acting ability that gave me reason to keep on *going* forever. I knew very strongly I never had the talent, and I didn't really have the great ambition, knowing I didn't have the talent to back it up with. I think I'd always felt that, when I began on the downhill thing [career-wise], I would *leave*. Because there's nothing sadder to see than an actor who's done quite a lot, to suddenly see him coming in for small parts and being asked to audition. The pecking order is quite severe at *all* times, and there is nothing more degrading. It's like seeing a wonderful boxer past his prime, a dancer past her prime. "Oh, *stop*, while people still have good memories of you! Don't leave this as a last impression!" It's very hard for a lot of people, the old ham in them, they just can't resist one final time—you need someone to butter you up a little bit, "Oh, you're marvelous!" But I think it was

Her aversion to horror movies made St. John think twice before accepting *Horror Hotel*—and made her think about retirement afterward!

Long-retired, and widowed since 1992, Betta St. John has residences in both the United States and England, where she enjoys activities like hiking the cliffs of Dorset.

always *very* much in my thinking: I don't want to lose that dignity or that self-respect, by sliding down the slippery slope! What did you say was my last film?

I don't know. Either Tarzan the Magnificent *or* Horror Hotel.

I'm sure it was *Horror Hotel*, because that probably *really* made me feel, "This is a good time to step out!" [*Laughs*] Pity, because apparently it *is*, as you've mentioned, kind of a cult film, and really very good in its way. But I never liked horror films. There are certain things you respond to more than other things. And certain things you feel you're more right for than other things.

So after that last movie, you just became wife and mother and....

Well, when you've got three children, it keeps you kind of busy. I missed it. I missed it terribly for a while. There wasn't the excitement of the phone ringing. As an actor, it was always what was unknown around the corner—a script would suddenly come to you, and it was always exciting. And, oh, for about ten years, I thought, "Oh, children *should* be fulfilling," but quite honestly, once you've had the adrenaline from working, and doing good things, life is a little bit gray [*laughs*]! But a family life was important to my husband Peter and me, and I didn't feel I was giving up very much at that point. My husband left the business for the same reason, though he regretted it afterwards. But, again, what are you going to do?, family life, children's education and so on. Very few actors, even if they're *very* successful, can keep a family and marriage together, and keep a good career going too. There's not many, just a few that have achieved it.

It sounds like you may never sit down to watch some of your movies again, but are you happy they're "out there" for your kids and grandkids?

Depending on their reaction to it. If they think they're as corny as I do, then no [*laughs*]! But my son is in the business now and doesn't seem to be as embarrassed about looking at some of my stuff as I do. As long as they're not too ashamed of me, fine!

HANS J. SALTER
(INTERVIEW BY PRESTON NEAL JONES)

> *Whenever a [horror movie] was done at another studio, they always ran for their composers one of* my *pictures, to show them how to treat it.*

Hans Julius Salter was a classically trained Viennese composer who in the late 1930s fled the horror of Hitler's frying pan and soon found himself in the fire of Universal's fright factory. Although adept at providing music for virtually any type of film, the scores that six-time Oscar nominee* Salter composed (sometimes in collaboration with Frank Skinner) for such scary tales as *The Wolf Man* (1941), *The Ghost of Frankenstein* (1942) and *The Invisible Man Returns* (1940) gave a special quality to the fearsome goings-on. Salter's unique gift was to write music which, even when it was eerie, ominous or explosive, was somehow still lyrical.

Born in Vienna in 1896, Salter conducted in opera houses and silent movie palaces—including performances of Fritz Lang's *Frau im Mond* (1929)—before writing music for early talkies at Berlin's famous UFA Studios. Once Salter reached Hollywood, he and his friend Skinner became the backbone of Universal's music department. In the early '50s, Salter began branching out to other studios as an independent agent, eventually scoring many TV series as well. At the time of this interview (1975), Salter had not scored a film since the 1967 TV-movie *Return of the Gunfighter*. But he never stopped getting fan mail from Monster Kids who had taped his horror movies off TV on their reel-to-reel recorders, and who never stopped dreaming of the seemingly impossible: a commercial recording of Salter's themes for Frankenstein's Monster, the Wolf Man, Dracula and the Mummy.

You've written scores for virtually every genre, from Westerns, dramas and comedies to musicals with Deanna Durbin and Elvis Presley. But your 1940s horror scores seem to be regarded as the highlight of your Hollywood career.

Do you know what they used to call me in those days? "The Master of Terror and Suspense" [*laughs*]! Pretty good? They couldn't understand how a nice, mild-mannered fellow from Vienna could develop such a sense of horror and mayhem. You know, I still get letters from people asking about those scores. This is very surprising, this renewed interest in the scores of the '40s. Why is it?

---

*It Started with Eve (1941), The Amazing Mrs. Holliday *(1943),* Can't Help Singing *(1944),* Christmas Holiday *(1944),* The Merry Monahans *(1944) and* This Love of Ours *(1945).*

I'm not surprised. They were wonderful scores for (sometimes) wonderful movies.

In those days, we had no idea we were writing for "eternity." We were just trying to keep up with the frantic pace of picture after picture. Let's say it was a Monday. The producer showed you his picture. You had to write a score, and orchestrate it, and be ready to rehearse and record with the orchestra on the following Monday. It was like a factory, where you'd have to produce a certain amount of red socks, a certain amount of green socks.... They'd screen one of those pictures for us without the music, and it would be *nothing*. All the pictures we saved for them! But those executives, they never knew what they had. We never heard a word from them. They were afraid if they gave us a compliment, we'd ask for a raise.

If you had to give yourself a compliment, which Salter scores are your own personal favorites?

Bend of the River [a 1952 James Stewart Western, directed by Anthony Mann], *Thunder on the Hill* [a 1951 Claudette Colbert mystery, directed by Douglas Sirk] and, especially, *Magnificent Doll* [a 1946 historical drama with Ginger Rogers, directed by Frank Borzage].

I notice you haven't mentioned any of the horror pictures.

Those horror pictures were a big challenge to me. When they presented those pictures to me in the projection room, there was nothing there, just a bunch of disjointed scenes that had no cohesion and didn't scare anybody. You had to create with the music all the horror, all the tension that was "in between the lines" and didn't come off on screen. And that was such a tremendous challenge that these pictures interested me, and I developed a very refined technique for this type of picture. But, as far as giving me a personal thrill, I can't say that they did. [*Smiles*] Sorry to disappoint you.

You had no special affinity for the fantastic subject matter in the horror films?

I must have had, because I mastered it in a short time. The musical devices at my command were evidently right at the right time and the right spot. And I know, whenever a picture of this type was done at another studio, they always ran for their composers one of *my* pictures, to show them how to treat it.

In some of the horror films there were moments which could have been used in a "straight" dramatic picture, such as the last-mile walk in Man Made Monster *[1941] or the more melancholy passages in* The Wolf Man. *Would you, perhaps, have felt as moved by these as you were by some of your "straight" scores?*

My basic approach to pictures is always the same. I ask myself, "What did the director want to tell the audience with this scene? Where does the picture, or the scene, need help?" Very often, I've told producers that they *didn't* need music for this scene, and they disagreed with me violently. There was a producer, who shall remain nameless, who showed me his picture, *Phantom Lady* [1944], directed by Robert Siodmak, and he said that he wanted a lot of music in it. I told him, "All you need is a main and end title. The picture plays just the way it is. You'll have a big success." He argued that they needed a lot of help with this scene, and this, and this.... I said, "Well, you're the boss, so I will write it, but it's just a waste of money, because in the dubbing room [where dialogue, music and sound effects are blended into the final soundtrack], you'll take out all this music." Okay, I wrote it, and, as I predicted, in the dubbing room, he took out the music for first this scene, then this, then this.... The picture went out with just the main and end title. Half a year goes by, and the same producer has another Siodmak picture, *The Strange Affair of Uncle Harry* [1945]. He says, "In this picture, we won't need any music. I've already used up the music budget for other things, bigger sets, better actors and so on." He shows me the picture, and it was a real lemon. And I told him, "Sorry to contradict you, but this picture needs an awful lot of help." He said, "You are really crazy! One time, you tell me I don't need any music, now you tell me I need a lot of music! You're wrong, and I'll tell you what we'll do. We'll take it out to a preview with just main and end title music, and then we'll release it that way." So they took the picture out for a preview that way, and it must have laid a big egg because the next morning the producer called me and said, "I need a hundred percent score!" He had to go to the front office on his hands and knees and beg for money for the music budget. I gave the picture, I would say, at least 60 percent music. The producer saw his picture and it was like [*Salter raises his hands and eyebrows in wonder*]—he was so amazed.

They shoot, *he* scores! Near the end of the assembly line at Universal, the studio that invented Hollywood movie horror, film factory worker Hans J. Salter made many celebrated shockers the beneficiary of his musical expertise.

You talked about the frantic, assembly-line pace of Universal. Did you, like most film composers, have to use an orchestrator to meet those deadlines?

Yes, whenever there was no time for orchestrating it myself. I started out as an orchestrator, for Frank Skinner. I orchestrated for him one of those early Frankenstein pictures, *Son of Frankenstein* [1939]. I remember, there was one stretch, pretty close to the recording date, where we didn't leave the studio for 48 or 50 hours. He would sit at the piano and compose a sequence, and then he would hand it to me. I would orchestrate it and he would take a nap on the couch in the meantime. Then, when I was through orchestrating, I would wake him up, and he had to go back and write another sequence while *I* would take a nap. And this went on for 48 hours or so, so that he could make the recording date.

That was one of Skinner's finest scores. Was it written in just those couple of days?

No, no, not a couple of days. But I don't think we had more than maybe two weeks to write the whole thing. There was always a release date staring us in the face, and my friend Charlie Previn, who was the head of the music department, would aggravate the situation by saying, "They want this picture on Thursday. Let's show 'em! We'll give it to them on Wednesday!" He was a bachelor, and he couldn't understand how some of us with wives and families might actually have some kind of a life away from the studio. He was a charming fellow, and I was very fond of him, but sometimes he just drove us nuts with these things.

Tower of London *was also released in 1939, had Rathbone and Karloff, supported by the same music as in* Son of Frankenstein.

I remember *Tower of London* very well. What we tried to do there was to record music of that period, Dowland and other early English composers' music, without regard to the scene, just for sort of a mood. And we used harpsichord, and flutes and violas da gamba—

Autographed photos of Charles Previn (left) and Frank Skinner, Salter's collaborators on various scores (including that of *The Wolf Man*).

all those old instruments. But when we went to the preview with this, it didn't work out. The executives were somehow startled. They didn't like it. They couldn't make heads or tails out of that sound. I think I had orchestrated some of that old music for strings and harpsichord, and I think I wrote a few sequences, too, in that style. It was a good idea, but it didn't work. So, after the preview, all this music was replaced by some other music, and some of it was from *Son of Frankenstein*.

You yourself would sometimes re-use parts of your scores in other films.
It was a matter of necessity, sometimes. When we were behind the eight ball with these recording dates and there wasn't time to write a completely new score, I would use bits and pieces of scores written by myself or my colleagues for other pictures. Charlie Previn called this process "Salterizing." I would try to create something that would be on an equal footing with a complete new score. And I'm sure that 90 percent of the people didn't know the difference.

At the factory that was Universal, did you have any voice in choosing which pictures would be assigned to you?
They made, in those days, an average of about 75 pictures a year. So, you can divide two men into 75, and what do you arrive at? In those days, everybody had to work on practically every picture. And the credits rarely reflected the whole story.

In Tower of London, *Previn is credited with the score and Skinner only receives credit for Orchestrations, even though most of the music was his. And Previn receives the only music credit on* The Wolf Man.

Once in a while, Previn wrote a sequence too. He had that ambition to keep his hand in.

Just how would you and Skinner collaborate on such a score?
We would split it up. Let's say, I would tell Frank, "I'm going to write this theme, and this theme, and this theme, and you write this theme, and this theme." And then we would exchange them, and use them as close as possible to their original form, and that would give the whole score a certain cohesion. We each tried to write in a style that was not too far apart.

How would you decide on that style? The Wolf Man *is a film score very much "of a piece."*
This can only be described in musical terms. We would stay within the bounds of tonality, so to speak, and not try to write anything too complicated which would stick out like a sore thumb. And, since we thought along more or less the same lines, musically.... Maybe I was a little ahead of him in certain respects.

Such as...?
Maybe in harmony, or in melodic development. If I held myself back a little, and he progressed a little, then we would meet somewhere in the middle. Frank Skinner was a real pal. He was such a wonderful fellow, so dependable. I don't think they make them any more like they did in those days, because Frank was, in many ways, a self-taught man. When I came to Universal in 1937, he was actually just learning the trade, so to speak. He had been a dance arranger before that. He came out of a dance band himself. I think he was a trombone player. How he adapted himself, with this limited knowledge, to write music for films, and to see how he grew with every assignment was wonderful to watch.

You say one of your first Universal jobs was orchestrating his music?
Yes, and then later on he orchestrated some of my music when it was necessary. When I first met him, he was not very talkative. He must have had some kind of inhibitions. He didn't open up easily to another person. But once you were his friend, you couldn't ask for a better friend than he was. He was very warm. He had a certain aura about him that was really wonderful. He would do some sequences in pictures when I couldn't get through in time. Frank Skinner was always there to the rescue, like the Marines.

Did he ever tell you what he considered his finest score?
I can't remember that he ever did. There were some pictures that he was fond of. [*Smiles:*] But the Frankenstein pictures were not among them.

Many people regard The Wolf Man *as a milestone score, and yet, neither you nor Skinner had any special feeling for it at the time...?*
No. I don't think anybody who created the basic material for a film like this, not even writers or directors, had that feeling at the time. Only time can tell if it has any lasting value. And I, personally, think that the horror films of that period will survive everything else. It's such a valid piece of Americana that it'll overshadow, not the Westerns, but all the romantic comedies, the adventure stories and so on. And this will survive into the twenty-first century, more than anything else. Because it was such a unique piece of work that couldn't be duplicated, no matter how hard they try. And it has retained its flavor to such a degree that, in spite of dated costumes and dated style, it still remains a valid piece of work. And it was such a good wedding between music and story and direction. I think film music, *per se*, is an art form, and the horror picture, *per se*, is an art form, and the wedding of these two elements created something unique.

There is much music in your scores which is complete in itself. In Man Made Monster, *Lon Chaney plays with his dog and there's a delightful scherzo with a beginning, a middle and an end....*

I always tried to do that, write set-pieces that made sense within themselves, if the scene required it. It was always my endeavor to write music that made sense as music and, within the flow of the music, to accentuate certain aspects of the film. But generally speaking, it's the wedding between the picture and the music that gives it that unique value. In picking my favorites from among my own scores, however, I can only judge by the way the music affected me while I was recording it on the stage. Some of the scores are just more or less a routine job, although I am happy they work out the way I had planned. But at other times the music affects me very deeply, and it gives me an exhilarating thrill, something that you can't get with any other endeavor. The laws that govern the flow of a scene, visually, and the laws that govern music, aurally, are diametrically opposed, and to bring these two disciplines in unison is not easy. Sometimes it made me cry, to see how well the music fitted the scene, how much it did for the scene or lifted the picture to some new heights that it didn't have before. I just couldn't believe it. Maybe other people were not affected the same way, but for me as the creator to see how all the musical devices I planned worked out to such perfection and improved what they had on the screen was a very big thrill. It's a unique feeling to get back what you have put in. Even in the horror scores, some of the sequences affected me deeply.

In looking through your copy of the House of Frankenstein *[1944] score, I find a section which must have been written for Boris Karloff and J. Carrol Naish's stormy exodus from prison, called here "The Gruesome Twosome Escape." That certainly indicates a less than reverent attitude.*

[*Smiles*] Yes, that was a great hobby of mine, developing those titles.

I notice, just before that sequence, a short section by yourself and Frank Skinner called "Lightning Strikes." And I see you share writing credit on many selections with "P. Dessau." Who was he?

Paul Dessau, a very talented man. It was one of those cases where there was very little time, and I needed some help to meet the recording date, so I called on him. He worked very fast and very well. I knew him from Berlin. He's a well-known opera composer now, in East Germany.

Did you work with him in the same manner as with Skinner on The Wolf Man?

It was similar. I would lay out themes for certain situations and certain characters in the film, and we would both use the same themes, only develop them differently. I discussed every sequence with him, how I would have done it, and then left it up to him to use his own musical language. But still, it created a certain unity and cohesion in the score, and it sounded like one composer. If you organize it right, and work it out, then it's bound to culminate in a good score.

On a film like House of Frankenstein *or* The Ghost of Frankenstein, *did you work with director Erle C. Kenton or with his producer?*

With Kenton. Kenton was a routine director. He was nothing particular. He was very matter-of-fact, and he left everything musical up to me. He had no opinion.

How about his House of Frankenstein *producer, Paul Malvern?*

He was the same kind of fellow, sort of a minus-B producer, you know? This was just a routine job for them. I don't think they had any particular love or feeling for these fantasies they were making. They trusted me and I was pretty much on my own.

Salter mastered the art of making macabre music at a time when Lon Chaney, Jr., was atop Univeral's family tree of iconic monsters. At left, he totes unconscious victim Anne Nagel in *Man Made Monster*, at right he strikes a jailhouse pose in *The Ghost of Frankenstein*; both were scored by Salter.

How about director Roy William Neill?

Neill? He did most of those Sherlock Holmes pictures, and *Frankenstein Meets the Wolf Man* [1943]. He impressed me at that time as a better grade director. But I don't recall that he expressed any likes or dislikes. He accepted pretty much what I gave him.

Did a fellow like Erle C. Kenton ever thank you for what you had done?

Oh, yes. And George Waggner, director of *The Wolf Man*, he appreciated it very much. I think he wrote the lyrics for that "Faro-La, Faro-Li," the song in *Frankenstein Meets the Wolf Man*. [Interviewer's note: Actually, Curt Siodmak, the movie's screenwriter, wrote the "Faro-La, Faro-Li" lyrics.]

Yes, that's the villager's song about death and eternal life which so upsets Larry Talbot [Lon Chaney, Jr.]. Was that actor, Adia Kuznetzoff, singing to a playback of his own voice or someone else's?

That was his own voice. [Kuznetzoff] was making several movies in those days. He was a very pleasant fellow. He was a Russian gypsy by heritage, and when we pre-recorded this song he just ate it up. He loved doing it.

Do you have any recollection of Rowland V. Lee, producer-director of Son of Frankenstein *and* Tower of London*?*

Very charming fellow. A typical Yankee. He embodied the best things in America. He had a wonderful sense of humor, and a wonderful outlook on life which was very heartening. While we were working on his pictures, Frank and I sometimes had lunch with him in the commissary, and he was always a lot of fun.

Fritz Lang's Scarlet Street *[1945] isn't one of his fantasies, but it was a bizarre murder story. Was that your first association with Lang since conducting a score for him in the silent days?*

Yes, and we became very friendly again. As a matter of fact, even long after the picture was finished, we used to eat lunch together in his office. He brought his lunch and I brought mine, and then he gave me half of his and I gave him half of mine, and it was a surprise every day, what we would bring. He told me a lot about his early days, and about some pet projects of his that he couldn't get anybody interested in producing. He was a very sophisticated, very intelligent fellow, and he had a strong feel for music in making pictures. Lang was basically an artist. He'd wanted to become a painter, originally, and then later he got into films. But he had the eye of a painter, and also a certain affinity for all other arts through that. So, you could talk to him in artistic terms and he understood what you were trying to do. And I can see how some people might find him hard to get along with, but he certainly has made his mark on the history of film.

Did you find him hard to get along with?

No, not the least bit. The only disagreement we had—not exactly disagreement—was a long discussion about the ending of *Scarlet Street*. It was one of the first films in those days that ended downbeat.

The film has a haunting ending, with Edward G. Robinson trudging off into the snow, haunted by the voices of Joan Bennett and Dan Duryea, the people for whose deaths he was responsible. How did you originally plan on scoring those last moments?

Well, very similarly to as it finally was. But at the very end, I wanted to go up a *little* more, and leave *some* ray of hope for the man. Musically, it seemed more natural—to develop it, and then end on a rise and a final redemption. But Lang didn't buy that. He said, "If we did that, it would defy the whole idea of my picture. This has to be downbeat, all the way to the very last frame." And he convinced me he was right. That's the way I scored it. Goes out, very somber to the very end, and just a few finishing chords, and that's it.

You scored two films produced by Val Lewton, unfortunately after his series of horror pictures. Did you work with him or with his directors?

I only dealt with Val Lewton, and it was a joy working with him. Such a wonderful fellow. He was a very literate guy, and he had a very highly developed sense of humor. *Please Believe Me* [1950] was at MGM and, to my surprise, he appeared a year later at Universal, and he asked for me. I did something interesting for him in *Apache Drums* [1951]. The main title is nothing but drums, running against each other in counterpoint. I recorded it on five different tracks and then combined them into one.

Had you discussed the idea with Lewton?

Oh, sure, he loved it. And with a title like *Apache Drums*, you couldn't ask for more. Another interesting development—I think it was this film, but it may have been some other Western that I did: There was a war chant in it, Indians dancing around the fire, so they had the brilliant idea to call in real Indians to do the pre-recording. Now, when these real Indians came in, none of them could speak any Indian dialect. None of them. They were real Hollywood Indians. I said, "We can't do it this way," so, what I did was I invented an Indian language. I did some research, studied different dialects from the part of the country where the picture took place. I wrote the chant and the dance that accompanies it, and I put these Indian words into it. And then I called back these Indians, but I added about eight good voices, because these Indians had no voices, they were just mumbling. And then, I, the guy from Vienna, the master of suspense and terror, taught these Indians how to sing in Indian!

How about the funeral chant in The Mummy's Hand *[1940]—did you have to do research on that?*

[*Laughs*] That was pure unadulterated Salter! Right from the tap! I had to get an extra provision in the budget to hire the eight vocalists for that sequence. I always liked to dress up certain scores with unexpected ingredients like the human voice.

According to the cue sheets, you wrote the main title to The Invisible Man Returns, *introducing the motif which receives many varied treatments throughout the score. Perhaps the loveliest variation occurs in the final scene when Vincent Price regains visibility. [A tape of the music is played.] Skinner shares credit with you on this sequence. This was a long time ago, of course, but can you recall which contribution was yours and which was Skinner's?*

The only thing I can say is that probably only those last three or four bars were Skinner's tacked on to the rest of it. I think it's all mine up to the point where it goes into that apotheosis at the end.

When you Salterized Son of Dracula *[1943], you used the same piece but for a totally different, unhappy ending. You superimposed a solo violin, which made a lot of difference. Now, in these selections from* The Ghost of Frankenstein, *the theme Ygor [Bela Lugosi] plays on his shepherd's pipe at the beginning takes many forms, for many different purposes, in the background scoring throughout the picture.*

At the time, it seemed a logical idea to devise a strange-sounding theme for Ygor's horn that could also be used and enlarged in all kinds of disguises and fashions in the rest of the score.

Frank Skinner took a similar approach in Son of Frankenstein, *using an instrument called a blute for the sound of Lugosi's horn.*

Mine was an English horn. It's probably that lowered fifth that repeats itself—*da-da-da-da-da*—which gives it that particular flavor.

For the opening graveyard sequence of Frankenstein Meets the Wolf Man, *as the ghouls approach the Talbot crypt, you wrote one of your moodiest themes. Is that an organ playing the melody over those low strings?*

It's a novachord. These string chords are based on fourths, which have a strange quality. Usually, chords are based on thirds, but these are based on fourths—there's a fourth interval between each voice. When you move these chords back and forth it gives a special, eerie and mysterious feeling. And then, if you put on top of it an eerie-sounding melody line with the novachord, it really adds up to something very strong.

When the grave robbers remove the wolfbane from Larry Talbot's coffin, the moonlight filters in and we hear the theme which will accompany the moonlight and warn us throughout the film whenever Talbot is about to become the Wolf Man.

There is a celeste in there, high strings, and high woodwinds. It's the interplay between these three elements that creates that effect.

No research went into the writing of the Egyptian funeral chant in *The Mummy's Hand*, the composer laughs. "That was pure unadulterated Salter! Right from the tap."

Your scores are usually very melodic, even in the most horrific passages. But when that animal hand reaches slowly for the thief's wrist, you merely build a few slow chords that are so low-pitched they're almost more sound effect than music. The effect is chilling.

That's the novachord again, but in a low register which is very rarely used. Most people use the instrument for melody line, higher, or screaming chords, higher. But that low register has an ominous quality. [*Audio tape of Salter music continues to play.*] Boy, oh boy. All that music that I've written. I never realized it!

How does it sound, being heard the first time in over 30 years?

Pleasing. I'm very critical of my own music. And if I hear, after 30 years, that I was on the right track even then, that gives you a good feeling.

In the 1950s, you participated in the science fiction boom at Universal through your contribution to the scores of This Island Earth *[1955] and* The Incredible Shrinking Man *[1957]. Do you recall working with producer William Alland or director Jack Arnold?*

As far as my work was concerned, Alland's contribution was a minor one compared to Jack Arnold's. Arnold was a very congenial man. We would discuss the scoring and we pretty much saw eye to eye on the approach. That *Shrinking Man* was a very interesting project. In scenes where his size reduced, we weren't able to work from the final product because the special effects team was still working on it, so we composers had to use our imaginations and score our own fantasies. The music cutters told us the rate of the character's reduction [for the climax] and how many seconds it would take, but that was all. But this was typical with a special effects picture; we often had to revise our scores or shorten them after the effects were finished. On those Invisible Man pictures we *never* had the finished product to work with. That was understandable, because John Fulton took great pains to see that every effect would come off as he had planned. We composers never saw the final product until the preview. I remember how mad I used to get when, after working frantically day and night to meet a certain recording date, Fulton still took his good time—maybe a week or ten days—before he was ready for the preview. I could have used some of this time to very good advantage.

I believe that Herman Stein and, to a lesser extent, Henry Mancini scored all of the early portions of This Island Earth *and that your work was on the finale, with the planet blowing up and the Metaluna Mutant running amok.*

I usually inherited the "colossal" sequences.

Although you wrote some melodic passages for Creature from the Black Lagoon *[1954], your scoring of the Creature and the Metaluna Mutant in* This Island Earth *was strikingly discordant, more so than for the Frankenstein and Wolf Man pictures.*

I can only tell you that what is right for one picture is not necessarily right for another picture. I tried to write music that would be appropriate for those particular scenes.

Do you have any recollections of the late Bernard Herrmann, whose fantasy scores have gained renewed interest in recent years?

I'd prefer not to discuss my memories of him. "De mortuis nil nisi bene." But I must say, he was a very talented man. I liked his early scores more than his later ones. His *Citizen Kane* [1941] was a landmark, a real breath of fresh air. Later, I think, he seemed to go off on a tangent as though he thought his music was more important than the picture, and this got him into a lot of trouble. *Psycho* [1960] was good. Not all the way through, but some of it was great. But in some pictures he started using outlandish orchestrations. It was as if he had the faculty of cutting out the director when they were discussing what kind of a score was needed. He would seem to be listening to the director but he listened only to himself. This is just my impression, however; I never discussed it with him.

Are you familiar with Miklos Rozsa's classic fantasy scores for The Thief of Bagdad *[1940] and* The Jungle Book *[1942]?*

Oh, yes. Of all the film composers, I would say that Miki is in a class by himself. He has developed his own unique style which is highly recognizable, and he has kept his high standards. He is really the only one of us who has managed to maintain a film career and still fulfill himself in the concert field.

Before you came to Universal, the studio had been blessed by distinguished scores by Heinz Roemheld for The Invisible Man *[1933] and, especially, by Franz Waxman for* Bride of Frankenstein *[1935]. Might they have had any influence on your work in the horror genre?*

I did not meet Roemheld until much later. I studied his score for *The Invisible Man* at the Universal library, because I was looking through all the scores, but it made no indelible impression that I can recall. I thought Franz did very well with his score for *Bride of Frankenstein*. I saw the film before coming to this country. But Franz and I knew each other from the very beginning when he was playing the piano with a German jazz band. I always thought he was a very fine composer. But when I came to Universal, he was with MGM, so the pic-

Attending Salter's (right) annual birthday celebration at the Sportsmen's Lodge in this early 1990s photo are Tony Thomas (left) and John Morgan, the men responsible for the CD release of some of Salter's greatest scores.

tures of his which we discussed were for that studio. His [*Bride of*] *Frankenstein* score was not really an influence on me.

What sort of compensation did Universal offer their composers? Were you paid per film, or per week, or what?

For a composer, that can work in one of several ways. He can be paid a weekly salary, or on commission, or by a package deal in which the composer acts as an independent contractor, not only writing the score but hiring the studio and the musicians and gambling on his own talents to get through in time—otherwise the overtime comes out of his own pocket. In my case, I started at Universal with a weekly salary which increased every year until I left in 1947 to work on a freelance commission basis. I came back to Universal in 1950 and signed a three-year contract. After that ran out, I worked freelance again, on a flat weekly salary with a three- to four-week guarantee.

And were you ever paid when your music would be reused, without screen credit, in later Universal films?

No. Once they paid you for the original assignment, they were free to use your music again and again, run it backwards, or mutilate it in any way they saw fit. A composer like Jerome Kern or Richard Rodgers could make arrangements for future credit and remuneration for his work, but we miserable plebes never had that chance.

Often the music credit would merely say "Musical Director: Joseph Gershenson."

When more than two composers contributed to a score, only the music director got the credit. I conducted most of my own scores, but when Gershenson came in, he liked to conduct sometimes. He would conduct, and I would sit in the control room and tell him what was wrong.

So it was wrong more often than right?

Well, naturally, I know better what I want to express in a sequence than he does. He was a good technician, but he had no sensitive feeling for what was in the music itself, sometimes he missed the meaning completely. So I had to tell him what was the idea behind this or that, and he would agree and do it the way I wanted.

Do you receive residuals when your films are shown on TV?

I get something from the three networks. That is, they pay a sum to ASCAP once a year for the use of their whole catalogue, and this is divided among the membership. We get nothing from the independents. I try to let ASCAP know when I see one of my pictures on an independent station, but there is no regular survey basis to keep track of these things, so there is no proof that the ASCAP material is used. There are many inequities in this business. Because of the United States' medieval copyright laws, the studio, and not the composer, is the "author" of his own music. There was a time when even ASCAP refused to pay film composers special compensation for their work. Revenue from film showings used to go into the pot for distribution to the whole ASCAP membership.

You've spoken of Universal as a factory and of the pressure to meet release dates. About how much time would usually elapse between your pre-production discussion with the producer and his showing you the rough cut of the film?

That differed. Sometimes they were in trouble or they had bad weather, so it took longer to shoot it and longer to cut it. but at the end of it was always a release date they had to meet. So the longer they took to cut a picture, the less time would be left between that point and the release date, and the people to suffer would be composers and sound-dubbing men, because these had to be squeezed together. Instead of one week, maybe in three days or so. On the average, it would take at least six weeks after pre-production discussions before they would show me their film.

After which you would run the film a couple of times for just yourself?

And then start a fight for the film. Because, in those days at Universal, each one of these departments wanted to have the film to work on it, and there was only one copy available. Later on, when they made color films, they made a dupe in black and white for us to work on. But in the early days, everything was black and white, so this was the only copy that was available. So the sound department would call up and say, "I'll give you Reel One if you'll give me Reel Six." And two hours later they said, "Okay, you can have Reel Six, but now we want Reel One back." And you couldn't make any marks on the film because this was to be the copy that was taken out for a preview later on.

How many instrumentalists did the budgets allow you for your orchestra?

For the horror pictures, something like 30 men.

Did you have to employ any technical tricks to get those 30 to sound like the larger orchestra we seem to hear on the films' soundtracks?

Oh, sure, you'd have to orchestrate in a way that hid all the weak points in an orchestra. Let's say you have only six violins. If you just let the six violins play, it sounds thin. But if you double up the six violins with two flutes and two clarinets and an oboe and bassoon, it hides it somehow. It sounds fuller and it takes on a different coloration altogether. Then there was the placing of the mikes and balancing certain parts of the orchestra against the rest of it. And in the dubbing you could help, too, by adding more to the lower end or the higher end of the frequencies on the soundtrack, according to what was necessary.

On a recording day, how much time would be allowed to rehearse before recording?

[*Laughs*] Very little. The less the better, because time was money. You had to write it in a way that the musi-

Salter died in 1994 in his Studio City, California, home, a few months after the passing of his wife Mausi.

cians could read it without difficulty, rehearse a few key spots that were a little harder, and then you would go for a take right away. Sometimes one sequence would be six minutes long, which would be too long to record. If there was a mistake at the end of six minutes you would have to go back to the beginning and record the whole thing all over again. You had to have one take that was immaculate. So you would break the sequence into two or three pieces which would segue one into the other. Even then, there could be problems. I remember one instance where I had already made a take on one sequence and the moment the red light was off, the film's cutter rushed in and said, "Hold everything! We just made another cut!" So he showed me the cut. I had to discard the whole take, make a cut in the music, and then record it. Things like this happened quite often. Rarely was a picture really finished when I got it.

But now you're free of all that madness, because you're retired?
Practically retired. These [modern] producers now want to get rich quickly on the music. They're not interested in helping their pictures. It's an entirely different ballgame now, and I'm not going to contribute to that.

Do you, however, still write music?
I'm working on a trio for piano, violin and cello, and also an orchestral piece, sort of a suite about four or five movements. I hope to have two movements finished within a short time. I'm taking my time. I'm in no hurry. That's not like writing for the movies, where you have to be ready on Thursday.

Postscript: When this interview was originally published by *Cinefantastique* magazine in 1978, it marked the unofficial beginning of a Salter Renaissance. Because of the vagaries of the business, although Hans had scored literally hundreds of features, not a single record album had ever been released featuring a Salter soundtrack. Tony Thomas finally broke this logjam by releasing on his private Citadel label Hans' music from the TV series *Maya*, following it up quickly with *The Horror Rhapsody*, a suite of original soundtrack selections from *The Mummy's Hand*, *Black Friday* [1940] and *Man Made Monster*. Other Salter LPs followed, and eventually the Film Music Society honored the composer with a luncheon in his honor at the Hollywood Bowl Museum. When Hans stepped up to the podium to accept his plaque, he said, "What took you so long?"

Hans—who always credited his longevity to his great wisdom in choosing his parents—lived to the age of 98. Not long before he died, the dream of Salter's fans came true when, thanks to the efforts of Tony Thomas, the Marco Polo classical music label hired composer John Morgan to reconstruct suites from *The Ghost of Frankenstein* and *House of Frankenstein* for CD. Conductor Andrew Penny recorded the suites in Ireland, and upon release the CD proved an instant success. Hans lived long enough to know that Marco Polo would soon be recording more of his (and Frank Skinner's) Universal monster music, including *The Wolf Man* and *Son of Frankenstein*, again reconstructed by Morgan, and now conducted by William Stromberg. When the Brentwood bookstore Dutton's scheduled Hans to sign copies of the *Ghost/House* CD, the line stretched out of the store and down the block. Not bad for a mild-mannered Viennese "Master of Terror and Suspense."—Preston Neal Jones

About the Interviewer: After studying drama and film at Carnegie-Mellon University and New York University respectively, writer-historian Preston Neal Jones journeyed from

Connecticut to Hollywood, as he puts it, "on a grant from *The $10,000 Pyramid*" (he was one of the game show's first winners). His winning streak resumed when he received the Classic Horror Film Board's 2002 "Book of the Year" Rondo Award for his *Heaven and Hell to Play With: The Filming of The Night of the Hunter*. In between, his work has appeared in *Cinefantastique, The Encyclopedia of Popular Culture, Groves' New Dictionary of Music and Musicians* and *Library of Congress Performing Arts: Film*.

JAY SAYER

> *You'll notice, I sort of divide the world*
> *between the sweetie-pies and the snotnoses.*

It's a movie that now stands out in the early career of maverick producer-director Roger Corman for a variety of reasons. First because of the title, a theater marquee dresser's worst nightmare: *The Saga of the Viking Women and Their Voyage to the Waters of the Great Sea Serpent*. Next for the record number of setbacks, mishaps and injuries that plagued the 1957 production. Then, and perhaps primarily, for the dottiness of the movie itself, an epic medieval tale (on a sandal-string budget) of Viking maidens, sailing the North Atlantic in search of their missing menfolk, washing ashore in a land of barbarians. Mix in the unmistakably twentieth-century "Corman stock company" in Viking and barbarian garb, a hand puppet sea serpent, a pig wearing a set of false teeth (*ad absurdum*), and the course has been charted to a grade-D cinema shipwreck unique in the logs of Hollywood fantasy adventure.

One last touch of *Viking Women* weirdness: the spectacle of a grown man, 24-year-old Jay Sayer, playing Senja, the barbarian king's whining-brat, weakling son—a sniveling role originally written to be played by an actor in his mid-teens! *Viking Women* was one of five Corman flicks for former New York casting agent Sayer, whose candle flamed in the Corman firmament for 11 months in 1957–58, starting with the showy supporting role of a young psycho in the j.d. actioner *Teenage Doll* and ending as a gay hoodlum in the Depression-era gangster drama *Machine-Gun Kelly*.

Disillusioned with show biz, Sayer later set aside his acting aspirations and began a career as an educator that has taken him around the globe and far away from the strange B-movie universe of Viking women, teenage dolls and warring satellites.

My career in show business started at a very early age. My parents allowed me to take tap dancing lessons and acting lessons and all of that good stuff, and I started performing at about the age of four, doing all kinds of benefits. I did some theater work on Broadway as a child actor, in plays like *Tomorrow the World* and Lillian Hellman's *Watch on the Rhine* and *Lady in the Dark* with Gertrude Lawrence. Then I went to the High School of Music and Art, as a music major, and pursued the arts in *that* direction. After I went to a college in Pennsylvania for a year, I went to Rollins College in Winter Park, Florida, where I was a theater arts major. Rollins was full of very wealthy kids who had flunked out of or couldn't get into the major Ivy League schools. And so Daddy would give Rollins a huge endowment and Rollins would admit Junior into the school. Needless to say, it was full of country club–behaving scions of major families, with too much money and not enough brains.

And then Rollins College took people like *me* in to help raise the average of the grades. My housemate at school was Anthony Perkins of *Psycho* fame—he was a little peculiar even then [*laughs*]. No, he really was! Tony didn't date when we were in school—that whole year, I don't remember him dating, *ever*. So when I'd come back from a date with a girl, he would start asking me questions. They would go from questions that were fine, like, "Where'd you go?" and "What did you eat?," to, "And *then* what did ya do?" and "Did ya blah blah blah?," and I'd suddenly realize what he was moving toward! So he was a bit of a voyeur—he was odd that way. *And*, Tony didn't treat people well, even his friends. He was somewhat competitive and somewhat defensive, and a little on the haughty side. He was *not* a star then and yet he was a little bit difficult, a little bit snobby. We saw each other quite a bit in Hollywood while he was going with Tab Hunter, and again we would have very abrupt conversations. Then he got mad at me, by the way, because some movie magazine found out that we had been at Rollins together and interviewed me. I really didn't say anything to get mad at, but he was angry that I gave an interview without asking his permission. Well, that was typically Tony.

After Rollins, what happened next on the Road to Roger Corman?

I came back to New York and, believe it or not, I went to work for the William Morris Agency, as a trainee, starting in the mailroom, much like Bernie Brillstein did. I became an assistant agent and then an agent, and I left William Morris and went to work for *another* agency in New York called the Robert Lantz Agency, a small but prestigious office. Our clientele were Louis Jourdan and Hedy Lamarr and so on—it was one of those agencies that was very, very classy. And then [producer] David Susskind of Talent Associates hired me to become a casting director, to work under Ethel Winant, who I notice just passed away a few months ago [in 2003] in L.A. Those were the golden days of live dramatic television. I did that for about a year or so.

What were some of the David Susskind shows you cast?

Armstrong Circle Theater, Mr. Peepers, Philco TV Playhouse, Appointment With Adventure. And of course we made some movies as well, we did *Edge of the City* [1957] with Sidney Poitier and John Cassavetes. Talent Associates was sort of a little Rolls-Royce production operation in New York City and David Susskind was the hot young man of *all* the entrepreneurs—and we had a *lot* of 'em. He was sort of the Hilly Elkins of his time. I worked with all those kinds of people in New York, in the management end.

Then Talent Associates went on hiatus, and I decided to go out to California for a coupla weeks, on vacation, and stay with a friend. I got out to California and I said, "I'm never going back [to New York]," because it was such a glorious place to live. L.A. in '56, there really was very little smog. Very little rain. No traffic problems. No racial problems. The first apartment I rented, I think for something like $45 a month, had no lock on the door. You could drive around in a convertible and leave your camera sitting on the seat and go inside to Schwab's or somewhere, and come out and the camera was still there. It was really Heaven.

How did you make your initial hookup with Corman?

I went to work at an agency in California, the Paul Kohner Agency. One thing led to another and I met Mitzi McCall of the nightclub act McCall and Brill. Mitzi had appeared with Jerry Lewis in a movie [*You're Never Too Young*, 1955] and now she was doing a featured role in a live production of *Best Foot Forward* on La Cienega Boulevard. She told me,

"We just lost one of our chorus boys. Why don't you come on over and audition? I bet you could get in." I said, "Sure, why not?"—I thought it'd be fun. So I went over and sang a chorus of "Tea for Two," did some soft-shoe dancing and whatever, and they hired me. And through Mitzi I met—you asked me about Corman, I know this story is a little circumlocutional! Through Mitzi I met her best friend, a gal named Barbara Crane, who is the mother of Melissa Gilbert and Sara Gilbert today.

And she's in Sorority Girl *[1957].*

Exactly! Barbara was going to go in to read for a role in a movie with Roger called *Teenage Doll* [1957], and she asked me to come in and read with her—she said, "They always have such terrible people to read with you." I did, and Roger said to her, "I can't use *you*," but he turned to me and said, "I want *you* to read for another role." Which I did, and he said, "The part is yours." That's how I got started.

Jay Sayer has spent most of his life in the entertainment industry, but his movie acting career was largely confined to the 11-month period in the 1950s when he appeared in *five* Roger Corman movies.

That was the first of your five pictures for Corman.

Roger is a phenomenon. First of all, I think almost everybody who works for Roger *loves* Roger. He's charming, he's very sweet, he's very kind, he's very bright. And he is very *cheap*. If Roger invites you to lunch, you've got to be prepared to pay for it! And you get paid scale. But as you know, half the people in the business today, he started them off on their careers. When I first started working for him, *those* were the days when people like Beverly Garland were the people he was discovering. Allison Hayes. Abby Dalton. Susan Cabot was very big with Roger, she was in four of the five movies I made with him. Et cetera. And he was very loyal, so that every time he was doing a film, if there was a part for you, you *got* it. He'd just call you and say, "I got a part I want you to do," and you didn't even ask what it was, you went in and got a script and you did it. *Teenage Doll* was the first one.

June Kenney was in three of your Corman movies—what was she like?

Oh, she was a sweetie-pie. (You'll notice, I sort of divide the world between the sweetie-pies and the snotnoses [*laughs*].) She was about as un–Hollywood as you can get. She was very little, a *tiny* little thing, diminutive. And just very sweet, very easy to work with, and a nice girl. You'd never guess she was an actress. You know, the cast of the film *Teenage Doll* was an interesting one, because Roger used all kinds of interesting young women to play the gang members. Ziva Rodann was Miss Israel. Barboura Morris for a while was in almost *every* movie that Roger made, and her husband Monte Hellman was a guy who got his first directing job from Roger—Monte went on to direct all kinds of things. So Roger was very clever not only in making exploitation films, but in discovering young talent … and exploiting them a *little* bit. But at least you were working and you got some film on yourself. And it was always *fun*, because you were working with some crazy kinda people [*laughs*]!

On Teenage Doll, *your first movie, did you get any direction from Corman?*

No. You never do. First of all, it was one take, and you knew that up front. Now, if the sound man or the light man said, "We need another take," then there was another take. If *you* [the actor] wanted another take with Roger, then you had to flub your lines up and say, "Oh, shit!" [*Laughs*] But you *had* to say, "Oh, shit!," 'cause then they had to redo it. If you just flubbed your lines, he'd keep it anyway!

You did a rehearsal, of course, 'cause Roger wanted to block it and make sure how it went. But that was it, and then you did one take. And, no, you never sat down with Roger and asked, "Now, what's the character's motivation?"—*no*. He assumed that you were gonna give him what he wanted. If you didn't, he kept it in anyway—but you didn't work for him again.

So everybody had to be on their toes at all times.

Absolutely. I think a lot of us that he used had done theater before. In fact, if you look at *Teenage Doll* where I play a psychopathic rapist, and then the next film I did for him [*Sorority Girl*], you'd think it was two different actors, because I overacted in the first one, being used to doing theater in New York, where you project and play to a live audience and to the balcony. No one had told me, and I hadn't quite figured it out yet, but in film, most people just *whisper*. So in *Teenage Doll* I was yelling and carrying on, and Roger loved it. When it came out and I went to see it, I ran out of the theater screaming, because I scared myself! So, you learn through experience with Roger. No, he doesn't really rehearse you except doing a run-through for the blocking, and no he doesn't really work with you very much as a, quote, director. Certainly not like, say, Coppola or Cassavetes or the New York directors.

You're only in Teenage Doll *for, what?, four or five minutes, but I thought that was a memorable scene you had there.*

It certainly was—I got hysterical [*laughs*]. As you said, it was only for a couple minutes, but who could ever forget you? That's why Roger hired me: When he auditioned me in the office, he said, "Let's do this scene," and I read it, and I was able to do a good cold reading—and got a little crazy and hysterical. He said, "Great! You got the role." And he said, "Gimme just that when we do the film." So I did.

Your character starts out so sympathetic to June Kenney, and then you "build" until you're ready to attack her. I not only thought your performance was effective, but that it was also an interesting piece of writing.

He's like a poor soul, but once he gets an erection, you gotta put him behind bars [*laughs*]! I believe it was that role that led Roger to think of me later for the role of "Senja, My Son" in *Viking Women*, because *that's* certainly an emotional role. By the way, I'll tell you a cute anecdote for *Teenage Doll*. Remember that June Kenney hits me over the head with the bottle? I was a little apprehensive, and they explained to me, "No, it's paraffin, very thin wax. When it hits your head, it just crumbles and you really will feel only a slight pressure, nothing at all." I went, "Oh. Okay!" Well, *some* idiot filled the bottle with liquid to make it look realistic. Therefore, instead of crumbling over my head like paraffin does, when she hit me over the head with the bottle, I went out like a light. Roger yelled *cut* and they went to set up for the next scene, and somebody must have said, "Uh ... Jay ... come *on*. Scene's over. Get up." Then they realized I was out like a light. Almost every picture I'm in, we had an incident like that. I'll tell you a story later about *Viking Women and the Sea Serpent* with Betsy Jones-Moreland, who by the way I got into the Roger Corman films. She was a friend of mine, we were in an acting workshop together.

Susan Cabot told me the same kind of story about a supposedly *harmless bottle. In a Corman picture called* The Wasp Woman [1959], *they threw a breakaway bottle at her but,* again, *somebody filled it first, so it hit like a rock.*

You spoke to Susan??

I was pretty friendly with Susan about 20 years ago.

Oh, for heaven's sake. Susan and I dated. Did you know that she had dated Sydney Pollock and was quite in love with him? That was a very serious relationship. How is Susan doing? Do you know what's happening with her now?

[Pause] You don't know what happened, do you?

No.

Well ... I don't wanna be the one to tell you!

No, it's all right. Because my life is full of violent stories of dear friends being killed or dying violent deaths.

Okay, then here's another one: She was murdered by her own son.

Oh my God ... oh my God.... Well, Susan was very passionate, as you know, and had a temper, and I imagine she probably produced a *son* who was volatile.

What else do you remember about Susan?

Susan was a delight. Susan was very intense. She had a great sense of humor. Susan also was from New York. When you say that somebody's from New York, that *says* something about them immediately. She was a New York girl and she was fun and she was great to work with. We became friends and we'd go out to the beach together and go out for dinner and stuff. Of course, Susan working for Roger Corman was a little bit of a [comedown] because at one point Susan was well on her way to becoming a movie star, playing every Indian princess at Universal. We just got along fine and had a lot of laughs together. She *could* be difficult—she was very strong-willed, had a very strong personality. And she had a trained soprano voice. I remember once sitting in a restaurant at Malibu, having dinner with her, and out of a clear blue sky with no warning, she let out a huuuge, fortissimo high C or a B or something—everybody in the restaurant turned around and looked! And she stopped and went back to eating her salad and said [*casually*], "Oh, that felt good." [*Laughs*] That singing in the restaurant, I was a little embarrassed by it—but it *was* funny.

I liked her a lot but I sometimes got a little nervous when I was out in public with her. You never knew what she was going to do next.

Or what was gonna come out of that mouth next! But that was what was kind of fun about Susan. Incidentally, she and Roger dated a little bit. And every gal that dated Roger, including Beverly, Susan, Abby Dalton, etc., made it a point to tell me that he was a perfect gentleman, he never came on to them. Maybe he was shy with women, but they all made the comment. And I think all of them really wanted to go to bed with him, and he disappointed them. Well, Roger was a very good-looking man when he was younger.

Funny you should say that. I was watching one of your movies today when it occurred to me that you looked *a little like him.*

A *little* bit, yeah. And Roger and I got along beautifully. I had done a lot of comedy, including some stand-up comedy. (Jerry Lewis once said to me, "You're very Chaplin-esque.") Everything I did, Roger would scream with laughter. He was over at the house frequently—I lived up on Wonderland, in the Canyon. He just thought I was a hoot and a riot, and he asked my opinion on things as a writer—he knew I wrote and had directed, etc. Like one of the things I did, I directed a production of *Bell, Book and Candle* in the Valley, at the Valley Playhouse [in 1960]. He would very often ask my advice and ask me, "How 'bout rewriting a scene?" or whatever—that was not uncommon.

What else were you doing to make a living in 1957–58 as you were doing all these pictures for Corman? You couldn't have been living off of a Corman salary!

Well, you collected unemployment. I also supplemented it by doing the theater work—for instance, when I was filming *Viking Women and the Sea Serpent*, at night I was appearing in a Billy Barnes Revue. Billy Barnes was a very famous comedy writer and songwriter in those days—he wrote the song "Something Cool," and also "Too Long at the Fair" that Barbra Streisand did. So there was *that*, and the movies for Roger, I did some voiceovers around town, and the unemployment. And I modeled at the Art Institute, I did some "life classes"—not in the complete nude, I wore a little posing strap. Like everybody, you sort of take whatever you can get. *And* you live fairly cheaply [*laughs*], to put it bluntly. As you must know, from talking to *any*body who's ever been an actor, you make certain sacrifices until you really make it big. You live a very conservative lifestyle.

Next you were in Sorority Girl *with Susan Cabot and Dick Miller.*

And Barbara Crane, who went on raise two stars [Melissa and Sara Gilbert]. For *Sorority Girl*, Roger rented out Ruta Lee's mansion up in Laurel Canyon. It had been some famous silent movie star's house, but I don't remember which one. Afterwards, Ruta wasn't very happy, because the living room was carpeted in *white* white carpeting, and of course there were oil stains all over it. And other damage was done to the house. When she agreed to rent it, I'm sure that assurances were given to her about the condition it would be left in. Roger, God bless him, probably said, "Oh, that was like that when we rented it," etc. I don't think she ever agreed to rent her house again!

You're the comedy relief in Sorority Girl.

Right, in a couple scenes with Dick Miller, one of them an exterior filmed down at USC. Dick Miller and Jonathan Haze were in almost every movie Roger made in those days. Dick and Jonathan, again, were both very New York. Friendly *professionally*, but not really friendly. I think part of the problem may have been, I'm from an upper-middle-class family and had certain privileges, and I think maybe they came from a less affluent background. I'm just guessing. But sometimes, as you know, that'll cause a little rift. Usually not in show business, though—most people in show business just bond. I'd run into Dick all the time for years after that and I'd always get a hello. But we never went to the movies, we never had dinner. Same thing with Jonathan—Jonathan was even, I think, *more* unfriendly in some respects. Now, also, they may have been into the drug scene and I wasn't, I don't know. That's another thing that separates people in Hollywood. I didn't even know about it in those days [*laughs*]. I was terribly naïve. I had smoked pot once in New York, with of all people Liz Smith the columnist and her girlfriend. I laughed myself to sleep—we laughed so hard, I fell asleep in their apartment. I woke up the next morning on the couch and I thought, "I don't think I wanna do *that* again." That was it for, like, *years*.

No, Jonathan and Dick were both very nice guys, I don't want to say I didn't like them. But they were more the type like ... Charlie Bronson's a good example. Charlie was the star of another movie with Roger, *Machine-Gun Kelly* [1958] — that's probably the most legit film I did with Roger. Charles Bronson never spoke to *any* of us. Never. He played cards with the stuntmen, with the extras. Because he had much more in common with them than he did with the actors. Years later my teenage son went to private school with Charlie Bronson's son, and I saw Charlie at Parents Day. Wouldn't even say hello. Yeah, Charlie Bronson was not pleasant. But, as I say, he played cards with the stuntmen, with the extras. Jonathan and Dick were a little bit like that, they were ... I dunno ... diamonds in the rough. Louie the Louse. Very Damon Runyon-esque.

Barboura Morris was in three of your five Cormans, including Sorority Girl. *What was she like?*

Oh, Barboura was a sweetheart. Like June Kenney. We never really had any bitches or difficult women. (Beverly Garland was a powerful and strong woman, but very sweet and lovely.) Barboura was a good actress ... interesting quality ... and just as nice as she could be. Now, again, I didn't get friendly with her, we didn't go out socially. I did go out with Abby Dalton and I did go out with Susan but I didn't go out with Barboura. But I liked her, she was very nice. I'm surprised nothing happened to her [career-wise], she had an interesting quality, like an Eva Marie Saint.

You keep mentioning Beverly Garland in connection with Corman — how did you know her when you were never in a movie with her?

I lived up in the hills, on Wonderland Avenue in Laurel Canyon, with a guy named Beach Dickerson, who was also in a lot of Roger's movies. So I lived with Beach, and Beach knew *all* the people from the previous chapter of the Roger Corman saga. All sorts of people came to parties that we had at Beach's. Beverly Garland, Tab Hunter, Michael Landon, Dennis Hopper, Natalie [Wood] and R.J. [Robert Wagner], Chad Everett and Ahna Capri, who he was going with at the time, Corey Allen, John Ashley — I can't even begin to name them all, just a lot of stars and other people coming and going to the parties. Helen Walker came to *all* of the parties! She lived next door to us in a little cottage that Beach owned, and by then of course she was an alcoholic and was no longer with 20th. Oh, I got to spend hours and hours with Helen, I adored her.

Then the third movie you did for Corman was the big one: Viking Women and the Sea Serpent.

You could do a whole book about *Viking Women* [*laughs*]. At the time there was a movie in production called *The Vikings* [1958] with Kirk Douglas and Tony Curtis and that's why Roger made *Viking Women*: He decided to do an exploitation film that could benefit from that other film, which was a maaajor production. When Roger called me about doing a part, he said, "It's really for a 15-year-old." I was 24. "But," he said, "I want you to do it anyway."

The role of Senja was written for a 15-year-old?

Yes, it was written for an actor named Robin something, who had been in a couple of Roger's movies. I knew him quite well — a little guy, blond curly hair, and much younger than I was. That's who Roger originally was going to use in the role, and then he called me in to his office at Ziv Studios and he said, "No, I want to use *you*. I know you're 24 but ... you'll be 15." He said he knew I could get away with it! So he told me the part was mine and then, "Go over to Western Costume and pick out your own costume." So I did, I went

The family that slays together stays together: Father-and-son barbarians Richard Devon (right) and Jay Sayer menace Viking maiden Abby Dalton in the unforgettable (we've tried) *The Saga of the Viking Women and Their Voyage to the Waters of the Great Sea Serpent.*

over to Western Costume and I literally grabbed every piece of junky jewelry they had there, which is why in the movie I'm wearing a tiara and bracelets and you name it. That diaper, that was the only thing I had to put around my bottom ... that fur vest ... the tacky, awful shoes, etc. When I first saw myself in that outfit, I went, "Oh, my God!"

I interviewed Richard Devon, who plays your father in the movie, and he wore the same kind of get-up. He said he thought he looked like Genghis Jerk.

Exactly! Incidentally, I did an interview for a Canadian magazine called *Take One* when I was teaching at the University of Western Ontario. The name of the article was "Senjamyocin" and the reason for *that* was: My name in *Viking Women* was Senja, and Dick Devon kept calling out, "Senja, my son! Senja, my son!" And I said to the interviewer, "It sounds like an antibiotic!" [*Laughs*] Senjamyocin! And when the magazine came out, on the cover was me in a horned Viking helmet, and then underneath in big type it said "Senjamyocin"!

There's a scene in *Viking Women* with all of us riding horses in Bronson Canyon and we're galloping pretty full-throttle, and then we slow down and we go into the cave. In the scene were Dick Devon, playing my father, and me, and a bunch of stuntmen. I was supposed to lead the charge into the cave. But as you know, you can never control what's going on when you're on horseback, so at the last second something happened, maybe my horse pulled back, and suddenly there Dick was, leading the charge. Well, it turned out that the opening to the cave wasn't big enough for a man and a horse. That's typically Roger—Roger had no idea, 'cause he didn't ride a horse, didn't know what any of this stuff entailed or involved. So as Dick went to go in, the horse scraped him along the right-side wall and it tore all the skin off his knee area. He spent the rest of the movie wearing a drain on his knee, and limping. Luckily, he wore a costume that covered it. That was another one of the famous Corman Incidents.

Another one is the one with Betsy Jones-Moreland that I said I would tell you. At Iverson's Ranch, Roger plans a scene where a group of us, a lot of stuntmen and Betsy and some of the other Viking women and myself come riding down onto a plateau at the edge of a cliff. A rather high cliff. Roger is going to shoot this as a long shot from another cliff a distance away from there—it made for an interesting shot. But what Roger doesn't realize is that, unlike a Jeep where you press the brake and it stops, with *horses* it doesn't quite work that way. You rein them in, but if *you're* the one closest to the edge of the cliff, and the horses behind you come in a little too fast, or your horse shies a little bit and doesn't stop, you go over the cliff. So we try to plan it and we see it's gonna be a real problem, we see that somebody could get killed. So Roger's on the other mountaintop and he's yelling into an electric megaphone, "All right, people, let's try this." On *our* cliff, Betsy takes the electric megaphone away from the assistant director who's standing there and she says, "Roger. This is *much* too dangerous. I'm not doing it." Roger yells back to her from the other mountaintop, "It's in your contract, Betsy." And *she* yells back, "In your *hat*, Roger!" [*Laughs*] I thought, "Well, she's never gonna work for him again," but of course she did—*many* times. But that's another Roger Corman-ism, where he has *no* idea what it's like to ride horses. If we had *done* that scene, somebody would have gotten killed, I think. They would have gone off the cliff. So thank heavens for Betsy!

Both Betsy and Susan Cabot told me the scenes on the Viking boat were no picnic.

We were on the beach at either Crystal Cove or Paradise Cove, I forget which, and they did a scene with the Viking women out on the ocean in their boat. They finished doing the scene and Roger yelled *cut*, and they went to do the next set-up. The Viking boat was being pulled around by [an off-camera] tugboat, and the tugboat came in ... but no one told the tugboat captain to bring the boat with the girls back in. Well, by the time they remembered that all the girls were on this boat, it was *well* on its way to Catalina Island [*laughs*].

Nobody noticed that all the girls suddenly weren't anywhere around?

No! Somehow or other, they didn't bother to notice that the girls' Viking boat hadn't come in until they were ready to do the next scene, and then it was like, "...Where are the girls?" And somebody said, "Oh, shit—they're still on the boat." We could still sorta see the boat, but way off in the distance! Well, the girls on it were hysterical—they were really frightened. When they came back and got off the boat, they were pretty upset, because they weren't sure anyone was ever gonna come and get them. The water wasn't rough that day, it was a nice day, but I would have been scared to death, too, to be on a boat that was just drifting out to sea, and nobody paying any attention.

Oh, the glamour of making movies: You'd come into the studio, Ziv Studios, at five o'clock in the morning, get made-up. Of course the grips and those people got to the doughnuts before you, so you'd have a cup of coffee and *maybe* a doughnut. Get on a bus, go out to Malibu, and you're standing in the sand all day, the sun beating down on you. And the wind is blowing, so you got all that sand caught in your makeup, which is practically eating your skin away. It was really "glamourous"!

The *Viking Women* role of Senja was written for a 15-year-old, but director Roger Corman insisted the part be played by Sayer—then in his mid-20s! Left to right, Richard Devon, Sayer, Michael Forest.

An actress named Kipp Hamilton was originally signed to star in Viking Women, *but she was replaced by Abby Dalton.*

That's right, Abby wasn't supposed to do the lead, Kipp Hamilton was. But Kipp's agent was Lillian Small, the sister of Dore Schary, and Lillian didn't want Kipp to do the movie—Lillian told her, "Your career's just starting and you've done a couple of prestigious things. Doing a B-movie for Roger Corman isn't the best way to go." And Kipp had already accepted the part—she'd come in, we'd met together, etc. But on the advice of Lillian Small, Kipp called and said, "No, I'm not doing it." Originally Abby was supposed to play Kipp's character's younger sister so Roger promoted through the ranks, he said to Abby, "You'll do the lead role." Abby asked, "Well, what about now having my [real-life] sister to play my younger sister?" and Roger said, "Great." So Abby's sister, Shirley [Wasden], came in. Very pretty. Very, *very* pretty.

And then she *got injured, falling off a horse.*

Yeah. I remember it only very vaguely, but there *was* an accident and she did get hurt. Not scarred for life, but she certainly couldn't go on with the movie, because those roles were very physical, and we all did our own stuntwork. Since June Kenney had worked in several other films for Roger, they put *her* in the role of the younger sister after Shirley got hurt. By the way, there *are* a couple of scenes in the movie where the younger sister *is* played by Shirley, Abby's real sister, and then in other scenes it's June Kenney. Roger wasn't about to re-shoot any footage—are you kidding? So you've got two different actresses playing the role, if you look real carefully!

I like June Kenney—I wish she'd made more than just a handful of movies!

You're right, nothing much happened after the Roger Corman flicks with June, it was like nobody else used her. Abby Dalton went on to have a very good career—

I remember The Jonathan Winters Show.

Oh, yeah, and *The Joey Bishop Show* and the show with Jackie Cooper [*Hennesey*]. Abby was a very physical person. She used to live out at a ranch in Topanga Canyon with a famous jazz bass player named Joe Mondragon—and one of her close friends was Robert Blake! Abby was a wild chick when she was young! It's funny because she became very much "the Fifth Avenue-Madison Avenue lady" later on in life. And she's got quite a mouth on her, God bless her [*laughs*]! But as you know, so did Susan. And so does Beverly. *Oh* boy! Which is part of the reason why they were so much fun. And, oh, and so does Ruta Lee—I mean, with Ruta you have to say, "Ruta—*stop*! You're worse than a Marine!"

You did your *own "stunt" in* Viking Women *too.*

Right, that scene where the tree branch knocks me off the horse. I had to ride at a canter right into that branch and bend down at literally the last second, so that it looked to the camera like the branch hit me. Then, of course, the next shot was of me landing on the ground. They cut it together cleverly enough so you *think* you see me fall off the horse onto the ground. It was weird: They *had* stunt people around, but we had to do our own.

Some of the other people in the cast: Betsy Jones-Moreland?

Oh! I adore and love Betsy, she was a sweetie-pie. Betsy and I were in an acting workshop together and became very, very good friends and talked about all kinds of stuff. No romantic interest, just buddies. I told Roger about Betsy and he read her for the movie and she got in. Betsy had a quality like a Patricia Neal, and she was a very big woman as you know, very tall. And very womanly, not girlish. June Kenney was a little girl; Betsy was a woman. Wonderful voice, *good* good actress. And a lovely human being. Sally Todd was another one who was in *Viking Women*—she wound up going with Troy Donahue.

Sally Todd: Sweetie-pie or snotnose?

Sally was a sweetie-pie. Sally looked like Lana Turner in those days, she was really gorgeous. She was probably the prettiest one in *Viking Women*.

I don't get very good reports on Brad Jackson.

Now *that's* a sad story. Brad Jackson and I were very, very, very close ... and he was crazy even then. I remember one night he asked me to stay over, we were going to go to the Easter Mass the next morning at the Hollywood Bowl, and.... [*Sigh*] He went into this whole thing, he thought he was the reincarnation of Rudolph Valentino, and he talked about himself in the third person: "Brad Jackson can't do this because it would interfere with his career," "Brad Jackson can't eat this food because it's not healthy for his body" and so on. He was a sweetie-pie—I knew him before he got crazy. And, as I say, we were *very* close. I mean, the other people and I were just friends, etc., but Brad and I were like buddy-buddies. He was *so* sweet. Very vulnerable. And gorgeous. He was a handsome, handsome man.

Richard Devon?

Richard's a sweetheart. But Richard again is another one who would probably, if he had his choice, be playing cards with the stuntmen. Richard's "one of the guys." And Richard had a very good career—he worked for a lot of other people besides Roger. The only other film that I did in Hollywood, other than Roger's, was *Will Success Spoil Rock Hunter?* [1957].

Devon had nothing good to say about Corman when I interviewed him—Corman was so cheap, Corman got him hurt—

First of all, Roger really *is* cheap. I mean, I wasn't kidding when I talked about the lunches. Roger and I went out to scout locations for *Viking Women*, and why he invited me to come along I don't know. Various people that I have worked for have had crushes on me. I don't mean sexual crushes, I mean ... like "talent crushes," where they got a kick out of me and they wanted to have me around almost 24 hours a day. Roger was a little bit like that; Jerry Lewis was *definitely* like that. I was with Jerry's Comedy Workshop over at Paramount for almost a year, and then one day I arrived at the Paramount gates and the guard told me, "I'm sorry, but I have instructions not to let you on the lot." That's the way he let me go. Jerry's very peculiar.

Anyway, Roger and I went out to scout *Viking Women* locations and I went along with him, as a favor I guess. We stopped somewhere to have lunch and he said, "Oh, I don't have any money on me, would you catch this, please?" That was basically what he did every time I had lunch with him! I always would say to him, "Roger, you are the cheapest son of a bitch I've ever worked for!" And he would say, "Yes, but you're *working* for me, aren't ya?" We'd both laugh, but there was a lot of truth to it: "I keep you working but, yeah, I stick ya for lunch!"

But Richard Devon got hurt [the knee incident]. I think the reason why Richard might be more "down" on Roger than myself or some other people is because Richard went on to have a fully expanded career so that, although he worked for Roger, he wasn't quite as grateful to him as some of us are. So he's dealing with what Roger was like on a very realistic level, and not getting sort of sucked in by the charm and the boyishness. Richard's seeing only the fact that he was exploited, and that he got hurt. And that he really didn't *need* to have gotten hurt. If you [the director] are gonna do a scene with your actors on horses galloping into a cave, you do your homework. Also, it raises the question, *why* did Roger have to have a group of mounted riders charging into a cave? You don't usually charge your horse into a cave, you get *off* the horse and you walk *into* the cave. So I can see where Richard would be a little more resentful!

And your performance in the movie...?
 I based it a little bit on Jay Robinson, who played the emperor in *The Robe* [1953]. I did sort of think about that as a possible role model.

The part does require a 15-year-old so you are not right for the part, can we agree on that?
 Oh, yeah!

So what's your most over-acted scene, what's the scene where you cringe the most when you watch Viking Women*?*
 I don't know whether you realize it, but *Viking Women* was run on *Mystery Science Theatre*, that series with the puppets who poke fun at B movies. During the scene where I first come in and I slap Abby in the face, the puppets were saying things about my performance, like, "Don't hate me because I'm beautiful!" and "This kid needs a conflict management seminar!" [*Laughs*] In answer to your question, it's either that scene, or the scene after Abby killed the boar—

The scene where you're whining, "I don't want to be saved by a gir-rel!"
 Yeah, that's it! I *wasn't* 15, and I was supposed to be a frightened teenager.

You were 24 so it's terrible. But if you'd been 15, it would have been a great *performance!*
 Exactly! In fact, I think I come across a little *gay* because I'm not the right age. Suddenly when a *man* is acting like that, it's like, "*Hmmmm....!*" [*Laughs*] By the way, remember the "wild boar"? We laughed so hard at it, and Roger said, "Stop it, you people! You gotta get serious, you gotta do this scene!" It was a pig with false teeth [*laughs*]! For the shot where you see the pig with the spear through it, the spear was one of those things like the arrow around your head that you wear on Halloween.
 By the way, another funny story—and this was my fault: Remember the scene where I set fire to Abby and Brad, who are tied to the stakes? And Susan calls upon Thor, god of the thunderbolt, and I get struck down by lightning? Well, I decided to be very "method": There was a puddle there, and I fell with my face in the puddle. I thought, "Oooh, that's gonna be good," "It'll be Orson Welles-ish," whatever. *Except*, stupid me doesn't realize that Roger has to film a fight scene between Brad Jackson and Dick Devon after that, and my body will be in the scene.

So you had to lie face-down in the puddle the whole time?
 Literally, I had to take a deep breath and stick my face in there, and then Roger would have to cut every time I couldn't hold my breath any more. I really got hoisted on my own petard with that one—I got a little *too* clever!

In the shots of Abby Dalton and Brad Jackson at the stakes and the kindling burning, it looks to me like the flames get awful close.
 Oh, yeah! If the wind had shifted, they might have gotten a little suntanned! That could happen in a Roger Corman film. It's all about money. He's the world's best businessman,

he's made, what?, billions of dollars, I think. "The movie *will* be made, and the movie will be made as quickly and as cheaply as possible"—I think it became his *raison d'être*. Incidentally, there was going to be a scene in *Viking Women* where I try to rape Abby Dalton. But that was cut 'cause it got a little too graphic. After the scene where Abby and I arm-wrestle, etc., she comes to my room and we get into a fight and I suddenly pin her down and I'm going to rape her. Then she reminds me that she just saved my life, saved me from the wild boar, so I let her go and I'm pretty shook up and so is she. Apparently we went too far in the scene, so they had to cut it. But I've got some stills where, literally, she's lying down with her legs apart and I'm on top of her—pretty racy!

Viking Women was your only good-sized movie part; you must have gone to see it when it came out.

I went to see *Viking Women* with Barbara Crane and Mitzi McCall. We were the Three Musketeers. What I *didn't* know was that sitting behind me were Billy Barnes and Bob Rogers, who were producing the Billy Barnes show that I was in at the time. Mitzi is rambunctious, and Barbara and Mitzi and I are sitting there screaming our heads off at this movie. Remember the scene where the Viking women's boat gets smashed and they wash up on the shore and they're lined up like sardines? Audiences *scream* with laughter. But here's what's interesting: People think Roger is camp and kitsch and that he does that stuff on purpose. Truth be known ... *no!* Roger didn't know that was funny. He just said, "Go lie down on the beach, all of you," and, "Scrunch up more, I gotta get ya into camera." So they wound up on the beach lying one by one like the Rockettes [*laughs*]! Then people who see the movie read into it and say, "Oh, God, Roger Corman is funny, that is marvelous." And I'm thinking, "He didn't do it on purpose!"

What's the punchline to the "Billy Barnes was sitting behind me" anecdote you started?

Only that they were sitting behind me and I didn't know it, and at the Billy Barnes show rehearsal the next day, as I walked in, Billy said, "Senja, my son!" And I said, "Oh, *shit!*" [*Laughs*] They kidded me for ... it must have been *weeks!*

You were back to just one scene in War of the Satellites *[1958].*

On *War of the Satellites*, Roger called me and said there was a scene in the script that takes place on location in Texas, with hundreds of head of cattle and 15 or 20 cowboys sitting around a campfire when a little missile comes down. Then he said, "*You* know how ridiculous that is for one of *my* films. I'm not going to Texas or getting hundreds of head of cattle and 15 cowboys!" [*Laughs*] He said, "Would *you* rewrite it for you and another person? And make it a comedy scene. Make it two teenagers. *You* figure out what the setting is and what they're doing, and rewrite the scene." So I wrote a scene for him and he said, "This is terrific, I love it," and Mitzi McCall and I did it, a scene of just the two of us in a convertible up in Mulholland Canyon smooching, and all kinds of teenage jokes and stuff.

Another funny Roger Corman story: After I did my scene for *War of the Satellites*, I showed up one day while they were doing interiors. And since I was on the set, Roger said, "Don't just stand there. Let's put ya to work." He wanted to use me as an extra in that scene—he said, "Just don't show your face to the camera 'cause they'll recognize you from the other scene." I put on the costume, but I didn't have any socks on. So they wrapped my ankles in black tape [*laughs*]. You see me getting on and getting off elevators. That's very Roger Corman. You go to visit the set when you've already finished your part, and he *will* put you to work as an extra!

His sword struck by lightning, Senja lies dead in a puddle as his father (Richard Devon) fumes in *Viking Women*.

Your final Corman: One creepy scene as a swishy gangland type in Machine-Gun Kelly.

There's a scene in a bar in *Machine-Gun Kelly* that starts with somebody lighting somebody else's cigarette, and as the camera pulls back, the cigarette's in *my* mouth, and then you see that it's a guy lighting it. A guy's lighting another guy's cigarette, and they're looking into each other's eyes, or whatever, and you realize it's a gay bar. Well, the guy lighting my cigarette was *Gene* Corman, Roger's brother. Now, as nice as Roger is, Gene is a *putz*. Gene is *not* a nice person. I had known Gene before I knew Roger, and he was not a friendly man at *all*. But here we go again: Roger used his *brother* as an extra! And his brother was an agent at MCA! But that's, again, a Roger-ism. Suddenly I was doing this scene with Gene and I said to Roger, "How does Gene feel about this? 'Cause I don't think he likes me very much." Roger said, "Oh, *you* know Gene, he doesn't like *anybody* very much."

"Unless they're important," I felt like saying. Then I thought, "No, no postscripts. Stop while you're ahead!"

I don't think that shot you describe is in the movie, the lighting of the cigarette.

That's funny ... when *Machine-Gun Kelly* was first released, it did have that shot. We had to do it two or three times because the members of the crew got hysterical with laughter, 'cause ... well, Gene Corman is *so* homophobic [*laughs*] that I'm sure he was very uncomfortable doing that scene.

Did you enjoy doing the rest of that scene with Susan Cabot?

That *was* fun to do, that dishy scene at the table. I said to Roger, "If I go too far, tell me," and Roger looked at me as if to say, "Yeah, *right*!"—'cause with Roger, you do it, it's one take and it's done. I think *Machine-Gun Kelly* was only one day's work but it was a delightful experience. Half the people in it I'd already worked with, and I again got Mitzi McCall in it. One thing that was a thrill was, Connie Gilchrist was in it—I remembered her from the old Judy Garland movie *Presenting Lily Mars* [1943]. But she wasn't particularly friendly—she was from the old days, and she couldn't be bothered with all this stuff. And as I say, I don't think Charlie Bronson talked to anybody at *all*, really.

Did you stop accepting roles from Roger Corman, or did he stop offering them to you?

I think he stopped offering them to me, and I got much more involved in directing and writing. I don't remember why [it ended], but there certainly was no argument, he certainly wasn't disappointed in me, or I in him. The last movie I made for him was *Machine-Gun Kelly* and he was very happy and satisfied with my work in that. So ... I don't know.

Why did you never make movies for anybody but Corman?

Well, I did the one at 20th Century–Fox, *Will Success Spoil Rock Hunter?*, and that was fun 'cause I used to ride out to the L.A. Airport in a limousine with Jayne Mansfield, Lili Gentle and Joan Blondell. And if you had *those* conversations on tape, you'd have another book. Blondell *loved* to poke fun at Mansfield. People keep saying Mansfield was really a very intelligent, bright woman just pretending to be a ditz. Uhn-uh! No! *Not*! She was *such* a ditz! Blondell I had known in New York when I was an agent—and you don't *start* with Blondell, she really was a bright, tough lady. So the whole ride was Blondell poking fun at Jayne Mansfield.

Right to her face?

Oh, yeah! Mansfield started laughing ... *halfway* knowing she was getting it, but the other half thinking, "*What* is she saying...?" [*Laughs*] Lili Gentle and I would sit there and watch this going on and, like, be pinching each other's legs or elbowing each other.

I think one of the main reasons why I primarily worked for Roger was, every time I turned around, he had another thing for me. And I didn't really pursue the career that hard. There's a movie called *The Way We Were* [1973] and Robert Redford plays a guy who writes a book called *The Ice Cream Man*, and the beginning of the book is, "He was like the coun-

Still acting, Sayer was seen as Norman Thayer in a 2002 production of *On Golden Pond* at the Very Little Theatre in Eugene, Oregon.

try in which he was born, everything came easily to him." Because I had been a casting director in New York and had been on the Broadway stage as a child actor, and then was an agent, both in New York and again in L.A., I *knew* everybody. So the stuff sorta just *came* to me — I got a lot of television, I did all the court shows and *Richard Diamond* and so on. But I didn't really push it that hard. And I guess my agent wasn't *that* fantastic.

*You probably got most of the work your*self.

Well, with Roger I certainly did, yeah. And then also I got sick of acting — I decided I preferred writing and directing instead, so I directed *Bell, Book and Candle* in the Valley, and I had a few other directing offers. And I wrote a film called *The Shirt Off Her Back.*

Was it ever made?

Yeah. It was an independent, sort of an exploitation film, with [in the cast] me and a Las Vegas comic name of Tommy Moe Raft. We filmed it in Las Vegas, at the ranch where

Elizabeth Taylor and Eddie Fisher spent their honeymoon. I had fun writing it, 'cause I got to do every slapstick joke in the world, a lot of puns and stuff. It was full of schtick. Tommy Moe Raft was a working comic in one of those burlesque shows in Las Vegas, literally with the tear-away dresses on the girls and the big shoes on the comic and the drumrolls [rimshots], etc. We hired him to play the lead because it was written for someone like that. What we didn't know was that he was illiterate. So when it was time to start shooting the film, he hadn't learned any of his lines 'cause he couldn't read. We shot that entire film with me feeding him his lines, and we would do three lines at a time. That was torturous. It also ruined the comic timing.

When were you in Jerry Lewis' Comedy Workshop? What movies did you work on for him?

No, I didn't make any movies. That was '58, '59. Mitzi McCall was in it and Jo Anne Worley was in it and I was in it and, oh, a whole bunch of people that you would know. Jerry used me to write a lot of material for TV specials or scenes in movies and things. He was also developing me as a talent, to put *into* the movies, but that never happened. He'd call me and say, "I got a small part for you in such-and-such a picture" and I'd say, "Great! When do I get a script?" Then it wouldn't happen. That happened, ooh, about five or six times. But that's typically Jerry. He's another one who, when he loves you he loves you too much, and then ... he doesn't love ya *enough*! Jerry's very difficult.

What did you do to get on his bad side, that he barred you from the Paramount lot?

No, nothing, it was just ... the thrill wore off.

Sayer working with his wife Constance on her singing act.

What wrap-up comments would you like to make about your Corman years? Well, year. Well, 11 months!

[*Laughs*] I was just very lucky, in one sense, that I had the career I did with Roger and with all those people. But I somehow knew that it wasn't something I necessarily wanted to devote my life to. And then I met my now-wife Constance, and she was a member of the Baha'i faith, and she introduced me to Baha'i and I became a Baha'i. That changed all my spiritual values. Suddenly, being a star in show biz....

Not that big a deal any more?

Lemme tell you something: I lived with Sammy Davis for a while and we did a play together called *The Desperate Hours*—he did an interracial version of it at the Hollywood Center Theater while he was making *Porgy and Bess* [1959] for Otto Preminger. That was the period when Sammy tried to marry Kim Novak, and [Novak's boss at Columbia Pictures] Harry Cohn sent the gangsters on the train to Las Vegas and headed them off and told Sammy that if he tried that again, they'd break every bone in his body. So Sammy was going through a bad depressive state and asked me if I'd come and stay with him up at the house for a while. What I'm saying is, I'd *seen* an awful lot of stuff [like that], on "the inside" of show biz. I'd hung around with a lot of movie stars, Garland, Shirley MacLaine, the whole Rat Pack thing through Sammy. And ... I dunno ... suddenly it started to seem *depressing*. Then when I became a Baha'i, that changed my whole life around. My world vision and my sense of why-I'm-here got a little more introspective, a little more philosophical, a little more altruistic than *just* my career. By the way, do you want to hear something *really* funky?: When I met Constance and she introduced me to Baha'i, her name was Constance *Sayer*. When we got married, she didn't have to change it! At the wedding, when the guy said, "Do you, Constance Sayer, take Jay Sayer...," everyone started smiling.

Sounds like an Ozarks wedding!

[*Laughs*] Exactly—"You're marryin' your cousin, how lovely!" Anyway ... talking to you today, it's interesting to find out from you how these people [his Corman movie co-stars] wound up. I was one of the few people who said, "I've had it with this business" because I got married and I wanted to have a family, and I knew that [an actor's salary] was not reliable. So my wife talked me into this, and I'm glad I did it: I went back to school and finished up my B.A. and then an M.A. and then a Ph.D., etc. I've been a professor all over the world—Australia, Canada, the West Indies....

Right now, if you asked me if I wanted to go back into the business, I'd have to say that I don't think the current Hollywood has any resemblance whatsoever to the business that I knew. I mean, when we're talking Britney Spears and Christina Aguilera and Janet Jackson's boob, instead of Katharine Hepburn, Audrey Hepburn, Sophia Loren, etc.—it just doesn't have the same class. But it was a fun thing to do and I loved it. I had *great* times and met some really lovely people.

OLIVE STURGESS

> *When Mr. Karloff would turn to talk to me during a scene, and when he was talking* about *me, I felt the chills go up my spine because of the way he said it! Oh, golly!*

Roger Corman was riding high as producer-director of the profitable American International Edgar Allan Poe series in 1962 when he decided to go with a spoof as its next entry. He lined up a Richard Matheson script suggested by the Poe poem "The Raven," an all-star horror cast of Vincent Price, Boris Karloff and Peter Lorre as rival sorcerers in fifteenth-century England, and offered the role of Price's daughter to a rare and radiant damsel named Olive Sturgess.

That busy young TV actress happily accepted her first major movie role, and gazed in star-struck awe as onto the medieval castle sets stepped Price, Karloff and Lorre, Hollywood greats of the saintly days of yore. She also found that horror moviemaking was "nevermore" fun than when working with Price and Lorre—monster men on movie screens, but just incorrigible "bad boys" between takes.

I was born in Ocean Falls, British Columbia, which is up the coast near Prince Rupert. When I was just a baby, two years old or so, we moved to Vancouver. Right at the beginning, in the very early years, when I was two or three years old, my mother saw talents that I had—abilities and tendencies that were showing. Both my parents were very, very supportive, which is so wonderful for children. I was in a dance and ballet class when I was three or four, and then I took piano lessons later. And when I was nine or ten, I went to see Mary Martin on the stage in *Peter Pan* and that was *it*, that did it. I felt like I was in another world, I was lifted *so* high. We were sitting in the front row of the balcony, and when Mary Martin came flying out, I felt like I was watching a magic thing happening, and I knew that [being an actress] was what I wanted to do with my life.

I joined Elsie Graham's Children's Theater Group in Vancouver—she was a well-known theater woman there, and taught children. My mom saved quarters in a jar on the kitchen window for my $3-a-week classes with the Children's Theater, and I took private lessons in speech and elocution from her. And my dad taught me singing. So I had lots of training in those early years.

Were you the first actress in your family?

No, I come from a theatrical family. It started in England: My aunt Olive Sturgess, my dad's sister, was an opera singer who sang at Covent Garden with Sir John Barbirolli. My dad sang on a national radio program in Canada. And my first cousin Joan Benham, my Aunt Olive's daughter, was one of the good actors on [the TV series] *Upstairs, Downstairs*, playing Lady Prudence Fairfax, the leading lady's best friend. Joan was a comedienne, very tall, almost six foot.

When did you and your family come from Canada to the U.S.?

We came here with my dad's business. He was in the shoe business and he went into a partnership with someone in this country.

How did you break into the movie business?

We came here in about 1954, and I started to go to Whittier College and I was also working at Grant's Department Store. Of course I wondered, "How in the *world* is this [a show biz break] going to happen? I don't know *any*body!" But I felt God would show me the way, and I had to just trust Him to do it. At Whittier College, I heard about the Beverly Hills Playhouse, and I got in touch with them and I tried for a role there and I got it right away.

When I was in my late teens, 18 or 19, there was a man living in the same house where my dad and mom and I were tenants; I have no idea now who he was, but he told me, "I hear there's an actor's sheet at CBS Radio in Hollywood. Some actors go and sign their names when they're in between movies or TV assignments, and they're looking for work in radio shows." So I started going to CBS. I would go to rehearsals at the Beverly Hills Playhouse, and then afterwards I would get on a bus and transfer to go to CBS, go upstairs and find the sheet and sit and write my name. (And I'd see other people's names on it that I sorta knew a little bit.) Then I'd go home.

I *never* heard anything. After about six times of doing that, I thought, "This isn't gonna happen"—I felt very discouraged. But ... you know how sometimes you feel compelled to do things? I got discouraged, and I said to myself, "I'm not getting off the bus and going up to sign that sheet any more"—but one Friday, *some*thing said to me, "*Get* off the bus. *Go* sign that sheet again. *Do* it." I did. And a man walked down the hallway and stood near me while I was signing the sheet. I saw his shoes, so I looked up at him and he asked, "Did you want to see somebody?" I said, "Well, I'd *like* to meet Elliott Lewis"—Elliott Lewis was a big radio man in those days. Turns out the man I was speaking to was Hank Garson, a well-known writer of radio comedy shows at CBS. He was then the writer of Barbara Whiting's readio show [*Junior Miss*]— Margaret Whiting the singer had a sister Barbara. Garson asked, "Would you come into my office?," and I thought, "Oh-oh!" [*Laughs*] I thought, "If anything funny is gonna happen, I'll just go back to Whittier College." Of

Olive Sturgess felt that God would show her the way to a break in Hollywood—and a highly productive television career (approximately 300 appearances) followed.

course, nothing "funny" happened; he asked me into his office and he gave me a copy of the next Barbara Whiting show script and he said, "I'd like you to read this part." I took the script out in the hallway and I read the part, and then I came back into his office and I read it for him. He said, "Come back Saturday and do the show." My mouth dropped open! It was for the part on Barbara Whiting's show as a girlfriend of Barbara's.

Now, here's what I found out later from Susie, Hank Garson's secretary: Earlier that afternoon, as he was trying to find somebody to play that part, he ran into all kinds of unexpected problems, and he was getting fed up and a little desperate. Finally he said to Susie, "I'm going out in the hallway and I'm gonna take the first person I see and give her this role." And the "first person" was me, because of that strange "something" which said to me, "*Get* off the bus. *Go* sign that sheet again." I did the show, and then I did one or two *more* as Barbara Whiting's girlfriend. Then they started a radio show called *The Cobbs*, where I was the daughter of Hope Emerson and Bill Demarest, which went on for some time. Hope Emerson and Bill Demarest were "country folk" and their child was going to college—I was the child. I was a very shy person, and I did a lot of sitting around *watching* people. Bill Demarest got so fed up with me sitting on the set being quiet, he came over during one of the rehearsals and picked me up and shook me and said, "Wake up! Come on! Get going!," 'cause I was just *watching* all the time [*laughs*]! I was kind of a Canadian shy person, you know? I kinda sit back and listen and watch. Anyway, it was so wonderful, the way that [inner voice] told me to get off that bus one more time, and that was the day that the door just opened up and I was on my way! It was just a great thing, and I felt so happy about it.

Then you were a contract player at Universal.
It was like the most magical thing! My agent Mel Shauer was a wonderful man—my father and he became great friends. He introduced me to all the people I needed to know, and then I got a contract at Universal Studios within six months. At Universal, I did my screen test with Clint Eastwood. It's amazing—he was just the same then as he is now, he was just Clint. (And I wasn't really impressed with Clint Eastwood 'cause he was kind of ... just a flat-talking person!) There were two purposes for my screen test: Universal could see if they wanted to sign me as a studio contract player, *and*, they were looking for a girl to play the daughter of Jane Wyman for *All That Heaven Allows* [1955]. I didn't get *All That Heaven Allows*, they gave Gloria Talbott that part, but I *was* put under contract. At Universal Studios, they taught you horseback riding by taking you out on the back lot, they taught you singing, dancing, fencing—it was the very end of the studio system. I also got to play a couple of small parts. I did one of the Ma and Pa Kettle movies, *The Kettles in the Ozarks* [1956], I was in a short with Harry James [probably *Leave It to Harry*, 1954] and I did *Lady Godiva* [1955]. That was sort of awesome, to meet Maureen O'Hara with her beautiful red hair. I was just very briefly in a scene with her, but at Universal that was how you learned, they put their contract players in small parts. Clint Eastwood was in *Lady Godiva* too. It was a very wonderful thing to have that experience.

You weren't there long, though.
After six months, my agent Mel Shauer and I decided that I wouldn't keep on at Universal 'cause the TV show world was really beginning to open up. We decided it was better for me to get right into the TV, and I did. Of course, Universal later changed, it became what it is today—they began to have tours and everything. I went on a tour with my family, probably into the '60s, and I couldn't hardly stand it, I never went back. The tour took

You sure did get into TV—in a big way.

You'd see me twice a week on TV in the '50s [*laughs*]—those were the great days! I ended up doing 300 television shows all told. I did, I counted them up! Other actors have said this to you, I'm sure, you've probably heard it over and over, but to be able to do what you love is wonderful. If it happens to you, it's just a beautiful thing.

How did you land the role of Vincent Price's daughter in The Raven [1963]*?*

The two *Thriller* episodes that I did preceded *The Raven*, and I have a feeling that Mel Shauer may have had the people who were doing *The Raven*, Roger Corman and those guys, see those *Thriller*s. I tried for *The Raven* and got it right away, of course. It was shot at Producers Studio.

When you were offered The Raven, *were you aware of the Roger Corman Poe series?*

Yes, and I think *The Raven* is really a unique movie, because it was [a horror spoof] and because of the great actors who were in it. I remember Roger Corman just being thrilled that he could get Boris Karloff. Mr. Corman's other Poe movies sort of "belonged" to Vincent Price, but *The Raven* belongs, literally, to all three equally, Vincent Price and Mr. Karloff and Peter Lorre.

Karloff and Lorre were getting pretty old by this time. Do you remember that being a problem?

I was aware that Peter Lorre and Boris Karloff were not well, but they were just marvelous, how they did their scenes, and so you didn't think of them that way. But Boris Karloff ... his skin color didn't look very good, even. And he *did* sit a lot. So then, when he was walking down the staircase in the film....

*[Laughs] Every*body *who talks to me about* The Raven *mentions the day he staggered down that staircase!*

I was watching him walk down those stairs and I thought, "Oh, I hope he makes it!," because I think he was just *aching*, walking down the stairs in that long shot when you first see him. But he did it, *one take*. Boris Karloff being from England knew of the name of my Aunt Olive, so that was kind of nice. I just dwelt on practically everything he did and everything Vincent Price did because of the way they used their voices and the way they spoke. It made you *chill* just to hear it. When Mr. Karloff would turn to talk to me during a scene, and when he was talking *about* me, I felt the chills go up my spine because of the way he said it! Oh, golly! It was a great education just being with them.

It's nice talking to somebody who really appreciates having the chance to meet and work with those three guys.

Oh, I was just in awe being there, because it was Boris Karloff, Peter Lorre and Vincent Price. My friends and I used to laugh at the Spike Jones album that had the guy imitating Peter Lorre's voice, and now, my gosh, here I was, standing right beside him! Remember the scene where Peter Lorre is getting all his magic props out of his bag, and being so grandiose? I think he made up [ad libbed some of the dialogue in] that scene. He said, "Vini vidi vici!" and other Latin phrases and made them sound like magic spells. With his great theater background, his great talent, he just *did* it. I just couldn't believe that there I was with *him*.

Olive with the title character in *The Raven*.

Vincent Price liked Peter Lorre, Price even read the eulogy at Lorre's funeral, but he also said that Lorre did so much ad libbing that one day on the set of one of the Poe pictures, he just said to Lorre, annoyed, "Oh, for Christ's sake, Peter, say the lines!!"

    Peter Lorre's ad libbing did make it very hard for the other actors to keep up with him. In the movie, I didn't have a lot to do with Peter Lorre myself—not as much as the others did. I was *in* the scenes, or around, but not as much with him directly. But I observed all this, so I could tell—

That the other people were challenged, coping with him?
Yeah.

What kind of physical condition was he in?
He had to rest a lot. Sometimes you didn't see him, sometimes he wasn't there, because he had to take time off.

Vincent Price?
Vincent Price was so darling and sweet to me and very helpful. I wish I could tell both their daughters, Karloff's and Vincent Price's, how much I enjoyed working with their fathers. It was a special thing to me, looking back on it. At the beginning of the film, Vincent Price reads Poe's poem "The Raven" and it's a classic rendition, beautifully read. He had wonderful training, and you *hear* it in that. He knew how to read Edgar Allan Poe's words with great style, and his *heart* was in it, his *feelings*. Beautiful resonant tones, and the diction was so clear—you don't *hear* that very much any more! Vincent Price was an accomplished actor, and *very* very nice. I felt so comfortable working with him because he ... he was my "dad" [*laughs*], he acted like that, and I felt very safe and comfortable with him in the scenes. Oh, I like the scene where Vincent and Peter Lorre are opening Vincent's wife's casket, and after it's been open for a while, Vincent looks over at Peter and notices that he's looking at the other end of the corpse! Vincent has to say, "No, up *here*," because Peter was looking at her feet! They did that in the rehearsal and then they decided to keep it, they put it into the scene.

Hazel Court?
Hazel Court read my palm—she would go around reading people's palms, just for fun! Hazel was an excellent actress. I worked with her on other shows.

Jack Nicholson?
I thought, "Who is *he*?" [*laughs*], because I'd never seen him before! He wasn't one of the younger people doing shows at that time that *I* ever saw, and I thought he was a bit ... you know ... hard to understand. A little *different*, Jack. But he and Peter Lorre had a ball during their scenes together. Jack was supposed to be playing kind of a dolt, kind of a dumb guy. Remember the scene where Jack started fussing over Peter Lorre, touching Peter's collar and saying things like "Mother wants you home...," and Peter was getting more and more impatient with him and slapping his hand away? Well, Jack kept right *on* doing it [touching Lorre], which was not in the script—he kept making such a fuss over Peter, and Peter pretended to be getting madder and madder. And the scene got better and better, I thought.

What do you mean when you say that Nicholson was "hard to understand"?
He was sort of "different." He was a quiet person, very quiet, and we worked together really nicely, but ... I can't explain it ... he was just *different*. When we were about to do the scene on top of the coach, when he falls under the spell and puts a crazy look on his face and starts driving too fast—he asked me before doing that, "How does it look if I snarl with my teeth?," and he tried different ways of holding his mouth and clenching his teeth. He and I worked on that, and he showed his teeth. After *The Raven*, I've seen some of his other movies, and I've seen him do that in different ways [*laughs*]! He is really quite a good actor,

"Just *different*" was Sturgess' impression of *The Raven*'s juvenile lead (Jack Nicholson in one of his early co-starring roles).

isn't he? He worked so hard to get where he is, and he deserves all his awards. [Back in *Raven* days] you could *feel* this talent of his, but he wasn't letting it out yet. But he was on his *way*. Roger Corman could see things in these young actors that other people *weren't* seeing. And Jack got to have a good relationship with [Price, Karloff and Lorre], he got to kinda *know* them.

All three of them?

Yeah. I was an awful square person, I was really a Goody Two-Shoes, I would just do the job and go home. But Jack spent time with them, getting to know them. Especially Vincent Price, I think—Vincent was very interested and caring about the young actors. I'm sure it would have been a marvelous thing, to get to know those men better.

And working with the raven itself?

The raven was cared for by Moe [Disesso], its trainer. It just did what it was told to do. It was wonderful to see it. I didn't have any problems with it, it didn't bother anybody.

Up close and in person, were the Raven *castle sets impressive?*

Oh, they were really terrible [*laughs*]! They were *old*! Roger Corman got the *oldest* stuff! Lots of those sets were used over and over and over again, so you got the sense that Roger Corman did the very least expensive work he could do. That's him all the way through! But you don't *need* to spend millions of dollars when you can spend *thousands* of dollars, I guess. I'd love to have done any [Corman] shows that he wanted to do, but *The Raven* was *it*.

Did you wear a wig in that movie?

That was practically all my own hair, but they put a little bit at the back, a "fall," to make it a bit longer. I *had* long hair in those days, because it was very useful and helpful to have long hair. Oh, and I want to tell you about the dress I wore. That dress was velvet and it weighed about 50 pounds, and it was the only thing I wore through the whole two weeks. My shoulders were just raw from holding that dress on! Then at the end, when the castle was burning, we had to run out of the place. Well, I didn't know it then, but I *learned*, that Peter Lorre was well-known for being a practical joker. Do you know what a stage weight is? It's a rectangular metal bar that they put just behind the sets, at the bases of flats, to keep them from falling over. Well, during the dress rehearsal for the scene where we run out of the castle, *some*body put one on the floor behind me, on the end of my dress. There was a long train on this 50-pound dress, and I don't know if they put one stage weight or *two* on there but I sure couldn't move [*laughs*]! I tried to start to run and I *couldn't* run. My arms were flailing around, and I was hollering and yelling because I couldn't *get* anywhere—and they were laughing their heads off at me. *Every*one was laughing! I had to laugh, too, because I was totally fooled, I did not see *any*body do that. So I tell everybody about Peter Lorre putting the stage weight on the end of my dress. Oh, gosh!

And you think it was Lorre who dreamed that up?

Yes, that was Peter Lorre, and Vincent Price too I think—but Vincent told me that was just *him* [Lorre]. Peter Lorre was always teasing everybody, in his own quiet way. I think he pulled some of his little tricks on Jack Nicholson too. Oh, when I couldn't run, Peter and Vincent were standing at the side, just having a fit. I was tied to a column in a dungeon in another scene, and I was also in the pillory, that heavy wooden frame with holes [for the prisoner's head and hands]. When I was tied to the column, Vincent Price was out there ready to do *another* thing to me, and that was to sneak up and tickle me when I was defenseless and helpless. I was trying to do the scene, and all *they* [Price and Lorre] wanted to do was have fun—at the expense of me [*laughs*]!

But it was just Price who tickled you?

That's right. Roger Corman was lucky that those guys were able to remember their lines, because they were hatching all these tricks to play on people. Two of the prime practical

Sturgess is at the mercy of treacherous Hazel Court and sorcerer Boris Karloff in *The Raven*.

jokers of all time were Vincent Price and Peter Lorre—they would let you have it. And when I was in the pillory, I had to stand there a looong time as they shot it from all the angles. The other actor [Aaron Saxon as Karloff's henchman] was there holding a hot poker, menacing me, and I was reacting and screaming. After that scene was all done, I was just exhausted and sweating and going [*Sturgess pants*]—I was out of breath. And that's when they said, "Well, it's lunch time, we'll see ya later," and off they went! I called after them, "No, don't *do* this, *noooo*!" but they left anyway!

In one part of the film, Vincent Price goes down into his father's old laboratory and opens a dusty old box and he sees that it's full of eyes, and he looks like he's about to throw up. Well, somebody put one of those eyes in my dressing room [*laughs*]! I don't know who that was, but an eye was on a table in my dressing room, staring back up at me when I went in there!

Did you get much direction from Roger Corman?
   Not really.

Aaron Saxon, another *Raven* baddie, gives trussed-up damsel Sturgess a hard time.

I didn't think so!

I felt like *we* sometimes directed *him* [*laughs*]—I really do! Often we'd do two takes, or maybe even just *one* take, and Mr. Corman would say, "That was *it*." I used to say to myself, "Oh, no!," 'cause I'd feel that it could have been better. When I saw the film and saw those scenes, I realized, "Well, it was okay after all," but at first, [on the set,] I thought, "This isn't gonna work. We oughta do it again."

Did you feel like anybody was in any danger in that big slapstick fight scene with the servant [William Baskin] with the axe?

Oh, yeah! When you scream in a scene like that, you scream because it's terrifying. Of course the axe is plastic, it's not a real axe, but it's frightening! And I'm *good* at screaming. If someone walks down the hallway in my house and surprises me, I scream!

Do you recall seeing The Raven *for the first time?*

My husband-to-be Dale [studio musician Dale Anderson] and I went to see it—we sat in the back row at a little theater in Santa Monica. I was worried about it because *The Raven was* done on a shoestring, really, and in so few takes. But it was okay. And Vincent Price, Boris Karloff and Peter Lorre were wonderful, because they were just doing what they *always* did. *The Raven* became very, very, very popular, and it's been a marvelous thing in my life.

You'd already done the two episodes of Karloff's Thriller *series ["The Watcher" and "The Closed Cabinet"] by the time you were in* The Raven. *Did you happen to meet him at that time?*

No, *The Raven* was my first time meeting him, because the prologues that he did for *Thriller* were shot at a separate time from the rest of the episode, and in them he would usually be alone. He would film several of them at a time. I have a special story about "The Watcher." I was pretty established by then, and John Brahm the director—that great German director—and [associate producer] Doug Benton and the production staff asked me if I would like to sit in on the readings as four young men tried out for a part, and choose who I'd like to have in it with me. So I sat in on the readings, and afterwards they asked me which one of the boys I liked the best, and I said, "Richard Chamberlain." Because as soon as I saw him, I said to myself, "Oh! *There's* somebody totally different." And he *was* wonderful—he was a serious actor and very well-prepared. So I felt like I discovered Richard Chamberlain, and I always used to tell people I did, 'cause *I* had never seen him before that. From "The Watcher," he got the *Dr. Kildare* TV series that he did later on. Anyway, I chose Richard Chamberlain to be my leading man in that, and then I worked with him later, a couple of times, on some of *his* shows.

What did you think of John Brahm?

John Brahm was very wonderful, one of the best people. He coached me through the scene in the car when I had to be scared. I was doing it myself, but also he would tell me *when* to turn my head and when to do *this* and when to do *that*—he would just whisper. He was the kind of director who could just *talk* to you until you understood, without making you feel "pushed." He kind of *let* you get to that place before you did the scene—do you know what I mean? He did a lot of takes in order to get exactly what he wanted, and that's what I appreciated too. Very strong and very authoritative. But very sweet too.

Your other Thriller *episode was set in the past, as was* The Raven, *as were all your Westerns—it seems like you did an awful lot of costume stuff. Did you enjoy that as much as contemporary roles?*

I did, because it was more fun. In my training, as a young girl, in Canada, in my teens, between 12 and 16, the teacher

Sturgess says she had a hand in the casting of Richard Chamberlain in the early *Thriller* episode "The Watcher."

had you walk around with a sheet tied around your waist, and a book on your head. So I was able to carry the [period] dresses. Sometimes you see actresses in long dresses these days, especially at the Academy Awards, and they sort of lope in and out [*laughs*]—they don't know how to "carry" these dresses. But the actors and actresses in the older days learned how to carry these gowns. As you walk, you also keep yourself "still" so the dress is floating along with you, not bouncing up and down. I had a lot of training in order to do that, and I just *loved* those clothes, I felt very much at home in them.

Ida Lupino directed your other Thriller, *"The Closed Cabinet." Was that your only time being directed by a woman?*

Yes, as far as I remember. I was shaky about that, because here was this great movie star [Lupino] and I was afraid what she would think of me, a TV actor. But I learned an *awful* lot from her, about underplaying.

Thriller's "The Closed Cabinet" found Sturgess reopening the vintage clothes cabinet.

She coached me and she helped me. *Every*thing you do is training—learning and training and growing. So it really was quite wonderful to work with Ida Lupino, close up and face to face, and have her tell me how to do things. And she made me look glamourous in some of the scenes, so *that* was good [*laughs*]! *She's* a tiny person too. I'm five-two, and she was not much taller than me.

I know you were friendly with the producers of Thriller, *William Frye and especially Doug Benton.*

William Frye and Doug Benton used to like to have me in the shows. William once said to me, "You know, Olive, you look like Debbie Reynolds, but you're a helluva better actress than *she* is!" [*Laughs*] He said that—and he was very serious! He said, "She's very good, but you have all these other dimensions...." He thought of me as a very good actress, and that was good! And Doug Benton was one of the finest people in Hollywood and one of the very best producers. I'm surprised that he didn't become more of a producer as time went on. But he was very, very popular and well-liked. Many wonderful things happened in my life because of Doug Benton. Well [*laughs*], he was responsible for me meeting my future husband! Doug introduced me to his wife Jacqui, and Jacqui said, "I know somebody [you'll like]." Doug and Jacqui Benton took me to a party, and that's how I met Dale.

They took you to that party in order for you to meet him.

That's right. But Dale was always being set up with blind dates, so he wasn't supposed to know that I was there for the purpose of meeting him. We were married in 1964, and Jacqui Benton was one of my bridesmaids in the wedding. Then my daughter was born in 1966. [Anderson died in 2003.]

And you started drifting away from the acting.

Yes, I would turn down things every once in a while, and I kind of aced myself out. For example, I was asked to do [an episode of] the *Flipper* series, I was asked, "Would you go to Florida?," and I had to say, "No, I can't leave and go to Florida." There were things that I couldn't *do* as freely as I did before, once I was married and had a daughter. I wanted to have a good, strong home, without me going here and there and everywhere else but home. So that's when I changed my life, in the mid–'60s.

With professional singers and an actress in her family, Sturgess' show biz career almost seemed preordained.

And no regrets, about that change?

I'd had ten full years of very busy career. I'm now the *grand*mother of a most wonderful little girl. These days I feel very *free*, I can just be my*self*, and do things with my friends and my family and my granddaughter. I was very fortunate to have had a wonderful career and a family as well.

FRANKIE THOMAS, AL MARKIM AND JAN MERLIN ON *TOM CORBETT, SPACE CADET*

"As roaring rockets blast off to distant planets and far-flung stars, we take you to the age of the conquest of space with Tom Corbett, Space Cadet*!"*
—*the television series' opening narration*

Ask science fiction fans "What was network TV's first outer space adventure series?" and their answers will often reflect their age and their level of interest in genre history. Many would probably say *Star Trek* or *Lost in Space* (both from the mid–1960s) while others might remember the earlier, Sputnik-era *Men Into Space*, and still others *all* the way back to shows like *Space Patrol*. But the correct answer predates those by one more small step, the giant leap into the genre being originally taken by the New York-made *Tom Corbett, Space Cadet*.

Starting its run in October 1950 as a 15-minute, three-times-a-week CBS series, the show focussed on three young cadets enrolled at Space Academy in the mid–2300s: Tom Corbett, brave, resourceful and a born leader; Astro, a hard-working and sensitive cadet from the planet Venus; and Roger Manning, courageous but also cocky and hot-headed. Despite the fact that it targeted a young audience, *Tom Corbett* was light on monsters and other outlandish elements, emphasizing instead comparatively "believable" stories involving deep space rescue missions, stranded rocketships, meteor storms and, most memorably, the interaction between the characters as they patrolled the solar system in their ship the *Polaris*. Scientific plausibility was assured through consultations with renowned space scientist Willy Ley, the show's technical advisor.

Tom Corbett jumped networks the way its young space aces planet-hopped: It ran on CBS, ABC, NBC and Dumont, always live, and always in the catch-as-catch-can style of early TV. On the golden anniversary of the conclusion of the cadets' five-year mission, the pioneer series' three stars Frankie Thomas (Tom), Al Markim (Astro) and Jan Merlin (Roger) reunited for a look-back at those wild and woolly days of early TV...

Jan, you were the first of the Tom Corbett *stars to be cast so we'll start with you. How did you land the role of Roger Manning?*

Jan Merlin: I was in *Mister Roberts* on Broadway at the time, and since they got a little stiff about giving the cast members of the biggest hit on Broadway a raise in pay, almost all of us in the cast, with the exception of the leads, began looking for outside jobs. I read about this television show [*Tom Corbett*] that was going to be put together by Rockhill Radio, and I went over to see them. Albert Aley, who was the head writer, and Stanley Wolfe the president of Rockhill were there, and our first producer, Mort Abrahams. When I came in, they explained that it was going to be a show about a Space Academy, with youngsters going through the Academy the way they do at West Point. I came in with a crew haircut which I had from *Mister Roberts*, so they thought maybe I could do Astro. I read the part of Astro, and ... it just didn't sound right. Then they discussed having me read the other cadets. They obviously didn't feel that I'd be right for the part of the youngest cadet [Corbett], so they had me read Roger Manning. Well, the moment I started on Roger, I was in like Flynn, because it was perfect. It was the sort of role I liked, a smart-ass cadet who could be a mean son of a bitch but he could also be honorable and trustworthy. I just fell into it.

I must have been the first one to show up for this thing because they asked if I would stay and read with other people. After I read with actors all day long for several days, Al Markim came in and he was chosen for Astro. With Al, what you see is what you get, Al's a likable, solid citizen, and he was intrigued with playing a Venusian. Then I was reading with other guys who were coming in for Corbett.

What brought you to the Tom Corbett *auditions, Frankie?*

Frankie Thomas: I was living in New York, working in radio, and I got a call about meeting with the producers of *Tom Corbett, Space Cadet*, which *then* they were intending to call *Cris Colby, Space Cadet*. I walked into this room and here was George Gould, our first director, and Mort Abrahams, and Jan Merlin and Al Markim—I'd never met any of them before. They asked Jan and Al and me to stand together, they lined the three of us up ... and it just clicked. There was no doubt. I didn't have to read a line. It was kind of weird! I know it sounds unbelievable, but that's the way it happened.

Merlin: The minute Frankie walked in, we all knew he was the one. He looked the part and he was bright and young-looking and—he was just *right*.

Do you know what other actors were considered for the part?

Thomas: They said they'd gone through everybody in New York [*laughs*]. Jack Lemmon was up for it, and Dickie Moore, and a chap who was quite active in New York, a nice young fella, Peter Fernandez, who played a lot of juveniles. But ultimately I was selected. Well, I'd had a lot of experience that was valuable for television. I was doing a lot of television shows at the time, and I'd had motion picture experience, which was important. I met everybody and was hired on a Friday. The following Monday, we started rehearsals, and we rehearsed almost a week. Then we went on after that. Boy, it was instantaneous. Those things don't happen too often!

Years before Mr. Spock, Al, you were playing an alien on an Earth spaceship crew. What do you remember about developing the character of Astro?

Al Markim: We talked about a great many things in the beginning, how to distinguish Astro, and *should* Astro look different because he's from Venus? He didn't *behave* any different than anybody else, except that he was very sincere, very hard-working—very much the *opposite* of Roger Manning [*laughs*]. Albert Aley and George Gould weren't sure whether Astro should have a different colored skin. At one point I said yes, it could be done, certainly we could give him a brownish hue, a tannish hue—he was, after all, a Venusian, who *knows* what color skin Venusians would have [*laughs*]? If you look at very early episodes, you

More than fifty years have passed since the stars of television's *Tom Corbett, Space Cadet* (left to right, Jan Merlin, Frankie Thomas, Al Markim) last blasted off for distant planets and moons, but the actors' bond of friendship endured. What you're reading was the first-ever three-way print interview with network television's first-ever sci-fi stars.

can also see that some things had been done with my ears and with my eyebrows—a number of cosmetic things were tried. But it became clear to everybody that all of that was really unnecessary, and it sort of just disappeared over time.

Thomas: There were changes made to my character, too. As I recall, the original idea was to have my character kind of a junior cadet, the youngest of the three, and following the other two, more experienced cadets around. [The producers] wanted what they assumed would be the show's largest TV audience, which would be children, oh, maybe from 10 up to 17 or 18, to identify with me. Well, when I got on the scene, they decided to switch the format around. They changed the name [from Cris Colby] to Tom Corbett—I can't remember why—and now they wanted him to be the dominant leader. Tom was the same class as the other two, but he wasn't going to be asking *them* questions, he was going to be more the take-charge type.

When the series began, your commanding officer Capt. Strong was played—briefly—by an actor named Michael Harvey.

Thomas: Awfully nice fellow. Physically perfect for the part. But he had a problem with the lines. Bless his dear heart, he just couldn't get it. If you ever get a chance to see [episode] number one—

He does stammer a lot.

Thomas: Remember his long speech? Well, he was up higher than a kite! He was very nervous about his lines. Some people are that way, they just don't memorize easily. [The producers] realized he wasn't going to work.

Merlin: Michael Harvey was our first "tragedy" in the show. When the red light went on, his mind went blank!

Markim: Michael I think was on the show for a month—maybe not even a month. When Michael didn't appear to be working out, they quickly needed somebody who could do Capt. Strong. I had been in summer stock as an actor the year before and been in a play with Ed Bryce, so I told George Gould, "Gee, I know a guy...." They called Ed in, and he became Capt. Strong. Ed was a wonderful guy, so sincere, such a real, honest person—he *was* Capt. Strong, he really was! If you know what the Capt. Strong character is, *that* was Ed Bryce. Terrific guy.

Merlin: Ed didn't fill out Michael's uniform, so they gave him chest padding instead of altering it. Ed took a ribbing from us, but was happy anyway.

Over the years, Tom Corbett *moved from network to network, and you guys went from one studio to another.*

Up, up and away with *Corbett* stars, left to right, Frankie Thomas, Al Markim, Jan Merlin and Ed Bryce.

Born in a trunk, the product of an acting family, Frankie Thomas was playing starring roles on stage and screen in childhood. He was previously profiled in this author's *Earth vs. the Sci-Fi Filmmakers* (McFarland, 2005).

Merlin: Our first studio had a cheesy name, Liederkranz Hall. It was situated in the CBS studios on East 56th Street, between Park and Lexington Avenues. From there also came *Captain Kangaroo* and *Love of Life*. In one episode they had to have the blast-off of the rocket. The lower part of the *Polaris* spaceship, showing its entry and the rocket exhausts above the leg fins, was built for our set and we actors had to climb a ladder to enter the ship through a doorway, which then slid closed after us. After a pause, there had to be a powerful burst of stuff out of the rocket exhaust tubes. They were trying it with dry ice and bee smoke dispensers, but none of it worked, and we were getting closer and closer to air time. Finally our technical director Ib Melchior exclaimed, "I *got* it!" Ib remembered that Liederkranz Hall had a stairway with little fire extinguishers lined up along it. He rushed out and picked four of the fire extinguishers, and they rigged 'em on the inside deck above those rocket exhaust tubes, and at the right moment they were discharged. And here came all these violent blasts of white, and it looked just like a real rocket takeoff! It worked! Of course CBS was a little upset, because you're not supposed to do that with their fire equipment [*laughs*], but they forgave us!

Thomas: I should mention that the show later developed something that revolutionized television, and that was the matting amplifier. That was developed by George Gould and two technical men at ABC. Before they came up with the matting amplifier, you could have on TV a superimposition, one image superimposed over another, but when you looked at it you *knew* that it was one image on top of another. But the matting amplifier created an electronic void in one image and fitted another image *into* it. In one episode, we landed on a planet of dinosaurs, and the "dinosaur" actually was a baby alligator. But, boy, on the screen, combined with a small image of *us*, it looked very large and very real! With the matting amplifier, in scenes where we were supposedly on the outside of the *Polaris*, we would be shot in miniature and the *Polaris* model would be shot in magnification, and it looked like we were walking on the deck of the *Saratoga*!

Markim: In that era of black-and-white 1950 television, you didn't have all of the gimmickry that we have available to us today, all of the electronics and digital effects and everything else. You had to imagine how to do *every*thing. For one sequence at the lip of a volcano, the camera shot down into thick oatmeal bubbling and boiling. The stagehands had planted dry ice in it and so steam was coming up from it, and they kept the heat underneath it, and the oatmeal continued to bubble, and that's how they made "magma"! So the producers and directors and *all* of us had to be very creative about it, and it was fun, it was challenging. And the fact that *Tom Corbett* was live always added an element of intensity to it. I always liked live television a lot better than taped television, I thought there was a great thrill and challenge to doing live television.

Merlin: One of the "panics" of live shows is either blowing your lines or forgetting them altogether. In one episode set out in space, Roger Manning is inside the ship with the other cadets and Capt. Strong is outside, floating off into space. The other cadets want to go out after him, and Roger insists, "No, what we should do is go back to Space Academy and get help and *then* go after him," and I had a long bunch of scientific gobbledygook reasons, those peculiar words that our technical advisor Willy Ley would have us say. And I couldn't remember *any of them*. So "live," on the air coast to coast, Al Markim turned to me and said, "You mean to say you'd leave Capt. Strong out there to die?!?" I looked at him, and I was still totally blank, and so I replied, "...Why *not*??" [*Laughs*] I thought he'd have a heart attack! And I thought our TV technical crew would never trust me again! Another time we had a guy playing a space pirate, and he used to read a comic book during rehearsals. When he was gonna come into the scene, he'd put the comic book in his boot and he'd play the scene. He did that all through rehearsals. Well, on air, to our great surprise, he forgot that he had the comic book in his boot, and when he got shot and fell down to die on the *Polaris* control deck, the camera panned down, and there was the comic book winking at you from the top of his boot [*laughs*]! We had wonderful moments....

Thomas: I'm reminded of an incident we had with an actor (who shall remain nameless) who was playing a warlord. He was a little weak on learning the lines, so he had his script pages planted on the floor near the microphone that he would be speaking into, in a scene where he was broadcasting to another rocketship or to ... whoever. He wanted to just stand there and *read*. Well, our technical crew had become very protective about the show—this was *their show*. One of them was sweeping up the set before the scene, and he swept up the script too! The actor made his entrance, he picked up the microphone and he said, "All right, now..." and he looked down to read ... and there was nothing there [*laughs*]! Ohhh boy! He fought his way through it, though!

The crew guy swept it up on purpose, you're saying?

Thomas: Sure he did! The sweeper's attitude was, "You're not gonna do that with our boys [the *Tom Corbett* regulars]! They have to learn *their* lines!" They were very protective!

Merlin: Since all three of us cadets had stage experience, we were accustomed to learning lines and doing a show from start to finish rather than in little bits and pieces as film actors do. So the tendency on *Tom Corbett* was to hire actors who also had stage experience. It didn't necessarily have to be the Broadway stage, but people who at least had done theater work. We had people like Tom Poston, John Fiedler, Jack Klugman, Ben Cooper, Jack Warden, Frank Sutton, Joe DeSantis and Jack Lord. Even Frankie's uncle, Calvin Thomas, was in one of the shows. We became a little family, it was very nice.

Markim: Doing the show live was always a challenge. And Jan, who was very much Roger Manning even *off*-camera, would always try to break me up before we went on to do a scene. Jan and I were standing off in the wings one day and the show was on the air live, and we were waiting for our cue line, waiting to make an entrance. And Jan turned to me and he said, "Let's quit the show." I guffawed, and then the cue line came up, and I couldn't contain myself [*laughs*]! I tried to pretend I was coughing. That was the kind of thing that Jan was likely to do!

Is that a good thing to have on a live show, somebody who's trying to break people up?

Merlin [*very earnestly*]: No...! [*Laughs*] Yeah, I used to do it to the other actors. I was terrible that way, I was really awful. Well, it was a way to loosen up, y'know? And if *they* entered laughing, that was okay with me [*laughs*]!

How long would a sorehead like Roger Manning really last in any man's army—land, air, sea or outer space?

Merlin: He'd have had his lights punched out quite a few times by the guys who didn't like him, and he probably would have spent some time in the brig. And he probably would not have gotten much of a rank. But he still did the job. So he just might have been one of those guys you put up with, only because you knew he could do the job. Roger did some awful things and yet he always made up for it.

Markim: The character, as it was originally written, was nastier and more bitter. Jan as he played it had this impish quality that made him rather endearing. A lot of kids liked Roger Manning and that impish quality.

A native of Wilkes-Barre, Pennsylvania, Al Markim began performing as a young man in little theater groups, acted for the Armed Forces Network in post–World War II Germany and attended NYC's New School's Dramatic Workshop in the days before television stardom as Astro.

Did you ever happen to ask why Rockhill Radio branched out into the production of a sci-fi TV series in the first place?

    Thomas: How they got into this, I imagine, was because Kellogg's was the sponsor of Rockhill's *Mark Trail* [radio show], and Kellogg's was looking now for a television series. They took the name *Space Cadet* from a Robert Heinlein novel, but the show had absolutely no connection with the book. The only character in *Tom Corbett* that was in Heinlein's book was Commander Arkwright—that's all there was. The story in the book was nowhere near what *we* did.

Commander Arkwright was played by Carter Blake, and Dr. Joan Dale was an actress named Margaret Garland.

Markim: Maggie and Carter were both on the show for a long time and they were in many, many episodes. They weren't in them *all*, but whenever we were in an episode that took place back at Space Academy, of course that's where Arkwright and Joan were working. Arkwright was the commander of Space Academy and Joan was a professor there, and occasionally they would go out on a mission with us. Everybody on that show got along very well together, there really was a lot of camaraderie. I didn't know either Maggie or Carter that well socially, away from the show, but they were nice people, and I have fond memories of both of them.

Merlin: Margaret Garland and I came directly from Broadway shows to *Tom Corbett*, she from *Anne of the Thousand Days* and I from *Mister Roberts*. Maggie was friendly but a bit aloof, and kept her private life to herself. Carter Blake was a charming gent. I think his very first job in show business was when he was about five years old and he got cast into some play. He had a lovely wife named Nancy and two or three sons. We never really got to know him because he lived quietly—went home and had a very pleasant family life.

Markim: At one point, Frank Sutton came on more or less regularly [as Cadet Eric Rattison], and Frank was a delight. I always got along well with him, I enjoyed him, and I enjoyed his work. He fit in. It was not easy coming in and fitting into our little group, but he did.

Tom Corbett *was only on CBS a few months before it jumped over to ABC.*

Thomas: We switched to ABC because ABC offered us more outlets. Outlets at that time were very important. I think, after about three, four months [of *Tom Corbett* being on the air], *The Milton Berle Show* had the greatest number of outlets and Catholic Bishop Fulton Sheen's show was number two, and *Tom Corbett* was number three.

But how long was it before you and the others realized that it was becoming a popular show?

Thomas: Now, here's another one that's hard to believe: Almost by the second week. The disc jockeys all picked up our lingo: "Blast your jets," "Don't fuse your tubes," "Spaceman's luck!" We were hearing all of this and we said, "Hey, if they're *saying* it, they're *watching* it." *Tom Corbett* really caught on very fast. When I say "the second week," I know *I* had a feeling that it was going great guns.

At first ABC had us in a studio in a new building uptown, around the 60s, off Central Park West. Then they secured a floor of a building on West 57th Street, a floor which *had* been a gymnasium, and *that* became our studio. No other show was in there, so now we had the benefit of having our big sets remain permanent, which was a lot of help for the crew. The control room, the exterior of the spaceship, the cadets' room at Space Academy, etc.—those didn't have to be put up and taken down any more.

Merlin: It was a two-story-high gymnasium, quite a large one, and all around the gymnasium, about halfway up the wall, about 14 feet up, was a running track for joggers. When special guests were invited to watch us shoot, there was no room for them on the stage floor, because of the cameras and all the sets. So the director and/or producer would have guests go up on that running track and they could wander around the whole perimeter, depending on where we were working. So long as they didn't make any disturbance or talk, they could watch what we were doing.

Thomas: After ABC we were on Dumont and we worked at the Dumont Studios, around 56th Street. Then, at the end, for NBC, we were at the NBC Studios, 30 Rockefeller. There was a large studio on the seventh or eighth floor, and that worked out fine.

Did being the stars of a series like Tom Corbett *provide you with a good living during those years, or were TV paychecks minimal?*

Markim: TV paychecks *were* minimal. But you have to look at "minimal" in the context of what the dollar value was in the early 1950s. You could still go to a movie for probably a half a dollar; today it's, what?, seven or eight dollars.

Try 10.50 in Manhattan!

Markim [*laughs*]: Well, I don't go to Manhattan much, I go in Rockland [Rockland County, New York]! But you could buy a new automobile in the '50s with eight or nine thousand dollars. So you gotta look at the value. We were earning probably $12,000 to 15,000 a year, which of course sounds puny today. But it was more money than any of *my* contemporaries were making, and it afforded me a very good lifestyle. In addition to that, we got paid extra for doing the commercials and we were doing other things; for example, we had a *Tom Corbett* radio show. So it was a nice composite income from all of that, and, yes, we lived well on it. Did it make us rich? It made *no*body rich [*laughs*].

Thomas: Ed Kemmer, who played the lead in *Space Patrol*, once he told me that he was making eight dollars a show—hard to believe! That was not the situation with *Tom Corbett*.

Markim: My recollection is that we were getting $75 a show, and we were doing three a week, so you made $225. *But*, we were making more money than almost anybody else was at that time. This was in 1950 dollars ... not so bad. I mean, I was driving a new car when my friends could not yet buy a car—and we were only kids in our twenties.

Did you have any interest in science fiction when you were a kid?

Thomas: Yes. As a matter of fact, I was a fan of Robert Heinlein, I thought his *The Puppet Masters* was one of the greatest political satires of all time and that he was a heckuva writer. And naturally, like all kids my age, I was brought up on the *Buck Rogers* comic strip and the radio show—mostly the radio show.

Jan Merlin saw seagoing (U.S. Navy) action in real life during World War II before his spacegoing stint on *Tom Corbett*. He subsequently made his film debut in *Six Bridges to Cross* with Sal Mineo and starred in a second television series, the post–Civil War Western *The Rough Riders*.

Markim: *Flash Gordon* was my favorite. As a young boy I read a lot of adventure stories with boy heroes, and my favorites were the space stories. Later I became a big fan of Isaac Asimov's books. Long before *I, Robot* was made into a movie [2004]!

Merlin: Did *I* have an interest in science fiction?, oh my, yes. Listen—when I was a little bitty kid, when we didn't have any money and we couldn't afford a thing like radio, my brother Joe made a crystal set and we would share the headset. He'd have one of the ear pieces and I'd have the other and we'd listen to all these shows on radio at night, things like *The Witch's Tale*. And Joe used to read these pulp magazines and science fiction magazines, *Amazing Stories* and *Astounding Stories*, and I picked up on that. I had a collection of many of those marvelous old magazines.

Tom Corbett being a live show, did you ever get to see it?

Merlin: We used to go in to Rockhill and they'd play the kinescopes for us, *if* we had time between the rehearsals and the show time. Al and I did see quite a few of 'em, but even I got tired of it and didn't do it any more. One of the problems was, I couldn't—I *still* can't—stand myself on the screen. I hate the sound of my voice, I hate the way I look, I don't like what I *do*. Very seldom do I think, "Okay, *that's* a good job." In those days, I was appalled by what I was looking at, and I couldn't believe I was *doing* it [*laughs*]!

Why was Tom Corbett *popular?*

Merlin: Because it had to do with the only thing that replaced the love of dinosaurs in children's hearts: It had to do with outer space. And there was nothing more fabulous than to go to another world—or *lots* of other worlds. That's why all of these space shows, to this day, have always been so exciting to the kids. Although that's kind of wearing off, isn't it? The kids have become jaded, which is sad.

Markim: *Tom Corbett* was popular, first of all, because it was well-written. Secondly, it wasn't hokey, it was *real*, it was about real people, it was about relationships as much as it was about adventure. And I think the three characters that Albert Aley and his original writers put together were interesting characters. The casting was done well enough, and the three of us pulled it off. We stayed together for a number of years and worked together very well, good working relationships, and a lot of that came across on the air. Now, television was extremely young at the time, and *Tom Corbett* was also very novel. It was the kind of thing you didn't see much of. The competition when we first went on the air were things like *Captain Video*. But *Captain Video* wasn't really a space show, it was a guy in a studio who ran cowboy movies.

Thomas: Captain Video [Richard Coogan] would be in his secret headquarters, high in the mountains somewhere, contacting his "agents in the field"—who were Buck Jones and Tom Tyler. In other words, he was running old B-Westerns! *Space Patrol* was also a totally different show. They had monster shows and Dracula-like characters and all sorts of weirdos, whereas we stuck close to what was scientifically possible. Willy Ley was our technical director—he had been the president of the German Rocket Society, he was Wernher Von Braun's closest friend, and he checked over every *Tom Corbett* script. When I was writing some of the *Corbett* shows with my writing partner Ray Morse, I would have a conference with Willy, and it was amazing, the things that he said we *could do*, things that he said *were* in the realm of scientific possibility. There was only one thing that he said would never work, and that was the Paralo-Ray, which froze victims into immobility with non-fatal results. However, we had the Paralo-Ray and *kept* it [*laughs*]!

The relationship between Astro (Markim, left), Manning (Merlin) and Corbett (Thomas), and their interaction with others at Space Academy like Commander Arkwright (Carter Blake, seated), was an important part of the show's success.

Did you just see Ley on the set, or also socially?

Thomas: When you as a writer were envisioning a *Tom Corbett* adventure, and they were going to have you write it, you checked it with *him*. Maybe over dinner together. (By the way, he could drink Manhattan cocktails faster than anybody I ever saw. It didn't bother him a bit!) He would check your story's "scientific possibility"—those were the words that he used—and if it was scientifically possible, okay, go ahead with the story! I had very few problems with him. Everything I came up with, he okayed.

What was he like personally?

Thomas: He was very interesting. After we'd finish our business about what was possible for the show or not, he had many a story to tell. I remember one time I asked, "Willy, what about these smalltime wars?" [like the Korean War], and he said, "Vell, vee are going to develop a small, miniature A-bomb. And when a var starts, vee just drop the A-bomb and dat *stops* it!" Say, it wasn't a bad idea now that I think about it! Willy was very nice, very pleasant to work with.

Merlin: Willy Ley was a funny little guy. He was a little, stout man with thick glasses like the bottoms of soda pop bottles, and this heavy German accent. At one point we did ask him when we'd get to the Moon, and he told us we'd be there within ten years. I was astounded.

Thomas: And he was not far off.

Merlin: The thing we all liked about the show was that, although it was considered a show for kids, they veered away from making it a kid's show by really trying to keep it technically accurate. And instead of it being one of those oater-type things where you'd get the same plot over and over again and there's not much change, the difficulties we had were very frequently the difficulties between the cadets. Personal things. The by-play between the three of them. It wasn't intended to *teach* the kids anything, but we were doing things that *did* teach them how to get along with each other, how to conduct yourself in bad situations, how to react to one another's quirks and whatnot. It was a much more serious show than one would have expected at that time; it was no *Uncle Don* [a then-current children's radio show].

Did you guys find yourself being recognized on the street once the show became popular?

Markim: Yes. While we were doing the show, in the second or third year, I got a running part in a soap opera called *Love of Life*. So now I was being seen in two different ways on television, and people began to recognize me and come to me and I didn't know *which* character they wanted an autograph for! Once I was asked for an autograph by a little old lady, at the roller derby or a wrestling match or something, because she watched the soap opera, and with her was a grandson who wanted an autograph because he knew I was Astro on *Tom Corbett* [*laughs*]!

Thomas: Rockhill made darn sure we never saw our fan mail. I heard something like 10,000 letters. And — I know this is true, because a fellow who worked in the office told me — I got three proposals of marriage [*laughs*]! Rockhill suppressed all the fan mail. They were worried that we were going to start to ask for more money, so they kept that quiet. I didn't find out about that until after the show was over.

Merlin: I was being followed home by kids — they'd follow me in the subways all the way to where I lived in Elmhurst, Queens. And whenever we made personal appearances, the kids would crowd around. They just thought that Roger was ... like one of *them*.

For a kid's show out of New York, you had a surprising number of soon-to-be "name" actors show up in guest roles.

Thomas: The show acted as a launch pad for a lot of young actors who went on to do very well. Some of them, it was their first jobs. Jack Lord was on *Tom Corbett* and he had some very nice things to say about the show in *Saturday Morning TV*, a very large book on television. Tommy Poston started out with us ... we had Woody Parfrey ... Jack Klugman was just the guest of honor at a Pacific Pioneer Broadcasters luncheon and, talking about his credits, he said, "It was a looong way from *Tom Corbett, Space Cadet* to *Quincy!*" [*Laughs*]

Jack Warden has had quite an illustrious career, a lot of very good parts. He came out of Newark, and I'm sure that *Tom Corbett* was the first job that he did. He played "Joe Yakker, chief construction engineer of the Venusian mud lake tunnel project." I had to memorize that line, and *say* it, and I worked on that one so hard I never forgot it! His first scene was with me, and I know what he did: He wanted to be good, this was his first job, and he memorized the whole scene. He memorized his part and mine as well — he was gonna be darn sure that he got the right cues. He made his entrance and he walked over to me, as was called for ... and he said my line. I had written that show and so I was kinda familiar with it, so ... I said *his*. And he said *mine*. And I said *his*. We went through the whole thing,

The stars of *Tom Corbett* safeguarded the Earth from space pirates, rogue asteroids and other interstellar threats in the early television days of black-and-white, roof aerials and "larger than life-sized" 20-inch screens. Left to right, Markim, Merlin, Thomas (seated), Ed Bryce and Margaret Garland.

reversing our characters. We came into the commercial, and the producer rushed over; by this time, that was Allen Ducovny. He said, "Gee, Frank, that was a great scene!" He didn't even *know* it had all been reversed [*laughs*]!

Markim: In one of the latter years of the *Tom Corbett* show, I was doing two other things. I was in the soap opera *Love of Life* a couple times a week and I was also doing a play at the Circle in the Square called *La Ronde*, a hit play that ran for six months down there. So I had a busy schedule: memorize a script for the soap opera, then I'd have a script to memorize for *Tom Corbett*, and at night a heavy makeup job for the character that I was playing in *La Ronde*. I would be at the makeup room at the Circle in the Square Theater and a friend at that time would come and coach me on the *Tom Corbett* lines. That fella was George Segal. George is a little younger than I am, and he kinda looked up to me and wanted to have the kind of career *I* was having then [*laughs*]. As a matter of fact, several years later, he was interviewed by the Hollywood columnist Sidney Skolsky and he said, "My favorite actor of all time was Al Markim." Of course, nobody knew who the hell Al Markim was [*laughs*]!

What were some of the "hidden" perils of a 1950s outer space show? Hot lights, cumbersome spacesuits—

Merlin: Oh, the spacesuits were terrible. I remember blacking out one time. For a scene where I was supposed to be floating out in space, they were pulling me, lying flat on my back on a little mechanic's creeper, across a floor which was painted black with little white stars on it.

With the camera up above you shooting down at you, I bet.

Merlin: I have no idea where the camera was, because they'd kept me in that suit throughout the whole damn day's rehearsal period, and the lights were hot, and I blacked out briefly while we were on air. Fortunately I "came to" about the time I reached whatever the end of the scene was, but ... it was awful, it was really terrible.

Thomas: The lights in those days were a lot hotter than they are now. You could really burn off a few pounds.

Markim: The spacesuits were clumsy, and the helmet had a great big open porthole in it, so you could breathe. The open porthole probably shows in all the shots [*laughs*], and often your face would poke through it! The suits were uncomfortable because you were in 'em all day long, rehearsing and whatever. We weren't in the spacesuits just for the 15 minutes that we were on the air but, really, all day long. It was a pain in the neck.

Frankie, what difficulties did you run into on Tom Corbett *that the average, casual fan might not know about?*

Thomas: Sometimes we'd have a guest actor who rehearsed just fine ... and then, when the red light came on and it was now or never, he suddenly was playing Hamlet, and everything got slowed down. See, with live television, that's your big problem—*time*. You had to finish on *time*.

And you'd cope with this situation by speeding up yourself?

Thomas: That's right. Tom Corbett was always looking through the porthole, to see where the *Polaris* was going. Well, looking out through the porthole, I would get the speed-up from the floor manager. Now, here's the funny thing: When I would turn away from the porthole, the boys [Merlin and Markim] *knew* that I had gotten the speed-up. Before I opened my mouth. How they sensed that, I don't know, but we played an awful lot of those last scenes *very* quickly!

Behind the scenes, who were some of the "unsung heroes" of Tom Corbett, Space Cadet?

Markim: Albert Aley is one for sure. Albert had a great talent for keeping this show going. He knew how to get the scripts out, he wrote many, many of them himself. Frankie later wrote some of them, and in the latter days *I* wrote a couple of them. I wrote them with a friend, Hal Rein, who got the name credit on it, but *we* wrote them. But Albert remained overall story editor and kept the storylines going and kept it always interesting and he had a lot of love and affection for all of this, and I think his contributions have probably not been as *well* sung as some of the others.

Merlin: Another unsung hero was a great gal who was not only *Tom Corbett*'s assistant producer, but sort of a general all-around go-fer and had a *heck* of a lot to do with the show. We used to call her Moo-Moo because her name was Muriel Maron. She was such an astonishing worker that we never had any problems regarding anything we wanted done or needed to know or *anything*. Our technical director Ib Melchior had a remarkable background: He's the son of Lauritz Melchior, the greatest tenor of the century, and during the Second World War, Ib had been with the O.S.S. and C.I.C. for the U.S. Army in Germany and he tracked down Nazis—for which he was specially honored by the U.S. and by the Danish king. Oddly enough, here was this *real* hero working with us "television heroes" and he never let on about all of this, he and I never discussed our wars at all. Actually, Rockhill didn't like us [the actors] to talk about war experience in the past. They certainly didn't want *me* to talk about my background, because they wanted fans to believe the actors playing the three cadets were about 18. At the time, I was 25 years old.

Thomas: Eddie Taliaferro, our costume designer, did something else he never got credit for: He was a quick-change artist!

You mean he helped you guys change quickly between scenes.

Thomas: That's right. And we were doing a *lot* of quick changes! For instance, we'd have to get out of our cadet uniforms and into the spacesuits, and sometimes I didn't think we were going to be able to *do* it in time, but we did! Eddie never seemed to be in a hurry, but he got things done awfully fast. Oh, and I remember another time, Jan, Al and myself were playing our regular parts, but the show also had scenes with Mercurians, and we all got into the Mercurian costumes and masks. In addition to playing Tom, Roger and Astro, we were also running around as Mercurians! If you want me to tell you how we made the change from our uniforms into those other outfits as quickly as we did, *I don't know* [laughs]. It was a strain, but we did it!

Markim: Then there were a couple of writers who haven't been talked about enough, who wrote a lot of the early episodes, Jack Weinstock, who was a doctor, and Willie Gilbert. You'll see their credit at the end of a lot of these shows. They would come in the studio and we knew them well, and they were good—they caught the feeling and the essence of the characters. Later on they wrote something that was on Broadway for quite a while [*How to Succeed in Business Without Really Trying*, 1961–65].

It occurred to me, re-watching a bunch of Tom Corbett*s, that Astro, who's from another planet and a bit of an "outsider" and is sometimes picked on, could possibly have become the show's "identification figure" for kids who had trouble fitting in, and for minority kids.*

Markim: What happened is that many, many minority kids picked up on this and Astro became a hero for a lot of them. One year the three of us were asked to be the grand marshals of the Thanksgiving Day Parade in Philadelphia.

Merlin: Oh, that was a glorious parade, I'd never seen anything like it. It had mummers in feathered costumes and they were having a great time prancing along the parade route ahead of us.

Markim: A *huge* parade. Probably a million, a million and a half people

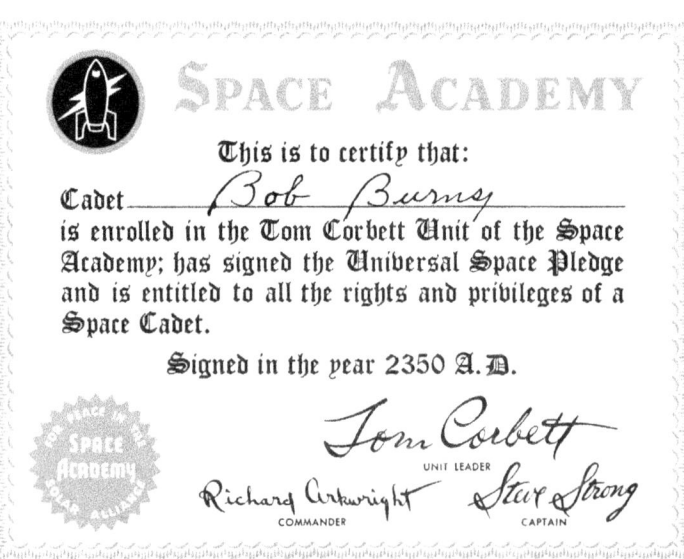

Kids didn't just watch *Tom Corbett* on TV; many bought the toys, read the comic—even enrolled in the Space Academy!

lined the streets. And all along that route, there were pockets of black kids and Hispanic kids and so on, all waving things, pictures and so on that they had of Astro. And when we got around to meeting and talking with some people afterwards and signing autographs, the black kids were mainly interested in Astro. He was their hero.

At one point there was a sequence where Astro was very ill, and there was concern that maybe Astro was gonna die. I don't quite remember—*you've* probably seen these episodes more recently than I have. Anyway, a lot of letters poured in, and lots of 'em (you could tell from the language and the addresses and everything else) were from minority groups. So, yes, your assumption is right, I think because Astro *was* a Venusian, and different in that sense, and picked on a little bit, they identified with that and they empathized with that.

Merlin: Incidentally, it was cold the day of that parade and we were all bundled up in our uniforms. They had a very nice mock-up of a rocketship built over a truck bed and angled above the driver's cab. All three of us, side by side, were riding in it, waving at the crowd as we went along. But just prior to getting into the rocket, Frank suddenly had to go off to the john. He hurried out and rushed back, and climbed back aboard the rocket setup. And he looked kind of harried. Finally he said to me, "Hey, hey ... come over here and block me, will ya?" His problem was that his pants zipper was jammed open—he was having a terrible time with it! There he was, trying to wave and smile and be nice, but he didn't want his uniform to come apart! And for the entire parade, I was guarding his treacherous, revealing zipper for him [*laughs*]!

At the end of the parade, we were led upstairs to a fellow on a balcony overlooking the area. He was a radio person whose name I don't remember, a guy who introduced us to the crowd below. "Here come the space cadets and we're going to have 'em say a few words to you." He announced, "Here's Frankie Thomas, who plays Tom Corbett. Frankie, say something to the crowd!" Well, Frank was his usual, charming self and said nice words to the people of Philadelphia. And then the fellow turned to me and he said, "Here's Roger Manning. Say something to Philadelphia, Roger!" And I guess I got irritated, because he didn't say that I was "Jan Merlin, who *played* Roger." I looked at him and I was kind of flustered, and then I looked out at that big crowd and I said [*sneering*], "Ahhhh, go blow your jets!" [*laughs*]—which was Roger's frequent way of saying "Shove it!" to others on the series. The crowd laughed heartily at the familiar phrase, but the radio guy was appalled. The radio crew hustled *me* out right away ... and we never got invited back to Philadelphia for Thanksgiving again!

Any idea what the budget of an average episode was?

Thomas: No, but it was pretty low, I'll tell you that. As low as Rockhill could make it. If we had had the budgets that they've got now, we'd still be running! I know that they allocated $50 for special business like an additional gun or something like that. It was crazy.

Merlin: For heaven's sake, our Paralo-Ray guns were soldering irons. I used to crack up the people in rehearsals—we'd be confronting some "heavy," and out of the blue I'd pull a different line on him, like, "Stop in your tracks, or I'll solder you to death!" [*Laughs*] And of course the guy would be thinking of that when we went on air. If my eyes were twinkling, he knew what *I* was thinking, and he had to start to wonder if I was gonna *say* it again or not [*laughs*]!

When you were doing three *Tom Corbetts a week, and radio, and p.a.s now and then,* Tom Corbett *was probably your whole life. How did that suit you at that point?*

Tom Corbett's stories were serialized and its stars "cerealized." Markim, pictured here, later worked behind-the-scenes on the prestige pictures *Long Day's Journey into Night* (1962) and *The Pawnbroker* (1965). Partnered with *Corbett* director George Gould, he also made history by producing 1950s television commercials on videotape and headed the world's largest video-duplicating company.

Merlin: Well, I was always happiest when I was working. I'm one of the few guys in the Screen Actors Guild who voted to *continue* working on weekends. For years you worked six days a week and *maybe* got Sunday off, and then the Guild wanted to have Saturdays *and* Sundays off and they took a vote on it—

And you voted against it.

Merlin: Sure! I'd rather work than sit at home and wonder what I was going to *do* next.

Did it ever start to "get old" for you, Frankie?

Thomas: No. Nope, nope, nope. There was always something new, something different, and I never got tired of it.

Markim: On the show, we all took turns doing commercials, some of which you can still see in the old kinescopes. We did the commercials *in* costume—like, Astro would sell the Kellogg's Pep, a Corn Flakes-like cereal. As a matter of fact, rather a cute story, at one point they alternated putting our pictures on the backs of the Pep boxes, Frankie's, Jan's, Margaret's, and then *my* picture was on the back of the Pep boxes. The *back* of the box. And in the stores, they would display the *front* of the box. Well, my mother would go into the stores and turn all the boxes around [*laughs*]!

Merlin: When they put our faces on the backs, the idea was for kids to cut out and use them for masks. So there were a lot of teeny *us* running around everywhere.

Kellogg's was your sponsor for a long time. Did you eat Kellogg's cereal?

Thomas: *Yes*! I liked 'em! I liked Kellogg's Pep—that became "the Solar Cereal"!

Merlin: Hey, I ate *all* those cereals. For a time I had one of those Tom Mix wooden pistols that I sent in a Ralston cereal box top for! I loved Kellogg's Corn Flakes.

Markim: *Did* I eat Kellogg's cereal? You know what?, I still *do* [*laughs*]! I'm a big cereal eater, every morning I have cereal, and most of my cereals happen to be Kellogg's cereals. I guess old loyalties die hard...!

Do you think it was the success of Tom Corbett, Space Cadet *that inspired the other outer space series of the '50s?*

Markim: Without question. As a matter of fact, after the first two years of our doing the show, George Gould left *Tom Corbett* and was instrumental in getting onto the air another space series called *Rod Brown of the Rocket Rangers* with Cliff Robertson. I went and appeared on *Rod Brown*—not as Astro, but just played some roles because George was directing it. I'd play little parts, because he and I were close and it was easy to do.

Thomas: There was a big fuss about *Rod Brown*, a lawsuit brought by [Rockhill president] Stanley Wolfe against CBS. CBS had gotten a-hold of George Gould along with two of our best writers, Jack Weinstock and Willie Gilbert, and *Rod Brown* looked like a carbon copy of *Tom Corbett*—it had a unit of three as the principals, it was all laid in space, *everything*. But that didn't slow *us* down, and we knocked *Rod Brown* off in 26 weeks [*laughs*]! We knocked off all the rest of those shows too, *except Space Patrol*—that stayed.

Jan, you left Tom Corbett *before it went off the air.*

Merlin: While I was working the show early on, I was happy as a clam because I was making a good salary. But I got nervous. I wanted to do *more* as an actor than that, and I really felt that I was in danger of being typed the way the people who played Dick Tracy and Tarzan did. So I began to make noises about quitting. The producers and the head writer Albert Aley didn't believe me at first, and at one point they thought "We'll give him

Merlin now has an Emmy to show for his days as a television soap opera writer. He is also the author of several books available via www.Xlibris.com/bookstore.

a scare" and they brought in a boy who could possibly replace me. And they discovered that I didn't care, I *liked* it! They brought in Frank Sutton, and Frank was a delightful actor to work with. What was nice was, he was playing as tough a character as I was, so we could really have some decent, belligerent scenes together. I still was determined to leave, and I stopped having the crewcut and began to grow my hair, and finally I quit. I took my first wife Patricia, a New York actress, off to Africa on a three-month safari, and when I came back, all through that late summer I did some summer stock. Getting back to New York in the fall ... times were hard, and I began to worry about getting work. Albert called me up and asked, "You comin' back to the show?" and I drawled reluctantly, "Wellll ... maybe," and I said I'd come back under other conditions.

What were your conditions?

Merlin: When we all first got together [in 1950] with Albert and Wolfe and those people, they wanted to know what kind of billing I wanted. I said, "I don't give a rap about the billing, just pay me my salary." But this time, having discovered that the kids identified with Roger and were pretty crazy about him, I said, "I want a raise," and they gave me a raise, and I said, "And I want billing after Frankie." (Up until that time, it was Frankie Thomas–Al Markim–myself.) I demanded second billing, so they changed it to Frankie Thomas–Jan Merlin–Al Markim. Al was very gracious, he never said anything to me about the change. But I still wasn't content, that wasn't really what I wanted, so I went through that season with them and I quit again when we came to the spring break.

So you quit, came back and quit again?

Merlin: Yeah, I quit a second time. And when I quit the second time, I did an Off-Broadway play called *Rope* and got fabulous reviews from the critics. That's how Universal found me and put me in *Six Bridges to Cross* [1955], which was shot in Boston and Hollywood. While I was in Hollywood, one of the best agencies there, William Morris, snapped me up and I thought, "Gee, I can work like a crazy man here." I telephoned my wife in New York and asked, "What would you think of moving out to California?" She replied instantly, "I'm packing!" [*Laughs*] That was *it*! I never returned to New York until 1975 when I went back to pick up an Emmy for writing scripts for the soap opera *Another World*.

After Jan quit the show, an actor named Jack Grimes came in as a new character, Cadet T.J. Thistle.

Markim: I thought Jack did a terrific job. He fit right in—he joined the group, he worked with us and there were no "bumps" when that happened. Did our audience miss Jan? I think they did. I think Jan had something and the character of Roger Manning had something that T.J. didn't quite have. But the show went in a different direction, and T.J. Thistle was an interesting character too, and it did bring some humor to the show, a type of humor that we hadn't had.

Thomas: Jackie Grimes was a very proficient actor who had been around a long time. Before *Tom Corbett* he did a CBS morning radio show called *Let's Pretend* for 20 years—our story editor Al Aley had played the lead in it! But with Jack Grimes in the part of the third cadet, it was not the same character, it wasn't like Roger Manning, the troublemaker and lovable rogue. We had good shows with Jack, but it wasn't quite the same.

Why did Tom Corbett *finally go off the air?*

Thomas: I guess we ran out of sponsors! At the end, Kraft Caramels was sponsoring *Tom Corbett*, and we couldn't sell enough of those. I mean, if we sold a *ton* of them, it didn't

A half-century after his space jockey days, Thomas (left) was still riding the film festival and autograph trail. Here he presses the flesh with another early rocket ranger, Ed Kemmer of the *Space Patrol* series.

make much difference—do you know what I mean? You've got a small-priced item, and—how many caramels can you sell [*laughs*]? We couldn't sell enough of 'em to warrant the expenditure of the show. Kellogg's, our first sponsor, had a variety of things—Kellogg's Corn Flakes, Kellogg's Rice Krispies, Kellogg's Raisin Bran, and they had our pictures on the boxes and everything. That was *big*.

Al, why do you think the show went off the air?

Markim: I guess the usual thing that makes television shows go off the air after four, five years. Maybe it had gotten a little stale. Maybe the competition from other types of television was getting stronger. And, yes, the sponsorship was no longer there—we lost Kellogg's after two or three years, and after that we went through a number of different sponsors. But eventually there were no sponsors, and that's what took a show off the air in those days.

Your reaction?

Markim: I was not terribly unhappy. I had had enough of it and I was doing other things, and I wanted to do yet *more* things. So the time had come and it was fine.

Starting in the late '50s, America had its own space program—exciting to a lot of people, but "old news" to you guys!

Markim: I remember sometimes we'd watch something [real-life space-related news coverage] and my kids would say, "Wow" and they'd ooh and aah and I would say, "Awww, I was there. I stood there. I walked on the Moon. I walked on Mars. That's nuthin'!" [*Laughs*] Because it felt, in my mind, sort of like I *had* done it!

When you'd hear "space news," would that make Tom Corbett *flash into your head every time?*

Merlin: Of course, because the whole concept was so similar and so close. The spacesuits resembled those that were actually used. The remarkable sight of those rockets going up into the air and taking Man into space was simply astonishing, and you felt very proud of your country. But I never thought of the show as having much to do with the real thing until I learned that many of the people who got into the space program were actually influenced by having *watched* the *Tom Corbett* series. It was startling. A number of prominent Air Force test pilots, some before they ever were involved with astronautical work, had come [onto the *Tom Corbett* show] to do commercials, for Kellogg's cereals. Chuck Yeager, a legendary idol for all of us, was one of those plugging Kellogg's Corn Flakes, and I realize it had been great luck to have met the authentic "gung ho" guys.

Thomas: On that momentous day when we landed on the Moon and the fellows came out of the hatch, "Boy," I said to myself, "They look just like our space costumes!" And they *did*. With the bulbous head piece and everything!

Merlin: When we actually went to the Moon, Patricia and I and my son Peter were visiting the home of Wright King, an actor, and his wife and children. My little boy was about six then. I had a little Sony TV set at poolside because the astronauts were going to land on the Moon that day, and I took a great shot of Peter standing there, gazing in awe at the TV screen just when Neil Armstrong was coming down the ladder. Nowadays, Pete *works* for NASA. His late mother would have been so proud of him. At NASA's Dryden Flight Research Center in California, Pete is the film archivist, and writes books for NASA. His latest is *The Smell of Kerosene*, about Donald L. Mallick, one of NASA's test pilots, and he also writes articles for various technical publications. Having been to the Cape to photograph takeoffs, he's got a remarkable shot of the exploding *Challenger*. It's a heartrending picture; part of the beach is at the bottom of the scene with the whole crowd looking up. You can see the trail of the rocket over the ocean beyond the people, and the vivid explosion above them, looking like an absolutely beautiful skyrocket bloom, as though something made for the Fourth of July. It's an extraordinary shot....

How have you enjoyed meeting Tom Corbett *fans at conventions in recent years?*

Thomas: Oh, they're a lot of fun. Look, it's always nice, we all have a little bit of ego. You see fellows who remember what you did and they like it and ... it's great. *Tom Corbett* is all over the Internet now. There's a site, Solar Guard [www.solarguard.com], and two or three others, and they've got the history of *Tom Corbett* and interviews and everything. I'm surprised that, after half a century, the show could be so well-remembered.

Markim: There are I-don't-know-*how*-many websites that have *Tom Corbett* memorabilia on it, and fan clubs. The fan clubs still exist! And I hear from these guys, I get letters from them, they send me a lunch pail and ask me to please autograph the lunch pail, that kind of thing. And these are 65-year-old men!

Did you save a lot of the memorabilia from the old days?
   Thomas: Oh, dear heavens. Oh, if I had just *done* it!

You didn't?
   Thomas [*groans*]: Noooo! We didn't know at that time that they'd be selling *Tom Corbett* lunchboxes for $1500. I mean, come on! Even the cereal boxes with our pictures on them command quite a bit of money. I never realized, and neither did any of the other boys, how valuable those things would become.

Save your memorabilia, Jan?
   Merlin: None. Absolutely none.
   Markim: I still have my uniform. I think I could probably get into it if I wanted to [*laughs*]!

At a 1993 Friends of Old-Time Radio convention in Newark, New Jersey, the three of you reunited for the first time in ... how long?
   Merlin: Four decades. We three had not seen one another in the same group since I left the show in 1954.
   Markim: That was terrific. It was a very warm and very wonderful thing. We hadn't been together in a *long*, long, long time and now here we were, and we were going to do a re-creation of one of our *Tom Corbett* radio shows. Well, the minute we got together and sat down with George Gould our director to go over the script, we just immediately fell right back into the characters and the kibitzing and the relationships, and everybody was sorta the same ... y'know? It was like, when you go home for Christmas, everybody becomes a kid again.
   Merlin: It was as though time rolled back. Everybody fell immediately into their characters, as if we'd never done anything else [*laughs*]! My present wife Barbara was with us, and I was delighted to be able to show her what shows were like in "the olden days." Barbara now gets to play roles in radio re-creations Frank and I do at festivals we attend as celebrities. She helps Tom Corbett and Roger come to life again!
   Thomas: And another funny thing

Both of Frankie Thomas' actor-parents lived beyond the age of 100 but Frankie "only" made it to 85. In this photo, Jan Merlin visits the grave on what would have been Frankie's 86th birthday. The marker reads, "Frank M. Thomas Jr.—Beloved Son, Husband, Stepfather, Actor—April 9, 1921–May 11, 2006—Love You Forever and Then Some—'Spacemans Luck.'"

happened—at least, it surprised *me*. I had a recording of that same radio show as we had done it originally, back in the '50s, and some time after the Newark convention a friend sent me a recording of the re-creation that we did. They sounded *just the same*. I mean, come *on*—40 years had gone by! But they sounded *identical*. I've had other people listen to both and they've confirmed it, so ... I guess we didn't change too much!

How often do you look at a Tom Corbett *these days?*

Markim: Not *too* often. I have a lot of grandchildren, and once in a while one of 'em gets old enough and they ask, "What was that all about?," and I say, "Would you like to see one?" I show it to them, and they *laugh* at it! So I'm not too eager to show it to them, because in a kid's eyes today, because of the kind of television that they're used to watching, this looks *so* primitive that they may as well be watching Abraham Lincoln [*laughs*]!

Did you know that in real life the Earth was almost hit by an asteroid a couple months ago? That made me think of your show!

Markim: Yeah, we were always chasing some asteroid, always bumping around through the asteroid belt!

We'll never live to see it, not even me, but—will there ever be a Space Academy with cadets shooting a rogue asteroid out of space or anything even remotely like what we saw on Tom Corbett?

Merlin: You'd do better to ask my son, Pete; he's closer to actual reality than any of us are. What do you guys feel about future space cadets being possible?

Thomas: I don't know why not *except* ... you're going to have an awful lot of trouble fusing the world into one nation. In theory, Space Academy was a training ground for spacemen who were working for *every*body. I think there *could* be a Space Academy someday. There might even be, eventually, two or three planets involved, if we find life on any of them. But now we're goin' *waaaay* out!

Markim: There *is* a Space Academy and it's in existence in Houston. It's where NASA trains the people who go into space now. It's very much like our Space Academy, and these people *are* beginning to go into space to do specific jobs, specific tasks. Space Academy was not unlike what happens now when we send a spaceship up to deposit two guys on a ship [in orbit], or send a spaceship up to take two Russian guys *off* of a ship and so on.

Shooting an asteroid out of space? You know what?, you probably *will* live to see that, Tom. An asteroid that's going to threaten the Earth in some way has got to be *fairly* close—"close" in astronomical terms, anyhow—so we probably *will* be capable of hitting it with a laser, or with this defense system that they've been talking about and working on. A lot of the advances depicted on *Tom Corbett* have already come to be, and they've come to be probably *sooner* than Willy Ley and others may have imagined.

INDEX

Numbers in *bold italics* indicate pages with photographs.

Abbott, Philip *248*
Abrahams, Mort 318
Ackerman, Forrest J 97
Adams, Julie 240
Adams, Ron vii
The Adventures of Sadie (1954) 140, 142
Agar, John 200, 201
Airport (1970) 18
The Alaskans (TV) 66
Albert, Eddie 2
Alden, Richard 1–9, *4*, *6*, *8*
Aletter, Frank 182
Aley, Albert 318, 327, 331, 335, 337
Alfred Hitchcock Presents (TV) 8
All My Children (TV) 186
All That Heaven Allows (1955) 306
All the Brothers Were Valiant (1953) 256
Alland, William 279
Allen, Corey 291
Allen, Irwin 49, 56, 57–58, 63–64, 66, 78–79, 80, 81, 83, 87, 88
Allen, Sheila 64
Allen, Steve 19
The Alligator People (1959) 90, 108
The Amazing Mrs. Holliday (1943) 269
Amazon Women on the Moon (1987) 66
Ameche, Don 53
Anders, Merry 107, 108, 109, 110
Andersson, Bibi 14
Anne of the Thousand Days (stage) 325
Another World (TV) 337
Antosiewicz, John vii
Apache Drums (1951) 276–77
Apocalypse Now (1979) 108
Appointment with Adventure (TV) 286
The Aquanauts (unmade movie) 21
Arkoff, Samuel Z. 117, 118–19
Arlen, Harold 144
Armstrong, Neil 339
Armstrong, Robert 171
Armstrong, Sam 200, 202
Armstrong Circle Theater (TV) 286
Arnaz, Desi 159
Arnold, Jack 279

Around the World in 80 Days (1956) 145
Ashley, John 291
Asimov, Isaac 327
Attack of the Puppet People (1958) 198, 200–02, *201*
Away All Boats (1956) 237–38, 243

Back from the Dead (1957) 90, 96
Bailey, Pearl 144
Ball, Lucille 159
Barbirolli, John 304
Bare, Richard L. 243, 245, 246
Baretta (TV) 121
Barnaby Jones (TV) 186, 189, 195
Barnes, Billy 290, 298
Barnum, Mike vii
Baron, Allen 24
Barry, Don "Red" 182
Barrymore, John 139, 144
Bartholomew, Freddie 178
Baskin, William 313
Batman (1966) 181, 189–95, *189*, *191*, *192*, *193*, 196
Batman (TV) 60, 181, 189, 192, 195
Batman Begins (2005) 197
Batman Returns (1992) 196
Baumann, Marty vii
Baumgarten, E.J. 94
Baxter, Anne 29–30
Beal, John 125, 126
Beall, Betty 113, *114*
Beatty, Robert 259
Beaumont, Charles 198
Beckett, Scotty 171, 172–73
Bell, Book and Candle (stage) 290, 301
Bend of the River (1952) 270
Bender, Russ 109
Bendix, William 40–41, *40*, 139
Benham, Joan 305
Bennett, Joan 276
Benson, Hugh 55, 135, 136
Benton, Doug 314, 315–16
Bercovici, Leonardo 14
Bergman, Ingmar 14
Berlin, Irving 253
Bernds, Edward 96, 202, 204, 206
Berry, Halle 196–97
Bethune, Zina 153, 156

The Beverly Hillbillies (TV) 2, 93
Bey, Turhan 182
The Big Beat (1958) 242
Biography (TV) 195
Bissell, Whit 49, 58, 81, *86*
Black Friday (1940) 283
Black Gold (1963) 53
Blake, Carter 325, *328*
Blake, Robert 295
The Blob (1958) 182, 183, 187
Blondell, Joan 300
Blondie Hits the Jackpot (1949) 36
Bluel, Richard 133, 134, 136–37
Blyth, Ann 256
Bogart, Humphrey 37
Bogart, Timothy Scott 158
Boggs, Haskell *118*
Bohus, Ted vii
Bonacci, Carmen 7
Bonniere, Rene 8
Boone, Pat 113
Borden, Marshall 60
Borzage, Frank 270
Bourbon Street Beat (TV) 235
Bowers, William 3
The Boy and the Pirates (1960) 159, 166–67, *167*
The Boy with Green Hair (1948) 40
Braeden, Eric 10–25, *11*, *12*, *14*, *15*, *17*, *20*, *24*
Brahm, John 314
Brandon, Henry 240
Brandt, Harry 143–44
Brenon, Herbert 27
Brent, Eve 260
Bride of Frankenstein (1935) 280, 281
Bridges, James 16
Broccoli, Albert "Cubby" 18
Broken Arrow (1950) 134
Bronco (TV) 233–34, 243
Bronson, Charles 291, 300
Brooks, Mel 153
Brooks, Stephen 246
Brown, Donald H. 91
Brown, Jim 11
Brown, Robert *134*
Brunas, John vii
Brunas, Michael vii
Bryce, Ed 320, *320*, *330*
Buck Rogers (comic strip) 326

343

344 Index

Buck Rogers (radio) 326
Buono, Victor 181, 196
Burnett, Carol 86
Burns, Bob vii
Burns, George 149
Burton, Richard 256
Burton, Tim 157

The Cabinet of Caligari (1962) 115, 116–17
The Cabinet of Dr. Caligari (1919) 116
Cabot, Susan 287, 289, 290, 291, 293, 295, 297, 300
Cagney, James 182
Caine, Irene 204
Cameron, James 10
Cameron, Rod 51
Campanella, Roy 119
The Canadians (1961) 1, 2, 5, 6–7
Cangey, Dick 70, 71, 75–76, 77
Cannell, Stephen J. 8
Cansino, Eduardo 216–17
Can't Help Singing (1944) 269
Capri, Ahna 291
Captain from Castile (1947) 225
Captain Kangaroo (TV) 322
Captain Video and His Video Rangers (TV) 327
Carey, Timothy 166
Carousel (stage) 250, 251, 252–53, *253*, 256
Carrie (1952) 232, 233
Carroll, John 215
Carson, Johnny 166
Carter, Ann 26–48, *27*, *28*, *29*, *31*, *33*, *34*, *36*, *37*, *38*, *40*, *41*, *43*, *44*, *45*, *46*, *47*, *48*
Carter, Lynda 24–25
Cassavetes, John 286
Castle, William 52, 164, 167, 256, 257
Cat People (1942) 26, 39, 126
Catching, Bill 71
Catwoman (2004) 196–97
Chamberlain, Richard 314, *314*
Chan, Jackie 73
Chaney, Lon, Jr. 182, 274, 275
Chapman, Lonny 182
Charisse, Cyd 91
Charlie's Angels (TV) 121
Chase, Stanley 11, 12, 16
Cheyenne (TV) 243
Chiles, Linden 85
A Christmas Carol (1951) 140, 142, *142*
Christmas Holiday (1944) 269
Ciannelli, Eduardo 61
The Cimarron Kid (1951) 234
Citizen Kane (1941) 279
Citron, Herman 18
City Beneath the Sea (1971) 58, 66
City of Angels (stage) 149
The City of the Dead see *Horror Hotel*
Clark, Susan 14–15, *15*
Clarkson, Lana 66
Clatterbaugh, Jim vii
Clement, Kevin vii

The Cobbs (radio) 306
Cohn, Harry 303
Colbert, Claudette 270
Colbert, Glen 61–62
Colbert, Robert 49–68, *50*, *56*, *57*, *60*, *64*, *67*, 78, 81, *82*, 83, *84*, 85, *86*, 87, 89, 188
Colman, Booth 151, 152
The Colossus of New York (1958) 159, *162*, 163
Colossus: The Forbin Project (1970) 10, 12–18, *12*, *14*, *15*, *17*
Colton, David vii
Commandos Strike at Dawn (1942) 27–29, 30, 31, 34–35, 43
Congdon, James 184, 186, 188
A Connecticut Yankee in King Arthur's Court (1949) 40–41, *40*
Connery, Sean 18
Connor, Kevin 136
Conrad, Robert 69–77, *70*, *72*, *73*, *75*, *76*, 77
Conried, Hans 125
Conway, Curt 182
Coogan, Jackie 212, *223*
Coogan, Richard 327
Cook, Tommy *209*
Cooper, Ben 323
Cooper, Gary 103, 230
Cooper, Jackie 295
Coppola, Francis Ford 108
Corday, Mara 228
Corky of Gasoline Alley (1951) 172
Corman, Gene 300
Corman, Roger 285, 286, 287–88, 289–90, 291, 293, 295, 296, 297–298, 299, 300, 301, 303, 304, 307, 310, 311, 312–13
Cornfield, Hubert 102
Corridors of Blood (1962) 250, 263–64, *263*, *264*
Cotten, Joseph 58
Coughlin, Kerwin 125
Coulouris, George 259
Court, Hazel 309, *312*
Cowan, Will 242
Coy, Walter *236*
Crane, Barbara 287, 290, 298
Crane, Richard 108, 171, *172*, 173, *174*, *177*, 179, 229
Creature from the Black Lagoon (1954) 279
Cregar, Laird 83
Crosby, Bing 40–41, *40*
Crosby, Floyd 103
Cross, Dennis 247
Cult of the Cobra (1955) 232, 234–37, *236*, 240
Curse of Dracula see *The Return of Dracula*
The Curse of the Cat People (1944) 26, *29*, 30–34, *31*, *33*, *34*, 35–40, *36*, *37*, 42, 45, 47–48
Curse of the Fly (1965) 90
Curtis, Tony 18, 199, 209, 291
Cyrano de Bergerac (1950) 55

Dalton, Abby 287, 289, 291, *292*, 295, 297, 298

Dalton, Audrey 125
Damato, Glenn vii
Dano, Royal 153
Dante, Joe vii, 25
Darren, James 49, 56, 57, *57*, 58–59, 63, 65, 67, 68, 78–89, *79*, *82*, *84*, *86*, 188
Davis, Lisa 206
Davis, Phyllis 67
Davis, Sammy, Jr. 303
Davison, Bruce 158
Dawson, Richard 8
Day, Doris 163
Day, Robert 260, 262, 263, 264
The Day Mars Invaded Earth (1962) 90, 110, *111*, 112–15, *114*
The Day the Earth Stood Still (1951) 56, 110
Dead Like Me (TV) 246
Dean, Julia 30, *34*, 37
Dear Brat (1951) 233
DeCamp, Rosemary 164, 167
Demarest, William 306
Depp, Johnny 39
DeSantis, Joe 323
The Desert Fox (1951) 234
Designing Woman (1957) 50
The Desperate Hours (stage) 303
Dessau, Paul 274
Destry Rides Again (1939) 251, *252*, 256
Devon, Richard vii, *292*, 293, *294*, 296–97, *299*
Dexter, Maury 90–120, *95*, *101*, *103*, *118*
Dickerson, Beach 291
di Dienes, Andre 226
Dietrich, Marlene 143, 144, 251
Dillman, Bradford 19
Disesso, Moe 311
Dix, Robert *101*
Dobson, James 237
Dr. Jekyll and Mr. Hyde (1941) 129
Dr. Kildare (TV) 121, 314
Doheny, Edward L. 112
Doheny, Edward L., Jr. 112
Domergue, Faith 235
Donahue, Troy 296
Donlan, Yolande vii, 258, 260
The Donna Reed Show (TV) 164
Don't Go Near the Water (1957) 50
Douglas, Donna 2
Douglas, Kirk 198–99, *199*, 291
Dozier, William 190
Dracula (novel) 122, 130, 131
Dream Wife (1953) 250, 254–56, *255*, 257
Ducovny, Allen 330
Duke, Patty 186
Dullea, Keir 8
du Maurier, George 139, 145
Duncan, David 121, 122
Dunn, Michael 74
Dupont, E.A. 228
Durbin, Deanna 269
Duryea, Dan 276
The Dynamiters (1956) 139

Eastwood, Clint 154, 306
Eberhardt, Norma *131*, 132
Edge of the City (1957) 286
Edward, My Son (1949) 140
Edward, My Son (stage) 139–40
Eegah (1962) 1
87th Precinct (TV) 149, 154, *155*
Eilers, Sally 174–75
Elfman, Jenna 158
Elias, Louie 70
Elliott, Ross 228
Elmo, Mike vii
Emerson, Hope 306
Erickson, Leif 215
Escape from the Planet of the Apes (1971) 10, 19–20, *20*, 21
Everett, Chad 291

Fairbanks, Douglas 73
Farentino, James 14
The F.B.I. (TV) 192, 232, 239, 246, *248*
Fell, Norman *155*
Fernandez, Peter 318
Ferrer, Mel 226
A Fever in the Blood (1961) 53
Fickett, Mary 186
Fiedler, John 323
Fielder, Pat 121–38, *124*, *136*, *137*
Fighting Trouble (1956) 198
Fine, Larry 52
The First Hundred Years (TV) 171
Fisher, Eddie 302
Fisher, Terence 139
Fitzsimons, Charles 190
The Flame Barrier (1958) 121, 129, 130, 133, *134*
Fleming, Eric 206, *207*
Flipper (TV) 316
The Fly (1958) 96, 159, 164–66, *165*, 168
"The Fly" (short story) 96
Fonda, Henry 230
Ford, Glenn 50
Forest, Michael *294*
Forrest, Steve 66
Foster, Ron 107, 108
4D Man (1959) 181–88, *184*, *185*
Fowler, Gene, Jr. 98
Francis Goes to West Point (1952) 234
Frankenstein (1931) 186
Frankenstein Meets the Wolf Man (1943) 275, 277
Franz, Arthur *134*
Frasier (TV) 192
Frau im Mond (1929) 269
Freaks (1932) 106
Freeman, Kathleen 165
Fried, Gerald 129
Frith, Christopher vii
Frye, William 315
Fugate, Caril 1
Fulton, John P. 279

Gabor, Zsa Zsa 198, 204, 205–06, 207–08
The Gallant Men (TV) 235
Gambina, Ralph *72*

Gammill, Kerry vii
Gardner, Arthur vii, 121, 122, 124, 129, 130, 132, 134, 137, *137*
Garland, Beverly 153–54, 228, 287, 289, 291, 295
Garland, Judy 303
Garland, Margaret 325, *330*
Garland, Richard 228
Garner, James 53, 54
Garrett, Betty 190
Garrison's Gorillas (TV) 149, 153, 156
Garson, Hank 305–06
Gasoline Alley (1951) 172
The Gelignite Gang see *The Dynamiters*
General Hospital (TV) 183
Gentle, Lili 300
George, Jimmy vii, 70, 74, 75, *75*, 76, 77
George, John *219*
Geronimo (1962) 121, 134–35
Gershenson, Joseph 281
The Ghost of Frankenstein (1942) 269, 274, *275*, 277, 283
Gibbons, Ayllene 107
Gibson, Mimi *127*
Gilbert, Melissa 287, 290
Gilbert, Sara 287, 290
Gilbert, Willie 332, 335
Gilchrist, Connie 300
Gilmore, John 106–07
Gingold, Mike vii
Girls in Prison (1956) 198
Glass Trap (2005) 146, 158
Glasser, Bernard 96
Goddard, Mark 81
Goddard, Paulette 130
The Godfather Part II (1974) 108
Goldstein, Bruce vii
Goliath Awaits (1981) 121, 135–36
Gordon, Alex vii, 141
Gordon, Bert I. 159, 166, 167, 201, 202
Gordon, Richard 139–45, *142*
Gordon, Susan 166, 167, *167*
Gorshin, Frank 181, 191, *193*, 194
Gould, George 318, 322, 335, 340
Grand Tour: Disaster in Time (1992) 66–67
Granger, Stewart 256
Grant, Cary 53, 163, 164, 169, 250, 254, *255*
Grant, Peter 254–56, *254*, 258, 267
Gray, Coleen 126
The Great Indoors (stage) 11
Green Acres (TV) 245
The Green Hornet (TV) 60
Greer, Dabbs 128
Greystoke: The Legend of Tarzan, Lord of the Apes (1984) 259
Gries, Tom 11
Griffith, James 128
Grimes, Jack 337
Gudegast, Christian 22, 25
Gudegast, Hans see Braeden, Eric
Guest, Val vii

Guilbert, Ann Morgan 186
The Gunfighter (1950) 3
Gunman's Walk (1958) 80
Gunn, Rex 137
The Guns of Navarone (1961) 79, 85
Gunsmoke (TV) 96, 97

Haley, Jackie Earle 153
Half Pint Panel (TV) 159
Hall, Arch, Jr. vii, 1, 2, 3, 5, *6*, *6*, 7
Hall, Arch, Sr. 1, 2, 3, 7
Hall, Jon 107
Hall, Juanita 254
Hamilton, Kipp 295
Hamilton, Margaret 164
Hamilton, Murray 91
Hammerstein, Oscar 250
Hand of Death (1962) 90, 115–16
The Hank McCune Show (TV) 93
Hanks, Tom 65, 85–86, 87
Harding, Ann 29–30
Harper, Ron 146–58, *148*, *150*, *152*, *154*, *155*, *157*
Harris, Jack H. 182, 187
Harris, Julie 41
Harvey, Michael 319–20
Harvey, Phil *238*, 240, *241*
Have Rocket—Will Travel (1959) 52
Hawaiian Eye (TV) 70
Hawks, Howard 226
Hayes, Allison 287
Hayward, Susan 119
Hayworth, Rita 216
Haze, Jonathan 290–91
Hedison, David 79, 165
Heflin, Van 80
Hefner, Hugh 7
Heft, Richard vii
Heinlein, Robert 324–25, 326
Hellman, Lillian 285
Hellman, Monte 287
Hell's Belles (1970) 117–19
Henderson, Jan vii
Hennesey (TV) 295
Herbert, Charles 159–170, *162*, *165*, *167*, *168*
Herman, Norman T. 117–18
Hermanos, W. 54
Herrmann, Bernard 279–80
Herron, Bob 71
Heston, Charlton 12
The High Powered Rifle (1960) 102, *107*, 115
High Tide at Noon (1957) 265, 266
Highway Patrol (TV) 70
Highway to Heaven (TV) 119
Hill, Mary see Hill, Paula
Hill, Paula 216, 218, *219*
Hitchcock, Alfred 131, 257
Hitler, Adolf 24
Hogan's Heroes (TV) 8
Holt, Tim 125
Hootenanny Hoot (1963) 116
Hoover, J. Edgar 246
Hopper, Dennis 291

Horror Hotel (1960) 250, 265–66, *266*, 267
Horvath, Charles 242–43
Horvath, Georgia vii
Horvath, Sandy vii
Hough, Stan 151, 153
House of Flowers (stage) 144
House of Frankenstein (1944) 274, 283
House of the Damned (1963) 90, 104–09, *105*
Houseboat (1958) 53, 163, 169
Hovey, Helen 1, 3, 4, *4*
How to Succeed in Business Without Really Trying (stage) 332
Howard, Moe 52
Hoyt, John 200
Hudson, Rock 18
Huff, Tommy 70–71, 75, 77
Hughes, Howard 226, 235
Hughes, J. Anthony 27
Hughes, Kathleen 240
Hughes, Robin 242, *244*
Hughes, Whitey vii, 70, *72*, 74, 76, *76*
Humberstone, H. Bruce 259–60
Hunter, Kim 19, *20*
Hunter, Tab 80, 286, 291
Huston, John 7
Hutchinson, Bruce 192
Hutton, Barbara 51–52
Hyde-White, Wilfrid 258, 260

I Married a Monster from Outer Space (1958) 98, *99*
I Married a Witch (1942) 27, *27*, *28*
I, Robot (2004) 327
Iden, Rosalind 144
The Incredible Shrinking Man (1957) 279
Indusi, Joe vii
Innerspace (1987) 25
Invasion of the Body Snatchers (1956) 182
The Invisible Man (1933) 280
The Invisible Man Returns (1940) 269, 277
Ireland, John 151
The Islanders (TV) 243, 245–46
It Started with Eve (1941) 269
It Waits (2005) 8
It's Good to Be Alive (1974) 119

Jack Armstrong (radio) 232
Jackson, Brad 296, 297
Jacobs, Arthur P. 21–22
Jailhouse Rock (1957) 51
James, Harry 306
Jane Eyre (1944) 251
Janssen, David 235, 237, 240
Jarman, Claude, Jr. 35
The Jean Arthur Show (TV) 149
Jeffries, Lionel 262
Jennie: Wife/Child see *Tender Grass*
The Joey Bishop Show (TV) 295
John, Elton 86
Johns, Glynis 116, 117

The Jonathan Winters Show (TV) 295
Jones, Kent vii
Jones, Preston Neal vii, 269–84
Jones, Robert 119
Jones-Moreland, Betsy 289, 293, 295–96
Jory, Victor 61
Jourdan, Louis 286
Joy Ride (1958) 52
Joyce, Elaine 2
The Jungle Book (1942) 280
Junior Miss (radio) 305, 306
Jurgens, Curt 11
Jurow, Martin 140, 141

Kahn, Ivan 225, 226
Kane, Joe vii
Karatnytsky, Christine vii
Karloff, Boris 250, 263, 264, *264*, 271, 274, 304, 307, 309, 310–11, *312*, 313, 314
Katzman, Sam 256, 257
Kay, Roger 116–17
Kearney, Carolyn 242, 243, *244*
Keel, Howard 252
Kelly, Jack 53, 54, 235, 237, 240, 243
Kemmer, Ed 326, *338*
Kenney, June *201*, 287, 288, 291, 295
Kenton, Erle C. 274, 275
Kerr, Deborah 254
The Kettles in the Ozarks (1956) 306
Kiel, Richard vii, *105*, 106, 107
Kilbride, Percy 234
Kiley, Richard 258
King, Bob vii
King, Wright 339
King Lear (stage) 144
Kismet (stage) 258
Kitt, Eartha 190, 195, 196
Klugman, Jack 323, 329
Knapp, Robert 218, *219*
Knef, Hildegard see Neff, Hildegarde
Knight, Ted 61
Knights of the Round Table (1953) 139
Knox, Harold E. 93, 94, 108
Kolb, Ken 71
Kolchak: The Night Stalker (TV) 24
Koster, Henry 256
Kramer, Earl 30, 42
Kramer, Stanley 30
Kronos (1957) 90, 96, *97*
Kubrick, Stanley 16
Kuznetzoff, Adia 275

Ladd, Alan 163
Lady Godiva (1955) 306
Lady in the Dark (stage) 285
LaFayette, Gregory 51
Laird, Connie 213
Lake, Veronica 27, *28*
Lamarr, Hedy 286
Lamas, Fernando 11

Lamour, Dorothy 258
Land of the Giants (TV) 66
Land of the Lost (TV) 146, 156, 158
The Land Unknown (1957) 232, 235, 237–42, *238*, *239*, *241*
Landis, James 1, 2, 3, 5, 7, 9
Landon, Michael *118*, 119, 291
Landres, Paul 133
Lane, Jocelyn 117
Lang, Fritz 269, 276
Langley, Noel 139–40, 142
Lansbury, Angela 192
Lansing, Robert *155*, 181, 183–85, *184*, *185*, 186, 187, 188
The Last Man on Earth (1964) 90
Last of the Duanes (1941) 27
The Last Time I Saw Archie (1961) 3
LaStarza, Roland 71, *72*
Late Night with Conan O'Brien 65, 85
Laven, Arnold 121, 124, 130, 134
Laveroni, Jerry 71, 76
LaVigne, Emile 202, 204, *205*
Law of the Plainsman (TV) 121
The Law vs. Billy the Kid (1954) 257
Lawrence, Barbara *97*
Lawrence, Gertrude 285
The Lawrence Welk Show (TV) 42
Lean, David 140
Lear, Bill 58
Leave It to Harry (1954) 306
Lederer, Francis *131*, 132
Lee, Bruce 73
Lee, Christopher 136, 250, 266
Lee, Rowland V. 275–76
Lee, Ruta vii, 290, 295
Lehman, Lew 7
Lemmon, Jack 209, 318
Lenard, Mark 151
The Leopard Man (1943) 126
Let's Pretend (radio) 337
Levy, Jules V. 121, 124, 125, 129, 130, 132, 134
Lewis, Elliott 305
Lewis, Jerry 286, 290, 296, 302
Lewton, Val 26, 30, 32–33, 38, 126, 276
Ley, Willy 317, 322, 327–29, 341
Ling, Eugene 115
Lippert, Robert L. 2, 90, 93, 94, 96, 97–98, 99, 100, 101–02, *101*, 109–10, 113, 115, 116, 117
Lisa, Anna 52
Little Big Horn (1951) 113
Little House on the Prairie (TV) 119
The Little Shepherd of Kingdom Come (1961) 98–100, *101*
Lloyd, Jimmy 91
Locher, Felix 107, 109
Lock Up (TV) 70
Locke, Sondra 154
Lockhart, June 81
The Lodger (1944) 83
Lohman, Augie 125
Long, Richard 235, *236*, 237, 240, 243

Long Day's Journey into Night (1962) 334
Long John Silver (TV) 141
The Long, Long Trailer (1954) 159
Lord, Jack 323, 329
Loren, Sophia 53, 163, 164, 169
Lorre, Peter 304, 307–09, 310–11, 312, 313
Lost in Space (TV) 79, 81, 88
Lotis, Dennis 266
Love of Life (TV) 322, 329, 330
Lucas, Donna vii
Lucas, Tim vii, 26
Lugosi, Bela 277
Lukather, Lee 116
Lumet, Sidney 177
Lundigan, William 166
Lupino, Ida 55–56, 126, 315
Lux Radio Theatre (radio) 42
Lyden, Robert *174, 176, 177*
Lydon, Jimmy 171–180, *172*, 173, *174, 176, 177, 179*
Lynn, Bambi 253
Lynn, Diana 35
Lyon, Francis D. 235, 236

Macabre (1958) 52
Machine-Gun Kelly (1958) 285, 291, 299–300
MacLaine, Shirley 303
MacQueen, Scott vii
Magers, Boyd vii
Magginetti, William 93–94, 96, 97, 98, 100
Magnificent Doll (1946) 270
Mahoney, Jock 237–38, *238, 239, 241, 242, 261*, 262
Main, Marjorie 234
Maltin, Leonard vii
Malvern, Paul 274
A Man Apart (2003) 25
The Man from U.N.C.L.E. (TV) 64
Man in the Attic (1953) 83
The Man in the Net (1959) 163
Man Made Monster (1941) 270, 274, *275*, 283
Mancini, Henry 279
Mank, Greg 32
Mann, Anthony 270
Manning, Marilyn 1, 3–4
Mansfield, Jayne 86, 300
Mansfield, Sally *172*, 173, *174, 176, 177*
March, Fredric 27
Marciano, Rocky 71
Mark Trail (radio show) 324
Markim, Al 317–40, *319, 320, 324, 328, 330, 334*
Maron, Muriel 331
Mars, Kenneth 24
Marsh, Jean 136
Marshall, Herbert 53
Martin, Andra 242
Martin, Mary 254, 304
Martin, Ross *70*, 71, 74, 75, 163
Martinson, Leslie H. 190, 192–93
Martucci, Mark vii
Maryjane (1968) 112, 117

Mason, James 140
Matheson, Richard 304
Mathews, Sheila *see* Allen, Sheila
Matinee Theater (TV) 182
Matthau, Walter 22
Matthews, Francis 264, *264*
Mattson, Denver 62
Mature, Victor 58
Maverick (TV) 53, 54, 235, 243
Maya (TV) 283
Maytime (1937) 139
McCall, Mitzi 286–87, 298, 300
McCarthy, Kevin 25, 182
McCune, Hank 93
McDonnell, Dave vii
McDougall, Don 152, 153
McDowall, Roddy 19, *20*, 146, 149, 150, *150*, 156
McGraw, Charles 243
McKinnon, Bob 23
McLaglen, Andrew V. *101*
McLaughlin, Emily 183, 184
McQueen, Steve 183
Meadows, Jayne 19
Meiklejohn, William 233
Mein Kampf (1961) 23
Melchior, Ib J. 322, 331–32
Melchior, Lauritz 331
Melton, Troy 113
The Member of the Wedding (1952) 30, 41
Men Into Space (TV) 166
Men of Annapolis (TV) 182
Meredith, Burgess 181, 191, 194, 195
Meriwether, Lee 49, 56, 58, 60, *60*, 68, 81, 83, *84, 86*, 89, 181–97, *184, 185, 189, 191, 192, 193, 195*
Merlin, Jan 317–40, *319, 320, 326, 328, 330, 336, 340*
The Merry Monahans (1944) 269
Mesa of Lost Women (1953) *213, 214, 216, 217, 219, 220*, 212–22 *223*, 226, 230, 231
Middleton, Burr vii
Miller, Dick 290–91
Miller, Ken vii, 200, 201, *211*
Milner, Martin 164, 168
The Milton Berle Show (TV) 325
Mims, William 112, 115
The Mini-Skirt Mob (1968) 117
Minter, George 139, 140, 141, 142, *142*, 143, 144, 145
The Miracle Worker (stage) 186
Mishkin, Meyer 234
Missile to the Moon (1958) 198, 208–09, *209, 210*
Mr. Peepers (TV) 286
Mister Roberts (stage) 317–18, 325
Mitchell, Laurie 198–211, *199, 201, 203, 205, 207, 208, 209, 210, 211*
Mitchum, Robert 3
Mondragon, Joe 295
The Monolith Monsters (1957) 198
Monroe, Marilyn 204, 209, 226
The Monster That Challenged the World (1957) 121–25, *123, 124*, 126, *127*, 129, 130, 133, 138

Moore, Dickie 318
Moore, Ida *177*
Moore, Roger 54, 66
Moret, Jim 86
Morgan, Boyd "Red" 71
Morgan, Cosmo 159
Morgan, John vii, *280*, 283
Morley, Robert 139
Morris, Barboura 287, 291
Morris, Wayne 139
Morrow, Jeff *97*
Morrow, Jo 167–68
Morse, Hollingsworth 174–75
Morse, Ray 327
The Mummy's Hand (1940) 277, *278*, 283
Muni, Paul 27, 28, 34
The Munsters Today (TV) 195
Murder My Sweet (1944) 228
Murder, She Wrote (TV) 192
Murphy, Audie 234, 240
Murphy, Barry vii
Musuraca, Nicholas 30, 178
Mystery Science Theatre 3000 (TV) 297

Naish, J. Carrol 274
The Naked Dawn (1955) 257–58
Naked Gun (1956) 93
Namu, the Killer Whale (1966) 183
National Velvet (1944) 225
Naughton, James 146, 147, 148, 149–50, 152, 153, 156
The Neanderthal Man (1953) 212, 229–30, *229*
Neff, Hildegarde 140, 141–42, 143–45, *143*
Neill, Roy William 275
Nelson, Gene 115–16
Nelson, Lori 240
Neumann, Kurt 96, 165
The New Andy Griffith Show (TV) 186
Newman, Dean 185, 186
Newmar, Julie 181, 189, 190, 195, 196
Newton, Robert 139, 140, 141, 142, 144, 145
Nicholson, Jack 309–11, *310*
Nicholson, James H. 117, 119
Nickolaus, John 108
Nielsen, Ray vii
Ninotchka (1939) 140
Niven, David 163
Nixon, Allan 218
No Questions Asked (1951) 233–34
Norlund, Evy 85
The North Star (1943) 29–30, 36
Not as a Stranger (1955) 42
Nott, Robert vii
Novak, Kim 303
Nowhere in Africa (2001) 261

Oberon, Merle 251
O'Brien, Chuck 70
O'Brien, Conan 65
O'Brien, Edmond 102
O'Connor, Carroll 53, 61
O'Connor, Donald 234

The Odd Couple II (1998) 146
Odd Man Out (1947) 140
O'Hanlon, George *97*
O'Hara, Maureen 190
O'Herlihy, Dan 116
Oklahoma! (stage) 251, 252, 253, 254
Oliver, Maurine 226
Oliver Twist (1948) 140
Olivier, Laurence 144, 232, 233
One Exciting Week (1946) 92, 104
100 Rifles (1969) 11
Ormond, June 221
Ormond, Ron 212, 221
Orr, William T. 54–55
Our Girl Friday see *The Adventures of Sadie*
Owen Marshall, Counselor at Law (TV) 121
Owens, Patricia 165

Page, Geraldine 11
Palance, Jack 83
Pall, Gloria 198
Parfrey, Woodrow 329
Parker, Willard *103*, 109
Parrish, Leslie 209
Pastore, John 149
Patterson, Floyd 71
The Pawnbroker (1965) 334
Pearl Harbor (2001) 146
Peck, Gregory 12, 50
Peckinpah, Sam 134
Penny, Andrew 283
Perkins, Anthony 286
Perreau, Gigi 35
Pete Kelly's Blues (1955) 243
Pete Kelly's Blues (TV) 243
Peter Pan (stage) 304
Peters, Erika *105*, 107
Peters, Jean 225
Petersen, Paul 160, 163
Peyton Place (TV) 60
Pfeiffer, Michelle 196
Phantom Lady (1944) 270
Philco TV Playhouse (TV) 182, 286
Phillips, Mark vii
Phipps, William 233, 234
Phobia (1980) 7
Picerni, Charles 80
Picerni, Paul vii, 80
Pickett, Bobby 2
The Pickwick Papers (1954) 140, 142
Pidgeon, Walter 230
Pierson, Arthur 174
Pinsent, Gordon 14
Piranha (1978) 25
The Pit (1981) 7
Planet of the Apes (1968) 148
Planet of the Apes (2001) 157
Planet of the Apes (TV) 146–57, *150*, *152*, *154*
Playhouse 90 (TV) 166
Please Believe Me (1950) 276
Please Don't Eat the Daisies (1960) 163
Poe, Edgar Allan 304, 309
Poitier, Sidney 286

Police Nurse (1963) 110
Police Woman (TV) 121
Pollexfen, Jack 229
Pollock, Sydney 289
Porgy and Bess (1959) 303
Porter, Cole 140
Portrait of a Sinner (1959) 139
Poston, Tom 323, 329
Power, Tyrone 225
Powers, Mala 55, 163, 213
Preminger, Otto 303
Presley, Elvis 51, 116, 269
Previn, Charles 271, 272, *272*, 273
Price, Vincent 164, 165, *165*, 277, 304, 307, 308, 309, 310–11, 312, 313
The Prisoner of Zenda (1952) 139
Problem Girls (1953) 226–229, 231
Project U.F.O. (TV) 247
Provost, Jeanne vii
Provost, Oconee vii
Psycho (1960) 279–80, 286
The Puppet Masters (novel) 326
The Purple Hills (1961) 115
Pushnik, Frieda 106

The Queen and I (TV pilot) 8
Queen of Outer Space (1958) 198, 202–08, *203*, *205*, *207*, *208*, 211
Quinn, Anthony 18
Quinn, Jeanette see Quinn, Tandra
Quinn, Tandra 212–31, *213*, *214*, *216*, *217*, *219*, *220*, *223*, *225*, *227*, *229*, *230*

Rackin, Henry 70
Raft, Tommy Moe 301–2
Randolph, Jane 30, 39, 40
The Range Rider (TV) 237–38
Rappaport, Fred vii
The Rat Patrol (TV) 10, 11, *11*, 24
Rathbone, Basil 271
The Raven (1963) 307–14, *308*, *310*, *312*, *313*
"The Raven" (poem) 304, 309
Ray, Fred Olen vii, 157–58
Raymond, Guy 186
Reader, Jim 7
Rear Window (1954) 257
Reed, Donna 168
Reed, Lydia 126
Rein, Hal 331
Rennie, Michael 56, 61, 110
The Return of Dracula (1958) 121, 129, 130–33, *131*
Return of the Fly (1959) 90
Return of the Gunfighter (1967) 269
Reventlow, Lance 51–52
Reynolds, Burt 11
Reynolds, William 232–49, *233*, *236*, *238*, *239*, *241*, *244*, *247*, *248*
Rice, Tim 86
Richard Diamond, Private Detective (TV) 301
Richards, Carol 256

Richardson, Ralph 144
The Rifleman (TV) 121, 134
Righter, Carroll 143
Ritchie, Sharon Kay 182
The Riverbusters (1960s documentary) 22–23
Rivers, Johnny 3
Robards, Jason 183
The Robe (1953) 250, 256, 265, 297
Robertson, Cliff 335
Robinson, Edward G. 58, 130, 276
Robinson, Jay 297
Robinson, Sugar Ray 86
Rocky Jones, Space Ranger (TV) 171–80, *172*, *174*, *176*, *177*
Rod Brown of the Rocket Rangers (TV) 335
Rodann, Ziva 287
Rode, Alan vii
Rodgers, Jimmie *101*
Rodgers, Richard 250, 253, 254
Roemheld, Heinz 280
Rogers, Ginger 270
Romero, Cesar 181, 191, *192*, 194, 195
Rooney, Mickey 226
Roos, Fred 107–08
Rope (stage) 337
Rose, Pat 125
Rostand, Edmond 55
Rotsten, Herman 204
Rotter, Robert vii
The Rough and the Smooth see *Portrait of a Sinner*
The Rough Riders (TV) 326
Rozsa, Miklos 280
Rubirosa, Porfirio 207–08
Rumble on the Docks (1956) 79, 85
Runser, Mary Ray vii
Russell, Don 1, 3, 4, *4*
Russell, Elizabeth 30
Ruthless (1948) 35
Ryan, Irene 93
Ryan, Robert 2, 6

The Sadist (1963) 1, 2–7, *4*, *6*, 9
The Saga of the Viking Women and Their Voyage to the Waters of the Great Sea Serpent (1957) 285, 288, 289, 290, 291–98, *292*, *294*, 299
St. John, Betta 250–68, *252*, *253*, *254*, *255*, *257*, *259*, *261*, *263*, *264*, *266*, *267*
Salter, Hans J. vii, 269–84, *271*, *280*, *282*
The Saracen Blade (1954) 257
Sargent, Joseph 13, 16
Saxon, Aaron 312, *313*
Sayer, Jay 285–303, *287*, *292*, *294*, *299*, *301*, *302*
Scapperotti, Dan vii
Scarlet Street (1945) 276
Schary, Dore 295
Schwalb, Ben 202, 204, 206
Schwarzkopf, Elisabeth 144
Science Fiction Theatre (TV) 168

Index

Scorsese, Martin 30
Scott, Gordon 250, 258, 259, *259*, 260, 262
Scrivani, Rich vii
Scrooge see *A Christmas Carol*
Seay, James 226–28
Segal, George 330
Self, William 64
Serling, Rod 113, 232, 243, 245
Seven Brides for Seven Brothers (1954) 256–57
77 Sunset Strip (TV) 235
The Shadow (radio) 232, 247
Shadow of a Doubt (1943) 131
Shamroy, Leon 256
Shaughnessy, Mickey 50, 51
Shayne, Robert *229*
She Devil (1957) 96
Sheen, Fulton 325
The Shirt Off Her Back (circa 1960?) 301–02
Silk Stockings (stage) 140, 143, 144
Simon, Neil 2
Simon, Simone 26, *29*, 31–32, *33*, 36, *36*, 39, 40
Simpson, O.J. 86
Sinatra, Frank 199
Sinclair, Molly 232, 233
Siodmak, Curt 275
Siodmak, Robert 139, 270
Sir Lancelot 32
Sirk, Douglas 236, 270
Six Bridges to Cross (1955) 337
Skinner, Frank 269, 271, 272, *272*, 273, 274, 277, 283
Skolsky, Sidney 330
Slate, Jeremy 117
Slattery's People (TV) 121
Sleepy Hollow (1999) 39
Small, Lillian 295
Smiley, Logan 129
Smith, Kent 30, 32, 39
Smith, Liz 290
Smith, Queenie 251
Smith, Shawn 238, *239*, 242
Smith, William 154
Snyders, Sammy 7
The Soldier (1982) 158
Some Like It Hot (1959) 199, 204, 209
Son of Dracula (1943) 277
Son of Frankenstein (1939) 271, 272, 275, 277, 283
Sorority Girl (1957) 287, 288, 290, 291
South Pacific (stage) 250, 253–54, *254*, 258
Space Master X-7 (1958) 90, 96
Space Patrol (TV) 171, 326, 327, 335
Spalding, Harry 100, 102, 104–06, 108, 109, 110, 112, 113, 114, 115, 116
Spector, Phil 66
Spielberg, Steven 10–11
Springsteen, Bruce 86–87
Stabler, Robert 96
Stader, Paul 61–62, 80
Stanwyck, Barbara 37

Stapp, Marjorie 133
Star Trek: Deep Space 9 (TV) 83, 85
Stark, Sally 146, 147, 148
Starkweather, Charles 1
The Starlost (TV) 8
State Trooper (TV) 50–51
Stehli, Edgar 186
Stein, Herman 279
Stein, Ron 151
Stevens, Connie 149
Stevens, Eileen 228
Stevens, Harmon 218
Stewart, James 18, 270
Stockwell, Dean 40, 243
Stoker, Bram 122, 130
Stone, Oliver 10
Story of a Woman (1970) 14
The Strange Affair of Uncle Harry (1945) 270–71
Strasberg, Lee 182
Strauss, Robert 186
Streisand, Barbra 290
Stricklyn, Ray 132
Stromberg, William 283
The Student Prince (1954) 256
Sturgess, Olive 304–16, *305*, *308*, *310*, 312, *313*, *314*, *315*, 316
Support Your Local Sheriff! (1969) 3
Surf Party (1964) 108
Susskind, David 286
Sutton, Frank 323, 325, 337
Svengali (1931) 139, 144
Svengali (1954) 139–45, *140*, *143*

Tabu (1931) 103
Talbott, Gloria *99*, 306
Tannen, Charles 131
Tarzan (1999) 250
Tarzan (stage) 250
Tarzan (TV) 64
Tarzan and the Lost Safari (1957) 250, 258–60, *259*
Tarzan the Magnificent (1960) 250, 260–63, *261*, 267
Taylor, Don 19
Taylor, Elizabeth 225, 251, 302
Taylor, Kent 109, 110, 112, 113, 115
Taylor, Robert 256
Taylor, Rod 60
Teenage Doll (1957) 285, 287–89
Temple, Shirley 251
Tender Grass (1968) 7
Tevos, Herbert 212, 213–15, 216, 217–21
That Girl (TV) *64*
Them! (1954) 122
The Thief of Bagdad (1940) 280
The Thing from Another World (1951) 126
The Thing That Couldn't Die (1958) 232, 235, 240, 242–43, *244*
The Third Voice (1960) 102
13 Ghosts (1960) 159, 164, 167–68, *168*
13 Rue Madeleine (1946) 182

This Island Earth (1955) 279
This Love of Ours (1945) 269
Thomas, Calvin 323
Thomas, Frankie 317–40, *319*, *320*, *321*, *328*, *330*, *338*
Thomas, Marlo *64*
Thomas, Tony *280*, 283
Thompson, Marshall 235
The Three Stooges 52, 91
Thriller (TV) 55–56, *56*, 307, 314–16, *314*, *315*
Thunder on the Hill (1951) 270
Tigger vii
Time Express (TV) 121
The Time Machine (1960) 60
The Time Tunnel (TV) 49, *50*, 56–66, *57*, *59*, *60*, 67–68, *82*, *84*, *86*, 188, 195
Timpone, Tony vii
Titanic (1997) 10
T.J. Hooker (TV) 80, 83, 85
Tobey, Kenneth 126
The Today Show (TV) 181, 182, 189
Todd, Michael 145
Todd, Sally 296
Toguri, Iva 137
Tom Brown's School Days (1940) 178–79
Tom Brown's Schooldays (1951) 140, 142
Tom Corbett, Space Cadet (radio) 326, 333, 340–41
Tom Corbett, Space Cadet (TV) 171, 317–40, *319*, *320*, *321*, *324*, *326*, *328*, *330*, *332*, *334*, *336*
Tomorrow the World (stage) 285
Topper, Burt 117
Touched (2005) 158
Tousey, Terry vii
Tower of London (1939) 271–72, 275
Tracy, Spencer 129
Travolta, Joey 66
Travolta, John 66
Trilby (novel) 139
Turner, Lana 129
20000 Leagues Under the Sea (1954) 198–99, *199*
The Twilight Zone (TV) 232, 242, 243–46, *247*
The Two Little Bears (1961) 2
The Two Mrs. Carrolls (1947) 30, 35, 37
2001: A Space Odyssey (1968) 12, 16
Tyler, Judy 51

Uncivil War Birds (1946) 91
Under Fire (1957) 51, 52
The Unknown Terror (1957) 90, 96, 97
Upstairs, Downstairs (TV) 305
Us (TV pilot) 119

Val Lewton: The Man in the Shadows (TV) 30, 32, 39, 47–48
The Vampire (1957) 121, 125–30
Veidt, Conrad 116

Venomous (2002) 146, 157–58
Vice Squad (1953) 130, 138
The Vikings (1958) 291
Vincent, Virginia 132
The Virginian (TV) 5
Vittes, Louis 98
Vogel, Virgil W. 237, 239–40
Von Braun, Wernher 327
von Fritsch, Gunther 32, *33*
von Homburg, Wilhelm 71
Voyage to the Bottom of the Sea (TV) 79, 81, 88
Vye, Murvyn 166

Waggner, George 275
Wagner, Robert 66, 291
Walcott, Gregory *155*
Walker, Helen 228, 291
Walker, Robert, Jr. 85
Wallach, Eli 8
Waltz, Patrick 206
War of the Satellites (1958) 298
Ward, Burt 181, 191, 193, *193*, 195
Ward, Robin 8
Warden, Jack 323, 329–30
Warner, Jack L. 53
Warren, Charles Marquis 96, 97
Wasden, Shirley 295
The Wasp Woman (1959) 289
Wasserman, Lew 11
Watch on the Rhine (stage) 285
Waxman, Franz 280–81
Weaver, Jon vii, 75, *76*
Webb, Jack 3, 243, 247
Week-end at the Waldorf (1945) 225
Weinstock, Jack 332, 335
Weis, Don *152*

Welch, Raquel 11
Welk, Lawrence 42
Wells, H.G. 60
Wendy and Me (TV) 149
Wengraf, John 132
West, Adam 181, 191, *191*, 193–94, 195
West, Red 70, 74, 75, 76, *76*, 77
Wetbacks (1956) 93
Whatley, Stephen B. vii, 231
What's Up Front! (1964) 7
White, Jules 91
White, Robb 52
Whiting, Barbara 305, 306
Whiting, Margaret 305
Whitman, Stuart 66
Widmark, Richard 182
The Wild Wild West (TV) 64, 69–77, *70*, *72*, *73*
Wilder, Billy 204
Wilder, Glenn 151
Wilder, Thornton 130–31
Will Success Spoil Rock Hunter? (1957) 296, 300
Williams, Clarence III 11
Williams, Esther 11
Williams, Lucy Chase vii
Willis, Marlene *201*
Wills, Chill *101*
Wilson, Marie 218
Winant, Ethel 286
Windsor, Marie 113
Wisberg, Aubrey 229
Wise, Robert 26, 32
Witchcraft (1964) 90
The Witch's Tale (radio) 327
Without Warning! (1952) 130
Witney, William 74

The Wizard of Oz (1939) 139, 164, 251
The Wolf Man (1941) 182, 269, 270, 272, 273, 274, 275, 283
Wolfe, Stanley 318, 335, 337
Wolff, Ed *162*, 163
Wolfit, Donald *140*, 142, *143*, 144
Woman in the Moon see *Frau im Mond*
Wonder Woman (TV) 24–25
Wood, Natalie 291
Woods, Donald 164, 167
Worley, Jo Anne 302
Wyatt, Jane 2
Wyler, William 232, 233
Wyman, Jane 306

Yates, George Worthing 133
Yeager, Chuck 339
The Yearling (1946) 35
Yeaworth, Irvin S., Jr. 182, 186, 187
Yeaworth, Jean 182
The Yellow Canary (1963) 113
York, Dick 245
The Young and the Restless (TV) 10, 18, 21
The Young Animals (1968) 117
Young Frankenstein (1974) 153
You're Never Too Young (1955) 286

Zanuck, Richard D. 22
Zaremba, John 49, 58, 81, *86*
Zastupnevich, Paul 56, 63
Zimbalist, Efrem, Jr. 53, 232, *248*
Zinnemann, Fred 41
Zsigmond, Vilmos 2, 7

www.ingramcontent.com/pod-product-compliance
Ingram Content Group UK Ltd.
Pitfield, Milton Keynes, MK11 3LW, UK
UKHW050543150426
5217IPUK00026B/2059